# WATCHMAN NEE

## ESPECIAL EDITION

THE NORMAL CHRISTIAN CHURCH

THE NORMAL CHRISTIAN LIFE

D1712955

# THE NORMAL CHRISTIAN CHURCH

# WATCHMAN NEE

# INTRODUCTION

## IMPORTANT TO UNDERSTANDING OF THE BOOK

The content of the following pages is the substance of a number of talks to my younger fellow workers during conferences held recently in Shanghai and Hankow. When the addresses were given, the present book was not in view, but only my immediate audience; and the fact that the messages were intended for the instruction of my young colleagues accounts for their intensely practical nature, and for the simplicity of the style adopted. At these two conferences we sought in the first place to examine the teaching of God's Word concerning His churches and His work, and in the second place to review our past missions in the light of our findings.²

The talks proved of value to my younger brethren, and, as longhand notes were taken, the messages were shared with others. This resulted in many requests that the addresses be put into book form. As the conferences were attended chiefly by my younger fellow workers, I felt at liberty to instruct and counsel them, and to discuss quite freely a number of intimate and rather delicate matters. Had the addresses been intended for a wider audience, or for publication, I should have felt obliged to omit many matters that were mentioned, and to speak in an altogether different strain. I naturally hesitated when the suggestion was made to publish them, but the Lord made it clear that that was

His mind, so I have no option but to acquiesce. I questioned the wisdom of preserving the original style of the addresses, with their bits of "elderbrotherly" counsel and their distinct personal strain; but as a number of friends testified to special help received through the more personal parts, I realized that the book would lose its greatest value if those were eliminated. Therefore, though I send the addresses forth somewhat revised, they still remain, both in matter and style, very much as they were when originally delivered.

We trust the readers of this book will bear in mind that its messages, as originally given, were never meant for them. They were intended exclusively for the inner circle of my most intimate associates in the work, but by request we share our findings with the wider circle of all our brethren. The book is something private made public; something originally intended for the few now extended to the many; so we trust our readers will pardon anything that seems unsuited to the wider public.

We should like to point out here the place of the teachings of this book in the great body of divine truth, for the former have spiritual value only as they are held in relation to the latter. During the past eighteen years, the Lord has led us through different experiences in order that we might learn a little of the principle as well as the fact of the cross and resurrection, and learn something of the Christ-life, the lordship of Jesus, the corporate life of the Body, the ground of the kingdom of God, and His eternal purpose. It is natural, therefore, that these things have been the burden of our ministry. But God's wine must have a wineskin to contain it. In the divine pattern, nothing is left for man to decide. God Himself has provided the best wineskin for His wine, which will contain and preserve it without loss, hindrance, or misrepresentation. He has shown us His wine, but He has shown us His wineskin also.

Our work, throughout the past years, has been according to certain definite principles; but never until now have we tried to define or teach them. We have sought rather, in the power of the Spirit, to stress those truths which are so dear to our hearts and which, we believe, have more direct bearing on the spiritual life of the believer and the eternal purpose of God. But the practical outworking of those truths in the Lord's service is by no means unimportant. Without that, everything is in the realm of theory, and spiritual development is impossible. So we would seek, by the grace of God, not only to pass on His good wine, but also the wineskin He has provided for its preservation. The truths set forth in this book must therefore be regarded in relation to those taught throughout the eighteen years of our ministry, and as the sequence, not the introduction, to them.

Within the scope of these pages, it has been impossible to deal with all the questions relating to the subject of the book. Some I have already dealt with elsewhere, and others I hope to deal with at a later date. The title of the book explains its nature. It is not a treatise on missionary methods, but a review of our past work in the light of God's will as we have discovered it in His Word. The Lord had most graciously led us by His Spirit in our past service for Him, but we wanted to be clear as to the foundations upon which all divine work should rest. I realized that the primary need of my younger brethren was to be led of the Spirit and to receive revelation from Him, but I could not ignore their need of a solid scriptural basis for all their ministry. Therefore, together we talked freely of what we had been doing and how we had been doing it, and sought to compare our work and methods with what God had set before us in His Word. We examined the scriptural reasons for the means we employed, and the scriptural justification for the end we pursued; and we made a note of various lessons we had learned by observation as well as by experience. There was no thought of criticizing the labors of others, or even of making any suggestion to them how the work of God ought to be conducted; we were merely seeking to learn from God's Word, from experience, and from observation, how to conduct the work in the days to come, so that we might be workmen "approved to God."

The book is written from the standpoint of a servant looking from the work towards the churches. It does not deal with the specific ministry to which we believe the Lord has called us, but only with the general principles of the work; nor does it deal with "the church, which is His Body," but with the local churches and their relation to the work. The book does not touch the principles of the work, or the life of the churches; it is only a review of our missions, as the title suggests.

The truths referred to in this book have been gradually learned and practiced during the past years. Numerous adjustments have been made as greater light has been received, and if we remain humble, and God still shows us mercy, we believe there will be further adjustments in the future. The Lord has graciously given us a number of associates in the work, all of whom have been sent forth on the basis mentioned in this book, and through their labors numerous churches have been established in different parts of China. Though conditions are vastly different in these many churches, and the believers connected with them differ greatly too—in background, education, social standing, and spiritual experience—yet we have found that if, under the absolute lordship of Jesus, we come to see the heavenly pattern of church formation and government, then the scriptural methods are both practicable and fruitful.

While the book itself may seem to deal with the technical side of Christianity, let us emphasize here that we are not aiming at mere technical correctness. It is spiritual reality we are after. But spirituality is not a matter of theory; it always issues in practice; and it is with spirituality in its practical out-working that this book deals.

It is wearisome to me, if not actually repulsive, to talk with those who aim at perfect outward correctness, while they care little for that which is vital and spiritual. Missionary methods, as such, do not interest me at all. In fact, it is a deep grief to meet children of God who know practically nothing of the hatefulness of a life lived in the natural energy of man, and know little of vital experience of the headship of Jesus Christ, yet all the while are scrupulously careful to arrive at absolute correctness of method in God's service. Many a time we have been told, "We agree with you in everything." Far from it! In reality we do not agree at all! We hope this book will not fall into the hands of those who wish to improve their work by improving their methods, without adjusting their relationship to the Lord; but we do hope it will have a message for the humble ones who have learned to live in the power of the Spirit and have no confidence in the flesh.

It is death to have a wineskin without wine, but it is loss to have wine without a wineskin. We must have the wineskin after we have the wine. Paul wrote the Ephesian Epistle, but he could also write the Corinthian Epistle; and Corinthians presents us with Ephesian truths in practical expression. Yes, the writer of Ephesians was also the writer of Corinthians! But why is it that the children of God have never had any serious contentions over Ephesian truths, but always over Corinthian truths? Because the sphere of Ephesians is the heavenlies, and its truths are purely spiritual, so if there is any diversity of opinion concerning them, no one feels it much; but Corinthian teachings are practical and touch the earthly sphere, so if there is the slightest difference of opinion, a reaction is felt at once. Yes, Corinthians is very practical! And it tests our obedience more than does Ephesians!

The danger, with those who know little about life and reality, is to emphasize mere outward correctness; but with those to whom life and reality are a matter of supreme importance, the temptation is to throw away the divine pattern of things, thinking it legal and technical. They feel that they have the greater and can therefore well dispense with the lesser. As a result, the more spiritual a man is, the freer he feels to do as he thinks fit. He considers that he himself has authority to decide on outward matters, and rather fancies that to ignore God's commands regarding them is an indication that he has been delivered from legality and is walking in the liberty of the Spirit. But God has not only revealed the truths that concern our inner life; He has also revealed the truths relating to the outward expression of that life.

God prizes the inner reality, but He does not ignore its outward expression. God has given us Ephesians, Romans, and Colossians, but He has also given us Acts, the Epistles to Timothy, and the Epistles to the Corinthians. We may think it sufficient for God to instruct us through Romans, Ephesians, and Colossians as to our life in Christ, but He has considered it necessary to instruct us through Acts, Corinthians, and Timothy, how to do His work and how to organize His Church. God has left nothing to human imagination or human will. Man is afraid to use a thoughtless servant, but God does not care to use an overthoughtful one; all He requires of man is simple obedience. "Who has become His counselor?" asked Paul (Rom. 11:34). Man would fain occupy the post, but God has no need of a counselor. It is not our place to suggest how we think divine work should be done, but rather to ask in everything, "What is the will of the Lord?"

The Pharisees cleansed the outside of the platter, but left the inside full of impurity. Our Lord rebuked them for setting so much store on outward things, and ignoring the inward; and many of God's people conclude from the Lord's rebuke that, providing we stress the inner side of spiritual truth, all is well. But God demands both inward and outward purity. To have the outer without the inner is spiritual death, but to have the inner without the outer is only spiritualized life. And spiritualization is not spirituality. Our Lord said, "These you should have done and not neglected the others" (Matt. 23:23). No matter how insignificant any divine command may seem, it is an expression of the will of God; therefore, we never dare treat it lightly. We cannot neglect the least of His commands with impunity. The importance of His requirements may vary, but everything that is of God has eternal purpose and eternal worth. Of course, the mere observance of outward forms of service has no spiritual value whatever. All spiritual truths, whether pertaining to the inner or the outer life, are liable to be legalized. Everything that is of God— whether outward or inward—if in the Spirit is life; if in the letter it is death. So the question is not whether it is outward or inward, but whether it is in the Spirit or in the letter. "The letter kills, but the Spirit gives life" (2 Cor. 3:6).

It is our desire to accept and proclaim the whole Word of God. We covet to be able to say with Paul, "I did not shrink from declaring to you all the counsel of God" (Acts 20:27). We seek to follow the leading of God's Spirit, but at the same time we seek to pay attention to the examples shown us in His Word. The leading of the Spirit is precious, but if there is no example in the Word, then it is easy to substitute our fallible thoughts and unfounded feelings for the Spirit's leading, drifting into error without realizing it. If one is not prepared to obey God's will in every direction, it is easy to do things contrary to His Word and still fancy one is being led of His Spirit. We emphasize the necessity of following both the leading of the Spirit and the examples of the Word, because by comparing our ways with the written Word we can discover the source of our leading. The Spirit's guidance will always harmonize with the Scriptures. God cannot lead a man one way in Acts and another way today. In externalities the leading may vary, but in principle it is always the same; for God's will is eternal, therefore changeless. God is the eternal God; He takes no cognizance of time, and His will and ways all bear the stamp of eternity. This being so, God could never act one way at one time and another way later on. Circumstances may differ and cases may differ, but in principle the will and ways of God are just the same today as they were in the days of the Acts.

God said to the Israelites, "Moses, because of your hardness of heart, allowed you to divorce your wives" (Matt. 19:8), but the Lord Jesus said, "What God has yoked together, let man not separate" (Matt. 19:6). Is there not a discrepancy here? No! "Moses, because of your hardness of heart, allowed you to divorce your wives, but from the beginning it has not been so" (Matt. 19:8). It is not that in the beginning it was permissible, and later it became forbidden, and still later became permissible again, as though God were a changeable God. No, the Lord said, "From the beginning it has not been so" showing that God's will had never altered. From the beginning right on until today it is just the same. Here is a most important principle. If we want to know the mind of God, we must look at His commands in Genesis and not look at His permissions later on, because every later permission has this explanation, "because of your hardness of heart." It is God's directive will we want to discover, not His permissive will. We want to see what God's purpose was from the beginning. We want to see things as they were when they proceeded in all their purity from the mind of God, not what they have become because of hardness of heart on the part of His people.

If we would understand the will of God concerning His Church, then we must not look to see how He led His people last year, or ten years ago, or a hundred years ago, but we must return to the beginning, to the "genesis" of the Church, to see what He said and did then. It is there we find the highest expression of His will. Acts is the "genesis" of the Church's history, and the Church in the time of Paul is the "genesis" of the Spirit's work. Conditions in the Church today are vastly different from what they were then, but these present conditions could never be our example, or our authoritative guide. We must return to the beginning. Only what God has set forth as our example in the beginning is the eternal will of God. It is the divine standard and our pattern for all time.

A word of explanation may be needed regarding the examples God has given us in His Word. Christianity is not only built upon precepts, but also upon examples. God has revealed His will, not only by giving orders, but by having certain things done in His Church, so that in the ages to come others might simply look at the pattern and know His will. God has not only directed His people by means of abstract principles and objective regulations, but by concrete examples and subjective experience. God does use precepts to teach His people, but one of His chief methods of instruction is through history. God tells us how others knew and did His will, so that we, by looking at their lives, may not only know His will, but see how to do it too. He worked in their lives, producing in them what He Himself desired, and He bids us look at them, so that we may know what He is after.

Shall we, then, say that because God has not commanded a certain thing we need not do it? If we have seen His dealings with men in days past, if we have seen how He led His people and built up His Church, can we still plead ignorance of His will? Is it necessary for a child to be told explicitly how to do everything? Must each item be separately mentioned of things permissible and not permissible? Are there not many things he can learn simply by watching his parents or his elder brothers and sisters? We learn more readily by what we see than by what we hear, and the impression upon us is deeper. That is why God has given us so much history in the Old

Testament, and the Acts of the Apostles in the New. He knows we learn more easily by example than by precept. Examples have greater value than precepts, because precepts are abstract, while examples are precepts carried into effect. By looking at them, we not only know what God's precepts are, but we have a tangible demonstration of their outworking. If we try to eliminate examples from Christianity and leave only its precepts, then we have not much left. Precepts have their place, but examples have no less important a place, though obviously conformity to the divine pattern in outward things is mere formality if there is no correspondence in inner life.

In closing, may I stress the fact that this is not a book on missionary methods. Methods are not to be despised, but in God's service what matters most is the man, not his methods. Unless the man is right, right methods will be of no use to him or to his work. Carnal methods are suited to carnal men, and spiritual methods to spiritual men. For carnal men to employ spiritual methods will only result in confusion and failure. This book is intended for those who, having learned something of the cross, know the corruption of human nature, and seek to walk, not after the flesh, but after the Spirit. Its object is to help those who acknowledge the lordship of Christ in all things, and are seeking to serve Him in the way of His own appointing, not of their choosing. To put it in other words, it is written for those who are already in the good of Ephesian truths, so that they may know how to express their service along Corinthian lines. May none of my readers use this book as a basis for external adjustments in their work, without letting the cross deal drastically with their natural life.

In God's work everything depends upon the kind of worker sent out and the kind of convert produced. On the part of the convert, a real Holy Spirit new birth is essential, and a vital relationship with God. On the part of the worker, besides personal holiness and enduement for service, it is essential that he have an experimental knowledge of the meaning of committal to God and faith in His sovereign providence. Otherwise, no matter how scriptural the methods employed, the result will be emptiness and defeat.

To the Lord and to His people I commend this book, with the prayer that He may use it for His glory, as He sees fit. Shanghai January 1938 W. Nee.

# CHAPTER 1: THE APOSTLES

God is a God of works. Our Lord said, "My Father is working until now." And He has a definite purpose toward the realization of which He directs all His works. He is the God "who works all things according to the counsel of His will." But God does not do everything directly by Himself. He works through His servants. Among the servants of God the apostles are the most important ones. Let us look into the Word of God to see what it has to teach on the matter of the apostles.

## THE FIRST APOSTLE

In the fullness of time, God sent forth His Son into the world to do His work. He is known as the Christ of God, that is, "the Anointed One." The term "Son" relates to His Person; the name "Christ" relates to His office. He was the Son of God, but He was sent to be the Christ of God. "Christ" is the ministerial name of the Son of God. Our Lord did not come to the earth or to the cross on His own initiative; He was anointed and set apart for the work by God. He was not self-appointed, but sent. Frequently throughout the Gospel of John we find Him referring to God, not as "God," or "the Father," but as "Him who sent Me." He took the place of a sent one. If that is true in the case of the Son of God, how much more should it apply to His servants? If even the Son was not expected to take any initiative in God's work, is it likely that we are expected to do so? The first principle to note in the work of God is that all His workers are sent ones. If there is no divine commission, there can be no divine work.

Scripture has a special name for a sent one, that is, an apostle. The meaning of the Greek word is "the sent one." The Lord Himself is the first Apostle because He is the first one specially sent of God; hence, the Word refers to Him as "the Apostle" (Heb. 3:1).

## THE TWELVE

While our Lord fulfilled His apostolic ministry on earth, He was all the time aware that His life in the flesh was limited. Therefore, even as He pursued the work committed to Him by the Father, He was preparing a group of men to continue it after His departure. These men were also termed apostles. They were not volunteers; they were sent ones. We cannot overemphasize this fact that all divine work is by commission, not by choice.

From among whom did our Lord choose these apostles? They were chosen from among His disciples. All those sent out by the Lord were already disciples. Not all disciples are necessarily apostles, but all apostles are necessarily disciples; not all disciples are chosen for the work, but those who are chosen are always selected from among the disciples of the Lord. An apostle then must have two callings; in the first place he must be called to be a disciple, and in the second place he must be called to be an apostle. His first calling is from among the children of the world to be a follower of the Lord. His second calling is from among the followers of the Lord to be a sent one of the Lord.

Those apostles chosen by our Lord during His earthly ministry occupy a special place in Scripture, and they also occupy a special place in the purpose of God, because they were with the Son of God while He lived in the flesh. They were not just called apostles; they were called "the twelve apostles." They occupy a special place in the Word of God, and they occupy a special place in the plan of God. Our Lord told Peter that one day they should "sit on thrones judging the twelve tribes of Israel" (Luke 22:30). The Apostle has His throne, and the twelve apostles are going to have their thrones too. This is a privilege not granted to other apostles. When Judas lost his office and God led the remaining eleven to choose one to make up the number, we read that they cast lots and the lot fell upon Matthias, "and he was counted with the eleven apostles" (Acts 1:26). In the next chapter we find the Holy Spirit inspiring the writer of the Acts to say, "Peter, standing with the eleven" (Acts 2:14), which shows that the Holy Spirit recognized Matthias to be one of the twelve. Here we see that the number of these apostles was fixed; God did not want more than twelve, nor would He have less. In the book of Revelation we find that the ultimate position which they occupy is again a special one—"And the wall of the city had twelve foundations, and on them the twelve names of the twelve apostles of the Lamb" (Rev. 21:14). Even in the new heaven and the new earth the twelve enjoy a place of particular privilege, which is assigned to no other workers for God.

## THE APOSTLES IN SCRIPTURE DAYS

The Lord as an apostle was unique, and the twelve, as apostles, were also unique; but neither the Apostle nor the twelve apostles could abide on earth forever. When our Lord departed, He left the twelve to continue His work. Now that the twelve have departed, who are here to carry it on?

The Lord has gone, but the Spirit has come. The Holy Spirit is come to bear all responsibility for the work of God on earth. The Son was working for the Father; the Spirit is working for the Son. The Son came to accomplish the will of the Father; the Spirit has come to accomplish the will of the Son. The Son came to glorify the Father; the Spirit has come to glorify the Son. The Father appointed Christ to be the Apostle; the Son while on earth appointed the twelve to be apostles. Now the Son has returned to the Father, and the Spirit is on earth appointing men to be apostles. The apostles appointed by the Holy Spirit cannot join the ranks of those appointed by the Son; nevertheless, they are apostles. The apostles we read of in Ephesians 4 are clearly not the original twelve, for those were appointed when the Lord was still on earth, while these date their appointment to apostleship after the ascension of the Lord—they were the gifts of the Lord Jesus to His Church after His glorification. The apostles then were the personal followers of the Lord Jesus, but the apostles now are ministers for the building up of the Body of Christ. We must differentiate clearly between the apostles who were witnesses to the resurrection of Christ (Acts 1:22, 26), and the apostles who are ministers for the edifying of the Body of Christ, for the Body of Christ was not in existence before the cross. There is no doubt that later on the twelve received the Ephesian commission, but the twelve, as the twelve, were quite distinct from the apostles mentioned in Ephesians. It is evident then that God has other apostles besides the original twelve.

Immediately after the outpouring of the Spirit we see the twelve apostles carrying on the work. Until Acts 12 they are seen as the chief workers; but with the opening of chapter thirteen we see the Holy Spirit beginning to manifest Himself as the Agent of Christ and the Lord of the Church. In that chapter we are told that in Antioch, when certain prophets and teachers were ministering to the Lord and fasting, the Holy Spirit said, "Set apart for Me now Barnabas and Saul for the work to which I have called them" (Acts 13:2). Now is the time that the Spirit begins to send men forth. At this point two new workers were commissioned by the Holy Spirit.

After these two were sent out by the Spirit, how were they designated? When Barnabas and Paul were working in Iconium, "the multitude of the city was divided, and some were with the Jews and some with the apostles" (Acts 14:4). The two sent forth in the previous chapter are in this chapter referred to as apostles, and in the same chapter (v. 14), the designation "the apostles" is used in apposition to "Barnabas and Paul," which proves conclusively that the two men commissioned by the Holy Spirit were also apostles. They were not among the twelve; nevertheless, they were apostles.

Who then are apostles? Apostles are God's workmen, sent out by the Holy Spirit to do the work to which He has called them. The responsibility of the work is in their hands. Broadly speaking, all believers are responsible for the work of God, but apostles are a group of people specially set apart for the work. In a particular sense the responsibility of the work is upon them.

Now we see the teaching of the Scriptures as touching apostles. God appointed His Son to be the Apostle; Christ appointed His disciples to be the twelve apostles; and the Holy Spirit appointed a group of men (apart from the twelve) to be the Body-building apostles. The first Apostle is unique; there is only one. The twelve apostles are also in a class by themselves; there are only twelve. But there is another order of apostles, chosen by the Holy Spirit, and as long as the building up of the Church goes on and the Holy Spirit's presence on earth continues, the choosing and sending forth of this order of apostles will continue too.

In the Word of God we find numerous other apostles besides Barnabas and Paul. There are many belonging to the new order chosen and sent forth by the Spirit of God. In 1 Corinthians 4:9 we read, "God has set forth us the apostles last." To whom do the words "us the apostles" refer? The pronoun "us" implies that there was at least one other apostle besides the writer. If we study the context, we note that Apollos was with Paul when he wrote (v. 6), and Sosthenes was a joint writer with Paul of the Epistle. So it seems clear that the "us" here refers either to Apollos or to Sosthenes, or to both. It follows then that either or both of these two must have been apostles.

Romans 16:7: "Greet Andronicus and Junia, my kinsmen and my fellow prisoners, who are of note among the apostles." The clause "who are of note among the apostles" does not mean that they were regarded as notable by the apostles, but rather that among the apostles they were notable ones.

Here we have not only another two apostles, but another two notable apostles.

First Thessalonians 2:6: "We could have stood on our authority as apostles of Christ." The "we" here refers clearly to the writers of the Thessalonian letter, that is, Paul, Silvanus, and Timothy (1:1), which indicates that Paul's two young fellow workers were also apostles.

First Corinthians 15:5-7: "He appeared to Cephas, then to the twelve; then He appeared to over five hundred brothers at one time,...then He appeared to James, then to all the apostles." Besides the twelve apostles there was a group known as "all the apostles." It is obvious, then, that apart from the twelve, there were other apostles.

Paul never claimed that he was the last apostle and that after him there were no others. Let us read carefully what he said: "Last of all He appeared to me also...for I am the least of the apostles, who am not fit to be called an apostle" (1 Cor. 15:8-9). Notice how Paul used the words "last" and "least." He did not say that he was the last apostle; he only said he was the least apostle. If he were the last, there could be no more after him, but he was only the least.

In the book of Revelation it is said of the Ephesian church: "You have tried those who call themselves apostles and are not, and have found them to be false" (2:2). It seems clear from this verse that the early churches expected to have other apostles apart from the original twelve, because, when the book of Revelation was written, John was the only survivor of the twelve, and by that time even Paul had already been martyred. If there were to be only twelve apostles, and John was the only one left, then no one would have been foolish enough to pose as an apostle, and no one foolish enough to be deceived, and where would have been the need to try them? If John were the only apostle, then testing would be simple indeed! Anyone who was not John was not an apostle!

## THE MEANING OF APOSTLESHIP

Since the meaning of the word "apostle" is "the sent one," the meaning of apostleship is quite plain, that is, the office of the sent one. Apostles are not primarily men of special gifts; they are men of special commission. Everyone who is sent of God is an apostle. Many called of God are not as gifted as Paul, but if they have received a commission from God, they are just as truly apostles as he was. The apostles were gifted men, but their apostleship was not based upon their gifts; it was based upon their commission. Of course, God will not send anyone who is unequipped, but equipment does not constitute apostleship. If God cared to send out a man totally unequipped, that man would be as much an apostle as a fully equipped one, since apostleship is not based on human qualification but on divine commission. It is futile for anyone to assume the office of an apostle simply because he thinks he has the needed gifts or ability. It takes more than mere gift and ability to constitute men apostles; it takes nothing less than God Himself, God's will, and God's call. No man can attain to apostleship through natural or other qualifications; God must make him an apostle if he is ever to be one. Whether or not a man is going to be of any spiritual worth, and his work serve any spiritual end, depends upon the sending of God. "A man sent of God" should be the main characteristic of our entering upon His service, and of all our subsequent movements.

Let us turn to the Scriptures. In Luke 11:49 we read, "I will send to them prophets and apostles, and some of them they will kill and persecute." From Genesis to Malachi we do not come across anyone who was explicitly called an apostle; yet the men here referred to as apostles lived between the time of Abel and Zachariah (v. 51). Therefore, it is clear that even in Old Testament times God had His apostles.

Our Lord said, "A slave is not greater than his master, nor the apostle [Greek] greater than the one who sends him" (John 13:16). Here we have a definition of the term "apostle." It implies being sent out—that is all; and that is everything. However good human intention may be, it can never take the place of divine commission. Today those who have been sent out by the Lord to preach the gospel and to establish churches call themselves missionaries, not apostles; but the word "missionary" means the very same thing as "apostle," that is, "the sent one." It is the Latin form of the Greek equivalent, apostolos. Since the meaning of the two words is exactly the same, I fail to see the reason why the true sent ones of today prefer to call themselves missionaries rather than apostles.

## APOSTLES AND THE MINISTRY

"But to each one of us grace was given according to the measure of the gift of Christ. Therefore the Scripture says, Having ascended to the height, He led captive those taken captive and gave gifts to men.' (Now this, 'He ascended,' what is it except that He also descended into the lower parts of the earth? He who descended, He is also the One who ascended far above all the heavens that He might fill all things.) And He Himself gave some[3] as apostles and some as prophets and some as evangelists and some as shepherds and teachers, for the perfecting of the saints unto the work of the ministry, unto the building up of the Body of Christ, until we all arrive at the oneness of the faith and of the full knowledge of the Son of God, at a full-grown man, at the measure of the stature of the fullness of Christ" (Eph. 4:713).

There are many ministries connected with the service of God, but He has chosen a number of men for a special ministry—the ministry of the Word for the building up of the Body of Christ. Since that ministry is different from others, we refer to it as "the ministry." This ministry is entrusted to a group of people of whom the apostles are chief. It is neither a one-man ministry, nor an "all-men" ministry, but a ministry based upon the gifts of the Holy Spirit and an experimental knowledge of the Lord.

Apostles, prophets, evangelists, and shepherds and teachers are our Lord's gifts to His Church to serve in the ministry. Strictly speaking, shepherds and teachers are one gift, not two, because teaching and shepherding are closely related. In enumerating the gifts, apostles, prophets, and evangelists are all mentioned separately, while shepherds and teachers are linked together. Furthermore, the first three are each prefixed by the word "some," whereas the word "some" is attached to shepherds and teachers unitedly, thus —"some as apostles," "some as prophets," "some as evangelists," and "some as shepherds and teachers," not "some as shepherds and some as teachers." The fact that the word "some" is used only four times in this list indicates that there are only four classes of persons in question. Shepherds and teachers are two in one.

Shepherding and teaching may be regarded as one ministry, because those who teach must also shepherd, and those who shepherd must also teach. The two kinds of work are interrelated. Furthermore, the word "shepherd" as applied to any person is found nowhere else in the New Testament, but the word "teacher" is used on four other occasions. In the New Testament we find reference elsewhere to an apostle (for example,

Paul), and a prophet (for example, Agabus), and an evangelist (for example, Philip), and a teacher (for example, Manaen), but nowhere in God's Word do we find anyone referred to as a shepherd. This confirms the fact that shepherds and teachers are one class of men.

Teachers are men who have received the gift of teaching. This is not a miraculous gift, but a gift of grace, which accounts for the fact of its being omitted from the list of miraculous gifts in 1 Corinthians 12:8-10, and included in the list of the gifts of grace in Romans 12. It is a gift of grace which enables its possessors to understand the teachings of God's Word, and to discern His purposes, and thus equips them to instruct His people in doctrinal matters. In the church in Antioch there were several persons thus equipped, Paul among the number. It is by the operation of God that such men are "placed...in the church," and their position is next to that of the prophets. A teacher is an individual who has received the gift of teaching from God, and has been given by the Lord to His Church for its upbuilding. The work of a teacher is to interpret to others the truths which have been revealed to him, to lead God's people to an understanding of the Word, and to encourage them to seek and receive for themselves divine revelation through the Scriptures. Their sphere of work is mainly among the children of God, though at times they also teach the unsaved (1 Tim. 4:11; 6:2; 2 Tim. 2:2; Acts 4:2-18; 5:21, 25, 28, 42). Their work is more one of interpretation than of revelation, whereas the work of the prophets is more one of revelation than of interpretation. They seek to lead believers to an understanding of divine truth, and they seek to lead unbelievers to an understanding of the gospel.

Evangelists are also our Lord's gift to His Church, but exactly what their personal gifts are we do not know. The Word of God does not speak of any evangelistic gift, but it does refer to Philip as being an evangelist (Acts 21:8), and Paul on one occasion encouraged Timothy to do the work of an evangelist and fill up the measure of his ministry (2 Tim. 4:5). Apart from these three occasions, the noun "evangelist" is not found in Scripture, though we frequently meet the verb which is derived from the same root.

In the Word of God the place of prophets is more clearly defined than that of teachers and evangelists. Prophecy is mentioned among the gifts of grace (Rom. 12:6), and among the miraculous gifts we find it again (1 Cor. 12:10). God has set prophets in the Church universal (1 Cor. 12:28), but He has also given prophets for the ministry (Eph. 4:11). There is both the gift of prophecy and the office of a prophet. Prophecy is both a gift of miracle and a gift of grace. The prophet is both a man set by God in His Church to occupy the prophetic office, and a man given by the Lord to His Church for the ministry.

Of the four classes of gifted men bestowed by the Lord upon His Church for its upbuilding, the apostles were quite different from the other three. The special position occupied by apostles is obvious to any reader of the New

Testament. They were specially commissioned of God to found churches through the preaching of the gospel, to bring revelation from God to His people, to give decisions in matters pertaining to doctrine and government, and to edify the saints and distribute the gifts. Both spiritually and geographically their sphere is vast. That their position was superior to that of prophets and teachers is clear from the Word: "God has placed some in the church: first apostles" (1 Cor. 12:28).

Apostles belong to the ministry, but they are quite different from the prophets, evangelists, and teachers, because, unlike these three, it is not their gifts that determine their office; that is, they are not constituted apostles by receiving an apostolic gift.

It is important to note that apostleship is an office, not a gift. An office is what one receives as the result of a commission; a gift is what one receives on the basis of grace. "I was appointed...an apostle" (1 Tim. 2:7). "I was appointed...an apostle" (2 Tim. 1:11). We see here that apostles are commissioned. Being an apostle is not subject to receiving an apostolic gift, but subject to receiving an apostolic commission. An apostle has a special call and a special commission. It is in this that he differs from the other three ministers, though he may have received the prophetic gift and thus be a prophet as well as an apostle. His personal gift constitutes him a prophet, but it is commission, not gift, that constitutes him an apostle. The other ministers belong to the ministry by virtue of their gifts; an apostle belongs to the ministry by virtue of his being sent. Their qualification is the possession of gifts; his is the possession of gifts plus a special call and commission.

An apostle may be a prophet or a teacher. Should he exercise his gift of prophecy or teaching in the local church, he does so in the capacity of a prophet or a teacher, but when he exercises his gifts in different places, he does so in the capacity of an apostle. The implication of apostleship is being sent of God to exercise gifts of ministry in different places. It is immaterial to his office what personal gift an apostle has, but it is essential to his office that he be sent of God. An apostle can exercise his spiritual gifts in any place, but he cannot exercise his apostolic gifts, because an apostle is such by office, not by gift.

Nevertheless, apostles have personal gifts for their ministry. "Now there were in Antioch, in the local church, prophets and teachers: Barnabas and Simeon, who was called Niger, and Lucius the Cyrenian, and Manaen, the foster brother of Herod the tetrarch, and Saul. And as they were ministering to the Lord and fasting, the Holy Spirit said, Set apart for Me now Barnabas and Saul for the work to which I have called them" (Acts 13:1-2). These five men had the gifts of prophecy and teaching, a miraculous gift and a gift of grace. From that company of five two were sent by the Spirit to other parts, and three were left in Antioch. As we have already seen, the two sent out were thereafter called apostles. They received no apostolic gift, but they did receive an apostolic commission. It was their gifts that qualified them to be prophets and teachers, but it was their commission that qualified them to be apostles. The three who remained in Antioch were still prophets and teachers, not apostles, simply because they had not been sent out by the Spirit. The two became apostles, not because they had received any gift in addition to the gift of prophecy and teaching, but because they received an additional office as a result of their commission. The gifts of all five were just the same, but the two received a divine commission in addition to their gifts, and that qualified them for apostolic ministry.

Then why does the Word of God say, "He Himself gave some as apostles"? It is not a question here of apostleship being a gift given to an apostle, but a gift given to the Church; it is not a spiritual gift given to a man, but a gifted man given to the Church. Ephesians 4:11 does not say that the Lord gave an apostolic gift to any person, but that He gave men as apostles to His Church. Men have received gifts of the Spirit which have qualified them to become prophets and teachers, but no man has ever received a spiritual gift which has qualified him to be an apostle. Apostles are a class of people the Church has received as our Lord's gift for its upbuilding.

The gifts referred to in this passage are not the gifts given to men personally, but the gifts given by the Lord to His Church, and the gifts mentioned here are gifted workers whom the Lord of the Church bestows upon His Church for its edification. The Head gives to the Church which is His Body certain men to serve the Body and build it up. We must distinguish between those gifts given by the Spirit to individuals and those given by the Lord to His Church. The former are given to believers personally; the latter are given to believers corporately. The former are things, and the latter are persons. The gifts given by the Spirit to individuals are their equipment to serve the Lord in prophesy, teaching, speaking in tongues, and healing the sick; the gifts given by the Lord to His Church as a Body are the persons who possess the gifts of the Spirit.

"For to one through the Spirit a word of wisdom is given, and to another a word of knowledge, according to the same Spirit; to a different one faith in the same Spirit, and to another gifts of healing in the one Spirit, and to another operations of works of power, and to another prophecy, and to another discerning of spirits; to a different one various kinds of tongues, and to another interpretation of tongues" (1 Cor. 12:8-10). This passage provides us with a list of all the gifts which the Holy Spirit gave to men, but it includes no apostolic gift. "And God has placed some in the church: first apostles, second prophets, third teachers; then works of power, then gifts of healing, helps, administrations, various kinds of tongues" (1 Cor. 12:28). The first passage enumerates the gifts given to individuals; the second enumerates the gifts given to the Church. In the former there is no mention of any apostolic gift; in the latter we find that apostles head the list of God's gifts to the Church. It is not that God has given His Church the gift of apostleship, but that He has given it men who are apostles; and He has not given the gifts of prophecy and teaching to His Church, but He has given it some men as prophets and some as teachers. God has set different kinds of workers in His Church for its edification, one of which is apostles. They do not represent a certain kind of gift; they represent a certain class of persons.

The difference between the apostles, and the prophets and teachers, is that the latter two represent both gifts given by the Spirit to individuals and at the same time gifts given by the Lord to His Church, whereas apostles are men given by the Lord to His Church, but they do not represent any special, personal gift of the Spirit.

"And God has placed some in the church: first apostles, second prophets, third teachers" (1 Cor. 12:28). What church is this? It comprises all the children of God; therefore, it is the Church universal. In this Church God has set "first apostles, second prophets, third teachers." In 1 Corinthians 14:23 we read that "the whole church comes together." What church is this? Obviously the local church, for the Church universal cannot gather together in one locality. It is in this local church that the brethren exercised their spiritual gifts. One would have a psalm, another a teaching, another a revelation, another a tongue, and another an interpretation (14:26), but more important than all these was the gift of prophecy (14:1). In chapter twelve, apostles took precedence over the other ministers, but in chapter fourteen, prophets take the precedence. In the Church universal, apostles are first, but in the local church, prophets are first. How does it come about that prophets take first place in the local church, since in the universal Church they only occupy the second place? Because in the Church universal the question is not of personal gifts of the Spirit, but of God's gift of ministers to the Church, and of these, apostles rank first; but in the local church the question is one of personal gifts of the Spirit, and of these, prophecy is chief, because it is most important. Let us remember that apostleship is not a personal gift.

## THE SPHERE OF THEIR WORK

The sphere of an apostle's work is quite different from that of the other three special ministers. That prophets and teachers exercise their gifts in the local church is seen from the statement: "Now there were in Antioch, in the local church, prophets and teachers." You can find prophets and teachers in the local church, but not apostles, because they have been called to minister in different places, while the ministry of prophets and teachers is confined to one locality (1 Cor. 14:26, 29).

As to evangelists, we do not know their special sphere, as very little is said of them in God's Word, but the story of Philip, the evangelist, throws some light on this class of ministers. Philip left his own locality and preached in Samaria, but while he did good work there, the Spirit did not fall upon any of his converts. It was not till the apostles came from Jerusalem and laid hands on them that the Spirit was poured out. This seems to indicate that the local preaching of the gospel is the work of an evangelist, but the universal preaching of the gospel is the work of an apostle. This does not imply that the labors of an evangelist are necessarily confined to one place, but it does mean that that is their usual sphere. In the same way the prophet Agabus prophesied in another place, but his special sphere of work was his own locality.

## THE EVIDENCE OF APOSTLESHIP

Is there any evidence that one is really commissioned of God to be an apostle? In 1 Corinthians 9:1-2, Paul is dealing with our question in writing to the Corinthian saints, and it is obvious from his argument that apostleship has its credentials. "For you in the Lord are the seal of my apostleship," he writes, as if to say, "If God had not sent me to Corinth, then you would not be saved today, and there would be no church in your city." If God has called a man to be an apostle, it will be manifest in the fruit of his labors. Wherever you have the commission of God, there you have the authority of

God; wherever you have the authority of God, there you have the power of God; and wherever you have the power of God, there you have spiritual fruits. The fruit of our labors proves the validity of our commission. And yet it must be noted that Paul's thought is not that apostleship implies numerous converts, but that it represents spiritual values to the Lord, for He could never send anyone forth for a lesser purpose. The Lord is out for spiritual values, and the object of apostleship is to secure them. In this case the Corinthians represent these values. But did not Paul say here, "Have I not seen Jesus our Lord?" Then is it only those who have seen the Lord Jesus in His resurrection manifestations who are qualified to become apostles? Let us follow carefully the trend of Paul's argument. In verse 1 he asks four questions: (1) "Am I not free?" (2) "Am I not an apostle?" (3) "Have I not seen Jesus our Lord?" (4) "Are you not my work in the Lord?" An affirmative answer to all four questions was taken for granted, for Paul's case demanded such an answer. Notice that in pursuing his argument in the second verse, Paul drops two of his questions and follows out the other two. He drops the first and third, and takes up the second and fourth, linking them together. For the purpose of his reasoning he sets aside, "Am I not free?" and, "Have I not seen Jesus our Lord?" and replies to the question, "Am I not an apostle?" and, "Are you not my work in the Lord?" Paul was clearly seeking to demonstrate the genuineness of his commission from the blessing that attended his labors, not from his being free or from his having seen the Lord.

Of the four questions asked by Paul, three relate to his person and one to his work. These three are on the same plane, and are quite independent of one another. Paul was not arguing that because he was free and because he was an apostle, therefore he had seen the Lord. Nor was he reasoning that because he was an apostle and because he had seen the Lord, therefore he was free. Neither was he seeking to demonstrate that because he was free and had seen the Lord, therefore he was an apostle. The facts are he was free, he was an apostle, and he had seen the Lord. These facts had no essential connection one with the other, and it is absurd to connect them. It would be as reasonable to argue that Paul's apostleship was based upon his being free, as that it was based upon his seeing the Lord. If he was not seeking to prove his apostleship from the fact of his freedom, neither was he seeking to prove it from his having seen the Lord. Apostleship is not based on having seen the Lord in His resurrection manifestations.

Then what is the meaning of 1 Corinthians 15:5-9? "He appeared to Cephas, then to the twelve; then He appeared to over five hundred brothers at one time,...then He appeared to James, then to all the apostles; and last of all He appeared to me also." The object of this passage is not to produce evidence of apostleship, but evidence of the resurrection of the Lord. Paul is recording the different persons to whom the Lord appeared; he is not teaching what effect was produced upon these persons by His appearing. Cephas and James saw the Lord, but they were Cephas and James after they saw the Lord, just as they were Cephas and James before; they did not become Cephas and James by seeing Him. The same applies to the twelve apostles and the five hundred brethren. Seeing the Lord did not constitute them apostles. They were twelve apostles before they saw the Lord, and they were twelve apostles after they saw the Lord. The same argument applies in Paul's case. The facts were that he had seen the Lord, and he was the least of the apostles; but it was not seeing the Lord that constituted him the least of the apostles. The five hundred brethren were not apostles before they saw the Lord, nor were they after. Seeing the Lord in His resurrection manifestations did not constitute them apostles. They were simply brethren before, and they were simply brethren after. The Word of God nowhere teaches that seeing the Lord is the qualification for apostleship.

But apostleship has its credentials. In 2 Corinthians 12:11-12, Paul writes, "In nothing am I inferior to the super-apostles...Indeed the signs of an apostle were wrought among you in all endurance by signs and wonders and works of power." There was abundant evidence of the genuineness of Paul's apostolic commission; and the signs of an apostle will never be lacking where there is truly an apostolic call. From the above passage we infer that the evidence of apostleship lies in a twofold power—spiritual and miraculous. Endurance is the greatest proof of spiritual power, and it is one of the signs of an apostle. It is the ability to endure steadfastly under continuous pressure that tests the reality of an apostolic call. A true apostle needs to be "empowered with all power, according to the might of His glory, unto all endurance and long-suffering with joy" (Col. 1:11). Yes, it takes nothing short of "all power, according to the might of His glory" to produce "all endurance and long-suffering with joy." But the reality of Paul's apostleship was not only attested by his patient endurance under intense and prolonged pressure; it was evidenced also by the miraculous power he possessed. Miraculous power to change situations in the physical world is a necessary manifestation of our knowledge of God in the spiritual realm, and this applies not to heathen lands only, but to every land. To profess to be sent ones of the omnipotent God, and yet stand helpless before situations that challenge His power, is a sad contradiction. Not all who can work wonders are apostles, for the gifts of healing and of miracle-working are given to members of the Body (1 Cor. 12:28) who have no special commission, but miraculous as well as spiritual power is part of the equipment of all who have a true apostolic commission.

## WOMEN APOSTLES

Have women any place among the ranks of the apostles? Scripture indicates that they have. There were no women among the twelve sent forth by the Lord, but a woman is mentioned among the number of the apostles who were sent forth by the Spirit after the Lord's ascension. Romans 16:7 speaks of two notable apostles, Andronicus and Junia, and good authorities agree that "Junia" is a woman's name. So here we have a sister as an apostle and a notable apostle at that.

# CHAPTER 2: THE SEPARATION AND MOVEMENTS OF THE APOSTLES

## ANTIOCH—THE MODEL CHURCH

The church in Antioch is the model church shown us in God's Word, because it was the first to come into being after the founding of the churches connected with the Jews and the Gentiles. In Acts 2 we see the church in connection with the Jews established in Jerusalem, and in chapter ten we see the church in connection with the Gentiles established in the house of Cornelius. It was just after the establishment of these churches that the church in Antioch was founded. In its transition stage the church in Jerusalem was not altogether free from Judaism, but the church in Antioch from the very outset stood on absolutely clear Church ground. It is of no little significance that "the disciples were first called Christians in Antioch" (Acts 11:26). It was there that the peculiar characteristics of the Christian and the Christian Church were first clearly manifested, for which reason it may be regarded as the pattern church for this dispensation. Its prophets and teachers were model prophets and teachers, and the apostles it sent forth were model apostles. Not only are the men sent forth an example to us, but the manner of their sending forth is our example too. Since the first recorded sending out of apostles by the Holy Spirit was from Antioch, we shall do well to look carefully into its details.

Since the completion of the New Testament the Holy Spirit has called many of God's children to serve Him throughout the world, but, strictly speaking, none of these can be regarded as our examples. We must always look at the first act of the Holy Spirit in any given direction to discover His pattern for us in that particular direction. Therefore, in order to see what example the Church must follow today in the sending forth of apostles, let us examine carefully the first recorded sending forth of workers from the first church established on absolutely clear Church ground.

# THE HOLY SPIRIT'S CALL

In the first two verses of Acts 13 we read, "Now there were in Antioch, in the local church, prophets and teachers: Barnabas and Simeon, who was called Niger, and Lucius the Cyrenian, and Manaen, the foster brother of Herod the tetrarch, and Saul. And as they were ministering to the Lord and fasting, the Holy Spirit said, Set apart for Me now Barnabas and Saul for the work to which I have called them." Let us note a few facts here. There was a local church in Antioch, there were certain prophets and teachers who were ministers in that church, and it was from among those that the Holy Spirit separated two for another sphere of service. Barnabas and Saul were two ministers of the Lord already engaged in the ministry when the call of the Spirit came. The Holy Spirit only sends to other parts such as are already equipped for the work and are bearing responsibility where they are, not those who are burying their talents and neglecting local needs while they dream of some future day when the call will come to special service. Barnabas and Saul were bearing the burden of the local situation when the Spirit put the burden of other parts upon them. Their hands were full of local work when He thrust them out to work further afield. Let us note first that the Holy Spirit chooses apostles from among the prophets and teachers.

"And as they were ministering to the Lord and fasting, the Holy Spirit said, Set apart for Me now Barnabas and Saul for the work to which I have called them." These prophets and teachers ministered so wholeheartedly to the Lord that when occasion demanded they even ignored the legitimate claims of their physical being and fasted. What filled the thoughts of those prophets and teachers at Antioch was ministry to the Lord, not work for Him. Their devotion was to the Lord Himself, not to His service. No one can truly work for the Lord who has not first learned to minister to Him. It was while Barnabas and Saul ministered to the Lord that the voice of the Spirit was heard calling them to special service.

It was to the divine call they responded, not to the call of human need. They had heard no reports of man-eaters or head-hunting savages; their compassions had not been stirred by doleful tales of child-marriage or footbinding or opium-smoking. They had heard no voice but the voice of the Spirit; they had seen no claims but the claims of Christ. No appeal had been made to their natural heroism or love of adventure. They knew only one appeal—the appeal of their Lord. It was the lordship of Christ that claimed their service, and it was on His authority alone that they went forth. Their call was a spiritual call. No natural factor entered into it. It was the Holy

Spirit who said, "Set apart for Me now Barnabas and Saul for the work to which I have called them." All spiritual work must begin with the Spirit's call. All divine work must be divinely initiated. The plan conceived for the work may be splendid, the reason adequate, the need urgent, and the man chosen to carry it out may be eminently suitable; but if the Holy Spirit has not said, "Set apart that man for the work to which I have called him," he can never be an apostle. He may be a prophet or a teacher, but he is no apostle. Of old all true apostles were separated by the Holy Spirit for the work to which He called them, and today all true apostles must just as surely be set apart for the work by Him. God desires the service of His children, but He makes conscripts; He wants no volunteers. The work is His, and He is its only legitimate Originator. Human intention, however good, can never take the place of divine initiation. Earnest desires for the salvation of sinners or for the edification of saints will never qualify a man for God's work. One qualification, and only one, is necessary—God must send him.

It was the Holy Spirit who said, "Set apart for Me now Barnabas and Saul for the work to which I have called them." Only the divine call can qualify for the apostolic office. In earthly governments there can be no service without commission, and the same holds true in the government of God. The tragedy in Christian work today is that so many of the workers have simply gone out; they have not been sent. It is divine commission that constitutes the call to divine work. Personal desire, friendly persuasions, the advice of one's elders, and the urge of opportunity—all these are factors on the natural plane, and they can never take the place of a spiritual call. That is something which must be registered in the human spirit by the Spirit of God.

When Barnabas and Saul were sent forth, the Spirit first called them, then the brethren confirmed the call. The brethren may say you have a call, and circumstances may seem to indicate it, but the question is whether or not you yourself have heard the call. If you are to go forth, then you are the one who must first hear the voice of the Spirit. We dare not disregard the opinion of the brethren, but their opinion is no substitute for a personal call from God. Even if they are confident that we have a call, and in that same confidence a company of God's people gladly sends us forth to the work, unless we ourselves know a direct speaking of God into our hearts, on the basis of the new covenant, then we go forth as the messengers of men, not as the apostles of God.

If God desires the service of any child of His, He Himself will call him to it, and He Himself will send him forth. The first requirement in divine work is a divine call. Everything hinges on this. A divine call gives God His rightful place, for it recognizes Him as the Originator of the work. Where there is no call from God, the work undertaken is not of divine origin, and it has no spiritual value. Divine work must be divinely initiated. A worker may be called directly by the Spirit, or indirectly through the reading of the Word, through preaching, or through circumstances; but whatever means God may use to make His will known to man, His voice must be the one heard through every other voice; He must be the one who speaks, no matter through what instrument the call may come. We must never be independent of the other members of the Body, but we must never forget that we receive all our directions from the Head; so we must be careful to preserve our spiritual independence, even while we cultivate a spirit of mutual dependence among the members. It is wrong to reject the opinion of fellow workers under the pretext of doing the will of God, but it is also wrong to accept their opinions as a substitute for the direct instructions of the Spirit of God.

## SEPARATION OF WORKERS

Yes, it was the Holy Spirit who called Barnabas and Saul, but He said to the other prophets and teachers as well as to them, "Set apart for Me now Barnabas and Saul for the work to which I have called them." The Holy Spirit spoke directly to the apostles, but He also spoke indirectly through the prophets and teachers. What was said privately to the two was confirmed publicly through the other three. All apostles must have a personal revelation of God's will, but to make that alone the basis of their going forth is not sufficient. On the one hand, the opinion of others, however spiritual and however experienced, can never be a substitute for a direct call from God. On the other hand, a personal call, however definite, requires the confirmation of the representative members of the Body of Christ in the locality from which the workers go out.

Let us observe that the Holy Spirit did not say to the church in Antioch, "Set apart for Me now Barnabas and Saul." It was to the prophets and teachers He spoke. For God to make His will known to the entire assembly would scarcely have been practicable. Some of its members were spiritually mature, but others were only babes in Christ. Some were wholeheartedly devoted to the Lord, but it is highly improbable that all the members sought the Lord with such singleness of purpose that they could clearly differentiate between His will and their own ideas. God therefore spoke to a representative company in the church, to men of spiritual experience who were utterly devoted to His interest.

And here was the result: "When they had fasted and prayed and laid their hands on them, they sent them away" (Acts 13:3). The setting apart of the apostles by the prophets and teachers followed the call which came to them from the Spirit. The call was personal, the separation was corporate; and the one was not complete without the other. A direct call from God, and a confirmation of that call in the setting apart of the called ones by the prophets and teachers, is God's provision against free lances in His service.

The calling of an apostle is the Holy Spirit speaking directly to the one called. The separating of an apostle is the Holy Spirit speaking indirectly through the fellow workers of the called one. It is the Holy Spirit who takes the initiative both in the calling and separation of workers. Therefore, if the representative brethren of any assembly set men apart for the service of the Lord, they must ask themselves, Are we doing this on our own initiative, or as representing the Spirit of God? If they move without absolute assurance that they are acting on behalf of the Holy Spirit, then the separation of the worker has no spiritual value. They must be able to say of every worker they send forth, He was sent out by the Holy Spirit, not by man. No separation of workers should be done hastily or lightly. It was for this reason that fasting and prayer preceded the sending forth of Barnabas and Saul.

When Barnabas and Saul were separated for the work, there was prayer and fasting and the laying on of hands. The prayer and fasting was not merely in view of the immediate need of clear discernment regarding the will of God, but in view also of the coming need when the apostles would actually go forth. And the laying on of hands was not by way of ordination, for Barnabas and Saul were already ordained by the Holy Spirit. Here, as in the Old Testament, it was an expression of the perfect oneness of the two parties represented. It was as though the three sending forth the two said to them, "When you two members of the Body of Christ go forth, all the other members go with you. Your going is our going, and your work is our work." The laying on of hands was a testimony to the oneness of the Body of Christ. It meant that those who remained behind were one with those who went forth, and in full sympathy with them; and that, as they went, those at the base pledged themselves to follow them continually with prayerful interest and loving sympathy.

As regards all sent ones, they must pay attention to these two aspects in their separation for the service of God.

On the one hand, there must be a direct call from God and a personal recognition of that call. On the other hand, there must be a confirmation of that call by the representative members of the Body of Christ. And as regards all who are responsible for the sending forth of others, they must on the one hand be in a position to receive the revelation of the Spirit and to discern the mind of the Lord; on the other hand, they must be able to enter sympathetically into the experience of those whom they, as the representative members of the Body of Christ, send forth in the name of the Lord. The principle that governed the sending forth of the first apostles still governs the sending forth of all apostles who are truly appointed by the Spirit to the work of God.

## THE EXPRESSION OF THE BODY

On what ground did these prophets and teachers set certain men apart as apostles, and whom did these prophets and teachers represent? Why did they, and not the entire church, separate those workers? What is the significance of such separation, and what is the qualification required on the part of those who assume responsibility in the matter?

The first thing we must realize is that God has incorporated all His children into one Body. He recognizes no division of His people into various "churches" and missions. He has designed that all who are His shall live a corporate life, the life of a body among whose many members there is mutual consideration, mutual love, and mutual understanding. And He has purposed that not only the life, but also the ministry of His children, should be on the principle of the body, that it should be a matter of mutual helpfulness, mutual edification, and mutual service —the activity of the many members of one body. There are two aspects of the Body of Christ— life and ministry. The first half of Ephesians 4 speaks of the Body in relation to its ministry; the second half speaks of the Body in relation to its life. "Out from whom all the Body, being joined together and being knit together through every joint of the rich supply and through the operation in the measure of each one part, causes the growth of the Body unto the building up of itself in love" (v. 16). Here it is work that is under consideration. But in verse 25 the question is clearly one of life: "Therefore having put off the lie, speak truth each one with his neighbor, for we are members one of another." In Romans 12 we see how the members should care one for another, so that the thought there again is the manifestation of the one life. But in 1 Corinthians 12 we see how the members should serve one another, so the thought in that passage is the manifestation of the one ministry.

When we speak of the one Body, we emphasize the oneness of the life of all God's children. When we speak of its many members, we emphasize the diversity of functions in that unity. The characteristic of the former is life; the characteristic of the latter is work. In a physical body the members differ one from another; yet they function as one, because they share one life and have the upbuilding of the whole body as their one aim.

Because the Body of Christ has these two different aspects—life and ministry—it consequently has two different outward manifestations. The church in a locality is used to express the life of the Body, and the gifts in the Church are used to express the ministry of its members. In other words, each local church should stand on the ground of the Body, regarding itself as an expression of the oneness of the life of the Body, and it should on no account admit of division, since it exists as the manifestation of an indivisible life. The various ministers of the Church should likewise stand on the ground of the Body, regarding themselves as an expression of the oneness of its varied ministries. Perfect fellowship and cooperation should characterize all their activity, for though their functions are diverse, their ministry is really one. No local church should divide into different sects, or affiliate with other churches under a denomination, thus departing from the ground of the Body; and no group of ministers should unite to form a separate unit, standing on other than Body ground. All their work should be performed as members of the Body, and not as members of an organization existing in distinction from it. A worker may employ his gifts in the capacity of an officer of an organization, but in so doing he departs from the ground of the Body.

A cursory reading of Ephesians 4:11-12 might lead us to conclude that apostles, prophets, evangelists, shepherds and teachers functioned outside the Body, because they were given by the Lord to His Church for her upbuilding (v. 12). But verse 16 makes it clear that they do not stand outside the Body to build it up; they seek to build it up from within. They themselves are part of the Body, and it is only as they take their rightful place in it, as ministering members, that the whole Body is edified.

That churches are the local expression of the Body of Christ is an established fact, so we need not go into that here; but some explanation is called for regarding the gifted ministers whom God has set in the Church as the expression of the ministry of the Body. In 1 Corinthians 12 Paul is clearly dealing with the question of Christian service. He likens the workers to different members of a body, and shows that each member has its specific use, and all serve the body as belonging to it, not as distinct from it. In verse 27 he writes, "Now you are the body of Christ, and members individually"; and in the following verse he says, "And God has placed some in the church: first apostles, second prophets, third teachers; then works of power, then gifts of healing, helps, administrations, various kinds of tongues." A study of these two verses makes it clear that the gifted ministers of verse 28 are the members of verse 27, and that the Church of verse 28 is the Body of verse 27; therefore, what ministers are to the Church, members are to the Body. They hold their position in the Body on account of their functions (the "hearing" and "smelling" of verse 17). The gifted ministers are the functioning members of the Body, and all their operations are as members. They are to the Church what hands, feet, mouth, and head are to the physical body. God's servants do not minister to the Church as apart from it, but as its members. They are in the Body, serving it by the use of those faculties which they, as members, possess. A church in any locality is an expression of the one life of the Body, while its ministers are the expression of the difference and yet oneness of its ministry.

First Corinthians 12 deals with the subject of the Body of Christ, not in its life aspect but in its work aspect. The whole chapter is taken up with the question of ministry, and that ministry is spoken of as the functioning of the different members, from which it is evident that in the thought of God all ministry is on Body ground. Ministry is the practical expression of the Body, an expression of the diversity in unity of its various members. Therefore, we see that when the life aspect of the Body of Christ is expressed, there you have a local church; and when the work aspect is expressed, there you have a manifestation of the gifts God has given to His Church.

In reading 1 Corinthians 12:28 one cannot but be arrested by the striking difference between the description of the first three gifts and the remaining five. Paul, under the inspiration of the Spirit, takes special care in enumerating them—"first apostles, second prophets, third teachers." The first three are specifically numbered, but not the rest; and they are quite distinct in their nature as well as in their numbering. They are men; the rest are things. The three first-named gifts of the Lord to His Church—apostles, prophets, and teachers—stand apart from all the others. They are ministers of God's Word, and their function, to edify the Body of Christ, is the most important function in the Church. They are the representatives of the ministry of the Body.

34

The only scriptural record of the sending forth of apostles is found in Acts 13, and there we see that it is the prophets and teachers who set them apart for their ministry. Scripture provides no precedent for the separation and sending forth of men by one or more individuals, or by any mission or organization; even the sending out of workers by a local church is a thing unknown in the Word of God. The only example provided us there is the separating and sending forth of apostles by the prophets and teachers.

What is the significance of this? In Antioch the prophets and teachers were chosen of God to separate Barnabas and Saul for His service, because they were the ministering members of the church, and this separation of the apostles was a question of ministry rather than of life. Had it related to life, and not specifically to service, then it would have been the concern of the whole local church, not merely of its ministering members. But let it be noted that, though Barnabas and Saul were not separated for the work by the entire church, they were sent out not as representatives of a few select members, but as representatives of the whole Body. Their being separated by the prophets and teachers implied that they did not go out on individualistic lines, or on the basis of any organization, but on the ground of the ministry of the Body. The emphasis, as we have seen, was on ministry, not on life, but it was a ministry representing the whole church, not representing any particular section of it. This is clearly expressed by the laying on of hands.

As we have seen, the laying on of hands speaks of oneness (Lev. 1:4), and the only oneness known among the children of God is the oneness of the Body of Christ; therefore, in laying hands upon the apostles, the prophets and teachers definitely stood on the ground of the Body, acting as its representative members. Their action identified the whole church with the apostles, and identified the apostles with the whole church. These prophets and teachers did not stand on individual ground to send the apostles forth as their personal representatives, nor did they stand on the ground of any select company to send them out as representatives of that particular company; but they stood on the ground of the Body, as its ministering members, and set these two apart for the work of the gospel. In their turn the two, being thus separated, went forth, not to represent any particular individuals or any special organization, but to represent the Body of Christ, and the Body of Christ alone. All work that is truly scriptural and truly spiritual must be out from the Body and must minister to the Body. The Body must be the ground on which the worker stands, and it alone must be the sphere in which he works.

On two different occasions Paul had the laying on of hands; first when he believed on the Lord (Acts 9:17), then on the occasion under consideration, when he was sent out from Antioch. The former expressed his identification with the life of the Body; the latter his identification with the ministry of the Body. The first proclaimed him a member of the Body by receiving life from the Head; the second proclaimed him a ministering member, working not as an isolated individual, but in relation to the other members, as a part of one great whole.

In sending Barnabas and Saul from Antioch, the prophets and teachers stood for no "church" or mission; they represented the ministry of the Body. They were not the whole Church; they were only a group of God's servants. They bore no special name, they were bound by no particular organization, and they were subject to no fixed rules. They simply submitted themselves to the control of the Spirit and separated those whom He had separated for the work to which He had called them. They themselves were not the Body, but they stood on the ground of the Body, under the authority of the Head. Under that authority, and on that ground, they separated men to be apostles; and under the same authority, and on the same ground, others can do the same. The separation of apostles on this principle will mean that the men sent out may differ, those who send them may differ, and the time and place of their sending may differ too; but since all is under the direction of the one Head, and on the ground of the one Body, there will still be no division. If Antioch sends men out on the basis of the Body, and Jerusalem sends men out on the basis of the Body, there will still be inward oneness despite all outward diversity. How grand it would be if there were no representatives of different earthly bodies, but only representatives of the Body, the Body of Christ. If thousands of local churches, with thousands of prophets and teachers, each sent out thousands of different workers, there would be a vast outward diversity, but there could still be perfect inward unity if all were sent out under the direction of the one Head and on the ground of the one Body.

That Christ is the Head of the Church is a recognized fact, but that fact needs emphasis in relation to the ministry as well as to the life of the Church. Christian ministry is the ministry of the whole Church, not merely of one section of it. We must see to it that our work is on no lesser basis than the Body of Christ. Otherwise, we lose the headship of Christ, for Christ is not the Head of any system, or mission, or organization: He is the Head of the Church. If we belong to any human organization, then the divine headship ceases to be expressed in our work.

In Scripture we find no trace of man-made organizations sending out men to preach the gospel. We only find representatives of the ministry of the Church, under the guidance of the Spirit and on the ground of the Body, sending out those whom the Spirit has already separated for the work. If those responsible for the sending out of workers sent them out, not as their own representatives or the representatives of any organization, but only as representatives of the Body of Christ, and if those sent out stood on the ground of no particular "church" or mission, but on the ground of the Church alone, then no matter from what places the workers came or to what places they went, cooperation and unity would always be possible and much confusion in the work would be avoided.

## THEIR MOVEMENTS

After the apostles were called by the Spirit and were separated for the work by the representative members of the Body, what did they do? We need to recall that those who separated them only expressed identification and sympathy by the laying on of hands; they had no authority to control the apostles. Those prophets and teachers at the base assumed no official responsibility in regard to their movements, their methods of work, or the supply of their financial needs. In Scripture we nowhere find that apostles are under the control of any individual or any organized company. They had no regulations to adhere to and no superiors to obey. The Holy Spirit called them, and they followed His leading and guidance; He alone was their Director.

In Acts 13 and 14 we find the first scriptural record of missionary movements. Though today the places we visit and the conditions we meet may be vastly different from those of the Scripture record, yet in principle the experience of the first apostles may well serve as our example. Let us glance for a moment at these two chapters.

"They then, having been sent out by the Holy Spirit, went down to Seleucia; and from there they sailed away to Cyprus. And when they were in Salamis, they announced the word of God in the synagogues of the Jews. And they also had John as their attendant. And when they had passed through the whole island as far as Paphos, they found a certain man, a magician" (13:4-6). From the very outset constant movement characterized those sent ones. A true apostle is a traveler, not a settler.

"And putting out to sea from Paphos, Paul and his companions came to Perga of Pamphylia; and John departed from them and returned to Jerusalem. And they passed through from Perga and arrived at Pisidian Antioch. And they went into the synagogue on the Sabbath day and sat down" (13:13-14). (The Antioch mentioned here is not the same as the Antioch from which Barnabas and Saul set forth on their first missionary tour.) The apostles were constantly on the move, proclaiming the Word of God wherever they went, but until they reached Antioch in Pisidia we are not told anything of the result of their labors. From this point there is a definite development in the work.

"And when the synagogue gathering had been dismissed, many of the Jews and the devout proselytes followed Paul and Barnabas, who spoke to them and urged them to continue in the grace of God" (13:43). Here is the outcome of a short period of witness in Antioch of Pisidia —many of the Jews and religious proselytes believed. A week later almost the whole city gathered together to hear the Word (v. 44), but this enthusiastic response on the part of the people provoked the Jews to jealousy, and they opposed the apostles (v. 45). At this point the apostles turned to the Gentiles (v. 46), and "as many as were appointed to eternal life believed" (v. 48). On the previous Sabbath a number of Jews had received the Word of life. This Sabbath a number of Gentiles believed on the Lord. So not long after the arrival of the apostles in Antioch of Pisidia we find a church there.

But the apostles did not argue, "Now we have a group of believers here. We must stay awhile and shepherd them." They founded a local church at Antioch of Pisidia, but they did not stay to build it up. On they went again, publishing the Word of the Lord "through the whole region" (v. 49). Their objective was not one city, but "all the region." The modern custom of settling down in one place to shepherd a particular flock has no precedent in Scripture.

Persecution followed (v. 50). The opponents of the gospel message expelled the apostles from their coasts, and they answered by shaking the dust from their feet (v. 51). Many a present-day missionary has no dust to shake from his feet! But those who gather no dust lack the characteristic of an apostle. The early apostles never settled down in comfortable homes, nor did they stop for long to pastor the churches they founded. They were constantly traveling. To be an apostle means to be a sent one, that is, to be always going out. A stationary apostle is a contradiction in terms. A true apostle is one who in times of persecution will always have dust to shake off his feet.

What effect had this early departure of the apostles upon the infant church? Here was a group of new believers, mere babes in Christ, and their fathers in the faith forsook them in their infancy. Did they argue, "Why should the apostles be afraid of persecution and leave us to face the opposition alone?" Did they plead with the apostles to remain awhile and care for their spiritual welfare? Did they reason, "If you leave us now we shall be as sheep without a shepherd. If both of you cannot stay, surely one at least can remain behind and look after us. The persecution is so intense, we shall never get through without your help." How amazing the Scripture record is: "And the disciples were filled with joy and with the Holy Spirit" (v. 52).

There was no mourning among the disciples when the apostles left, but great gladness. The disciples were glad, for they knew the Lord; and they might well rejoice, because the apostles' departure meant an opportunity for others to hear the gospel. What was loss to them was gain to Iconium. Those believers were not like the believers of today, hoping for a settled pastor to instruct them, solve their problems, and shelter them from trouble. And those apostles were not like the apostles of today; they were pioneers, not settlers. They did not wait till believers were mature before they left them. They dared to leave them in mere infancy, for they believed in the power of the life of God within them.

But those disciples were not only filled with joy; they were filled with the Holy Spirit. The apostles might go, but the Spirit remained. Had the apostles remained to pastor them, it would have mattered little whether they were filled with the Spirit or not. If they had had a pastor to throw light on all their problems, they would have felt little need of the Spirit's instruction; and they would have felt little need of His power if they had had one in their midst who was bearing all responsibility for the spiritual side of the work while they attended to the secular. In Scripture there is not the slightest hint that apostles should settle down to pastor those they have led to the Lord. There are pastors in Scripture, but they are simply brethren raised up of God from among the local saints to care for their fellow believers. One of the reasons why so many present-day converts are not filled with the Spirit is that the apostles settle down to shepherd them and take upon themselves the responsibility that belongs to the Holy Spirit.

Praise God that the apostles moved on to Iconium, for "a great multitude of both Jews and Greeks believed" (14:1). Before long "the multitude of the city was divided, and some were with the Jews and some with the apostles" (v. 4). The saved were obviously a great multitude, since their coming out from the unsaved so vitally affected the place as to cause a division in the city. Only a short time after the apostles left Antioch in Pisidia, there was a church established in Iconium; and here, as in the previous place, opposition was intense. The apostles might well have argued that to leave a great multitude of mere babes in Christ exposed to fierce persecution was heartless, and bad policy besides. But the apostles were true to their apostolic calling, and off they went "to the cities of Lycaonia, Lystra and Derbe" (v. 6). And what did they do when they came to Lystra? As elsewhere, so here, "they announced the gospel" (v. 7), and as elsewhere, so here, there was opposition and persecution (v. 19). It is difficult to estimate the number of believers at Lystra, but judging by the remark that the disciples surrounded Paul (v. 20), there must have been at least half a dozen, and there may have been scores or even hundreds. So now there is a church in Lystra!

Does Paul stay to shepherd them awhile, or at least to tend them till the fierceness of the opposition has subsided? No! "On the next day he went out with Barnabas to Derbe" (v. 20). And there again the glad tidings are proclaimed and many disciples are made (v. 21). So another church is formed! And with the founding of a church in Derbe the first missionary tour of the apostles closes.

Looking back over these two chapters, we note that a fundamental principle governs the movements of the apostles. They travel from place to place, according to the leading of the Spirit, preaching the gospel and founding churches. Nowhere do we find them settling down to shepherd and instruct the converts, or to bear any local responsibility in the churches they have founded. In days of peace the apostles were on the move, and in days of persecution likewise. "Go!" was the word of the Lord, and "Go!" was the watchword of the apostles. The outstanding trait of a sent one is that he is always on the move.

## ON THEIR RETURN

But the question arises, How were these new converts shepherded and instructed? How were the newly-founded churches established? In studying the Word we find that the missionary tour of the apostles consisted of an outward and a return journey. On their outward journey their first concern was to found churches. On their return journey their chief business was to build them up.

Having "made a considerable number of disciples, they returned to Lystra and to Iconium and to Antioch, establishing the souls of the disciples, exhorting them to continue in the faith and saying that through many tribulations we must enter into the kingdom of God" (14:21-22). Here we see Paul and Barnabas returning to do some construction work in the churches already founded; but as before on their outward journey, so now on their return, they never settle down in any one place.

It is clear then that the apostles did not just move from place to place founding churches; they also did definite construction work. Merely to found churches without establishing them would be like leaving newborn babes to their own resources. The point to note here is that, while the instruction of the new converts and the building up of the churches was a very vital part of the apostles' work, they did it, not by settling down in one place, but rather by visiting the places where they had been before. Neither in their initial work of preaching the gospel, nor in their subsequent work of establishing the churches, did the apostles take up their permanent abode in any one place.

Before they left a place where a church had been founded and some construction work done, they appointed elders to bear responsibility there (14:23). This is one of the most important parts of an apostle's work. (This subject will be dealt with more fully in a subsequent chapter.)

Thus the early apostles worked, and the blessing of the Lord rested on their labors. We shall do well if we follow in their steps, but we must realize clearly that even though we adopt apostolic methods, unless we have apostolic consecration, apostolic faith, and apostolic power, we shall still fail to see apostolic results. We dare not underestimate the value of apostolic methods—they are absolutely essential if we are to have apostolic fruits— but we must not overlook the need of apostolic spirituality, and we must not fear apostolic persecution.

## BACK TO ANTIOCH

"And from there they sailed away to Antioch, where they had been commended to the grace of God for the work which they fulfilled. And when they arrived and gathered the church together, they declared the things that God had done with them and that He had opened a door of faith to the Gentiles" (14:26-27). On their return to Antioch the apostles "declared the things that God had done with them." It was from Antioch that Paul and Barnabas had gone out, so it was only fitting that on their return they should give an account of the Lord's dealings with them to those from whom they had gone forth. To give reports of the work to those who are truly bearing the burden with us, is sanctioned by God's Word. It is not only permissible, but necessary, that the children of God at the base should be informed of His doings on the field; but we do well to make sure that our reports are not in the nature of advertisements.

In the matter of reporting, we should on the one hand avoid all unnatural reticence and soulish seclusiveness; on the other hand, we must carefully guard against the intrusion of any personal interest. In all reports of the work our aim should be to glorify God and bring spiritual enrichment to those who share them. To utilize reports as a means of propaganda, with material returns in view, is base in the extreme, and unworthy of any Christian. When the motive is to glorify God and benefit His children, but at the same time to make known the needs of the work with a view to receiving material help, it is still far from acceptable to the Lord, and is unworthy of His servants. Our aim should be this alone—that God shall be glorified and His children blessed. If there were this perfect purity of motive in our reports, how differently many of them would be worded!

Each time we write or speak of our work, let us ask ourselves these questions: (1) Am I reporting with a view to gaining publicity for myself and my work? (2) Am I reporting with the double object of glorifying the Lord and advertising the work? (3) Am I reporting with this aim alone, that God shall be glorified and His children blessed? May the Lord give us grace to report with unmixed motives and perfect purity of heart!

# Chapter 3: The Elders Appointed by the Apostles

"Elders" is a designation of Old Testament origin. We find reference made in the Old Testament to the elders of Israel and also to the elders of different cities. In the Gospels we meet the term again, but still in relation to the Israelites. Even the elders referred to in the first part of Acts are of the Old Testament order (4:5, 8, 23; 6:12).

When were elders first instituted in the Church? Acts 11:30 refers to them in connection with the church in Jerusalem, and this is the first mention of elders in connection with any church; but though their existence is mentioned, nothing is said of their origin. Not till Acts 14:23, when we read of Paul and Barnabas returning from their first missionary journey, do we discover who they were, how they were appointed, and by whom. "When they had appointed elders for them in every church and had prayed with fastings, they committed them to the Lord."

## The Appointment

We have seen that the apostles themselves could not remain with the new believers to shepherd them and to bear the responsibility of the work locally. How then were the new converts cared for, and how was the work carried on? The apostles did not request that men be sent from Antioch to shepherd the flocks, nor did one of them remain behind to bear the burden of the local churches. What they did was simply this: "When they had appointed elders for them in every church and had prayed with fastings, they committed them to the Lord into whom they had believed" (v. 23). Wherever a church had been founded on their outward journey, they appointed elders on their return journey. They did not wait until any arbitrary standard was reached before appointing elders in a church, but "in every church" they chose a few of the more mature members to care for their fellow believers.

The apostolic procedure was quite simple. The apostles visited a place, founded a church, left that church for a while, then returned to establish it. In the interval certain developments would naturally take place. When the apostles left, some of the professing believers would leave too. Others would continue to attend the meetings, and would prove themselves to be truly the Lord's, but would make no appreciable progress. Others again would eagerly press on in the knowledge of the Lord and show real concern for His interests. Those who had more spiritual life than others would spontaneously come to the front and take responsibility for their weaker brethren. It was because they had proved themselves to be elders that the apostles appointed them to hold office as elders, and it was their business to shepherd and instruct the other believers, and to superintend and control the church affairs.

Nowhere did the apostles settle down and assume responsibility for the local church, but in every church they founded they chose from among the local believers faithful ones upon whom such responsibility could be placed. When they had chosen elders in each church, with prayer and fasting they committed them to the Lord, just as, with prayer and fasting, they themselves had been committed to the Lord by the prophets and teachers when they were sent out on their apostolic ministry. If this committal of elders to the Lord is to be of spiritual value, and no mere official ceremony, a vital knowledge of the Lord will be required on the part of the apostles. It is easy to become so occupied with the problems and needs of the situation, that one instinctively takes the burden upon oneself, even while admitting the truth that the Lord is responsible for His own Church. We need to know Christ as Head of His Church in no mere intellectual way if we are to let all its management pass out of our hands at the very outset. Only an utter distrust of themselves, and a living trust in God, could enable the early apostles to commit the affairs of every local church into the hands of local men who had but recently come to know the Lord. All who are engaged in apostolic work, and are seeking to follow the example of the first apostles in leaving the churches to the management of local elders, must be spiritually equipped for the task; for if things pass out of human hands and are not committed in faith to divine hands, the result will be disaster. Oh, how we need a living faith and a living knowledge of the living God!

The Word of God makes it clear that the oversight of a church is not the work of apostles, but of elders. Although Paul stayed in Corinth for over a year, in Rome for two years, and in Ephesus for three years, yet in none of these places did he assume responsibility for the work of the local church. In Scripture we read of the elders of Ephesus, but never of the apostles of

Ephesus. We find no mention made of the apostles of Philippi, but we do find reference to the bishops of Philippi. Apostles are responsible for their own particular ministry, but not for the churches which are the fruit of their ministry. All the fruit of the apostles' work had to be handed over to the care of local elders.

In God's plan provision has been made for the building up of local churches, and in that plan pastors have a place, but it was never His thought that apostles should assume the role of pastors. He purposed that apostles should be responsible for the work in different places, while elders were to bear responsibility in one place. The characteristic of an apostle is going; the characteristic of an elder is staying. It is not necessary that elders resign their ordinary professions and devote themselves exclusively to their duties in connection with the church. They are simply local men, following their usual pursuits and at the same time bearing special responsibilities in the church. Should local affairs increase, they may devote themselves entirely to spiritual work, but the characteristic of an elder is not that he is a "fulltime Christian worker." It is merely that, as a local brother, he bears responsibility in the local church. Locality determines the boundary of a church, and it is for that reason that the elders are always chosen from among the more mature believers in any place, and not transferred from other places. Thus, the local character of the churches of God is preserved, and consequently also their independent government and spiritual unity.

According to the usual conception of things, one would think it necessary for a considerable time to elapse between the founding of a church and the appointment of elders, but that is not according to God's pattern. The first missionary tour of the apostles covered less than two years, and during that period the apostles preached the gospel, led sinners to the Lord, formed churches, and appointed elders wherever a church had been formed. The elders were chosen on the apostles' return journey, not on their first visit to any place; but the interval between their two visits was never long, at the most a matter of months. On their return journey the apostles would naturally find some places progressing more favorably than others, but they did not reason that, because of the low state of any church, they would make an exception and appoint no elders. They appointed elders in every church. Some may ask, If all the members of a church are in a low spiritual condition, how is it possible to appoint elders among them? It may solve the problem of many if they only consider the implication of the term "elder." The existence of an elder implies the existence of a junior. The word "elder" is relative, not absolute. Among a group of men in their seventy-ninth year it takes a man in his eightieth year to be their elder; but it only takes a child of eight to be "elder" to a company of children of seven. Even among the spiritually immature there are bound to be those who, in comparison with the others, are more mature and have spiritual possibilities, which is all the qualification they require to be their elders.

A church may come far short of the ideal, but we cannot on that account deprive it of the status of a church. Our responsibility is to minister to it and so seek to bring it nearer the ideal. In the same way, even the comparatively advanced ones in a locality may not reach the ideal of elders, but we cannot for that reason deprive them of the status of elders. In comparison with the elders of other places they may seem very immature, but if they are more advanced than the other believers in the same locality, then in their own church they are elders. We must remember that the office of an elder according to Scripture is limited to a locality. Being an elder in Nanking does not qualify a man to be an elder in Shanghai; but even if his spiritual state is far from what it should be, provided he is in advance of his fellow believers in the same church, then he is qualified to be an elder there. You can only have pattern elders where you have a pattern church. Where a church is immature, the elders will naturally be immature; where a church is mature, the elders will also be mature. The model elders of 1 Timothy 3 and of Titus 1 are to be found in model churches.

The appointing of comparatively spiritual brothers to be elders is a principle set forth in the Word of God, though it runs counter to the modern conception of things. But even while we recognize this principle, we must not seek to apply it in any legal way. That would spell death. We must force nothing, but must be continually open to the leading of the Spirit. He will indicate the right time for the appointment of elders in any church. Should there be no leading of the Holy Spirit, and circumstances not permit an immediate appointment of elders on the second visit of the apostles, then a Titus could be left behind to see to their appointment later. This is the first subject dealt with in the book of Titus, and it is a most important one. Paul gives Titus injunctions to establish elders in every city in Crete (Titus 1:5).

In the appointment of elders the apostles did not follow their personal preferences; they only appointed those whom God had already chosen. That is why Paul could say to the elders in Ephesus, "The Holy Spirit has placed you as overseers" (Acts 20:28). The apostles did not take the initiative in the matter. They merely established as elders those whom the Holy Spirit had already made overseers in the church. In a man-made organization the appointment of an individual to office entitles him to occupy that office; but not so in the Church of God. Everything there is on a spiritual basis, and it is only divine appointment that qualifies a man for office. If the Holy Spirit does not make men bishops, then no apostolic appointment will ever avail to do so. In the Church of God everything is under the sovereignty of the Spirit; man is ruled out. Elders are not men who think themselves capable to control church affairs, or men whom the apostles consider suitable, but men whom the Holy Spirit has set to be overseers in the Church. Those whom the Spirit chooses to be shepherds of the flock, to them He also gives grace and gifts to qualify them for spiritual leadership. It is their spiritual call and their spiritual equipment, not their official appointment, that constitutes them elders. In a spiritual sense they are already elders before they hold the position officially, and it is because they actually are elders that they are publicly appointed to be elders. In the early Church it was the Holy Spirit who first signified His choice of elders; then the apostles confirmed the choice by appointing them to office.

## APOSTLES AND ELDERS

Elders were local men appointed to oversee affairs in the local church. Their sphere of office was limited by the locality. An elder in Ephesus was not an elder in Smyrna, and an elder in Smyrna was not an elder in Ephesus. In Scripture there are no local apostles, nor are there any extra-local elders; all elders are local, and all apostles are extra-local. The Word of God nowhere speaks of apostles managing the affairs of a local church, and it nowhere speaks of elders managing the affairs of several local churches. The apostles were the ministers of all the churches, but they had control of none. The elders were confined to one church, and they controlled affairs in that one. The duty of apostles was to found churches. Once a church was established, all responsibility was handed over to the local elders, and from that day the apostles exercised no control whatever in its affairs. All management was in the hands of the elders, and if they thought it right, they could even refuse an apostle entry into their church. Should such a thing occur, the apostle would have no authority to insist on being received, since all local authority had already passed from his hands into the hands of the elders.

How did Paul deal with the adulterous believer in Corinth? He did not just notify the church that he had excommunicated the man. The utmost he could do was to instruct its members regarding the seriousness of the situation and seek to admonish them to remove the wicked person from their midst (1 Cor. 5:13). If the church was right spiritually they would pay attention to Paul, but if they disregarded his exhortations, while they would be wrong spiritually, they would not be wrong legally. In the event of their despising his counsel, Paul could only bring his spiritual authority to bear on the situation. In the name of the Lord Jesus he could "deliver such a one to Satan for the destruction of his flesh" (v. 5). He had no official authority to discipline him, but he had spiritual authority to deal with the case. He had his spiritual "rod."

The affairs of the local church are entirely independent of the apostles. Once elders have been appointed, all control passes into their hands, and while thereafter an apostle may still instruct and persuade, he can never interfere. But this did not hinder Paul from speaking authoritatively to the Corinthians. Even a casual reader will notice how authoritative his statements were in both Epistles. It was quite within his province to pass judgment where doctrinal and moral questions were concerned, and when Paul did so he was most emphatic; but the actual enforcing of such judgments was outside his province and entirely a matter for the local church.

An apostle can deal with the disorders of a church whenever his advice and counsel are sought, as was the case with Paul and the church in Corinth. It was because of their inquiries that he could say to them, "And the rest I will set in order when I come" (1 Cor. 11:34). But the point to note here is that the rest of the matters which Paul intended to set in order on his arrival in Corinth were to be attended to in the same way as those he had dealt with in his Epistle, and they were dealt with doctrinally. In like manner as he had instructed them concerning certain affairs there, so he would instruct them concerning the remaining matters on his arrival; but the Corinthians themselves, not Paul, were the ones who would have to deal with the situation.

Since Peter and John were apostles, how did it come about that they were elders of the church in Jerusalem? (1 Pet. 5:1; 2 John 1; 3 John 1). They were elders as well as apostles because they were not only responsible for the work in different places, but also for the church in their own place. When they went out, they ministered in the capacity of apostles, bearing the responsibility for the work in other parts. When they returned home, they performed the duties of elders, bearing the responsibility of the local church. (Only such apostles as are not traveling much could be elders of the church in their own locality.) When Peter and John were away from their own church, they were apostles; when they returned, they were elders. It was not on the ground of their being apostles that they were elders in Jerusalem; they were elders there solely on the ground of their being local men of greater spiritual maturity than their brethren.

There is no precedent in Scripture for a visiting apostle to settle down as elder in any church he visits; but, provided circumstances permit him to be at home frequently, he could be an elder in his own locality, on the ground of his being a local brother. If the local character of the churches of God is to be preserved, then the extra-local character of the apostles must also be preserved.

Paul was sent out from Antioch, and he founded a church in Ephesus. We know he did not hold the office of elder in any church, but it would have been possible for him to be an elder in Antioch, not in Ephesus. He spent three years in Ephesus, but he worked there in the capacity of an apostle, not an elder; that is, he assumed no responsibility and exercised no authority in local affairs, but simply devoted himself to his apostolic ministry. Let us note carefully that there are no elders in the universal Church and no apostles in the local church.

## THEIR RESPONSIBILITIES

It is the responsibility of every saved man to serve the Lord according to his capacity and in his own sphere. God did not appoint elders to do the work on behalf of their brethren. After the appointment of elders, as before, it is still the brethren's duty and privilege to serve the Lord. Elders are also called bishops (Acts 20:28; Titus 1:5, 7). The term "elder" relates to their person; the term "bishop" to their work. Bishop means overseer, and an overseer is not one who works instead of others, but one who supervises others as they work. God intended that every Christian should be a "Christian worker," and He appointed some to take the oversight of the work so that it might be carried on efficiently. It was never His thought that the majority of the believers should devote themselves exclusively to secular affairs and leave the church matters to a group of spiritual specialists. This point cannot be overemphasized. Elders are not a group of men who contract to do the church work on behalf of its members; they are only the ones who superintend affairs. It is their business to encourage the backward and restrain the forward ones, never doing the work instead of them, but simply directing them in the doing of it.

The responsibility of an elder relates to matters temporal and spiritual. They are appointed to "lead," and also to "instruct" and "shepherd." "Let the elders who take the lead well be counted worthy of double honor, especially those who labor in word and teaching" (1 Tim. 5:17). "Shepherd the flock of God among you, overseeing not under compulsion but willingly, according to God; not by seeking gain through base means but eagerly; nor as lording it over your allotments but by becoming patterns of the flock" (1 Pet. 5:2-3).

The Word of God uses the term "lead" in connection with the responsibilities of an elder. The ordering of church government, the management of business affairs, and the care of material things are all under their control. But we must remember that a scriptural church does not consist of an active and a passive group of brethren, the former controlling the latter, and the latter simply submitting to their control, or the former bearing all the burden while the latter settle down in ease to enjoy the benefit of their labors. "That the members would...care for one another" is God's purpose for His Church (1 Cor. 12:25). Every church after God's own heart bears the stamp of "one another" on all its life and activity. Mutuality is its outstanding characteristic. If the elders lose sight of that, then their leading the church will soon be changed to lording it over the church. Even while the elders exercise control in church affairs, they must remember that they are only fellow members with the other believers; Christ alone is the Head. They were not appointed to be lords of their brethren, but to be their examples. What is an example? It is a pattern for others to follow. Since they were to be a pattern to the brethren, then obviously it was neither God's thought for them to do all the work and the brethren none, nor for the brethren to do the work while they simply stood by and commanded. For the elders to be a pattern to the brethren implied that the brethren worked and the elders worked as well. It also implied that the elders worked with special diligence and care, so that the brethren should have a good example to follow. They were overseers, but they were not lords of their brethren, standing aloof and commanding; and they did direct the work, but they did it more by example than by command. Such is the scriptural conception of the leading of the elders.

But their responsibility does not merely relate to the material side of church affairs. If God has equipped them with spiritual gifts, then they should also bear spiritual responsibility. Paul wrote to Timothy, "Let the elders who take the lead well be counted worthy of double honor, especially those who labor in word and teaching" (1 Tim. 5:17). It is the responsibility of all elders to control the affairs of the church, but such as have special gifts (as of prophecy or teaching) are free to exercise these for the spiritual edification of the church. Paul wrote to Titus that an elder should "be able both to exhort by the healthy teaching and to convict those who oppose" (Titus 1:9). The preaching and teaching in the local church is not the business of apostles but of local brethren who are in the ministry, especially if they are elders. As we have already seen, the management of a church is a matter of local responsibility; so also is teaching and preaching.

On the spiritual side of the work the elders help to build up the church not only by teaching and preaching, but by pastoral work. To shepherd the flock is particularly the work of elders. Paul said to the Ephesian elders, "Take heed to yourselves and to all the flock, among whom the Holy Spirit has placed you as overseers to shepherd the church of God" (Acts 20:28). And Peter wrote in the same strain to the elders among the saints of the Dispersion, "Shepherd the flock of God among you" (1 Pet. 5:2). The present-day conception of pastors is far removed from the thought of God. God's thought was that men chosen from among the local brethren should shepherd the flock, not that men coming from other parts should preach the gospel, found churches, and then settle down to care for those churches. A clear understanding of the respective responsibilities of apostles and elders would clear away many of the difficulties that exist in the church today.

## THE PLURALITY OF ELDERS

This work of leading, teaching, and shepherding the flock, which we have seen to be the special duty of the elders, does not devolve upon one man only in any place. To have pastors in a church is scriptural, but the present-day pastoral system is quite unscriptural; it is an invention of man.

In Scripture we see that there was always more than one elder or bishop in a local church. It is not God's will that one believer should be singled out from all the others to occupy a place of special prominence, while the others passively submit to his will. If the management of the entire church rests upon one man, how easy it is for him to become self-conceited, esteeming himself above measure and suppressing the other brethren (3 John). God has ordained that several elders together share the work of the church, so that no one individual should be able to run things according to his own pleasure, treating the church as his own special property and leaving the impress of his personality upon all its life and work. To place the responsibility in the hands of several brethren, rather than in the hands of one individual, is God's way of safeguarding His church against the evils that result from the domination of a strong personality. God has purposed that several brothers should unitedly bear responsibility in the church, so that even in controlling its affairs they have to depend one upon the other and submit one to the other. Thus, in an experimental way, they will discover the meaning of bearing the cross, and they will have opportunity to give practical expression to the truth of the Body of Christ. As they honor one another and trust one another to the leading of the Spirit, none taking the place of the Head, but each regarding the others as fellow members, the element of mutuality, which is the distinctive feature of the church, will be preserved.

# CHAPTER 4: THE CHURCHES FOUNDED BY THE APOSTLES

## THE CHURCH AND THE CHURCHES

The Word of God teaches us that the Church is one. Why then did the apostles found separate churches in each of the places they visited? If the Church is the Body of Christ, it cannot but be one. Then how does it come about that we speak of churches?

The word "church" means "the called-out ones." The term is used twice in the Gospels, once in Matthew 16:18 and once in Matthew 18:17, and we meet in quite frequently in the Acts and the Epistles. In the Gospels the word is used on both occasions by our Lord, but it is employed in a somewhat different sense each time.

"You are Peter, and upon this rock I will build My church, and the gates of Hades shall not prevail against it" (Matt. 16:18). What church is this? Peter confessed that Jesus was the Christ, the Son of the living God, and our Lord declared that He would build His Church upon this confession—the confession that as to His Person He is the Son of God, and as to His work He is the Christ of God. This Church comprises all the saved, without reference to time or space, that is, all who in the purpose of God are redeemed by virtue of the shed blood of the Lord Jesus, and are born again by the operation of His Spirit. This is the Church universal, the Church of God, the Body of Christ.

"And if he refuses to hear them, tell it to the church" (Matt. 18:17). The word "church" is used here in quite a different sense from the sense in Matthew 16:18. The sphere of the church referred to here is clearly not as wide as the sphere of the Church mentioned in the previous passage. The Church there is a Church that knows nothing of time or place, but the church here is obviously limited both to time and place, for it is one that can hear you speak. The Church mentioned in chapter sixteen includes all the children of God in every locality, while the church mentioned in chapter eighteen includes only the children of God living in one locality; and it is because it is limited to one place that it is possible for you to tell your difficulties to the believers of whom it is composed. Obviously the church here is local, not universal, for no one could speak at one time to all the children of God throughout the universe. It is only possible to speak at one time to the believers living in one place.

We have clearly two different aspects of the Church before us—the

Church and the churches, the universal Church and the local churches. The Church is invisible; the churches are visible. The Church has no organization; the churches are organized. The Church is spiritual; the churches are spiritual and yet physical. The Church is purely an organism; the churches are an organism, yet at the same time they are organized, which is seen by the fact that elders and deacons hold office there.[4]

All Church difficulties arise in connection with the local churches, not with the universal Church. The latter is invisible and spiritual, therefore beyond the reach of man, while the former is visible and organized, therefore still liable to be touched by human hands. The heavenly Church is so far removed from the world that it is possible to remain unaffected by it, but the earthly churches are so close to us, that if problems arise there we feel them acutely. The invisible church does not test our obedience to God, but the visible churches test us severely by facing us with issues on the intensely practical plane of our earthly life.

## THE BASIS OF THE CHURCHES

In the Word of God we find "the church of God" spoken of in the singular (1 Cor. 10:32), but we find the same Word referring to the "churches of God" in the plural (1 Thes. 2:14). How has this unity become a plurality? How has the Church which is essentially one become many? The Church of God has been divided into the churches of God on the one ground of difference of locality.[5] Locality is the only scriptural basis for the division of the Church into churches.

The seven churches in Asia, referred to in the book of Revelation, comprised the church in Ephesus, the church in Smyrna, the church in Pergamos, the church in Thyatira, the church in Sardis, the church in Philadelphia, and the church in Laodicea. They were seven churches, not one. Each was distinct from the others on the ground of the difference of locality. It was only because the believers did not reside in one place that they did not belong to one church. There were seven different churches simply because the believers lived in seven different places. Ephesus, Smyrna, Pergamos, Thyatira, Sardis, Philadelphia, and Laodicea are clearly all the names of places. Not only were the seven churches in Asia founded on the basis of locality, but all the churches mentioned in Scripture were founded on the same basis. Throughout the Word of God we can find no name attached to a church save the name of a place, for example, the church in Jerusalem, the church in Lystra, the church in Derbe, the church in Colosse, the church in Troas, the church in Thessalonica, the church in Antioch. This fact cannot be overemphasized, that in Scripture no other name but the name of a locality is ever connected with a church, and division of the church into churches is solely on the ground of difference of locality.

Spiritually the Church of God is one; therefore, it cannot be divided—but physically its members are scattered throughout the earth; therefore, they cannot possibly live in one place.[6] Yet it is essential that there be a physical gathering together of believers. It is not enough that they be present "in the spirit"; they must also be present "in the flesh." Now a church is composed of all "the called-out ones assembled" in one place for worship, prayer, fellowship, and ministry. This assembling together is absolutely essential to the life of a church. Without it, there may be believers scattered throughout the area, but there is really no church. The Church exists because of the existence of its members, and it does not require that they meet in a physical way; but it is essential to the very existence of a church that its members gather together in a physical way. It is in this latter sense that the word "church" is used in 1 Corinthians 14. The phrase "in the church" (vv. 19, 23, 28) means "in the church meetings." A church is a church assembled. These believers are not separated from other believers in any respect but that of their dwelling places. As long as they continue in the flesh, they will be limited by space, and this physical limitation, which in the very nature of things makes it impossible for God's people to meet in one place, is the only basis sanctioned by God for the forming of separate churches. Christians belong to different churches for the sole reason that they live in different places. That division is merely external. In reality the church as the Body of Christ cannot be divided; therefore, even when the Word of God refers to the different assemblies of His people, the places named vary, but it is still "the church" in every one of these places, such as "the church in Ephesus,"

"the church in Smyrna," "the church in Pergamos."

*In the New Testament there is one method and one alone of dividing the Church into churches, and that God-ordained method is division on the basis of locality.* All other methods are man-made, not God-given. May the Spirit of God engrave this truth deeply on our hearts, that the only reason for the division of God's children into different churches is because of the different places in which they live.

What is a New Testament church? It is not a building, a gospel hall, a preaching center, a mission, a work, an organization, a system, a denomination, or a sect. People may apply the term "church" to any of the above; nevertheless they are not churches. A New Testament church is the meeting together for worship, prayer, fellowship, and mutual edification, of all the people of God in a given locality, on the ground that they are Christians in the same locality. The Church is the Body of Christ; a church is a miniature Body of Christ. All the believers in a locality form the church in that locality, and in a small way they ought to show forth what the Church should show forth. They are the Body of Christ in that locality, so they have to learn how to come under the headship of the Lord, and how to manifest oneness among all the members, guarding carefully against schism and division.

## THE BOUNDARY OF A LOCALITY

We have seen that all the churches in Scripture are local churches, but the question naturally arises, What is a scriptural locality? If we note what places are mentioned in God's Word in connection with the founding of churches, then we shall be able to determine what the extent of a place must be to justify its being regarded as a unit for the forming of a church. In Scripture the localities which determine the boundary of a church are neither countries, nor provinces, nor districts. Nowhere do we read of a national church, or a provincial church, or of a district church. We read of the church in Ephesus, the church in Rome, the church in Jerusalem, the church in Corinth, the church in Philippi, and the church in Iconium. Now what kind of places are Ephesus, Rome, Jerusalem, Corinth, Philippi, and Iconium? They are neither countries, nor provinces, nor districts, but simply places of convenient size for people to live together in a certain measure of safety and sociability. In modern language we should call them cities. That cities were the boundaries of churches in the apostolic days is evident from the fact that on the one hand Paul and Barnabas "appointed elders for them in every church" (Acts 14:23), and on the other hand Paul instructed Titus to "appoint elders in every city" (Titus 1:5).

In the Word of God we see no church that extends beyond the area of a city, nor do we find any church which does not cover the entire area. A city is the scriptural unit of locality. From Genesis and Joshua we learn that cities in olden days were the places where people grouped together to live; they were also the smallest unit of civil administration, and each possessed an independent name. Any place is qualified to be a unit for the founding of a church which is a place where people group together to live, a place with an independent name, and a place which is the smallest political unit. Such a place is a scriptural city and is the boundary of a local church. Large cities such as Rome and Jerusalem are only units, while small cities such as Iconium and Troas are likewise units. Apart from such places where people live a community life, there is no scriptural unit of the churches of God.

Questions will naturally arise concerning large cities such as London. Are they counted as one unit-locality, or more than one? London is clearly not a city in the scriptural sense of the term, and it cannot therefore be regarded as a unit. Even people living in London talk about going "into the city," or "into town," which reveals the fact that, in their thinking, London and "the city" are not synonymous. The political and postal authorities, as well as the man on the street, regard London as more than one unit. They divide it respectively into boroughs and postal districts. What they regard as an administrative unit, we may well regard as a church unit.

As to country-places which could not technically be termed cities, they may also be regarded as unit-localities. It is said of our Lord, when on earth, that He went out into the cities and villages (Luke 13:22), from which we see that country-places, as well as towns, are considered to be separate units.

This division of churches according to locality is a demonstration of the marvelous wisdom of God. Had God ordained that the Church be divided into churches with the country as their boundary, then in the event of one country being vanquished and absorbed by another, the church would have to change its sphere. Were a province to mark the limit of a church, the sphere of the churches would be frequently altered because of the frequent change of provincial boundary. The same holds true in respect of a district. The most stable of all political units is a village, a town, or a city.

Governments, dynasties, and countries may change, but cities are seldom affected by any political change. There are cities that have passed from one country to another and still have their original name, and there are cities in existence today that have retained the same name for centuries. So we see the divine wisdom in decreeing that a locality should fix the boundary of a church.

Since the limits of a locality mark the limits of a church, then no church can be narrower than a locality, and none wider. The Word of God recognizes only two churches, the universal Church and the local churches; there is no third church whose sphere is narrower than the local, or else wider than the local and yet narrower than the universal Church. A local church admits of no possible division, and it admits of no possible extension. You cannot narrow its sphere by dividing it into several smaller churches, nor can you widen its sphere by linking several local churches together. Any church smaller than a local church is not a scriptural church, and any church larger than a local church, and yet smaller than the universal Church, is not a scriptural church either.

## NOT NARROWER THAN A LOCALITY

We read in 1 Corinthians 1:2 of "the church of God which is in Corinth." Corinth was a unit-locality, and the church in Corinth, a unit church. When discord crept in and its members were on the point of splitting the church into four different factions, Paul wrote, rebuking them: "Each of you says, I am of Paul, and I of Apollos, and I of Cephas, and I of Christ....Are you not men of flesh?" (1 Cor. 1:12; 3:4). Had these people formed four different groups, they would have been sects, not churches, for Corinth was a city, and that is the smallest unit which warrants the forming of a church. The church of God in Corinth could not cover a lesser area than the whole city, nor could it comprise a lesser number of Christians than all the Christians who lived there. This is Paul's definition of the church in Corinth—"to those who have been sanctified in Christ Jesus, the called saints" (1:2). To form a church in an area smaller than a unit-locality is to form it on a smaller basis than a scriptural unit, and it follows that it cannot be a scriptural church. Any group of believers less than all the believers in a place is not qualified to be a separate church. The unit of the church must correspond with the unit of the locality. A church must cover the same area as the locality in which it is found. If a church is smaller than a locality, then it is not a scriptural church; it is a sect.

To say, "I am of Paul," or "I am of Cephas," is obviously sectarian; but to say, "I am of Christ," is sectarian too, though less obviously so. The confession, "I am of Christ," is good as a confession, but it is not an adequate basis for forming a separate church, since it excludes some of the children of God in a given locality by including only a certain section who say, "I am of Christ." That every believer belongs to Christ is a fact, whether that fact be declared or not; and to differentiate between those who proclaim it and those who do not, is condemned by God as carnal. It is the fact that matters, not the declaration of it. The sphere of a church in any place does not merely include those in that place who say, "I am of Christ," but all in that place who are of Christ. It extends over the entire area of the locality, and includes the entire number of the Christians in the locality.

To take one's stand as belonging to Christ alone is perfectly right, but to divide between Christians who take that stand and Christians who do not, is altogether wrong. To brand as sectarian those who say, "I am of Paul," or "I am of Cephas," and feel spiritually superior as we separate ourselves from them and have fellowship only with those who say, "I am of Christ," makes us guilty of the very sin we condemn in others. If we make nonsectarianism the basis of our fellowship, then we are dividing the church on a ground other than the one ordained of God, and thereby we form another sect. The scriptural ground for a church is a locality and not nonsectarianism. Any fellowship that is not as wide as the locality is sectarian. All Christians who live in the same place as I do, are in the same church as I am, and I dare exclude none. I acknowledge as my brother, and as a fellow member of my church, every child of God who lives in my locality.

There were a great number of believers in Jerusalem. We read of a multitude who turned to the Lord; yet they are all referred to as the church in Jerusalem, not the churches in Jerusalem. Jerusalem was a single place; therefore, it could only be counted as a single unit for the founding of a single church. You cannot divide the church unless you can divide the place. If there is only one locality, there can only be one church. In Corinth there was only the church in Corinth; in Hankow there is only the church in Hankow. We do not read of the churches in Jerusalem, or the churches in

Ephesus, or the churches in Corinth. Each of these was counted as only one place; therefore, it was permissible to have only one church in each. As long as Jerusalem, Ephesus, and Corinth remain unit-localities, just so long do they remain unit-churches. *If a locality is indivisible, then the church formed in that locality is indivisible.*

## NOT WIDER THAN A LOCALITY

We have just seen that the boundary of a church cannot be narrower than the locality to which it belongs. On the other hand, its boundary cannot be wider than the locality. In the Word of God we never read of the church in

Macedonia, or the church in Galatia, or the church in Judea, or the church in Galilee. Why? Because Macedonia and Galilee are provinces, and Judea and Galatia are districts. A province is not a scriptural unit of locality; neither is a district. Both include a number of units; therefore, they include a number of separate churches and do not constitute one church. A provincial church or a district church is not according to Scripture, since it does not divide on the ground of locality, but combines a number of localities. It is because all scriptural churches are local churches that there is no mention of state churches, provincial churches, or district churches in the Word of God.

"Then had the churches rest throughout all Judea and Galilee and Samaria" (Acts 9:31, KJV). The Holy Spirit did not speak here of the church, but of the churches. Because there were a number of localities, there were also a number of churches. It was not God's plan to unite the churches of different places into one church, but to have a separate church in each place. There were as many churches as there were places.

"He passed through Syria and Cilicia, confirming the churches" (Acts 15:41). Again the reference is not to one single church, because Syria and Cilicia were vast districts, each comprising a number of different places. It is permissible in political circles to unite many different places into a district and call it Syria or Cilicia, but God does not unite the believers in a number of different places and call them the church in Syria, or the church in Cilicia. There may be unions or mergers in the commercial or political world, but God sanctions no combinations among the churches. Each separate place must have a separate church.

"All the churches of the Gentiles" (Rom. 16:4). The churches of God were not formed on national lines but on local lines; therefore, there is no mention of the church of the Gentiles, but of the churches of the Gentiles.

"The churches of Asia greet you" (1 Cor. 16:19). "The churches of Macedonia" (2 Cor. 8:1). "The churches of Galatia" (Gal. 1:2). "I was still unknown by face to the churches of Judea, which are in Christ" (Gal. 1:22). Asia, Macedonia, Galatia, and Judea were all areas comprising more than one locality-unit; therefore, the Word of God refers to the churches in these areas. A church according to the divine thought is always a church in one locality; any other kind of church is a product of the human mind.

God sanctions no division of the church within any one locality, and He sanctions no denominational combination of the churches in a number of localities. In Scripture there is always one church in one place, never several churches in one place, nor one church in several places. God does not recognize any fellowship of His children on a basis narrower, or wider, than that of a locality.

Nanking is a city, and so is Soochow. Because each is a separate unit, each therefore has a separate church. The two places are both in the same country, and even in the same province, but because they are two separate cities, they must form two separate churches. Politically Glasgow and Nanking do not belong to the same province, or even the same country; yet the relationship between Nanking and Soochow is exactly the same as between Nanking and Glasgow. Nanking and Soochow are as truly separate units as Nanking and Glasgow are. In the division of churches the question of country or province does not arise; it is all a question of cities. Two cities of the same country, or the same province, have no closer relationship than two cities of different countries or different provinces. God's intention is that a church in any one locality should be a unit, and in their relationship one to the other the different churches must preserve their local character.

When God's people throughout the earth really see the local character of the churches, then they will appreciate their oneness in Christ as never before. The churches of God are local, intensely local. If any factor enters in to destroy their local character, then they cease to be scriptural churches.

## THE INDEPENDENCE OF THE CHURCHES

It was never God's purpose that a number of churches in different places should be combined under any denomination or organization, but rather that each one should be independent of the other. Their responsibilities were to be independent and their government likewise. When our Lord sent messages to His children in Asia, He did not address them as "the church in Asia," but "the seven churches which are in Asia." His rebuke of Ephesus could not be applied to Smyrna, because Smyrna was independent of Ephesus. The confusion in Pergamos could not be laid to the charge of Philadelphia, because Philadelphia was independent of Pergamos. And the pride of Laodicea could not be attributed to Sardis, because Sardis was independent of Laodicea. Each church stood on its own merits and bore its own responsibility. Since God's children lived in seven different cities, they consequently belonged to seven different churches. And since each was independent of the other, each had its own special commendation, or exhortation, or rebuke.

And not only were there these seven churches on earth; there were seven lampstands representing them in heaven. In the Old Testament there was only one lampstand with seven different branches, but in the New Testament there were seven distinct lampstands. Had the New Testament representation been the same as the Old, then believers in the seven Asiatic churches might have united to form one church; but there are now seven separate lampstands, each upon its own base, so that the Lord is able to walk "in the midst of the seven golden lampstands" (Rev. 2:1). Therefore, though all churches stand under the authority of the one Head and express the life of the one Body (for they are all made of gold), still they are not united by any outward organization, but each stands on its own base, bearing its own responsibility, maintaining its local independence.

## AMONG THE CHURCHES

This does not imply that the different local churches have nothing to do with one another, and that each can simply do as it pleases without considering the rest, for the ground of a church is the ground of the Body. Although they are unit-churches in outward management, still their inner life is one, and the Lord has made their members the members of one Body. There is no outward organization forming them into one big combined unit, but there is a strong inward bond uniting them in the Lord. They have a oneness of life which knows nothing of the bounds of locality, and which leads the separate churches to uniform action despite the absence of all outward organization. In organization the churches are totally independent of one another, but in life they are one, and consequently interdependent. If one church receives revelation, the others should seek to profit by it. If one is in difficulty, the others should come to its aid. But while the churches minister one to the other, they should always preserve their independence of government and responsibility.

On the one hand, each church is directly under the authority of the Lord and responsible to Him alone; on the other hand, each must listen not only to His direct speaking, but to His speaking through the others. "He who has an ear, let him hear what the Spirit says to the churches," is our Lord's injunction to all (Rev. 2 and 3). In the introduction of His letters to the seven churches we find our Lord addressing the angel of each church, but at their close we find that His message to one particular church was also a message to all the churches. From this it is clear that what one church ought to do, all the churches ought to do. The responsibility of the churches is individual, but their actions should be uniform. This balance of truth ought to be carefully preserved.

We find the same teaching in the Epistles. "Because of this I have sent Timothy to you...who will remind you of my ways which are in Christ, even as I teach everywhere in every church" (1 Cor. 4:17). What Paul has taught "everywhere in every church," the Corinthians are called upon to lay to heart. There is not one kind of instruction for Corinth, and another kind of instruction for another place. What the apostles have been teaching to some of the churches, the believers in other churches must also note. And that applies to commandments as well as to matters of doctrine. "As the Lord has apportioned to each one...so let him walk. And so I direct in all the churches" (1 Cor. 7:17). The Lord could never give a command to one church which in any way contradicted His command to another church. His requirements for one group of His children were His requirements for all His children. "But if anyone seems to be contentious, we do not have such a custom of being so, neither the churches of God" (1 Cor. 11:16). The church in Corinth was apt to strike out on individual lines. All the other churches were going on together with the Lord. It was only Corinth that was out of step; therefore, Paul sought to bring it into line with the others. Today, alas! it is not just one church that has departed from God's way, but the majority of the so-called churches. It is a tragedy that today an injunction to follow "all the churches" would lead, not into, but away from, the will of God!

"Now concerning the collection for the saints, just as I directed the churches of Galatia, so you also do" (1 Cor. 16:1). Paul is saying in effect, "Although you are independent of other churches, yet you must not disregard their example." A willingness to help one another, and to learn from one another, should mark the relationship between the various churches. What the more mature churches have learned from the Lord, the less experienced should be ready to learn from them. "For you, brothers, became imitators of the churches of God which are in Judea in Christ Jesus," wrote Paul to the Thessalonians (1 Thes. 2:14). The church in Thessalonica was younger than the churches in Judea; therefore, it was only fitting that they should learn from them.

There is a beautiful balance in the teaching of God's Word regarding the relationship between the various churches. On the one hand, they are totally independent of one another in matters relating to responsibility, government, and organization. On the other hand, they are to learn from one another and to keep pace with one another. But in everything it is essential to have both the guidance of the Holy Spirit and the pattern in God's Holy Word.

## THE HIGHEST COURT

Since there is a spiritual relatedness between the various local churches, no one church may strike out on an individualistic line, and taking advantage of its independence, decide things after its own good pleasure. Each must rather cultivate a relationship with the other churches, seeking their sympathy and working with their spiritual good in view. On the other hand, since each is totally independent of the other, the decision of a church in any locality is absolutely final. There is no higher court of appeal; the local court is the supreme court. There is no organization to whose control it must submit, nor is there any organization over which it exercises control. It has neither superiors nor subordinates. If any one is received or refused by a local church, its judgment in the matter must be regarded as absolutely decisive. Even should the decision be wrong, all that can be done is to appeal for a reconsideration of the case. The local church is the highest church authority. If other churches object to its decisions, all they can do is resort to persuasion and exhortation. There is no alternative course, because the relationship which exists between the churches is purely spiritual, not official.

If a brother who has been disciplined in Nanking moves to Soochow, and there proves himself to be innocent of the charge brought against him, then Soochow has full authority to receive him, despite the judgment of Nanking. Soochow is responsible for its actions to God, not to Nanking. Soochow is an independent church, and has therefore full authority to act as it thinks best. But because there is a spiritual relationship with Nanking, it is well for the brother in question not to be received before Nanking's mistake in judgment is pointed out to Nanking. If Nanking's relationship with the Lord is right, then it will pay attention to what Soochow has to say. But if it refuses to do so, Soochow cannot press anything against Nanking, because Nanking as a local church is directly responsible to the Lord alone, and has full authority to decide and act independently of Soochow. If the churches are spiritual, there will be no difficulty in their relationship one with the other.

But if they are not, and difficulties should arise, we must not seek to solve them by interfering in any way with their independence, for it is ordained by an all-wise God.

The organization of no one church is superior to another, nor is its authority greater. Many Christians regard Jerusalem as the mother-church, possessing supreme authority, but such a conception has its source in the human mind, not in the divine Word. Every church is locally governed and is directly responsible to God, not to any other church or organization. A local church is the highest Christian institution on earth. There is none above it to whom appeal can be made. A local church is the lowest scriptural unit, but it is also the highest scriptural organization. Scripture warrants no centralization in Rome which could give Rome authority over other local churches. This is God's safeguard against any infringement of the rights of His Son. Christ is the Head of the Church, and there is no other head in heaven or on earth.

There must be a spiritual relatedness among the churches if the testimony of the Body is to be preserved, but there must at the same time be an absolute independence of government if the testimony of the Head is to be maintained. Each church is under the immediate control of Christ, and is directly responsible to Him alone.

Then why, when a question arose concerning circumcision, did Paul and Barnabas go to Jerusalem to see the apostles and elders there? Because those who were responsible for the erroneous teaching in Antioch had come from Jerusalem. Jerusalem was the place where this problem originated; therefore, it was to Jerusalem the apostles went to have it settled. If a boy were caught in mischief, we would report his misdeeds to his father. In going to Jerusalem Paul and Barnabas were bringing the case to those who had control of the brethren who had created trouble, and once they brought the matter to the responsible source, a speedy settlement was effected. The elders in question were not the elders in Jerusalem, but the elders of Jerusalem; and the apostles were not the apostles of Jerusalem, but the apostles in Jerusalem. The former were the representatives of the church; the latter, the representatives of the work. Paul and Barnabas referred the matter to the apostles and elders, because the apostles had been responsible for teaching in the churches, and the elders for any decision made regarding local matters. When the apostles and elders both repudiated responsibility concerning the teaching propagated by these troublesome brethren from Jerusalem, Paul and Barnabas on their later visits to different places were able to show to the churches there "the decrees to keep which had been decided upon by the apostles and elders in Jerusalem" (Acts 16:4). We must not infer from this that the elders of Jerusalem had any authority over other churches, but merely that they, as well as the apostles, repudiated the teaching of those who had gone out from them. Besides, in Jerusalem some of the apostles occupied the double office of elder and apostle.

## How to Preserve the Local Character of the Churches

Since the churches of God are local, we must be careful to preserve their local character, their local sphere, and their local boundary. Once a church loses these, it ceases to be a scriptural church. Two things call for special attention if the local nature of a church is to be safeguarded.

In the first place, no apostle must exercise control in any official capacity over a church. That is contrary to God's order, and destroys its local nature by putting the imprint of an extra-local minister upon it. No apostle has the authority to establish a private church in any place. The church belongs to the locality, not to the worker. When people are saved by the instrumentality of any man, they belong to the church in the place where they live, not to the man through whom they were saved, nor to the organization he represents. If one or more churches are founded by a certain apostle, and that apostle exercises authority over them as belonging in a special sense to him or to his society, then those churches become sects, for they do not separate themselves from other Christians (saved through the instrumentality of other apostles) on the ground of difference of locality, but on the ground of the difference of instrumentality of salvation. Thus apostles become the heads of different denominations, and their sphere the sphere of their respective denominations, while the churches over which they exercise control become sects, each bearing the particular characteristic of its leader instead of the characteristic of a local church.

The Epistle to the Corinthians throws light on this subject. There was division among the believers in Corinth simply because they failed to realize the local character of the church and sought to make different apostles—Paul, Apollos, and Cephas—the ground of their fellowship. Had they understood the divinely-ordained basis for the division of the Church, they could never have said, "I belong to Paul," or "I belong to Apollos," or "I belong to Cephas," for, despite their especial love for certain leaders, they would have realized that they belonged not to any one of them, but to the church in the locality in which they lived.

No worker may exercise control over a church or attach to it his name or the name of the society he represents. The divine disapproval will always rest on "the church of Paul," or "the church of Apollos," or "the church of Cephas." In the history of the Church it has frequently happened that when God has given special light or experience to any individual, that individual has stressed the particular truth revealed or experienced, and gathered round him people who appreciated his teaching, with the result that the leader, or the truth he emphasized, has become the ground of fellowship. Thus sects have multiplied. If God's people could only see that the object of all ministry is the founding of local churches and not the grouping of Christians around any particular individual, or truth, or experience, or under any particular organization, then the forming of sects would be avoided. We who serve the Lord must be willing to let go our hold upon all those to whom we have ministered, and let all the fruits of our ministry pass into local churches governed entirely by local men. We must be scrupulously careful not to let the coloring of our personality destroy the local character of the church, and we must always serve the church, never control it. An apostle is servant of all and master of none. No church belongs to the worker; it belongs to the locality. Had it been clearly seen by the men who have been used of God throughout the history of the Church that all the churches of God belong to their respective localities, and not to any worker or organization used in their founding, then we should not have so many different denominations today.

Another thing is essential for the preservation of the local character of the church—its sphere must not become wider than the sphere of a locality. The current method of linking up companies of believers in different places who hold the same doctrinal views, and forming them into a church, has no scriptural foundation. The same applies to the custom of regarding any mission as a center, linking together all those saved or helped by them to constitute a "church" of that mission. Such so-called churches are really sects, because they are confined by the bounds of a particular creed, or a particular mission, not by and within the bounds of locality.

The reason God does not sanction the establishing of churches which combine companies of believers in different places is that the divinelyordained basis for the forming of churches is thereby destroyed. Any "church" formed with a mission as its center is bound to be other than local, because wherever there is a center, there is also a sphere; and if the center of the church is a mission, then obviously its sphere is not the scriptural sphere of locality but the sphere of the mission. It clearly lacks the characteristic of a church, and can only be regarded as a sect. In the purpose of God, Jesus Christ is the center of all the churches, and the locality is their sphere.

Whenever a special leader, or a specific doctrine, or some experience, or creed, or organization, becomes a center for drawing together the believers of different places, then because the center of such a church federation is other than Christ, it follows that its sphere will be other than local. And whenever the divinely-appointed sphere of locality is displaced by a sphere of human invention, there the divine approval cannot rest. The believers within such a sphere may truly love the Lord, but they have another center apart from Him, and it is only natural that the second center becomes the controlling one. It is contrary to human nature to stress what we have in common with others; we always emphasize what is ours in particular. Christ is the common center of all the churches, but any company of believers that has a leader, a doctrine, an experience, a creed, or an organization as their center of fellowship, will find that that center becomes the center, and it is that center by which they determine who belongs to them and who does not. The center always determines the sphere, and the second center creates a sphere which divides those who attach themselves to it from those who do not.

Anything that becomes a center to unite believers of different places will create a sphere which includes all believers who attach themselves to that center and excludes all who do not. This dividing line will destroy the God-appointed boundary of locality, and consequently destroy the very nature of the churches of God. Therefore, the children of God must see to it that they have no center of union apart from Christ, because any extra-local union of believers around a center other than the Lord enlarges the sphere of fellowship beyond the sphere of locality, and thus the specific characteristic of the churches of God is lost. There are no other churches in Scripture but local churches!

## The Benefits of Independence

The divine method of making locality the boundary line between the different churches has various obvious advantages:

1.  If each church is locally governed, and all authority is in the hands of the local elders, there is no scope for an able and ambitious false prophet

to display his organizing genius by forming the different companies of believers into one vast federation, and then satisfy his ambition by constituting himself its head. Rome could never sway the power it does today had the churches of God maintained their local ground. Where churches are not affiliated, and where local authority is in the hands of local elders, a pope is an impossibility. Where there are only local churches, there can be no Roman Church. It is the federation of different companies of believers that has brought such evils as dabbling in politics into the Church of God. There is power in a federated "church," but it is carnal power, not spiritual. God's thought for His Church is that she should be like a mustard seed on earth, full of vitality, yet scarcely noticed. It is federation that has brought the Church of today to the state of Thyatira. The failure of Protestantism is that it has substituted organized churches—State and Dissenting—for the Church of Rome, instead of returning to the divinelyordained local churches.

2. Further, if the churches retain their local character, the spread of heresy and error will be avoided, for if a church is local, heresy and error will be local too. Rome is a splendid illustration of the reverse side of this truth. The prevalence of Romish error is because of Romish federation. The sphere of the federated churches is vast; consequently the error is widespread. It is a comparatively simple matter to quarantine error in a local church, but to isolate error in a vast federation of churches is quite another proposition.

3. The greatest advantage of having locality as the boundary of the churches is that it precludes all possibility of sects. You may have your special doctrines and I mine, but as long as we are out to maintain the scriptural character of the churches by making locality the only dividing line between them, then it is impossible for us to establish any church for the propagation of our particular beliefs. As long as a church preserves its local character, it is protected against denominationalism, but as soon as it loses that, it is veering in the direction of sectarianism. A believer is sectarian when he belongs to anyone or anything apart from the Lord and the locality. Sects and denominations can only be established when the local character of the church is destroyed.

In the wisdom of God He has decreed that all His churches be local. This is the divine method of safeguarding them against sects. Obviously, it can only protect the Church against sectarianism in expression. It is still possible for a sectarian spirit to exist in a non-sectarian church, and only the Spirit of God can deal with that. May we all learn to walk after the Spirit and not after the flesh, so that both in outward expression and inward condition the churches of God may be well-pleasing to Him.

# CHAPTER 5: THE BASIS OF UNION AND DIVISION

## THE FORMING OF LOCAL CHURCHES

In the previous chapter we observed that the word "church" was only mentioned twice in the Gospels. It is used frequently in the Acts, but we are never explicitly told there how a church was formed. The second chapter speaks of the salvation of about three thousand men, and the fourth chapter of a further five thousand, but nothing whatever is said about these believers forming a church. Without a single word of explanation they are referred to in the following chapter as the church—"And great fear came upon the whole church" (5:11). Here the Scriptures call the children of God "the church," without even mentioning how the church came into being. In Acts 8:1, immediately after the death of Stephen, the word is again used, and the connection in this case is clearer than before. "There occurred in that day a great persecution against the church which was in Jerusalem." From this passage it is obvious that the believers in Jerusalem are the church in Jerusalem. So we know now what the church is. It consists of all the saved ones in a given locality.

Later on, in the course of the apostles' first missionary tour, many people were saved in different places through the preaching of the gospel. Nothing is mentioned about their being formed into churches, but in Acts 14:23, it is said of Paul and Barnabas that "they had appointed elders for them in every church." The groups of believers in these different places are called churches, without any explanation whatever as to how they came to be churches. They were groups of believers, so they simply were churches. Whenever a number of people in any place were saved, they spontaneously became the church in that place. Without introduction or explanation of any kind, the Word of God presents such a group of believers to us as a church. The scriptural method of founding a church is simply by preaching the gospel; nothing further is necessary, or even permissible. If people hear the gospel and receive the Lord as their Savior, then they are a church; there is no need of any further procedure in order to become a church.

If in a given place anyone believes on the Lord, as a matter of course he is a constituent of the church in that place; there is no further step necessary in order to make him a constituent. No subsequent joining is required of him. Provided he belongs to the Lord, he already belongs to the church in that locality; and since he already belongs to the church, his belonging cannot be made subject to any condition. If, before recognizing a believer as a member of the church, we insist that he join us, or that he resign his connection elsewhere, then "our church" is decidedly not one of the churches of God. If we impose any conditions of membership upon a believer in the locality, we are immediately in an unscriptural position, because his being a member of the local church is conditioned only by his being a believer in the locality. All the saved ones who belong to the place in which we live belong to the same church as we do. I mean by the church a scriptural church, and not a man-made organization. A local church is a church which comprises all the children of God in a given locality.

Let us note well that the ground of our receiving anyone into the church is that the Lord has already received that one. "Him who is weak in faith receive...for God has received him" (Rom. 14:1, 3). "Therefore receive one another, as Christ also received you" (15:7). Our receiving anyone is merely our recognition that the Lord has already received him. Our receiving him does not make him a member of the church; rather, it is that we receive him because he is already a member. If he is the Lord's, he is in the church. If he is not the Lord's, he is not in the church. If we demand anything beyond his reception by the Lord before admitting him to fellowship, then we are not a church at all, but only a sect.

Within and Without the Circle

In any place where the gospel has been proclaimed and people have believed on the Lord, they are the church in that place, and they are our brethren. In the days of the apostles the question of belonging or not belonging to a church was simple in the extreme. But things are not so simple in our days, for the question has been complicated by many socalled churches that exclude those who should be in the church, and include those who should be outside. What sort of a person can be rightly considered a constituent of the church? What is the minimum requirement we can insist upon for admission to church fellowship? Unless the qualifications for church membership are clearly defined, there will always be the danger of excluding from the church those who truly belong to it and including those who do not.

Before we proceed to discover who really belongs to a local church and who does not, let us first inquire who belongs to the universal Church and who does not, since the condition of membership in a church is essentially the same as in the Church. When we know what kind of persons belong to the Church, then we know also what kind of persons belong to a church.

How can we know who is a Christian and who is not? "If anyone does not have the Spirit of Christ, he is not of Him" (Rom. 8:9). According to the Word of God, every person in whose heart Christ dwells by His Spirit is a true Christian. Christians may differ from one another in a thousand respects, but in this fundamental matter there is no difference between them: one and all have the Spirit of Christ dwelling within them. If we wish to know who belongs to the Lord, then we only need to discover whether he has the Spirit of Christ or not. Whoever has the Spirit of Christ is inside the Church circle, and whoever does not have the Spirit of Christ is outside the circle. A participant of the Spirit of God is an essential part of the Church of God; a non-participant of the Spirit of God has no part in the Church. In the Church universal this is true; in the church local this is also true. "Test yourselves whether you are in the faith; prove yourselves. Or do you not realize about yourselves that Jesus Christ is in you, unless you are disapproved?" (2 Cor. 13:5). There is a subjective line of demarcation between the Church and the world; all within that line are saved, and all without that line are lost. This line of demarcation is the indwelling Spirit of Christ.

## THE ONENESS OF THE SPIRIT

The Church of God includes a vast number of believers, living at different times, and scattered in different places throughout the earth. How has it come about that all have been united into one universal Church? With such differences in age, social position, education, background, outlook, and temperament, how could all these people become one church? What is the secret of the oneness of the saints? By what means has Christianity caused these people, with their thousand differences, to become truly one? It is not that, having a grand convention and agreeing to be one, Christians become united. Christian unity is no human product; its origin is purely divine. This mighty mysterious oneness is planted in the hearts of all believers the moment they receive the Lord. It is "the oneness of the Spirit" (Eph. 4:3).

The Spirit who dwells in the heart of every believer is one Spirit; therefore, He makes all those in whom He dwells to be one, even as He Himself is one. Christians may differ from one another in innumerable ways, but all Christians of all ages, with their countless differences, have this one fundamental likeness—the Spirit of God dwells in every one of them. This is the secret of the oneness of believers, and this is the secret of their separation from the world. The reason for Christian unity and for Christian separation is one.

It is this inherent unity that makes all believers one, and it is this inherent unity that accounts for the impossibility of division between believers, except for geographical reasons. Those who do not have this are outsiders; those who have it are our brethren. If you have the Spirit of Christ and I have the Spirit of Christ, then we both belong to the same Church. There is no need to be united; we are united by the one Spirit who dwells in us both. Paul besought all believers to endeavor "to keep the oneness of the Spirit" (Eph. 4:3); he did not exhort us to have the oneness, but merely to keep it. We have it already, for obviously we cannot keep what we do not have. God has never told us to become one with other believers; we already are one. Therefore, we do not need to create oneness; we only need to maintain it.

We cannot make this oneness, since by the Spirit we are one in Christ, and we cannot break it, because it is an eternal fact in Christ; but we can destroy the effects of it, so that its expression in the Church is lost. Alas! that we have not only failed to preserve this precious oneness, but have actually so destroyed the fruits of it, that there is little outward trace of oneness among the children of God.

How are we going to determine who are our brothers and our fellow members in the Church of God? Not by inquiring if they hold the same doctrinal views that we hold, or have had the same spiritual experiences; nor by seeing if their customs, manner of living, interests, and preferences tally with ours. We merely inquire, Are they indwelt by the Spirit of God or not? We cannot insist on oneness of opinions, or oneness of experience, or any other oneness among believers, except the oneness of the Spirit. That oneness there can be, and always must be, among the children of God. All who have this oneness are in the Church.

In your travels has it not sometimes happened that on a boat or train you have met a stranger, and after only a few moments of conversation you have found a pure love for him welling up in your heart? That spontaneous outgoing of love was because of the one Spirit dwelling in both hearts. Such inner spiritual oneness transcends all social, racial, and national differences.

How can we know whether or not a person has this oneness of the Spirit? In the verse immediately following Paul's exhortation to keep the oneness of the Spirit, he explains what those have in common who possess this oneness. We cannot expect believers to be alike in everything, but there are seven things which all true believers share, and by the existence or absence of these we can know whether or not a person has the oneness of the Spirit. Many other things are of great importance, but these seven are vital. They are indispensable to spiritual fellowship, and they are at once the minimum and the maximum requirements that can be made of any person who professes to be a fellow believer.

## SEVEN FACTORS IN SPIRITUAL ONENESS

"One Body and one Spirit, even as also you were called in one hope of your calling; one Lord, one faith, one baptism; one God and Father of all, who is over all and through all and in all" (Eph. 4:4-6). A person is constituted a member of the Church on the ground that he possesses the oneness of the Spirit, and that will result in his being one with all believers on the above seven points. They are the seven elements in the oneness of the Spirit, which is the common heritage of all the children of God. In drawing a line of demarcation between those who belong to the Church and those who do not, we must require nothing beyond these seven lest we exclude any who belong to the family of God; and we dare not require anything less, lest we include any who do not belong to the divine family. All in whom these seven are found belong to the Church; all who lack any of them do not belong to the Church.

(1)ONE BODY. The question of oneness begins with the question of membership of the Body of Christ. The sphere of our fellowship is the sphere of the Body. Those who are outside that sphere have no spiritual relationship with us, but those who are inside that sphere are all in fellowship with us. We cannot make any choice of fellowship in the Body, accepting some members and rejecting others. We are all part of the one
Body, and nothing can possibly separate us from it, or from one another.

Anyone who has received Christ belongs to the Body, and he and we are one. If we do not wish to extend fellowship to anyone, we must first make sure that he does not belong to the Body; if he does, we have no reason to reject him (unless for such disciplinary reasons as are clearly laid down in the Word of God).

(2)ONE SPIRIT. If anyone seeks fellowship with us, however he may differ from us in experience or outlook, provided he has the same Spirit as we have, he is entitled to be received as a brother. If he has received the Spirit of Christ, and we have received the Spirit of Christ, then we are one in the Lord, and nothing must divide us.

(3)ONE HOPE. This hope, which is common to all the children ofGod, is not a general hope, but the hope of our calling, that is, the hope of our calling as Christians. What is our hope as Christians? We hope to be with the Lord forever in glory. There is not a single soul who is truly the Lord's in whose heart there is not this hope, for to have Christ in us is to have "the hope of glory" in us (Col. 1:27). If anyone claims to be the Lord's, but has no hope of heaven or glory, his is a mere empty profession. All who share this one hope are one, and since we have the hope of being together in glory for all eternity, how can we be divided in time? If we are going to share the same future, shall we not gladly share the same present?

(4)ONE LORD. There is only one Lord, the Lord Jesus, and all who recognize that God has made Jesus of Nazareth to be both Lord and Christ are one in Him. If anyone confesses Jesus to be Lord, then his Lord is our Lord, and since we serve the same Lord, nothing whatever can separate us.

(5)ONE FAITH. The faith here spoken of is the faith— not our beliefs in regard to the interpretation of Scripture, but the faith through which we have been saved, which is the common possession of all believers; that is, the faith that Jesus is the Son of God (who died for the salvation of sinners and lives again to give life to the dead). Anyone who lacks this vital faith does not belong to the Lord, but all who possess it are the Lord's. The children of God may follow many different lines of scriptural interpretation, but in regard to this fundamental faith they are one.
Those who lack this faith have no part in the family of God, but all
who possess it we recognize as our brothers in the Lord.

(6)ONE BAPTISM. Is it by immersion or by sprinkling? Is it single or triune? There are various forms of baptism accepted by the children of God, so if we make the form of baptism the dividing line between those who belong to the church and those who do not, we shall exclude many true believers from our fellowship. There are children of God who even believe that a material baptism is not necessary, but since they are the children of God, we dare not on that account exclude them from our fellowship. What then is the significance of the one baptism mentioned in this passage? Paul throws light on the subject in his first letter to the Corinthians. "Is Christ divided? Was Paul crucified for you? Or were you baptized into the name of Paul?" (1:13). The emphasis is not on the form of baptism, but on the name into which we are baptized. The first question is not whether you are sprinkled or immersed, dipped once or three times, baptized literally or spiritually; the important point is this: Into whose name have you been baptized? If you are baptized into the name of the Lord, that is your qualification for church membership. If anyone is baptized into the name of the Lord, I welcome him as my brother, whatever the manner of his baptism. By this we do not imply that it is of no consequence whether we are sprinkled or immersed, or whether our baptism is spiritual or literal. The Word of God teaches that baptism is literal, and is by immersion, but the point here is that the manner of baptism is not the ground of our fellowship, but the name into which we are baptized. All who are baptized into the name of the Lord are one in Him.

(7)ONE GOD. Do we believe in the same personal, supernatural God as our Father? If so, then we belong to one family, and there is no adequate reason for our being divided.

The above seven points are the seven factors in that divine oneness which is the possession of all the members of the divine family, and they constitute the only test of Christian profession. They are the possession of every true Christian, no matter to what place or period he belongs. Like a sevenfold cord the oneness of the Spirit binds all the believers throughout the world; and however diverse their character or circumstances, provided they have these seven expressions of an inner oneness, then nothing can possibly separate them.

If we impose any conditions of fellowship beyond these seven—which are but the outcome of the one spiritual life, then we are guilty of sectarianism, for we are making a division between those who are manifestly children of God. If we apply any test but these seven, such as baptism by immersion, or certain interpretations of prophecy, or a special line of holiness teaching, or a so-called Pentecostal experience, or the resigning from any denominational church—then we are imposing conditions other than those stipulated in the Word of God. All who have these seven points in common with us are our brothers, whatever their spiritual experience, or doctrinal views, or so-called church relationships. Our oneness is not based on our appreciation of the truth of our oneness, nor on our coming out from all that would contradict our oneness, but upon the actual fact of our oneness, which is made real in our experience by the indwelling Spirit of Christ.

## LOCAL CHURCHES

Now what is true of the universal Church is also true of a local church.

The universal Church comprises all those who have the oneness of the Spirit. The local church comprises all those who, in a given locality, have the oneness of the Spirit. The Church of God and the churches of God do not differ in nature, but only in extent. The former consists of all throughout the universe who are indwelt by the Spirit of God; the latter consists of all in one locality who are indwelt by the Spirit.

Anyone wishing to belong to a church in a given locality must answer two requirements—he must be a child of God, and he must live in that particular locality. Membership in *the Church of God* is conditioned only by being a child of God, but membership in a church of God is conditioned, firstly, by being a child of God and, secondly, by living in a given locality.

*In nature the Church is indivisible as God Himself is indivisible. Therefore, the division of the Church into churches is not a division in nature, life, or essence, but only in government, organization, and management. Because the earthly church is composed of a vast number of individuals, a measure of organization is indispensable. It is a physical impossibility for all the people of God, scattered throughout the world, to live and meet in one place; and it is for that reason alone that the Church of God has been divided into churches.*

We must realize clearly that the nature of all the local churches is the same throughout the whole earth. It is not that the constituents of one local church are of one kind, and the constituents of another local church are of another kind. In nature there is no difference whatever. The only difference is in the localities that determine their respective boundaries. The Church is indivisible; therefore, in nature the churches are indivisible too. It is only in outward sphere that there is any possibility of dividing them. Physical limitations make geographical divisions inevitable, but the spiritual oneness of believers overcomes all barriers of space.

Locality is the divinely-appointed ground for the division of the Church, because it is the only inevitable division. Every barrier between all believers in the world is avoidable, except this one. As long as believers remain in the flesh they cannot exist apart from their dwelling places; therefore, the churches which consist of such believers cannot but be restricted by their dwellings. Geographical distinctions are natural, not arbitrary, and it is simply because the physical limitations of the children of God make geographical divisions inevitable, that God has ordained that His Church be divided into churches on the ground of locality. Such division is scriptural, and all other divisions are carnal. *Any division of the children of God other than geographical implies not merely a division of sphere, but a division of nature. Local division is the only division which does not touch the life of the Church.*

Most believers of today are so utterly blind to the scriptural basis of a church that if one asks another, "To what church do you belong?" The first thought of the one questioned is of the specific line of teaching he approves of, or the group of people with whom he has special fellowship, or how his group of Christians is different from others, or perhaps the name that particular group bears, or the form of organization they have adopted—in short, anything but the place in which he lives. Few would answer that question with, "I belong to the church in Ephesus," or "I belong to the church in Shanghai," or "I belong to the church in Los Angeles." It is our being in Christ that separates us from the world, and it is our being in a given locality that separates us from other believers. It is only because we reside in a different place from them that we belong to a different church. The only reason I do not belong to the same church as other believers is that I do not live in the same place as they do. If I wish to be in the same church, then I must change my residence to the same place. If, on the other hand, I wish to be in a different church from others in my locality, then the only solution to my problem is to move to a different locality. Difference of locality is the only justification for division among believers.

## SEVEN FORBIDDEN GROUNDS OF DIVISION

On the positive side we have just seen the ground on which God has ordained that His Church be divided. Now, on the negative side, we shall see on what ground the Church ought not to be divided.

(1) SPIRITUAL LEADERS. "Now I mean this, that each of you says, I am of Paul, and I of Apollos, and I of Cephas, and I of Christ" (1 Cor. 1:12). Here Paul points out the carnality of the Corinthian believers in attempting to divide the church of God in Corinth, which, by the divine ordering, was

indivisible, being already the smallest scriptural unit upon which any church could be established. They sought to divide the church on the ground of a few leaders who had been specially used of God in their midst. Cephas was a zealous minister of the gospel, Paul was a man who had suffered much for his Lord's sake, and Apollos was one whom God certainly used in His service, but though all three had been indisputably owned of God in Corinth, God could never permit the church there to make them a ground of division. He ordained that His Church be divided on the basis of localities, not of persons. It was all right to have a church in Corinth and a church in Ephesus, and quite all right to have several churches in Galatia and a number in Macedonia, for difference of locality justified division into these various churches. It was also all right for the believers to esteem those leaders whom God had used among them, but it would have been quite wrong to divide the churches according to the respective leaders by whom they had been helped.

Paul, Cephas, and Apollos were true-hearted servants of God who allowed no party-spirit to separate them; it was their followers who were responsible for the separation. Hero worship is a tendency of human nature, which delights to show preference for those who appeal to its tastes. Because so many of God's children know little or nothing of the power of the cross to deal with the flesh, this tendency to worship a man has expressed itself frequently in the Church of God, and much havoc has been wrought in consequence. It is in keeping with God's will that we should learn from spiritual men and profit by their leadership, but it is altogether contrary to His will that we should divide the Church according to the men we admire. The only scriptural basis for the forming of a church is difference of locality, not difference of leaders.

(2) INSTRUMENTS OF SALVATION. Spiritual leaders are no adequate reason for dividing the Church; neither are the instruments used of God in our salvation. Some of the Corinthian believers proclaimed themselves to be "of Cephas," others "of Paul," others "of Apollos." They traced the beginning of their spiritual history to these men, and so thought they belonged to them. It is both natural and common for persons saved through the instrumentality of a worker, or a society, to consider themselves as belonging to such a worker or society. It is likewise both natural and common for an individual, or a mission, through whose means people have been saved, to consider the saved ones as belonging to them. It is natural, but not spiritual. It is common, but nevertheless, contrary to God's will. Alas! that so many of God's servants have not yet realized that they are servants of the local church, not masters of a private "church." *Churches are divided on*

*the ground of geography, not on the ground of the instruments of our salvation.*

(3) NON-SECTARIANISM. Some Christians think they know betterthan to say, "I am of Cephas," or "I am of Paul," or "I am of Apollos." They say, "I am of Christ." Such Christians despise the others as sectarian, and on that ground start another community. Their attitude is—"You are sectarian;
I am non-sectarian. You are hero worshippers; we worship the Lord alone."

But God's Word condemns not only those who say, "I am of Cephas," "I am of Paul," or "I am of Apollos." It just as definitely and just as clearly denounces those who say, "I am of Christ." It is not wrong to consider oneself as belonging only to Christ; it is right and even essential. Nor is it wrong to repudiate all schism among the children of God; it is highly commendable. God does not condemn this class of Christians for either of these two things; He condemns them for the very sin they condemn in others— their sectarianism. As a protest against division among the children of God, many believers seek to divide those who do not divide from those who do, and never dream that they themselves are divisive! Their ground of division may be more plausible than that of others who divide on the ground of doctrinal differences, or personal preference for certain leaders, but the fact remains that they are dividing the children of God. Even while they repudiate schism elsewhere, they are schismatic themselves.

When you say, "I am of Christ," do you mean to say others are not? It is perfectly legitimate for you to say, "I am of Christ," if your remark merely implies to whom you belong; but if it implies, "I am not sectarian; I stand quite differently from you sectarians," then it is making a difference between you and other Christians. The very thought of distinguishing between the children of God has its springs in the carnal nature of man, and is sectarian. If we look on other believers as sectarian and consider ourselves to be non-sectarian, we are immediately differentiating between God's people and thereby manifesting a divisive spirit even in the very act of condemning division. No matter by what means we distinguish between the members of God's family—even if it be on the pretext of Christ Himself —we are guilty of schism in the Body.

What then is right? All exclusiveness is wrong. All inclusiveness (of true children of God) is right. Denominations are not scriptural, and we ought to have no part in them, but if we adopt an attitude of criticism and think, "They are denominational; I am undenominational. They belong to sects; I belong to Christ alone"—such differentiating is definitely sectarian.

Yes, praise God I am of Christ, but my fellowship is not merely with those who say, "I am of Christ," but with all who are of Christ. What is of vital importance is not the confession, but the fact. Although these other believers say they are of Paul, of Cephas, and of Apollos, yet in fact they are of Christ. I do not so much mind what they say, but I very much mind what they are. I do not inquire whether they are denominational or undenominational, sectarian or unsectarian; I only inquire, "Are they of Christ?" If they are of Christ, then they are my brethren.

Our personal standing should be undenominational, but the basis of our fellowship is not undenominationalism. We ourselves should be nonsectarian, but we dare not insist on non-sectarianism as a condition of fellowship. Our only ground of fellowship is Christ. Our fellowship must be with all the believers in a locality, not merely with all the unsectarian believers in that locality. They may make denominational differences, but we must not make undenominational requirements. We dare not differentiate between ourselves and them, because they differentiate between themselves and others. They are the children of God, and because they make distinctions between themselves and other children of God, they do not on that account cease to be the children of God. Their denominationalism or sectarianism will mean that severe limitations are imposed upon the Lord as to His purpose and mind for them, and this will mean that they will never go beyond a certain measure of spiritual growth and fullness. Blessing there may be, but fullness of divine purpose never.

*All believers living in the same locality belong to the same church.* This is an unchanging principle. We dare not alter "all the believers in a locality" to "all the undenominational believers in a locality." If we make undenominationalism or unsectarianism the boundary of our church, instead of locality, then we lose our local standing as a church and become a sect. It is not a denominational church, nor an interdenominational church, nor even an undenominational church we are after, but a local church. The difference between a local church and an undenominational church is as vast as the difference between heaven and earth. A local church is undenominational, but an undenominational church is denominational. "The church in Corinth" is scriptural, but "the church of all those who say, 'I am of Christ' in Corinth" is unscriptural. Our work is positive and constructive, not negative and destructive. We are out to establish churches, not to destroy denominations.

Human nature is prone to go to extremes; it is so easy for us either to be undenominational ourselves and demand undenominationalism of others, or else to tolerate denominationalism in others and gradually become denominational ourselves. We ourselves must be undenominational, but we must not demand undenominationalism of other Christians as the basis of our fellowship.

Therefore, if we come to a place where Christ is not named, we must preach the gospel, win men to the Lord, and found a local church. If we come to a place where there are already Christians, but on various grounds these believers separate themselves into denominational "churches," our task is just the same as in the other place— we must preach the gospel, lead men to the Lord, and form them into a church on the scriptural ground of locality. All the while we must maintain an attitude of inclusiveness, not exclusiveness, towards those believers who are in different sects, for they, as we, are children of God, and they live in the same locality; therefore, they belong to the same church as we do. For ourselves, we cannot join any sect or remain in one, for our church connection can only be on local ground, but in regard to others we must not make leaving a sect the condition of fellowship with those believers who are in a sect. That will make undenominationalism our church ground, instead of locality. Let us be clear on this point, that an undenominational church is not a local church.

There is a vast difference between the two. A local church is undenominational, and it is positive and inclusive; but an undenominational church is not a local church, and it is negative and exclusive.

Let us be clear as to our position. We are not out to establish undenominational churches, but local churches. We are seeking to do a positive work. If believers can be led to see what a local church is—the expression of the Body of Christ in a locality—they will certainly not remain in any sect. On the other hand, it is possible for them to see all the evils of sectarianism, and leave them, without knowing what a local church is. We must help those, to whom God has been pleased to use us, to understand clearly the truth regarding local churches, and not to lay emphasis on the question of denominations. They must realize that whenever they use the term "we" in relation to the children of God, they must include all the children of God, not merely those who are meeting with them. If when we say "our brethren," we do not include all the children of God, but only those who continually meet with us, then we are schismatic.

I do not condone sectarianism, and I do not believe we should belong to any sect, but it is not our business to get people to leave them. If we make it our chief concern to lead people to a real knowledge of the Lord and the power of His cross, then they will gladly abandon themselves to Him, and will learn to walk in the Spirit, repudiating the things of the flesh. We shall find there will be no need to stress the question of denominations, for the Spirit Himself will enlighten them. If a believer has not learned the way of the cross and the walk in the Spirit, what is gained by his coming out of a sect?

(4) DOCTRINAL DIFFERENCES. In the Greek the word rendered "heresies" in Galatians 5:20 [KJV] does not necessarily convey the thought of error, but rather of division on the ground of doctrine. The Interlinear New Testament translates it as "sects," while Darby in his New Translation renders it "schools of opinion." The whole thought here is not of the difference between truth and error, but of division based upon doctrine. My teaching may be right or it may be wrong, but if I make it a cause of division, then I am guilty of the "heresy" spoken of here.

God forbids any division on doctrinal grounds. Some believe that rapture is pre-tribulation; others, that it is posttribulation. Some believe that all the saints will enter the kingdom; others believe that only a section will enter. Some believe that baptism is by immersion; others, that is by sprinkling. Some believe that supernatural manifestations are a necessary accompaniment to the baptism in the Holy Spirit, while others do not. None of these doctrinal views constitute a scriptural basis for separating the children of God. Though some may be right and others wrong, God does not sanction any division on account of difference as to such beliefs.[2] If a group of believers split off from a local church in their zeal for certain teaching according to the Word of God, the new "church" they establish may have more scriptural teaching, but it could never be a scriptural church. To bring error into a church is carnal, but to divide a church on account of error may also be carnal. It is carnality that so often destroys the oneness of the church in any place.

If we wish to maintain a scriptural position, then we must see to it that the churches we found in various places only represent localities, not doctrines. If our "church" is not separated from other children of God on the ground of locality alone, but stands for the propagation of some particular doctrine, then we are decidedly a sect, however true to the Word of God our teaching may be. The purpose of God is that a church should represent the children of God in a locality, not represent some specific truth there. *A church of God in any place comprises all the children of God in that place, not merely those who hold the same doctrinal views.*

Should we arrive at a place where a church has already been established on clear local ground, and discover that its members hold views which we consider unscriptural, or that they consider the views we hold as unscriptural, if we then refuse to recognize them as the church of God in that locality and withdraw from fellowship, we are divisive. The question is not whether they agree with our presentation of truth, but whether they are standing on clear church ground.

If our hearts are set to preserve the local character of the churches of God, we cannot fail to come up against problems in our work. Unless the cross operates mightily, what endless possibilities of friction there will be if we include in one church all the believers in the locality with all their varying views. How the flesh would like just to include those holding the same views, and to exclude all whose views differ from ours. To have constant and close association with people whose interpretation of Scripture does not tally with ours, is hard for the flesh, but good for the spirit. God does not use division to solve the problem; He uses the cross. He would have us submit to the cross, so that through the very difficulties of the situation, the meekness and patience and love of Christ may be deeply wrought into our lives. Under the circumstances, if we do not know the cross, we shall probably argue, lose our temper, and finally go our own way. We may have right views, but God is giving us an opportunity to display a right attitude; we may believe aright, but God is testing us to see if we love aright. It is easy to have a mind well stored with scriptural teaching, and a heart devoid of true love. Those who differ from us will be a means in God's hand to test whether we have spiritual experience, or only scriptural knowledge, to test whether the truths we proclaim are a matter of life to us, or mere theory.

Romans 14 shows us how to deal with those whose views differ from ours. What would we do if in our church there were vegetarians and Sabbatarians? Why, we should consider it almost intolerable if in the same church some of the believers kept the Lord's Day and others the Sabbath, and some ate meat freely, while others were strict vegetarians. That was exactly the situation Paul was facing. Let us note his conclusions. "Now him who is weak in faith receive, but not for the purpose of passing judgment on his considerations" (v. 1). "Who are you who judge another's household servant? To his own master he stands or falls; and he will be made to stand, for the Lord is able to make him stand" (v. 4). "Therefore let us judge one another no longer, but rather judge this: not to put a stumbling block or cause of falling before your brother" (v. 13). Oh, for Christian tolerance! Oh, for largeness of heart! Alas! that many of God's children are so zealous for their pet doctrines that they immediately label as heretics, and treat accordingly, all whose interpretation of Scripture differs from theirs. God would have us walk in love toward all who hold views contrary to those views that are dear to us (v. [15]).

This does not mean that all the members of a church can hold whatever views they please, but it does mean that the solution to the problem of doctrinal differences does not lie in forming separate parties according to the different views held, but in walking in love toward those whose outlook differs from ours. By patient teaching we may yet be able to help all to "the oneness of the faith" (Eph. 4:13). As we wait patiently on the Lord, He may grant grace to the others to change their views, or He may grant us grace to see that we are not such good teachers as we thought we were. Nothing so tests the spirituality of a teacher as opposition to his teaching.

The teachers must learn humility, but so must all the other believers. When they recognize their position in the Body, they will know that it is not given to everyone to determine matters of doctrine. They must learn to submit to those who have been equipped of God for the specific ministry of teaching His people. Spiritual gifts and spiritual experience are necessary for spiritual teaching; consequently not everyone can teach.

"Make my joy full, that you think the same thing, having the same love, joined in soul, thinking the one thing, doing nothing by way of selfish ambition nor by way of vainglory, but in lowliness of mind considering one another more excellent than yourselves; not regarding each his own virtues, but each the virtues of others also" (Phil. 2:2-4). When the churches have laid to heart what Paul wrote to the church in Philippi, then it will be perfectly possible to have only one church in one locality with no friction whatever among its many members.

(5) RACIAL DIFFERENCES. "For also in one Spirit we were all baptized into one body, whether Jews or Greeks, whether slaves or free, and were all given to drink one Spirit" (1 Cor. 12:13). Jews have always had the strongest racial prejudice of all peoples. They regarded other nations as unclean, and were forbidden even to eat with them; but Paul made it very clear, in writing to the Corinthians, that in the Church both Jew and Gentile are one. All distinctions in Adam have been done away with in Christ. A

racial "church" has no recognition in the Word of God. Church membership is determined by place of residence, not by race.

Today in the large cosmopolitan cities of the world there are churches for the whites and churches for the blacks, churches for the Europeans and churches for the Asiatics. These have originated through failure to understand that the boundary of a church is a city. God does not permit any division of His children on the ground of difference of color, custom, or manner of living. No matter to what race they belong, if they belong to the same locality, they belong to the same church. God has placed believers of different races in one locality, so that, by transcending all external differences, they might in one church show forth the one life and the one Spirit of His Son. All that comes to us by nature is overcome by grace. All that was ours in Adam has been ruled out in Christ. The whole matter hinges here—are all carnal differences done away with in Christ, or is there still a place for the flesh in the Church? Are our resources in Christ sufficient to overcome all natural barriers? Let us remember that the church in any locality includes all the believers living there and excludes all who live elsewhere.

NATIONAL DIFFERENCES. Jews and Gentiles represent nationals well as racial distinctions, but in the Church of God there is neither Jew nor Greek. There is no racial distinction there, and there is no national distinction either. All believers living in one place, no matter what their nationality, belong to the one church. In the natural realm there is a difference between Chinese, French, British, and Americans, but in the spiritual realm there is none. If a Chinese believer lives in Nanking, he belongs to the church in Nanking. If a French believer lives in Nanking, he also belongs to the church in Nanking. The same holds good for Britishers, Americans, and all other nationalities, provided they are born again. The Word of God recognizes the church in Rome, the church in Ephesus, and the church in Thessalonica, but it does not recognize the Jewish church, or the Chinese church, or the Anglican church. The reason the names of cities appear in Scripture in connection with the churches of God is that the difference of dwelling place is the only difference recognized by God among His children. Their life is essentially one, and is therefore indivisible, but the place in which that life is lived cannot but vary as long as they remain in the flesh.

Since the churches are all local, if a believer—whatever his nationality—moves from one place to another, he immediately becomes a member of the church in the latter place, and has no church connection in the place of his former residence. You cannot live in one place and be a member of the church in another. There is no extraterritoriality in connection with the churches of God. As soon as you exceed the city limit, you exceed the church limit. If a Chinese brother moves from Nanking to Hankow, he becomes a member of the church in Hankow.

In like manner, a British brother coming from London to Hankow immediately becomes a member of the church in Hankow. A change of residence necessarily involves a change of church, whereas naturalization has no effect on church membership.

Our fellow workers who have gone from China to the South Sea Islands must be careful not to form an Overseas Chinese church there. It is possible to have an Overseas Chinese Chamber of Commerce, or an Overseas Chinese College, or an Overseas Chinese Club. Anything you like can be Overseas Chinese, but not a church. A church is always local! If you go to any city in a foreign land, then it follows as a matter of course that you belong to the church in that city. There is nothing Chinese about the churches of God.

How glorious it would be if the saved in every city could overlook all natural differences and only consider their spiritual oneness. "We are the believers in Christ in such-and-such a place" is the finest confession a company of Christians can make. Whether Christ is in you or not, determines whether or not you belong to the Church; where you live determines the particular church to which you belong. The question put by God to the world is, "Do they belong to Christ?" The question put by God to believers is, "Where do they live?" Not nationality but locality is the question raised. The churches of God are built on city ground, not on national ground.

The usual conception of an indigenous church, while quite right in some respects, is fundamentally wrong at the most vital point. Since the divine method of dividing the Church is according to locality, not nationality, then all differentiation between Christian and heathen countries is contrary to God's thought. The Church of God knows neither Jew nor Greek; therefore, it knows neither native nor foreigner, neither heathen country nor Christian country. The Scriptures differentiate between cities, not between countries, heathen and Christian. So if we would be in full accord with the mind of God, we must make no difference whatever between the Chinese and foreign church, between Chinese and foreign workers, or between Chinese and foreign funds.

The thought of the indigenous church is that the natives of a country should be self-governing, self-supporting, and self-propagating, while the thought of God is that the believers in a city—whether native or foreign— should be self-governing, self-supporting, and self-propagating. Take, for instance, Peking. The theory of the indigenous church distinguishes between Chinese and foreigners in Peking, whereas the Word of God distinguishes between the believers in Peking—whether Chinese or foreign —and the believers in other cities. That is why in Scripture we read of the churches of the Gentiles, but never of the church of the Gentiles. The attempt to form all Chinese believers into one church shows a lack of understanding in regard to the divine basis of forming churches.

On the one hand, there is no church of the Gentiles in Scripture; on the other hand, we read of "the church of the Thessalonians." It is suggestive that this is the only expression of its kind used in the New Testament. The Word does not speak of the church of the Greeks (a race, or nation), but of the church of the Thessalonians (a city). There is no such thing in the thought of God as the church of the Chinese, but there is such a thing as the church of the Pekinese. Scripture knows nothing of the church of the French, but it does recognize the church of the Parisians. A clear apprehension of the divine basis of church formation —according to the difference of cities and not of countries —will save us from the misconception of the indigenous church. There should be no distinction whatever between

Chinese and foreign Christians, between Chinese and foreign workers, or between Chinese and foreign money in any given locality.

(7) SOCIAL DISTINCTIONS. In Paul's day, from a social point of view, there was a great gulf fixed between a free man and a slave; yet they worshipped side by side in the same church. In our day, if a rickshaw coolie and the president of our republic both belong to Christ and live in the same place, then they belong to the same church. There may be a mission for rickshaw coolies, but there can never be a church for rickshaw coolies. Social distinctions are no adequate basis for forming a separate church. In the Church of God there "cannot be slave nor free man."

In Scripture we have at least seven definite things referred to which are forbidden by God as reasons for dividing His Church. As a matter of fact these seven points are only typical of all other reasons the human mind may devise for dividing the Church of God. The two millenniums of Church history are a sad record of human inventions to destroy the Church's oneness.

The sphere of the church is local, and the local church should on no account be divided. The question naturally arises, if the spiritual life of a local (not denominational) church is very low, can a few of the more spiritual members not gather together and form another assembly? The answer from the Word of God is emphatically, No! God's Word only warrants the establishment of churches on local ground. Even lack of spirituality is no adequate reason for dividing the church. Should local methods, government, and organization be far from ideal, that still constitutes no reason for division. Even wrong teaching (2 John 9 excepted) is no ground for those who know better to form a separate church. We must lay it to heart that the difference of locality is the only ground for dividing the Church of God. No other ground is scriptural.

We who live in the same locality cannot but belong to the same church. This is something from which there is no escape. If I am dissatisfied with the local church, the only thing I can do is to change my locality; then automatically I change my church. We can leave a denomination, but we can never leave a church. To leave a sect is justifiable, but to leave a church — whether on account of unspirituality, wrong doctrine, or bad organization — is utterly unjustifiable. If you leave the local church and form a separate assembly, you may have greater spirituality, purer teaching, and better government; but you have no church; you have only a sect.

In the second and third chapters of Revelation we see seven different churches in seven different localities. Only two were not rebuked but actually praised by the Lord. The other five were all definitely censured. Spiritually those five were in a sad state. They were weak, defeated churches; but they were churches for all that, not sects. Spiritually they were wrong, but positionally they were right; therefore, God only commanded those in them to be overcomers. The Lord said not a word about leaving the church. A local church is a church which you cannot leave; you must remain in it. If you are more spiritual than the other members, then you should use your spiritual influence and your authority in prayer to revive that church. If the church does not respond, you have only two alternatives; you must either remain there, keeping yourself undefiled, or else you must change your dwelling place. But this does not apply to a sect. It is futile to seek by a wrong application of these two chapters to keep Spirit-taught believers within a sect, for the seven churches referred to are local churches, not sectarian "churches."

90

However weak they may have been, they were still on the scriptural ground of the Body in the locality. The Word of God has never authorized anyone to leave a church. All groups of believers who base their fellowship on other ground than that of locality are sects, even though they may term themselves churches. It is all right to leave a sect, but it is never right to leave a local church. If you leave a local church, you do so without the authority of the Lord, and you become guilty of the sin of schism in the Body.

What a tragedy it is when a few spiritual members leave a local church, and form another assembly, simply because the other members are weak and immature. Those stronger members should remain in that church as overcomers, seeking to help their weaker brothers and sisters, and claiming the situation there for the Lord. Oh, how prone we are to despise the believers we consider inferior to us, and how we delight to associate with those whose fellowship we find specially congenial. Pride of heart, and a selfish enjoyment in spiritual things, causes us to overlook the fact that a church in any given place should consist of all the children of God in that place; so we narrow down Christian fellowship and make selection among the children of God. This is sectarianism, and it is a grief of heart to the Lord.

# CHAPTER 6: THE WORK AND THE CHURCHES

## THE APOSTLES AND THE CHURCHES

In regard to the universal Church, God first brought it into being, and thereafter set apostles to minister to it (1 Cor. 12:28); but in regard to the local churches the order was quite otherwise. The appointment of apostles preceded the founding of local churches. Our Lord first commissioned the twelve apostles, and thereafter the church in Jerusalem came into existence. The Holy Spirit first called two apostles—Paul and Barnabas—to the work, and thereafter a number of churches sprang into being in different places. So it is clear that the apostolic ministry precedes the existence of the local churches, and consequently it is obvious that the work of apostles does not belong to the local churches.

As we have already observed, the Holy Spirit said, "Set apart for Me now Barnabas and Saul for the work to which I have called them." The service that followed the apostles' separation, which we generally refer to as their missionary campaigns, the Holy Spirit referred to as "the work." "The work" was the object of the Spirit's call, and all that was accomplished by Paul and his associates in the days and years that followed, all that for which they were responsible, was included in this one term, "the work." (The term "the work" is used in a specific sense in this book, and relates to all that is included in the missionary efforts of the apostles.)

Since churches are the result of the work, they cannot possibly include it. If we are to understand the mind of God concerning His work, then we must differentiate clearly between the work and the churches. These two are quite distinct in Scripture, and we must avoid confusing them; otherwise we shall make serious mistakes, and the outworking of God's purposes will be hindered. The word "churches" appears frequently in Scripture, so it has been easy for us to arrive at a clear understanding of its meaning and content, but the word "work" is not often used in the specific sense in which it is employed here, with the result that we have paid little heed to it. But the Spirit has used the expression in an inclusive way to cover all that related to the purpose of the apostolic call. Let us then abide by the term which the Spirit has chosen to employ.

It has been repeated again and again, but let us point it out once again, that the churches are local, and nothing outside the locality must interfere with them, nor must they interfere with anything beyond that sphere. Church affairs are to be managed by local men who, on account of their comparative spiritual maturity, have been appointed to be elders. As the work of the apostles is to preach the gospel and found churches, not to take responsibility in the churches already established, their office is not a church office. If they go to work in a place where no church exists, then they should seek to found one by the proclamation of the gospel; but if one exists already, then their work must be distinct from it. In the will of God "the church" and "the work" follow two distinct lines.

The work belongs to the apostles, while the churches belong to the local believers. The apostles are responsible for the work in any place, and the church is responsible for all the children of God there. In the matter of church fellowship the apostles regard themselves as the brethren of all believers in the city, but in the matter of work, they regard themselves as its personnel, and maintain a distinction between themselves and the church. As members of the Body, they meet for mutual edification with all their fellow members in the locality; but as ministering members of the Body, their specific ministry constitutes them a group of workers apart from the church. It is wrong for the apostles to interfere with the affairs of the church, but it is equally wrong for the church to interfere with the affairs of the work. The apostles manage the work; the elders manage the church. It follows then that we must be clear about our call. Has God called us to be elders, or to be apostles? If elders, then our responsibility is confined to local affairs; if apostles, then our responsibility is extra-local. If elders, then our sphere is the church; if apostles, then our sphere lies beyond the church, in the work.

The reason God called apostles and entrusted the work to them is that He wished to preserve the local character of the church. If any church exercises control over work in another locality, it at once becomes extralocal, and thereby loses its specific characteristic as a church. The responsibility of the work in different places is committed to apostles, whose sphere extends beyond the locality. The responsibility of the church is committed to elders, whose sphere is confined to the locality. An Ephesian elder is an elder in Ephesus, but he ceases to be an elder when he comes to Philippi, and vice versa. Eldership is limited to locality. When Paul was at Miletus, he wished to see the representative members of the church in Ephesus, so he sent for the Ephesian elders. But no request was sent to the Ephesian apostle, for the simple reason that there was none. The apostles belong to different places, not to one place alone, whereas the sphere of the elders is strictly local, for which reason they take no official responsibility beyond the place in which they live. Whenever the church tries to control the work, the church loses its local character. Whenever an apostle tries to control a church, he loses his extra-local character. Much confusion has arisen because the divine line of demarcation between the churches and the work has been lost sight of.

## RESPONSIBILITY—SPIRITUAL AND OFFICIAL

Just as the apostles have spiritual but no official responsibility regarding the church, so the elders, and the whole church, have spiritual but no official responsibility regarding the work. It is commendable if a local church seeks to help in the work; but it is under no official obligation to do so. If the members of the church are spiritual, they cannot but regard the work of God as their work, in which case they will count it a joy to help in any way. They will recognize that, while the official responsibility for the work rests on the apostles, the spiritual responsibility is shared by all the children of God, and consequently by them. There is a vast difference between spiritual and official responsibility. In the matter of official responsibility there are certain prescribed duties, and one is in the wrong if one fails to perform them. But in the matter of spiritual responsibility there are no legal obligations. Therefore, any neglect of responsibility does not register as an official shortcoming, but it does register as a low spiritual state. From an official point of view, the responsibility of the work rests upon the apostles. If they lack the needed help, they cannot demand it; but if the church is spiritual, its members will see the meaning of the Body and will gladly assist in the work and give towards it. If the church fails in spiritual responsibility, the apostles may have difficulties which they should not have, and the church will suffer spiritually. On the other hand, the responsibility of the church rests officially upon the elders; therefore, the apostles should not take upon themselves to do anything directly there. They may and should assist the church by their counsel and exhortations. If the local believers are spiritual, they will willingly receive such help; but should they be unspiritual, and in consequence reject the help the apostles offer, their failure is spiritual and not official, and the apostles have no option but to leave them to their own resources. The church does not come within the sphere of the work and is consequently outside the sphere of their authority. Again let us repeat, the churches are local, intensely local; the work is extra-local, and always extra-local.

## REPRESENTATIVES OF THE MINISTRY OF THE BODY — INDIVIDUALS, NOT CHURCHES

There is a definite divine reason for the fact that the work is entrusted to individual apostles and not to local churches; but before we enter into that, let us examine the fundamental difference between the activities of a church as a body and the activities of a brother as an individual. It may be all right for a brother (or for several brothers) to go into business, but it would be all wrong for a church to do so. It might be quite in order for one or more brothers to open a restaurant or a hotel, but that would not be in order for a church. What may be perfectly permissible in the case of brothers, as individuals, is not necessarily permissible in the case of a church, as a company. The business of the churches consists in the mutual care of their various members, such as the conduct of meetings for breaking of bread, for the exercise of spiritual gifts, for the study of the Word, for prayer, for fellowship, and for gospel preaching. The work is beyond the sphere of any church as a corporate body; it is the responsibility of individuals, though not of individuals as such.

There is no scriptural precedent for such work being undertaken by a church, as, for instance, hospitals, or schools, or even something on a more definitely spiritual plane such as foreign missions. It is perfectly in order for one or more members of a church to run a hospital, or a school, or to be responsible for mission work, but not for any church as a whole. A church exists for the purpose of mutual help in one place, not for the purpose of bearing the responsibility of work in different places. According to God's Word, all the work is the personal concern of individual brothers called and commissioned by God, as members of the Body, and not the concern of any church as a body. The responsibility of the work is always borne by one or more individuals.

The important point to note is that the Body of Christ in its ministry aspect is not represented by local churches, but by individuals who are the gifts given by God to His Church. A local church has not been chosen by God to represent the Body where ministry is in view. When God wants any representatives of the Body to express its ministry, He chooses certain individuals, who are the functioning members, to represent that Body. The whole thing is clear in the last part of 1 Corinthians 12.

It was never the thought of God that His work should be done on any other basis than that of the Body, because it is actually the natural functioning of the Body of Christ. It is the activity, under the direction of the Head, of those members who possess special faculties. We have already pointed out that the local church represents the Body in its life aspect, and the functioning members represent the Body in its ministry aspect. The local church is called to manifest not so much the service, as the life of the Body, while the apostles, prophets, and teachers, as such, are called to manifest not so much the life, as the service of the Body. That is the reason God did not entrust the work to any local church as a body, but to individuals. But it is the latter, not the former, who represent the Body, if the latter are functioning members of the Body.

Therefore, we find that the two apostles who went out from Antioch were not sent forth to the work by the whole church but by several ministers in the church, because in the matter of service and work it is the latter, not the former, who represent the Body. So the work is the responsibility of individuals who are called and commissioned by God, and not the responsibility of the whole church.

But, let it be clearly understood, by individuals we do not mean individuals as individuals, but as functioning members representing the Body. God has never sanctioned that anyone take up an individualistic line in His work. Free-lancing, without due coordination with other members of the Body, has never been a divine manner of work. This cannot be too strongly emphasized; nor can it be too strongly emphasized that in His work God uses individuals to represent the Body, not local churches. Therefore, while the work is the responsibility of individuals, it is not the business of just any individual who cares to take it up, but only of such as are called and sent forth by God, and are equipped with spiritual gifts for the task. Only those who represent the ministry of the Body can bear the official responsibility of the work. The work is undertaken by individuals, but only by such as represent the Body in its ministry aspect, for they, not the entire church, are responsible for it. It is not individuals, as individuals, that undertake the work, but individuals as representing the Body of Christ.

If our work is that of an apostle, it must be clearly distinguished from the local church. It may seem quite unimportant to some that any distinction be made between the work and the church. They may think it of no consequence that the responsibility of the work be in the hands of individual members, not the whole church, and that the apostles be responsible only for the work, not for the church; but the principle is a scriptural principle, and its outworking is of great importance and has tremendous effects, as we shall presently see.

## "HIS OWN RENTED DWELLING"

The church in Rome is a good illustration of the foregoing. Before Paul visited Rome, he had written to the church there expressing an intense desire to see them (Rom. 1:10-11). From his letter it is obvious that a church had been established in that city prior to his arrival. When he actually reached Rome, the church there did not hand over local responsibility to him, nor did they say (as a church today probably would), "Now that an apostle has come into our midst, he must take over the responsibility and be our pastor." Instead, we find this amazing record in the Word: "And he remained two whole years in his own rented dwelling and welcomed all those who came to him, proclaiming the kingdom of God and teaching the things concerning the Lord Jesus Christ with all boldness, unhindered" (Acts 28:30-31). Why did Paul live in "his own rented dwelling" and preach and teach from there and not from the already existing church? Some may suggest that because he was a prisoner he would not have been allowed to take meetings in the church; but there would have been little difference between taking meetings in the church and in the house. If he was granted permission to rent a house and preach and teach there, why should he have been refused permission to preach and teach in connection with the church? Moreover, we need to remember that the Word does not state the reason Paul rented a house and preached and taught there; it only mentions the fact. The fact is that he did rent a house and did preach and teach there, and that fact is enough for us. It is enough for our guidance. Further, God has made it clear that he was under no necessity to do so. No pressure whatever was brought to bear upon him, for he acted "with all boldness unhindered."

Then what is the meaning of the rented house? We must remember the divine economy of words in Scripture, and we must realize that neither the occurrence, nor the record of it, was accidental. There is no room for chance happenings or unimportant records in God's Word. All that is written there is written for our learning, and even a seemingly casual remark may enfold a precious lesson. Moreover, this book is the book of the Acts of the Apostles, who moved under the direct guidance of the Holy Spirit, so the record in question is also one of the acts of the apostles, and is therefore not a chance happening, but an act under the guidance of the Holy Spirit. Here in two short sentences we have an important principle, namely, that the apostolic work and the local church are quite distinct. A church had already been established in Rome; therefore, the members must have had at least one meeting place, but they did not request that Paul take control of the local church, nor did they make their place of meeting Paul's center of work. Paul had his own work in his own rented house quite apart from the church, and apart from their meeting place, and he did not take over the responsibility of the local church affairs.

Every apostle must learn to live in "his own rented dwelling" and work with that as his center, leaving the responsibility of the local church to the local brethren.[8] The work of God belongs to the workers, but the church of God belongs to the locality. Any work in a given place is only temporary, but any church in a given place is always permanent. The work is movable; the church is stationary. When God indicates that an apostle should move, his work moves with him, but the church remains. When Paul thought of leaving Corinth, the Lord showed him He had further ministry for him in the city, so Paul remained for eighteen months — not permanently. When Paul left Corinth, his work left, but the church in Corinth continued, although the fruits of his work were left in the church. A church should not be influenced by the movements of the workers. Whether they are present or absent, the church should move steadily forward. Every one of God's workmen must have a clean-cut line of demarcation between his work and the church in the place of his labors.

The work of the apostles and the work of the local church run parallel; they do not converge. When the apostles are working in any place, their work goes on side by side with the work of the church. The two never coincide, nor can the one ever be a substitute for the other. On leaving a place, an apostle should hand over all the fruit of his work to the local church. It is not God's will that the work of an apostle should take the place of the work of the church, or be in any wise identified with it.

The principle of Paul living in his own rented house shows clearly that the work of the church is unaffected by the presence or absence of an apostle. After Paul's arrival in Rome, the work of the church went on as before, independently of him. Since it was dependent on him neither for its origin nor its continuance, it would be unaffected by his departure. Work is work, and church is church, and these two lines never converge, but keep running parallel one to the other.

Suppose we go to Kweiyang to work; what should be our procedure? On arrival in Kweiyang we either live in an inn, or rent a room, and we begin to preach the gospel.

When men are saved, what shall we do? We must encourage them to read the Word, to pray, to give, to witness, and to assemble for fellowship and ministry. One of the tragic mistakes of the past hundred years of foreign missions in China (God be merciful to me if I say anything amiss!) is that after a worker led men to Christ, he prepared a place and invited them to come there for meetings, instead of encouraging them to assemble by themselves. Efforts have been made to encourage the young believers to read the Word themselves, pray by themselves, witness themselves, but never to meet by themselves. Workers never think of reading, praying, and witnessing for them, but they do not see any harm in arranging meetings for them. We need to show the new converts that such duties as reading, praying, witnessing, giving, and assembling together are the minimum requirement of Christians. We should teach them to have their own meetings in their own meeting place. Let us say to them, "Just as we cannot read the Word, or pray, or witness for you, so we cannot take the responsibility of preparing a meeting place for you and leading your meetings. You must seek out suitable premises and conduct your own meetings. Your meetings are your responsibility, and a regular assembling of yourselves is one of your chief duties and privileges."

Many workers regard their meetings and the meetings of the church as one and the same thing, but they are not. (See chapter nine.) Therefore, as soon as a few believers are saved, we must instruct them to take full responsibility for their private reading, prayer, and witness, and also for the public meetings of the church.

As for ourselves, while we go on working and keep our work distinct from the work of the church, we must go and have fellowship with the believers in their various local gatherings. We must go and break bread with them, join with them in the exercise of spiritual gifts, and take part in their prayer meetings. When there is no church in the place to which God has sent us, we are only workers there, but as soon as there is a local church, we are brothers as well as workers. In our capacity as workers we can take no responsibility in the local church, but in our capacity as local brothers we go and meet with all the members of the church as their fellow members.

As soon as there is a local church in the place of our labors, we automatically become members. Here is the chief point to observe in the relationship between the church and the work—the worker must leave the believers to initiate and conduct their own meetings in their own meeting place, and then he must go to them and take part in their meetings, not ask them to come to him and take part in his meetings. Otherwise, we shall become settlers in one place and shall change our office from apostle to pastor; then when we eventually leave, we shall have to find a successor to carry out the church work. If we keep "church" and "work" parallel and do not let the two lines converge, we shall find that no adjustment will be needed in the church when we depart, for it will not have lost a "pastor," but only a brother. Unless we differentiate clearly in our own minds between church and work, we shall mix the work with the church and the church with the work; there will be confusion in both directions, and the growth both of the church and the work will be arrested.

"Self-government, self-support, and self-propagation" has been the slogan of many workers for a number of years now. The need to deal with these matters has arisen because of the confusion between the church and the work. In a mission, when people are saved, then the missionaries prepare a hall for them, arrange for prayer meetings and Bible classes, and some of them go as far as to manage the business and spiritual affairs of the church as well. The mission does the work of the local church! Therefore, it is not surprising that in the process of time, problems arise in connection with self-government, self-support, and selfpropagation. In the very nature of things, such problems would never have come up for consideration if the principles shown us in God's Word had been adhered to from the very beginning.

Anyone who cares enough to be a Christian ought to be taught from the outset what the implications are. Believers must pray themselves, study the Word themselves, and assemble themselves, not merely go to a meeting place prepared by others and sit down and listen to others preach. Going to a mission compound or a mission hall to hear the Word is not scriptural assembling, because it is in the hands of a missionary, or of his mission, not in the hands of the local church. It is a mixture of work and church. If from the outset Christians learned to gather together according to the Scriptures, many problems would be avoided.

## The Results of the Work

When a servant of God reaches a new place, his first business must be to found a local church, unless there is one already in existence, in which case his one concern must be to help the church. The one aim of the work in any place is the building up of the church in that place. All the fruit of a worker's labors must go to the increase of the church. The work in any place exists for the church alone, not for itself. The apostle's goal is to build up the church, not to build up his work or any group of people that may have sent him out.

Wherein lies the failure of missions today? They keep the results of their work in their own hands. In other words, they have reckoned their converts as members of their mission, or of their mission church, instead of building them into, or handing them over, to the local churches. The result is that the mission extends all the while and becomes quite an imposing organization, but local churches are scarcely to be found. And because there are no local churches, the mission has to send workers to different places as "pastors" of the various companies of Christians. So church is not church, and work is not work, but both are a medley of the two. There seems to be no scriptural warrant for forming companies of workers into missions; nevertheless, to regard a mission as an apostolic company is not definitely unscriptural, but for missions to enlarge their own organization instead of establishing local churches is distinctly so.

## Two Lines of Work

An apostle should go and work in a certain place if the local church invites him, or if he himself has received a revelation from the Lord to work there. In the latter case, if there is a church in the place, he can write notifying them of his coming, just as Paul notified the churches in Corinth and in Rome. These are the two lines which regulate the work of an apostle —he must either have a direct revelation of God's will, or an indirect revelation through the invitation of a church.

Wherever an apostle goes, he must learn to bear his own responsibility, having his own rented dwelling. It may be all right to work in a place, living as the guest of the local church, but it would not be right to impose upon them by taking advantage of their hospitality over an extended period. If a worker expects to stay for any length of time in one place, then he must have his own center of work, and he must not only bear his own personal responsibilities, but also all responsibilities in connection with the work. A local church must bear entire responsibility for its own work, and so must the worker for his. The church as such must not be involved in any financial outlay in connection with the work; the worker alone is liable for all expenses incurred, and he must learn from the very outset of his ministry to look to the Lord for the supply of his needs. Of course, if the church is spiritual, its members will recognize their spiritual responsibility, and will be willing to assist in material ways so that the work of God may go forward, but the worker should take nothing for granted and should bear the entire financial burden, so that it may be manifest that the church and the work are absolutely distinct.

When an apostle comes to a place where a local church already exists, he must never forget that no church authority rests with him. Should he desire to work in a place where the local church does not wish to have him, then all he can do is to pass on to some other part. The church has full authority either to receive or reject a worker. Even should the worker in question have been used of God to found the very church that rejects him, he can claim no authority in the church on that account.

Should he know unmistakably that God has led him to work in that place, yet the local church refuse to welcome him, if they persist in their attitude, then he must obey the command of God and go and work there despite them. But he must not gather believers around him, nor must he on any account form a separate church. There can only be one church in one place. If he forms a separate company of believers where a local church already exists, he will be forming a sect and not a church. Churches are founded on the ground of locality, not on the ground of receiving a certain apostle. Even if the local church refused to receive him, and his work had to be done without its sympathy and cooperation, or even despite its opposition, still all the results of his labors must be for their benefit. Despite its attitude toward the apostle personally, all the fruit of his labors must be contributed to that church. The sole aim of all work for God is the increase and up-building of the local churches. If they welcome the worker, the result of his labors goes to them; if they reject him, it goes to them just the same.

We require deeper spiritual experience and clearer spiritual light if we are to be workers acceptable to God and to His Church. If we wish to overcome difficulties, we must learn to overcome by spirituality, not by official authority. If we are spiritual, we shall submit to the authority of the local churches. It is lack of submission on the part of God's servants that is responsible for the forming of numerous sects. Many so-called churches have been established because workers have been rejected by the churches and have gathered groups of people around them, who have supported them and the doctrines they taught. Such a procedure is sectarian.

If we are truly led of God, surely we can trust God to open doors for us. If a church receives us, let us praise Him; if not, let us look confidently to Him to unlock closed doors. Many servants of God trust Him to open up spiritual truths to them, but they cannot trust Him to open doors for the reception of those truths. They have faith to believe God will give them light, but they have no faith to believe that He will also supply the keys to open human hearts to the light He has given. So they resort to carnal methods, and the consequence is much division among the children of God. If God Himself does not remove the obstacles in our circumstances, then we must quietly remain where we are, and not have recourse to natural means, which will assuredly work havoc in the Church of God.

## THE SPECIFIC MINISTRIES OF THE WORD

All God's servants are engaged in the ministry of building up the Body of Christ, but it does not follow that, because all are in the ministry of the Word, all ministries are the same. Everyone has a different line of ministry. Time and again God has raised up some new witness, or group of witnesses, giving them fresh light from His Word, so that they could bear a special testimony for Him in the particular time and circumstances in which they live. All such ministry is new and specific and is of great value to the Church; but we must bear it well in mind that if God commits a specific ministry to any man relating to certain truths, he must not make his particular ministry, or his particular line of truth, the basis of a new "church." No servant of God should cherish the ambition that his truth be accepted as the truth. If doors are closed to it, let him wait patiently upon God who gave it until He opens doors for its reception. No separate "church" must be formed to bear a separate testimony. The work of God does not sanction the establishment of a church for the propagation of any particular line of teaching. It knows only one kind of church—the local church; not a sectarian church, but a New Testament church.

Let us lay it to heart that our work is for our ministry and our ministry is for the churches. No church should be under a specific ministry, but all ministries should be under the church. What havoc has been wrought in the Church because so many of her ministers have sought to bring the churches under their ministry, rather than by their ministry serve the churches. As soon as the churches are brought under any ministry, they cease to be local and become sectarian.

When a specific ministry has been raised up of God to meet a specific need in His Church, what should be the attitude of the minister? Whenever a new truth is proclaimed, it will have new followers. The worker to whom God has given fresh light upon His truth should encourage all who receive that truth to swell the ranks of the local church, not to range themselves around him. Otherwise, the churches will be made to serve the ministry, not the ministry the churches, and the "churches" established will be ministerial "churches," not local ones. The sphere of a church is not the sphere of any ministry, but the sphere of the locality. Wherever ministry is made the occasion for the forming of a church, there you have the beginning of a new denomination. From the study of Church history we can see that almost all new ministries have led to new followings, and new followings have resulted in new organizations. Thus ministerial "churches" have been established and denominations multiplied.

If the Lord delays His coming and His servants remain true to Him, He will certainly raise up new ministries in the Word. He will open up special truths to meet the specific needs of His children. Some of the hearers will question the truths, others reject them, and others condemn, while there will be those who gladly respond. What should the attitude of God's servants be? They must be fully persuaded in their own minds that there can only be one church in one place, and that all truth is for the enrichment of that church. If it receives the truths God's ministers proclaim, let them praise Him; if not, let them praise Him still. No thought must be entertained of forming a separate "church" comprising those believers who support the special doctrines emphasized. If in the local church a number of people receive their teaching, then they must still remain there. No divisive work must be done in the local church. Those who receive the truth may use their spiritual teaching and spiritual power to help their fellow members, but they must not use any divisive methods to support the truth they have embraced. If we always bear in mind that the churches of God are only formed on the basis of locality, much division among the children of God will be avoided.

Should God entrust us with a special ministry and lead us to a place where no church exists, our first duty is to establish one in the locality, and then contribute our ministry to it. We can establish local churches and contribute our ministry to such churches, but we dare not establish ministerial churches.

Let me illustrate the relation between various ministries and various local churches. One man is a florist, another a grocer. The most obvious way for them to extend their business is to establish branches in various districts. The florist opens branch shops to sell flowers, and the grocer opens branch shops to sell groceries. This is just like the various ministers trying to establish "churches" according to their ministry. God's plan for His Church is on quite a different line. It is not that the grocer and the florist each seek to open as many branches as they possibly can in order to sell their respective commodities, but that the grocer or the florist, arriving in any place, opens a department store, and having duly established that, he contributes his goods to it, and other tradesmen coming along contribute their wares to the same store. A department store does not just deal in one line of goods; it has a varied stock. The thought of God is not that we should open branch florist shops or branch grocery stores, or stores that specialize in other lines, but department stores. His plan is that His servants should just establish a local church, and then contribute their different ministries to that church. The church is not controlled by one ministry but served by all the ministries. If any company of God's people are open to receive one truth only, then they are a sect.

As apostles our first concern on arrival in a place which has no church is to found one there. As soon as it has been formed, we should seek to serve it with whatever ministry the Lord has entrusted to us, and then leave it. We dare to exercise our ministry faithfully, but having done so, we dare to leave the church open to other ministry. This should be the attitude of all God's workmen. We should never cherish the hope that only "our" teaching will be accepted by any church. There must be no thought of dominating a church by our personality or by our ministry; the field must be left clear for all God's servants. There is no need to build a wall of protection around "our" particular "flock" to secure them against the teachings of others. If we do so, we are working along popish lines. We can safely trust God to protect our ministry, and we must remember that for "the perfecting of the saints" the varied ministries of all God's faithful servants are necessary. Local responsibility is with the elders; they must watch the interests of the flock in the matter of ministries.

## INSTITUTIONS OF FAITH

It must not be inferred from the foregoing that God has no other workmen but apostles and the various ministers of the Word. Those who work in the ministry of the Word are only a section of God's servants. The work is not the only work. God has many servants who are bearing the burden of various works of faith, such as schools, orphanages, and hospitals. Looked at superficially, their work does not seem as spiritual as the work of the apostles or ministers we have just referred to, but in reality it is. Although such faith workers do not go forth as apostles, or teach the Word like the special ministers, yet they are used just as definitely as the others to strengthen the Church of God.

George Muller's orphanage is just such a faith work. It has resulted in the salvation of many souls. The question arises, where should the fruits of such a work go? Not into an orphanage "church," but into the local church. A work such as that is not a unit sufficiently large to form a church. It is the city which is a church unit, not an institution. No matter how prosperous a work of faith may be, and no matter how many souls may be saved through it, no church can be formed on such a basis; for should there be various workers in one city engaged in various kinds of work, then there would be as many churches as there were such institutions. The boundary of a church is a city, not any institution in a city.

Several years ago I was in Tsinan. Some brothers in Cheloo University asked me if I thought it time for them to begin a meeting for the breaking of bread. I asked, "Do you represent Cheloo University or Tsinan city?" They answered, "Cheloo." "Then I do not think it is right," I said. Of course, they wanted to know why, so I explained: "The Word of God sanctions the forming of a church in Tsinan, but not in Cheloo. The sphere of Cheloo is too narrow to justify the existence of a separate church. The standard scriptural unit for the forming of a church is a city, not a university."

The fruits resulting from various institutions of faith must not be retained by such institutions. All must be handed over to the local church. Workers must not argue that because they have been the means of salvation to certain souls, therefore they have a special claim upon them and special responsibility for them, and consequently withhold them from uniting with their fellow believers in the locality. Even though there may be regular prayers, and preaching, and a variety of meetings in connection with a Christian institution, those can never serve as a substitute for church fellowship, and no such institution, however spiritual, can be regarded as a church, since it is not founded on the divinely appointed basis of locality. All Christians engaged in efforts of this kind must differentiate clearly between church and work, and they must realize that any sphere narrower than a locality does not justify the forming of a separate church. They dare not pride themselves on their successful work and think it will serve well as a church, but they must humbly join in fellowship with all the other members of the Body of Christ in the place where they live.

All the various God-given ministries have one aim, the establishing of local churches. In the thought of God only one company of people exists, and all His designs of grace center in that one company—His Church. The work is not a goal in itself; it is only a means to an end. If we regard our work as an end, then our purpose is at variance with God's, for His end is the Church. What we regard as an end in itself is only the means to His end.

There are three things which we must bear clearly in mind. (1) The work and other works are the special concern of the workers, not of the churches, and the sphere of any work is not wide enough to justify its being regarded as a church. (2) All workers must be humble enough to take the place of brothers in the local church. In the sphere of their work they hold the position of God's servants, but in the sphere of the church they are only brethren. In the church there are only children of God; therefore, none of its members are "workers," all are brethren. (3) The goal of all work is the establishment of local churches. If we make our work the basis of a separate unit of God's people, then we are building up a sect, not a church.

# CHAPTER 7: AMONG THE WORKERS

The churches in Scripture are intensely local. We never find any federation of churches there; they are all independent units. The position is quite otherwise as regards the workers. Among them we find a certain amount of association; we see here a little group, and there another, linked together for the work. Paul and those with him—as for instance Luke, Silas, Timothy, Titus, and Apollos— formed one group. Peter, James, John, and those with them formed another. One group came out from Antioch, another from Jerusalem. Paul refers to those who were with him (Acts 20:34), which indicates that while there was no organization of the workers into different missions, still they had their own special associates in the work. Even in the beginning, when our Lord chose the twelve, He sent them out two by two. All were fellow workers, but each had his special fellow worker. Such grouping of workers was ordained and ordered by the Lord.

*These apostolic companies were not formed along partisan or doctrinal lines;* they were formed under the sovereignty of the Spirit, who so ordered the circumstances of the different workers as to link them together in the work. It was not that they were really divided from other workers, but merely that in the Spirit's ordering of their ways, they had not been led into special association with them. It was the Holy Spirit, not men, who said, "Set apart for Me now Barnabas and Saul." Everything hinged on the sovereignty of the Spirit. The apostolic companies were subject to the will and ordering of the Lord. As we have seen, the twelve were divided into pairs, but it was not left to their personal discretion to choose their associates; it was the Lord who coupled them together and sent them forth. Each had a special fellow worker, but that fellow worker was of the Lord's appointing, not of their choosing. It was not because of natural affinity that they associated specially with some, nor was it because of difference in doctrine or practice that they did not associate specially with others. The deciding factor was always the ordering of the Lord.

We recognize that the Lord is the Head of the Church, and that the apostles were the first order "placed" by the Lord in the Church (1 Cor. 12:28). Although they were formed into associations, having their special fellow workers appointed by the Lord, still they had no special name, system, or organization. They did not make a company smaller than the Body to be the basis of their work; all was on the ground of the Body. Therefore, although on account of difference of locality and the providential ordering of their ways, they formed different groups, still they had no organization outside the Body; their work was always an expression of the ministry of the Body. They were constituted into separate companies, but each company stood on the ground of the Body, expressing the ministry of the Body.

The Lord is the Head of the Body and not the Head of any organization; therefore, whenever we work for a society, a mission, or an institution, and not for the Body alone, we lose the headship of the Lord. We must see clearly that the work is the work of the Body of Christ and that, while the Lord did divide His workers into different companies (not different organizations), their work was always on the ground of the Body. And we must recognize that every individual worker and every company represents the ministry of the Body of Christ, each office held being held in the Body, and for the furtherance of the work of God. Then, and only then, can we have one ministry—the up-building of the Body of Christ. If we recognized clearly the oneness of the Body, what blessed results we should see! Wherever the principle of the oneness of the Body operates, all possibility of rivalry is ruled out. It does not matter if I decrease and you increase; there will neither be jealousy on my part, nor pride on yours. Once we see that all the work and all its fruits are for the increase of the Body of Christ, then no man will be counted yours and no man mine; it will not matter then whether you are used or I. All carnal strife among the workers of God will be at an end once the Body is clearly seen as the principle of the work. But life and work in the Body necessitate drastic dealings with the flesh, and that in turn necessitates a deep knowledge of the cross of Christ.

The early apostles were never free lances; they worked together. In the story of Pentecost we read of "Peter, standing with the eleven" (Acts 2:14). At the Beautiful Gate we see Peter and John working together, and again they were the two who visited Samaria. When Peter went to the house of Cornelius, six other brothers accompanied him. When the apostles went out, it was always in companies, or at least by twos, never alone. Their work was not individual, but corporate. As to those with Paul at Antioch and elsewhere, it is unfortunate that so much emphasis has been placed upon Paul as an individual, with the result that his fellow workers are almost lost sight of. We see that at Troas, Luke joined their company and was of one mind with Paul in considering that the Macedonian cry should be responded to. Later on when they returned from Macedonia, they brought with them as fellow workers Sopater, Aristarchus, Secundus, Gaius, Timothy, Tychicus, and Trophimus. Later on we find Apollos, Priscilla, and Aquila joining them. Still later we find Paul sending

Timothy to Corinth and encouraging Apollos and Titus to go there; and some time afterwards we see Epaphroditus joining them as a fellow worker. And it is good to read at the head of Paul's Epistles words like these:

"Paul...and Sosthenes the brother," "Paul...and Timothy the brother," "Paul...Silas and Timothy."

So we see no trace of organized missions in Scripture on the one hand, nor do we see any workers going out on individual lines on the other hand, each being a law to himself. They are formed into companies, but such companies are on a spiritual basis, not on the basis of organization. Scripture gives no warrant for an organized mission on the one hand, nor does it sanction free-lance work on the other hand; the one is as far from the thought of God as the other. Therefore, while we must guard against the snare of man-made organizations, we must also guard against the danger of being too individualistic. We must not be organized into a mission and thus become schismatic; at the same time we must have associates in the work with whom we cooperate on a spiritual basis, and thus maintain the testimony of the Body.

We need to emphasize this fact, that the apostles worked in association with others, but their companies were not organized. Their relationship one to another was only spiritual. They loved and served the same Lord, they had one call and one commission, and they were of one mind. The Lord united them; therefore, they became fellow workers. Some were together from the outset; others joined at a later date. They were one company, yet they had no organization, and there was no distribution of offices or positions. Those who joined them did not come in response to some "Help Wanted" advertisement, nor did they come because they were equipped by a special course of training. On their journeys the Lord so ordered circumstances that they met; He drew them one to another, and being of one mind and one spirit, linked together by the Lord, they spontaneously became fellow workers. In order to join such a company there was no need of first passing an examination, or of fulfilling some special conditions, or of going through certain forms or ceremonies. The Lord was the One who determined everything. He ordered; man only concurred. In such groups none held special positions or offices; there was no director, or chairman, or superintendent. Whatever ministry the Lord had given them, that constituted their position. They received no appointments from the association. The relationship which existed between its members was purely spiritual, not official. They were constituted fellow workers, not by a human organization, but by a spiritual bond.

## SPIRITUAL AUTHORITY

Before considering the question of spiritual authority, let us read a few passages of Scripture bearing on the relationship between the workers, as they throw considerable light on our subject. "Timothy...Paul wanted this one to go forth with him" (Acts 16:1-3). "When he [Paul] had seen the vision, we immediately endeavored to go forth into Macedonia, concluding that God had called us to announce the gospel to them" (Acts 16:10). "And those who conducted Paul brought him as far as Athens; and receiving a command for Silas and Timothy to come to him as quickly as possible, they went off" (Acts 17:15). Paul "resolved to return through Macedonia. And Sopater of Berea, the son of Pyrrhus, accompanied him" (Acts 20:3-4). "We, going ahead onto the ship, set sail for Assos, from there intending to pick up Paul, for so he had arranged" (Acts 20:13). "If Timothy comes, see that he is with you without fear....Send him forward in peace that he may come to me....And concerning our brother Apollos, I urged him many times to come to you" (1 Cor. 16:10-12). "We entreated Titus" (2 Cor. 8:6). "Titus...received the entreaty....And we sent together with him the brother" (2 Cor. 8:16-18). "We sent with them our brother" (2 Cor. 8:22). "Tychicus, the beloved brother..I have sent to you" (Eph. 6:21-22). "But I considered it necessary to send to you Epaphroditus" (Phil. 2:25). "All the things concerning me, Tychicus...will make known to you" (Col. 4:7). "Luke, the beloved physician, greets you, as well as Demas" (Col. 4:14). "And say to Archippus, Take heed to the ministry" (Col. 4:17). "We sent Timothy" (1 Thes. 3:1-2). "Be diligent to come to me quickly....Take Mark and bring him with you....But Tychicus I have sent to Ephesus" (2 Tim. 4:9-12). "Trophimus I left at Miletus sick. Be diligent to come before winter" (2 Tim. 4:20-21). "For this cause I left you in Crete, that you might set in order the things which I have begun that remain and appoint elders in every city, as I directed you" (Titus 1:5). "When I send Artemas to you or Tychicus, be diligent to come to me at Nicopolis, for I have decided to spend the winter there. Zenas the lawyer and Apollos send forward diligently that nothing may be lacking to them" (Titus 3:12-13).

The above Scriptures show us that among the workers of God dependence upon Him does not render us independent of one another. We saw that Paul left Titus in Crete to complete the work he himself had left unfinished, and that he afterwards sent Artemas and Tychicus to replace him when he instructed him to proceed to Nicopolis. On various occasions he appointed Timothy and Tychicus to do certain work, and we read that he persuaded Titus and Apollos to remain in Corinth. We observe that these workers not only learned to work in teams, but the less experienced learned to submit to the direction of the more spiritual. God's workers must learn to be left, to be sent, and to be persuaded.

It is important to recognize the difference between official and spiritual authority. In an organization all authority is official, not spiritual. In a good organization the one who holds office has both official and spiritual authority; in a bad organization the authority wielded is only official. But in any organization, no matter whether the office-bearer himself has spiritual authority or not, the authority he holds in the organization is actually only official. What is the meaning of official authority? It means that because a man holds office, therefore, he exercises authority. The authority is exercised solely on account of the office he holds. As long as the officebearer retains his position, just so long can he exert his authority; as soon as he resigns office, his authority ceases. Such authority is altogether objective; it is not inherent in the man himself. It is connected not with the person, but merely with his position. If he holds the office of superintendent, it follows as a matter of course that he superintends affairs, no matter whether he is spiritually qualified to do so or not. If he holds the office of director, then automatically he directs, even if lack of spirituality should really disqualify him from exercising control over other lives. The life of an organization is position; it is position that determines authority.

But in divinely constituted companies of workers there is no organization. Authority is exercised among them, but such authority is spiritual, not official. It is an authority based upon spirituality, an authority which is the outcome of a deep knowledge of the Lord, and intimate fellowship with Him. Spiritual life is the source of such authority. The reason Paul could direct others was not because of his superior position, but because of his greater spirituality. If he had lost his spirituality, he would have lost his authority. In an organization those who are spiritual do not necessarily hold any office, and those who hold office are not necessarily spiritual; but in Scripture it is otherwise.

There it is those who know the Lord who superintend affairs. It is those who are spiritual that direct others, and if those others are spiritual, they will recognize spiritual authority and will submit to it. In an organization its workers are obliged to obey, but in a spiritual association they are not, and from an official point of view no fault can be found with them if they do not obey. In a spiritual association there is no compulsion; direction and submission alike are on the ground of spirituality.

Apart from the question of spiritual authority there is also the question of different ministries. All servants of the Lord are in the ministry, and each has his own special ministry. In an organization, positions are allotted by man, but in spiritual work ministries are appointed by the Lord. Because of difference of ministry, we must on the one hand obey the Lord, and on the other we must obey the brethren. Such obedience is not on the ground of their superior position, but because their ministry differs from ours, and yet both are intimately related. If the head is moving the tips of my fingers, the muscles of my arms cannot take an independent attitude and refuse to move with them. The principle of being in one Body necessitates the closely related members to move with one another. In moving with the other members, we are not really obeying them; we are obeying the Head. In many things we can claim a direct guidance from the Head, but in just as many things the Head moves others and we simply move with them. Their movement is reason enough for us to fall in. It is most important to recognize this relatedness of various ministries in the Body of Christ. We have to know our ministry and to recognize the ministry of others, so that we can move as one obeying those who have a greater ministry. Since our ministry is interrelated in such a way, we dare not take an individual or independent attitude.

All positions held by God's ministers are spiritual, not official. Alas! men have only seen half the truth, so they try to organize the work and appoint a director to superintend the service of others, but their directing is based upon their position in the organization, not upon their position in the ministry. The reason Paul could direct others was that the ministry committed to him by the Lord put him in a position of authority over them; and the reason Titus, Timothy, and Tychicus could submit to being directed was that the ministry committed to them by the Lord put them in a position under his authority. Unfortunately, the directing of today is based upon neither depth of spirituality nor greatness of ministry.

Timothy was a man of God. He lived close to the Lord, obeying and serving Him faithfully; yet many a time he was sent here or there by Paul. He did not say, Do you think I am incapable of working by myself? Do you think I do not know how to preach the gospel and how to found churches? Do you think I do not know how to go about things? Although Timothy knew a lot, he was willing to obey Paul. In spiritual work there is such a thing as being directed by others; there is the position of a Paul, and there is also the position of a Timothy, but these are spiritual, not official, positions.

Today we must learn on the one hand to maintain a right relationship with our fellow workers, and on the other hand to be guided by the Holy Spirit. We must maintain both relationships and also maintain the balance between the two. In the first and second Epistles to Timothy there are many passages which illustrate how fellow workers should cooperate, and how a younger worker should submit to an older one. A young Timothy ought to obey the commands of the Holy Spirit, but he ought also to receive the instructions of an elderly Paul. Timothy was sent out by Paul, Timothy was left by Paul at Ephesus, and Timothy obeyed Paul in the Lord. Here is an example for young servants of God. It is most important in His work to learn how to be led by the Spirit and how, at the same time, to cooperate with our fellow workers. The responsibility must not be wholly upon Timothy; neither must it rest wholly upon Paul. In the work Timothy must learn to fit in with Paul, and Paul must also learn to fit in with Timothy. Not only must the younger learn to submit to the instructions of the elder, but the elder must learn how to instruct the younger. The one who is in a position to leave, send, or persuade must learn not to follow the dictates of his own nature, acting according to personal inclination or desire, for in that case he will make it difficult for those under his authority. Paul must direct Timothy in such a way that he will not find it hard to obey both the Holy Spirit and the apostle.

God's servants must work together in companies, but there is a kind of co-working which is to be avoided, that is, co-working in a man-made organization which restricts its members so that they cannot really respond to the leading of the Spirit. When workers are entirely subject to the direction of men, then their work is not the outcome of a spiritual burden placed on them by God, but merely the doing of a piece of work in response to the dictates of those holding higher positions than they. The trouble today is that men are taking the place of the Holy Spirit, and the will of men in official position is taking the place of the will of God. Workers have no direct knowledge of the divine will, but simply do the will of those in authority over them, without bearing any personal burden from the Lord for His work.

There are others again who know the mind of God, have a call from Him, and depend entirely upon Him for the meeting of all their needs; but while they know what it is to be led of Him individually, they fancy they can just go their own way and do their own work in independence of others.

The teaching of God's Word is that, on the one hand, human organizations must not control the servants of God; on the other hand, His servants must learn to submit to a spiritual authority which is based on the difference of ministry. There is no organized cooperation, yet there is a spiritual fellowship and a spiritual oneness. Individualism and human organization alike are out of line with the will of God. We should seek to know His will, not independently, but in conjunction with the other ministering members of the Body. The call of Paul and Barnabas was on this principle. It was not a case of two prophets and teachers only, but of five, waiting upon God to know His will. Acts 13 gives us a good example of a working company, all the workers being mutually related, and the guidance of one confirmed by the others.

## THE SPHERE OF THE WORK

The sphere of the work, unlike the sphere of the local church, is very wide. Some of the workers are sent to Ephesus, some go to Paul at Nicopolis, some stay on in Corinth, some are left in Miletus, some remain in Crete, some return to Thessalonica, and others go on to Galatia. Such is the work! We see here not the movements of the local church but of the work, for the movements of the local church are always confined to one locality. Ephesus only manages the affairs of Ephesus, and Rome the affairs of Rome. The church confines herself to matters in her own locality. There is no need for the church in Ephesus to send a man to Corinth, or for the church in Corinth to leave a man in Rome. The church here is local, the work extralocal. Ephesus, Corinth, and Rome are all the concern of the workers. The church only manages the affairs in any given locality, but the workers of God regard as their "parish" the sphere which the Lord has measured out to them.

## NO CENTRAL CONTROL, BUT FELLOWSHIP

In Scripture the workers were formed into companies, but that does not imply that all the apostles formed themselves into one company and placed everything under one central control. Although Paul had "those with him," and Peter his associates, they comprised only a number of apostles, not all the apostles. That all the apostles should combine into one company is not shown in the Word of God. It is quite in order for scores of men, or even hundreds, who have received the same trust from God, to join together in the same work; but in the Scriptures we find no centralization of authority for the control of all the apostles. There is a company of apostles, but it is not great enough to include all the apostles. That is Romish, not scriptural.

The parties referred to in Philippians 1:15-17, 2 Corinthians 11:12-13, 22-23, and Galatians 4:17 all indicate that the work in the early days was not centralized. Had it been centralized, those groups could not have remained in existence, for they could have been dealt with effectively. The Scriptures show that in divine work there is no universal organization or central control, which accounts for the fact that the apostle had no authority to deal with those groups of people who were creating such difficulty in the churches.

The explanation is this: God does not wish the power of organization to take the place of the power of the Holy Spirit. Even though there is no central control, provided all the workers follow the leading of the Spirit, everything will run smoothly and satisfactorily, and there will be the coordination of a body. Whenever people cease to obey the

Spirit and labor in the power of the flesh, then it is best if the work is simply allowed to fall to pieces. A good organization often serves as a bad substitute for the power of the Holy Spirit, by holding a work together even after all its vitality is gone. When life has departed from the work and the scaffolding of organization still supports it, its collapse is prevented; but that is doubtful gain, for a splendid outward organization may be blinding God's servants to a deep inward need. God would rather His work be discontinued than that it go on with such a counterfeit for spiritual power. When the glory of God had departed from the temple, He himself left it to utter ruin. God desires that the outward and inward conditions should correspond, so that if death invades a work, His workers may awaken at once to their need and in humility of heart seek His face.

Central control has many evils. It makes it easy for God's servants to disregard the leading of the Spirit, and readily develops into a popish system,

116

becoming a great worldly power. It is a scriptural fact that God's servants are formed into companies, but they are not formed into one single company.

However, that does not mean that every company could just go on independently, knowing no relatedness or fellowship with other companies. The principle of the oneness of the Body holds good here as in all other relationships between the children of God. In Scripture we not only see the principle of "the laying on of hands," but also that of giving "the right hand" (Gal. 2:9). The former speaks of identification; the latter of fellowship. In Antioch hands were laid on Paul and Barnabas; in Jerusalem there was no laying on of hands, but the right hand of fellowship given them by James, Cephas, and John. In Antioch the sphere in view was one apostolic company, and the point emphasized was identification; consequently, hands were laid on them. But in Jerusalem the sphere in view was the relationship between different apostolic companies, and the point emphasized was fellowship; consequently, the right hand was extended to them.

Many are called to work for the Lord, but their sphere of service is not the same, so it follows that their associates cannot be the same. But the various companies must all be identified with the Body, coming under the headship of the Lord, and having fellowship among themselves. There is no laying on of hands between Antioch and Jerusalem, but there is the giving of the right hand of fellowship. So the Word of God does not warrant the forming of one central company; neither does it warrant the forming of various scattered, unrelated, and isolated companies. There is no one central place for the laying on of hands, nor is there merely the laying on of hands and nothing else in any one of the various groups; but among them there is also the giving of the right hand of fellowship one to the other. Each company should recognize what God is doing with the other companies and should extend fellowship to them, acknowledging that they are also ministers in the Body. Under the ordering of God they may work in different companies, but all must work as one Body. The extending of the right hand of fellowship implies a recognition that other people are in the Body and we are in fellowship with them, working together in a related way, as becomes functioning members of the same Body. "Seeing that I had been entrusted with the gospel to the uncircumcision...and perceiving the grace given to me, James and Cephas and John, who were reputed to be pillars, gave to me and to Barnabas the right hand of fellowship that we should go to the Gentiles, and they, to the circumcision" (Gal. 2:7-9). The unrelated, scattered, disrupted, and conflicting organizations in Christendom, which do not recognize the principle of the Body and do not come under the sovereignty and headship of Christ, are never according to

## COOPERATION AMONG THE WORKERS

The question naturally arises, how should workers and working associations cooperate? To one company God gives one kind of ministry, and to another an altogether different form of ministry. How should the various groups work together? Peter and his associates, and Paul and those with him, were appointed to different spheres, but in the event of their work overlapping, how should they act? Since there is no centralization of work, yet at the same time there are various groups of workers, how should these different groups cooperate? We must note two fundamental points in regard to the work:

(1)The first responsibility of every worker—no matter what his ministry or what his special line of work— whenever he comes to a place where there is no local church, is to establish one in the locality. (What applies to the individual worker applies also to any group of workers.)

(2)Should he come to a place where a local church already exists,then all his teaching and all his experience must be contributed to that church, that it may be strengthened and edified, and no attempt should be made to attach that church to himself or to the society he represents.

If a worker goes to a place where there is no church and founds one there for the propagation of his particular doctrine, then we cannot cooperate with him because he is building up a sect, and not a church. On the other hand, should a worker go to a place where there is already a local church, and instead of contributing his teaching and experience to its upbuilding, seek to make it a branch-church of the society to which he belongs, then again it is impossible for us to cooperate, because he is building up a denomination. The basis of fellowship in the church is the common possession of life in Christ and living in the same locality. The basis of cooperation in the work is the common aim of the founding and building up of local churches. Denominational affiliations do not hinder us from reckoning anyone as belonging to the Body, but the aim of denominational extension will certainly keep us from any cooperation in the service of God. The greatest harm a worker can do is, instead of establishing and edifying the local churches, to attach to his society the believers he finds in a place, or to form those brought to the Lord through his labors into a branch of his particular denomination. Both these procedures are condemned by the Word of God.

Paul came from Antioch to Corinth and there he preached the gospel. People believed and were saved, and soon there was a group of saints in Corinth. Into what kind of church did Paul form them? Into the church in Corinth. Paul did not establish an Anitochian church in Corinth. He did not form a branch-church of Antioch in Corinth, but simply established a church in Corinth. Thereafter Peter came to Corinth and preached the gospel, with the result that another group of people believed. Did Peter say, "Paul came from Antioch, but I am come from Jerusalem, so I must set up another church: I will establish a Jerusalemic church in Corinth, or, I will form a branch-church of Jerusalem here in Corinth"? No, he contributed all those he led to the Lord to the already existing local church in Corinth. After a while Apollos came along. Again people were saved, and again all the saved ones were added to the local church. So in Corinth there was only one church of God; there were no schismatic denominations. Had Paul established the precedent of founding a church in Corinth to enlarge the sphere of the church from which he went out, calling it the Antiochian church in Corinth, then when Peter came to Corinth he might well have argued, "It is all right for Paul to found an Antiochian church in Corinth since he came from Antioch, but I have nothing to do with Antioch; my church is in Jerusalem, so I must establish a Jerusalemic church here." Apollos coming to Corinth would in turn follow their example and establish another church as a branch of the one from which he came out. If every worker tried to form a branch of the church he represented, then sects and denominations would be utterly inevitable. If the aim of a worker in any place is not to establish a local church there, but to enlarge the church from which he has gone out, then he is not establishing a church of God in that locality, but only building up his own society. Under such circumstances there is no possibility of cooperation.

Conditions have greatly changed since the days of the early apostles. Christianity has lost its original purity, and everything connected with it is in a false and confused state. Despite that fact, our work today is still the same as in the days of the early apostles—to found and build up local churches, the local expressions of the Body of Christ. So if we are in a place where there is no church, we should seek the Lord's face that He may enable us to win souls for Himself and form them into a local church. If we are in a place where there are missions, or churches, standing on sectarian or denominational ground, but no church standing on the ground of the Body and the locality, then our duty is just the same, that is, to found and build a local church. Many will still persist in their old ways; hence, the persons standing on clear church ground may be far fewer than the total number of Christians in the locality. But the area of the ground on which they stand is just as wide as that on which the church ought to stand, so it is still our duty to maintain that ground. We can only cooperate with those who are building up the Body of Christ as expressed in local churches, and not with those who are building up something else. Denominational connection does not hinder us from fellowship in the Lord, but denominational extension does hinder us from cooperation in the work of God.

Here is the most important principle in the work of God —a worker must not seek to establish a branch of the church from which he goes out, but to establish a church in the locality to which he comes. He does not make the church in the place to which he goes to be an extension of the church in the place from which he comes, but he founds a church in that locality. Wherever he goes, he establishes a church in that place. He does not extend the church of his place of origin, but establishes the church in the place of his adoption. Since in Scripture all churches are local, Jerusalem and Antioch can have no branch-churches. We cannot extend one local church to another locality; we can only form a new church in that locality. The church which the apostles established in Ephesus is the church in Ephesus; the church which they established in Philippi is the church in Philippi; the churches which they established in other places are the churches of those different places. There is no precedent in Scripture for establishing any other than local churches. It is all right to extend the Church of God, but it is all wrong to extend a local church of God. What is the place in which I intend to work? It is the church in that place I must seek to establish.

Now there are two kinds of workers, namely, those who stand on scriptural ground, and those who stand on denominational or mission ground. But even with those who stand on denominational or mission ground, the principle of cooperation is just the same—the one aim of founding and building up the local church.

The work of evangelization is primarily for the salvation of sinners, but its spontaneous result is a church in the place where such work is done. The immediate object is the salvation of men, but the ultimate result is the formation of churches. The danger which confronts the missionary is to form those he has led to the Lord into a branch of the society he represents. Since workers represent different societies, they naturally form different branches of their respective societies, and the consequence is great confusion in the work and churches of God. The immediate aim of the various workers is no doubt the same—what preacher does not hope that many souls will be won to the Lord?—but there is a lack of clarity and definiteness regarding the ultimate issue. Some workers, praise God, are out to establish local churches; others, alas! are out to extend their own denomination or to form mission churches.

This is a point on which my fellow workers and I cannot see eye to eye with many of God's children. From the depths of our hearts we thank God that in the past century He has sent so many of His faithful servants to China, so that those who were sitting in darkness should hear the gospel and believe in the Lord. Their self-sacrifice, their diligence, and their godliness have truly been an example to us. Many a time, as we looked at the faces of missionaries suffering for the gospel's sake, we have been moved to pray, "Lord, make us to live like them." May God bless and reward them! We acknowledge that we are utterly unworthy to have any part in the work of God, but by the grace of God we are what we are, and since God in His grace has called us to His service, we cannot but seek to be faithful. We have nothing to criticize, and much to admire, as far as the gospel work of our missionary brethren is concerned; yet we cannot but question their methods in dealing with the fruits of such work. For in the past hundred years it has not resulted in the building up of local churches but in the forming of missionary churches, or of branch churches of the various denominations which the missionaries represented. In our opinion this is contrary to the Word of God. There is no such thing in Scripture as the building up of denominations; we only find local churches there. May God forgive me if I am wrong!

## LOCAL CHURCHES AND MISSION CHURCHES

Permit me to mention a personal incident. Some time ago I met a certain missionary in Shanghai who asked me if it would not be possible for me to cooperate with his mission. Not knowing quite what to say, I did not commit myself. Later on I came across him in another part of the country, and again he repeated his question and asked if I had anything against the mission. I answered, "I dare not criticize your mission, though I do not believe it is according to the full thought of God. I believe it was God's will to establish it so that the servants of God in Western lands could come to China to preach the gospel. I have nothing to say regarding the mission as a body, for the Scriptures speak of companies of workers, and if you feel it should be organized, should have officers, and should bear a specific name, you must answer to God and not to man for that. Who am I that I should criticize the servants of the Lord? But while I do not criticize, I cannot copy, because God has not revealed that as His will and way for me. Regarding the mission as a mission, I have nothing to say, but I have serious questions regarding the churches formed by the mission. To illustrate, you represent the 'X' Mission. Now, do those saved by your instrumentality become the 'X' Church, or do they become the church of the particular locality in which they live? It may be all right for missionaries to belong to the 'X' Mission, but it is all wrong for them to form the fruits of the mission into the X' Church. The Word of God has not definitely forbidden the forming of an 'X' Mission, but it clearly does not sanction the founding of other than local churches."

Then I mentioned the apostolic examples, pointing out that they always sought to found or build up churches in the locality of their labors with the fruit of such labors. They never used such fruit to form branches of the companies in which they worked; otherwise, the Church of God would have been rent by numerous factions from its very inception.

I then took as an illustration the work at T——. "There at T——," I said, "God has used you to win many souls. If the people saved by your instrumentality are the church in T——, then if I come to T—— I shall certainly join them, no matter what their spiritual state, or what their form of organization; otherwise, I should be guilty of sectarianism.

But if you build up an 'X' Church in T-with the people saved there, then you are not building the Church of God in T-, and such a church' I regret to say I cannot join. I shall be obliged to work separately in T—— unless there is a church there standing on the scriptural ground of locality.

"If we are all out to establish local churches, then there is every possibility of cooperation. It is permissible to establish an 'X' Mission, but it is not scriptural to establish an 'X' Church. Suppose your 'X' Mission coming to T——establishes an 'X' Church; thereafter, various other missions come to T——, each establishing a separate mission church.' That would be the same as Paul establishing an Antiochian church in Corinth, and Peter coming along shortly after and establishing a Jerusalemic church there. On such a basis cooperation is impossible, for we should be disregarding the pattern which God has clearly shown us in His Word—the establishment of local churches.

"If we come to a place to found a church, then it must be local, intensely local, without anything extraneous to rob it in the slightest of its local

character. If you come to T —— with the establishing of the church in T —
— as your one aim, and I come to T—— with the establishing of the church
in T—— as my one aim, then cooperation will be no problem. Even if a
hundred and one missionaries, representing a hundred and one missions, all
come to T —— with this as their one aim, to establish the church in T ——
, then there will be no possibility of sectarianism, and cooperation will be a
matter of course. If the aim of the 'X' Mission is only to preach the gospel,
then it is possible for us to work together; but if there is a twofold aim—the
preaching of the gospel and the extension of the mission— then cooperation
is not possible. If a worker seeks on the one hand to preach the gospel, and
on the other hand to extend his own society, it is impossible for us to work
together." Whether or not a man is out to establish local churches determines
whether or not we can cooperate with him. No matter to what mission a man
may belong, if he comes to a place not seeking to establish his own "church,"
but a church in the locality, then we are perfectly willing to work with him.
Although we are not a mission, we are quite prepared to cooperate with any
mission if they have no private end in view, but only the one end which God
has shown as His will regarding His work.

May God grant us grace to see that His churches are all local churches.

# CHAPTER 8: THE QUESTION OF FINANCE

It is a remarkable fact that, while the book of Acts supplies many minute details regarding the work of an apostle, the one subject which from a human standpoint is of paramount importance in the carrying on of any work is not dealt with at all. No information whatever is given as to how the needs of the work or the personal needs of the workers were supplied. This is certainly amazing! What men consider of supreme importance, the apostles regarded of least consequence. In the early days of the Church, God's sent ones went out under the constraint of divine love. Their work was not just their profession, and their faith in God was not intellectual, but spiritual; not just theoretical, but intensely practical. The love and the faithfulness of God were realities to them, and that being so, no question arose in their minds concerning the supply of their temporal needs. Today as then, the matter of finance will present no problems to those who have a vital faith in God and a real love for Him.

This question of finance has most important issues, so let us devote a little time to it. In grace God is the greatest power, but in the world mammon is the greatest. If God's servants do not clearly settle the question of finance, then they leave a vast number of other questions unsettled too. Once the financial problem is solved, it is amazing how many other problems are automatically solved with it. The attitude of Christian workers to financial matters will be a fairly good indication as to whether or not they have been commissioned of God. If the work is of God, it will be spiritual; and if the work is spiritual, the way of supply will be spiritual. If supplies are not on a spiritual plane, then the work itself will speedily drift on to the plane of secular business. If spirituality does not characterize the financial side of the work, then the spirituality of its other departments is merely theoretical. There is no feature of the work that touches practical issues as truly as its finance. You can be theoretical in any other department, but not in that one.

## THE IMPORTANCE OF THE LIFE OF FAITH

Every worker, no matter what his ministry, must exercise faith for the meeting of all his personal needs and all the needs of his work. In God's Word we read of no worker asking for, or receiving, a salary for his services. Paul made no contract with the church in Ephesus, or with any other church, that he should receive a certain remuneration for a certain period of service. That God's servants should look to human sources for the supply of their needs has no precedent in Scripture. We do read there of a Balaam who sought to make merchandise of his gift of prophecy, but he is denounced in no uncertain terms. We read also of a Gehazi who sought to make gain of the grace of God, but he was stricken with leprosy for his sin. No servant of God should look to any human agency, whether an individual or a society, for the meeting of his temporal needs. If they can be met by the labor of his own hands, or from a private income, well and good. Otherwise, he should be directly dependent on God alone for their supply, as were the early apostles. The twelve apostles sent out by the Lord had no fixed salary, nor had any of the apostles sent out by the Spirit; they simply looked to the Lord to meet all their requirements. The apostles of today, like those of the early days, should regard no man as their employer, but should trust Him who has sent them forth to bear the responsibility of all that the doing of His will involves, in temporal as well as spiritual matters.

If a man can trust God, let him go out and work for Him; if not, let him stay at home, for he lacks the first qualification for the work. There is an idea prevalent that if a worker has a settled income he can be more at leisure for the work, and consequently will do it better; but as a matter of fact, in spiritual work there is need for an unsettled income, because that necessitates intimate fellowship with God, constant clear revelation of His will, and direct divine support. In worldly business, all a worker needs by way of equipment is will and talent; but human zeal and natural gift are no equipment for spiritual service. Utter dependence on God is necessary if the work is to be according to His will; therefore, God wishes His workers to be cast on Him alone for financial supplies, so that they cannot but walk in close communion with Him and learn to trust Him continually. A settled income does not foster trust in God and fellowship with Him; but utter dependence on Him for the meeting of one's needs certainly does. The more unsettled a worker's living is, the more he will be cast on God; and the more an attitude of trustful dependence on God is cultivated, the more spiritual the work will be. So it is clear that the nature of the work and the source of its supply are closely related. If a worker receives a definite salary from man, the work produced can never be purely divine.

Faith is a most important factor in God's service, for without it there can be no truly spiritual work; but our faith requires training and strengthening, and material needs are a means used in God's hand toward that end. We may profess to have faith in God for a vast variety of intangible things, and we may deceive ourselves into believing we really trust Him when we have no trust at all, simply because there is nothing concrete to demonstrate our distrust. But when it comes to financial needs, the matter is so practical that the reality of our faith is put to the test at once. If we cannot trust God to supply our temporal needs, then we cannot trust Him to supply our spiritual needs; but if we truly prove His trustworthiness in the very practical realm of material wants, we shall be able also to trust Him when spiritual difficulties arise either in connection with the work or with our personal lives. What a contradiction it is if we proclaim to others that God is the living God, yet we ourselves dare not trust Him for the meeting of our material needs.

Further, he who holds the purse holds authority. If we are supported by men, our work will be controlled by men. It is only to be expected that if we receive an income from a certain source, we should have to account for our doings to such a source. Whenever our trust is in men, our work cannot but be influenced by men. It is a serious misconception to fancy that we can take money from men to do the work of God. If we are supported by men, then we must seek to please men, and it is often impossible at the same time both to please men and God.

In His own work God must have the sole direction. That is why He wishes us to depend on no human source for financial supplies. Many of us have experienced that again and again God has controlled us through money matters. When we have been in the center of His will, supplies have been sure, but as soon as we have been out of vital touch with Him, they have been uncertain. At times we have fancied God would have us do a certain thing, but He has showed us it was not His will by withholding financial supplies. So we have been under the constant direction of the Lord, and such direction is most precious. If we cease to be dependent on Him, how can our trust be developed?

The first question anyone should face who believes himself truly called of God is the financial question. If he cannot look to the Lord alone for the meeting of his daily wants, then he is not qualified to be engaged in His

126

work, for if he is not financially independent of men, the work cannot be independent of men either. If he cannot trust God for the supply of needed funds, can he trust Him in all the problems and difficulties of the work? If we are utterly dependent on God for our supplies, then we are responsible to Him alone for our work, and in that case it need not come under human direction. May I advise all who are not prepared for the walk of faith, to continue with their secular duties and not engage in spiritual service. Every worker for God must be able to trust Him.

If we have real faith in God, then we have to bear all the responsibility of our own needs and the needs of the work. We must not secretly hope for help from some human source. We must have faith in God alone, not in God plus man. If the brethren show their love, let us thank God, but if they do not, let us thank Him still. It is a shameful thing for a servant of God to have one eye on Him and one eye on man or circumstance. It is unworthy of any Christian worker to profess to trust in God and yet hope for help from other sources. This is sheer unbelief. I have constantly said, and say it again, that as soon as our eyes turn to the brethren, we bring disgrace on our fellow workers and on the name of the Lord. Our living by faith must be absolutely real, and not deteriorate into a "living by charity." We dare to be utterly independent of men in financial matters, because we dare to believe utterly in God; we dare to cast away all hope in them, because we have full confidence in Him.

If our hope is in men, then when their resources dry up, ours will dry up too. We have no board behind us, but we have a Rock beneath us; and no one standing on this Rock will ever be put to shame. Men and circumstances may change, but we shall carry on in a steady course if our reliance is on God. All the silver and the gold are His, and none who walk in His will can ever come to want. We are apt to trust in the children of the Lord who in bygone days have sent us gifts, but they will all pass away. We must keep our eyes fixed on the unchanging God whose grace and faithfulness continue forever.

The two initial steps in the work of God are—first, the prayer of faith for needed funds, then the actual undertaking of the work. Today, alas! many of God's servants have no faith; yet they seek to serve Him. They undertake the work without having the essential qualification for it; therefore, what they do has no spiritual value. Faith is the first essential in any work for God, and it should be exercised in relation to material as well as other needs. If there is no faith for funds, then no matter how good the work is, sooner or later it will fail. When money stops, the work will stop too.

## LIVING FROM THE GOSPEL

Our Lord said, "The worker is worthy of his wages" (Luke 10:7); and Paul wrote to the Corinthians, "So also the Lord directed those who announce the gospel to live from the gospel" (1 Cor. 9:14). What is the meaning of living from the gospel? It does not mean that God's servant should receive a definite allowance from the church, for the modern system of paid service in the work of God was unknown in Paul's day. What it does mean is that the preachers of the gospel may receive gifts from the brethren; but no stipulations are made in connection with such gifts. No definite period of time is named, no definite sum of money, and no definite responsibility; all is a matter of freewill. As the hearts of believers are touched by God, they give gifts to His servants, so that while these servants receive gifts through men, their trust is still entirely in God. It is upon Him their eyes are fixed, it is to Him their needs are told, and it is He who touches the hearts of His children to give. That is what Paul meant when he spoke of living from the gospel. Paul himself received the gift from the church in Philippi (Phil. 4:16), and when he was in Corinth, he was helped by the brothers in Macedonia (2 Cor. 11:9). These are examples of living from the gospel. Paul received occasional gifts from individuals and from churches, but he received no definite remuneration for his preaching.

Yes, "the worker is worthy of his wages," and he should certainly live from the gospel. But we do well to ask ourselves, Whose laborers are we? If we are the laborers of men, then let us look to men for our support; but if we are the laborers of God, then we must look to no other but Him, though He may meet our needs through our fellow men. The whole question hinges here: Has God called us and sent us out? If the call and the commission have come from Him, then He must and surely will be responsible for all that our obedience to Him involves. When we make our needs known to

Him, He will certainly hear, and He will move the hearts of men to supply us with all we need. If we are only volunteers in God's service, then God will not be responsible for the liabilities we incur, so we shall be unable to live from the gospel.

When Miss M. E. Barber thought of coming to China to serve the Lord, she foresaw the difficulties of a woman setting out on her own for a foreign country, so she asked advice of Mr. Wilkinson of the Mildmay Mission to the Jews, who said, "A foreign country, no promise of support, no backing of any society—all these present no problem. The question is here: Are you going on your own initiative, or are you being sent by God?" "God is sending me," she replied. "Then no more questions are necessary," he said, "for if God sends you, He must be responsible." Yes, if we go on our own initiative, then distress and shame await us, but if we go as sent ones of God, all responsibility will be His, and we need never inquire how He is going to discharge it.

But in Corinth Paul did not live from the gospel; he made tents with his own hands. So there are evidently two ways by which the needs of God's servants may be met— either they look to God to touch the hearts of His children to give what is needful, or they earn it by doing part-time secular work. To work with our hands may be very good, but we need to note that Paul does not regard that as the usual thing. It is something exceptional, a course to be resorted to in special circumstances.

"If we have sown to you the spiritual things, is it a great thing if we shall reap from you the fleshly things? If others partake of this right over you, should not rather we? Yet we did not use this right, but we bear all things that we may not cause any hindrance to the gospel of Christ. Do you not know that those who labor on the sacred things eat the things of the sacred temple, that those who attend to the altar have their portion with the altar? So also the Lord directed those who announce the gospel to live from the gospel. But I myself have not used any of these things; and I have not written these things that it may be so with me; for it is good for me rather to die than—No one shall make my boast void....What then is my reward? That in preaching the gospel I may present the gospel without charge, so as not to use to the full my right in the gospel" (1 Cor. 9:11-15, 18). There are certain rights which are the privilege of all preachers of the gospel. Paul did not receive anything from Corinth, because he was in special circumstances at the time; but though he did not avail himself of his privileges as a gospel preacher on that occasion, that he did so at other times is quite clear. "Or did

I commit a sin, abasing myself that you might be exalted, because I announced the gospel of God to you free of charge? I robbed other churches, taking wages for the ministry to you. And when I was present with you and lacked, I was not a burden to anyone; for the brothers who came from Macedonia filled up my lack, and in everything I kept myself from being burdensome to you, and will keep myself. The truthfulness of Christ is in me, that this boasting shall not be stopped as it regards me in the regions of Achaia" (2 Cor. 11:7-10).

## THE PRINCIPLE OF RECEIVING GIFTS

It is not permissible to receive a definite salary from a church, and at times it is not even permissible to receive an indefinite gift. Paul was demonstrating this principle in not receiving anything from the Corinthian church. If anyone gives us a gift out of pity for us, then for the Lord's sake we dare not accept it; or if gifts are offered, the reception of which would either bring us under obligation to the givers, or bring us under their control, we must refuse them too. All the servants of God must not only trust Him entirely for the supply of their needs, but when gifts are freely offered them, they must be able to discern clearly whether or not such gifts could be received by God.

In the Old Testament the tithes of the Israelites were handed over to the Levites. The Israelites made their offerings to God, not to the Levites, but the latter stood in the place of God to receive the offerings. Today we are standing in the position of the Levites, and the gifts that are proffered to us are really offered to God. We do not receive gifts from any man; therefore, we are under obligation to none. If anyone wants thanks, he must seek it from God, for God is the One who receives the offerings. Therefore, whenever a gift is given to us, it is essential for us to be clear whether or not God could receive that gift. If God could not receive it, neither dare we. We dare not accept gifts indiscriminately lest we put God into a false position. (I say this reverently.) There are many people whose lives are not wellpleasing to God; how then could God receive their offerings? If He cannot, then we dare not do so in His stead. We should only receive money when our doing so involves no obligation on our part, and on God's part no misrepresentation of His nature.

It may happen at times that the gift is right, and also the attitude of the giver; but on the strength of his gift the giver may consider himself entitled to a say in the work. It is quite in order for the offerer to specify in what direction his offering be used, but it is not in order for him to decide how the work should be done. No servant of God should sacrifice his liberty to follow the divine leading by accepting any money which puts him under human control. A giver is at perfect liberty to stipulate to what use his gift should be put, but as soon as it is given, he should take hands off, and not seek to utilize it as a means of exercising indirect control over the work. If he can trust a servant of God, let him trust him; if not, then he need not give his money to him.

In secular work the man who supplies the means exercises authority in the realm to which his means are devoted, but not so in spiritual work. All authority in the work rests with the one who has been called of God to do it. In the spiritual realm it is the worker who controls the money, not the money the worker. The one to whom the call has come, and to whom the work has been entrusted by God, is the one to whom God will reveal the way the work must be carried out, and he dare not receive money from anyone who would use his gift to interfere with the Lord's will as it is revealed to him concerning the work. If a giver is spiritual, we shall gladly seek his counsel, but his advice can be sought solely on the ground of his spirituality, not on the ground of his gift. If he can trust us, and if he is clear the Lord is leading him to give it to us, then we may receive his offering; otherwise, let him keep his money, and let us go on with God's work in the way He has directed, looking to Him alone to supply its needs and ours.

In all our service for God we must maintain an attitude of utter dependence on Him. Whether funds are abundant or low, let us steadfastly pursue our work, recognizing it as a trust committed to us by God, and a matter for which we must answer to Him alone. "Am I seeking to please men? If I were still trying to please men, I would not be a slave of Christ" (Gal. 1:10). We must remain absolutely independent of men as regards the financial side of the work, but even in our independence we must preserve an attitude of true humility and willingness to accept advice from every member of the Body who is in close contact with the Head; and we should expect through them confirmation of the leading we have received direct from God. But all the counsel we seek and receive from others is on account of their spirituality, not on account of their financial position. We are willing to seek advice of the richest member of the Body, neither because of nor despite his money, and we are just as ready to seek the counsel of the poorest member, neither because of nor despite his poverty. In matters of finance we must maintain this ground, that it is God alone we have to do with. Let Paul's boasting be ours too!

## ATTITUDE TOWARD THE GENTILES

The principle is "taking nothing from the Gentiles" (3 John 7). We dare not receive any support for the work of God from those who do not know Him. If God has not accepted a man, He can never accept his money, and only what God can accept dare His servants accept. If anyone engaged in God's service accepts money for the furtherance of the work from an unsaved man, then he virtually places God under obligation to sinners. Let us never receive money on God's behalf which would enable a sinner before the great white throne to charge God with having taken advantage of him. However, this does not mean that we need reject even the hospitality of the Gentiles. If in the providence of God we visit some Miletus, then we should do well to accept the hospitality of a friendly Publius. But this must be definitely under the ordering of God, not as a matter of regular occurrence. Our principle should always be to take nothing from the Gentiles. When we begin to use their money, our work will have fallen into a sorry state.

## THE CHURCHES AND THE WORKERS

Should the churches provide for the needs of the workers? God's Word supplies a clear answer to our question. We see there that the money collected by the churches is used in three different ways:

(1)For the poor saints. The Scriptures pay much attention to the needy children of God, and a large proportion of the local offerings goes to relieve their distress.

(2)For the elders of the local church. Circumstances may make it necessary for elders to give up their ordinary business in order to devote themselves wholly to the interests of the church, in which case the local brothers should realize their financial responsibility toward them, and seek at least in some measure to make up to them what they have sacrificed for the church's sake (1 Tim. 5:17-18).

(3)For the working brothers and the work. This must be regarded asan offering to God, not as a salary paid to them.

"I robbed other churches, taking wages for the ministry to you. And when I was present with you and lacked, I was not a burden to anyone; for the brothers who came from Macedonia filled up my lack, and in everything I kept myself from being burdensome to you, and will keep myself" (2 Cor. 11:8-9). "And you yourselves also know, Philippians, that in the beginning of the gospel, when I went out from Macedonia, no church had fellowship with me in the account of giving and receiving except you only....But I have received in full all things and abound; I have been filled, receiving from Epaphroditus the things from you, a sweet-smelling savor, an acceptable sacrifice, well-pleasing to God" (Phil. 4:15, 18). Where the members of a church are spiritual, they cannot but care for the interests of the Lord in places beyond their own locality, and the love of the Lord will constrain them to give both to the workers and to the work. If the members are unspiritual they will probably reason that, since the church and the work are separate, they have no obligations towards the work, and it is enough that they bear responsibility for the church. But those members who are spiritual will always be alive to their responsibility in regard to the work and the workers, and will never seek to evade it on the ground that they have no official responsibility. They will count it both a duty and a delight to further the Lord's interests by their gifts.

While in the Epistles the churches are encouraged to give to the poor saints and also to the local elders and teachers, there is no mention made of encouraging the giving to the apostles, or to the work in which they were engaged. The reason is obvious. The writers of the Epistles were themselves apostles; therefore, it would not have been fitting for them to invite gifts for themselves or their work, nor had they any liberty from the Lord to do so. It was quite in order for them to encourage the believers to give to others, but for the meeting of their own needs and the needs of the work they could only look to God. As they cared for the needs of others, He did not overlook their needs, and He Himself moved the hearts of His saints to supply all that was required. So the workers of today should do as the apostles did of old, concern themselves only with the needs of others, and God will make all their concerns His.

That was a great and noble statement that our brother Paul made to the Philippians. He dared to say to those who were almost his sole supporters, "I have received in full all things and abound." Paul gave no hint of need, but took the position of a wealthy child of a wealthy Father, and he had no fears that by doing so further supplies would not be forthcoming. It was all very well for apostles to say to an unbeliever who himself was in distress, "Silver and gold I do not possess," but it would never have done for a needy apostle to say that to believers who would be ready to respond to an appeal for help. It is a dishonor to the Lord if any representative of His discloses needs that would provoke pity on the part of others. If we have a living faith in God, we shall always make our boast in Him, and we shall dare to proclaim under every circumstance, "I have received in full all things and abound." There is nothing petty or mean about God's true servants; they are all great souls. The following lines were penned by Miss M. E. Barber on Psalm 23:5 when she had used her last dollar:

There is always something over,
When we trust our gracious Lord;
Every cup He fills o'erfloweth,
His great rivers all are broad.
Nothing narrow, nothing stinted,
Ever issued from His store;
To His own He gives full measure,
Running over, evermore.
There is always something over,
When we, from the Father's Hand,
Take our portion with thanksgiving,
Praising for the path He planned.
Satisfaction, full and deepening,
Fills the soul, and lights the eye,
When the heart has trusted Jesus All its need to satisfy.
There is always something over,
When we tell of all His love;
Unplumbed depths still lie beneath us,
Unscaled heights rise far above.
Human lips can never utter All His wondrous tenderness.
We can only praise and wonder And His Name for ever bless.

We are the representatives of God in this world, and we are here to prove His faithfulness; therefore, above all in financial matters we must be totally independent of men, and wholly dependent upon God. Our attitude, our words, and our actions must all declare that He alone is our source of supply. If there is any weakness here, He will be robbed of the glory that is His due. As God's servants, we must show forth the abundant resources of our God. We must not be afraid to appear wealthy before people. We must never be untrue, but such an attitude is perfectly consistent with honesty. Let us keep our financial needs secret, even if our secrecy should lead men to conclude that we are well off when we have nothing at all. He who sees in secret will take note of all our needs, and He will meet them, not in stinted measure, but "according to His riches, in glory, in Christ Jesus" (Phil. 4:19). We dare to make things difficult for God, because He requires no assistance from us in order to perform His miracles.

From the study of God's Word we note two things concerning the attitude of His children to financial matters. On the one hand, workers should be careful to disclose their needs to none but God; on the other hand, the churches should be faithful in remembering the needs both of the workers and their work, and they should not only send gifts to those who are working in their vicinity, or to those who have been called out from their midst, but, like the Philippians and the Macedonians, they should frequently minister to a far-off Paul. The horizon of the churches should be much wider than it is. The present method of a church supporting its own "minister" or its own missionary was a thing unknown in apostolic days. If, with the present-day facilities for transmitting money to distant parts, the children of God only minister to the material needs of those in their own locality, they certainly lack spiritual insight and largeness of heart. On the part of the workers there must be no expectation from man, and on the part of the churches there should be a faithful remembrance of the work and the workers both at home and abroad. It is essential to the spiritual life of the churches that they take a practical interest in the work. *God has no use for an unbelieving worker, nor has He any use for a loveless church.*

The distinction between the church and the work must be clearly defined in the mind of the worker, especially as regards financial matters. Should a worker pay a short visit to any place on the invitation of the church, then it is quite right for him to receive their hospitality. But should he stay for an indefinite period, then he must bear the burden alone before God; otherwise, his faith in God will wane. Even should a brother willingly offer free hospitality, it ought to be declined, for the life of faith must be carefully maintained. It is right for the brethren to give occasional gifts to the workers, as the Philippians did to Paul, but they must not bear the responsibility of any. The churches have no official obligations regarding the workers, and the latter must see to it that the former do not take such obligations upon themselves. God permits us to accept gifts, but it is not His will that others become responsible for us. Gifts of love may be sent to the workers from their brethren in the Lord, but no believers must regard themselves as under any legal obligations towards them. Not only have the churches no official responsibility towards the workers; they are not even responsible for their board, lodgings, or traveling expenses. The entire financial responsibility of the work rests upon those to whom it has been committed by God.

"We have wronged no one, we have corrupted no one, we have taken advantage of no one" (2 Cor. 7:2). "I will not be a burden" (2 Cor. 12:14). "For neither were we found at any time with flattering speech, even as you know, nor with a pretext for covetousness; God is witness" (1 Thes. 2:5). "Nor did we eat bread as a gift from anyone, but in labor and hardship we worked night and day so that we would not be burdensome to any of you" (2 Thes. 3:8). From these passages we see clearly the attitude of the apostle. He was not willing to impose any burden upon others or in any way to take advantage of them. And this must be our attitude too. Not only should we receive no salary, we should be careful not to take the slightest advantage of any of our brethren. Apostles should be willing to be taken advantage of, but on no account should they ever take advantage of others. It is a shameful thing to profess trust in God and yet play the role of a pauper, disclosing one's needs and provoking others to pity. A servant of God who really sees the glory of God, and his own glorious position as one of His workmen, can well afford to be independent of others, and even liberal. It is only right for us to enjoy the hospitality of our brethren for awhile, but we should most rigidly guard against taking advantage of them in trifles such as a night's lodging, an odd meal, or the use of light and coal, or of household utensils, or even of a daily paper. Nothing reveals smallness of character so readily as taking petty advantages. If we are not careful in such matters, we may as well relinquish our task.

All the movements of workers vitally affect the work, and unless we have a living trust in God, our movements are liable to be determined by prospective incomes. Money has great power to influence men, and unless we have true faith in God and a true heart to do His will, we are likely to be influenced by the rise and fall of funds. If our movements are governed by financial supplies, then we are hirelings working for pay, or beggars seeking alms, and we are a disgrace to the name of the Lord. We should never go to a place because of the bright financial prospects of working there, nor should we refrain from going because the financial outlook is dark. In all our movements we must ask ourselves, Am I in the will of God? or am I influenced at all by financial considerations? We are out to serve the Lord, not to make a living.

## THE WORKERS AND THEIR WORK

Let us be clear that we must not only bear the burden of our own personal needs, but of the needs of the work as well. If God has called us to a certain work, then all financial outlay connected with it is our affair. Wherever we go, we are responsible for all expenses relating to it, from its inception to its close. If we are called of God to do pioneering work, though the expenses of rent, furniture, and traveling, may amount to a goodly sum, we alone are responsible for them. He is not worthy to be called God's servant who cannot be responsible for his own needs and the needs of the work to which God has called him. Not the local church, but the one to whom the work has been committed, must bear all financial burdens connected with it.

Another point to which we must give attention is a clear discrimination between gifts intended for personal use and gifts given for the work. It may seem superfluous to mention it, and yet it needs emphasis, that no money given for the work should be used by the worker to meet his personal needs. It must either be used to defray expenses in connection with his own work, or be sent on to another worker. We must learn righteousness in relation to all money matters. If there is any lack in connection with the work, the worker must bear the burden, and if there is any surplus, he cannot divert it to the meeting of his own requirements.

When I had just begun to serve the Lord, I read an incident in Hudson Taylor's life which was a great help to me. If I remember it correctly, this is the gist of it: Mr. Taylor was in St. Louis, U.S.A., and was due in Springfield for meetings. The carriage taking him to the station was delayed, with the result that when he arrived there the train had already left, and there seemed no possible way for him to keep his appointment. But, turning to Dr. J. H. Brookes, he said, "My Father runs the trains; I'll be there in time." Upon inquiry of the agent, they found a train leaving St. Louis in another direction, which crossed the line going to Springfield; but the train on the other line always left ten minutes before this train arrived, as they were opposing roads. Without a moment's hesitation, Mr. Taylor said he would go that way, in spite of the fact that the agent told him they never made connections there. While they waited, a gentleman came to the station and handed Mr. Taylor some money. He turned to Dr. Brookes with the remark, "Do you not see that my Father has just sent me my train fare!" meaning that, even had he arrived in time for the other train, he could not have taken it. Dr. Brookes was amazed. He knew Mr. Taylor had quite a good sum of money in hand, which had been given him for his work in China, so he asked, "What do you mean by saying you had no money for your fare?" Mr. Taylor replied, "I never use anything for personal expenses that is specified for the work. The money earmarked for my own use has just come in!" For almost the first time in the history of that road the St. Louis train arrived ahead of the other, and Mr. Taylor was able to keep his appointment at Springfield!

## MAKING OUR NEEDS KNOWN

As we have already said, an apostle may encourage God's people to remember the needs of the saints and of the elders, but he can mention nothing of his own needs or the needs of the work. Let him only draw the attention of the churches to the wants of others, and God will draw their attention to his wants. Let him be concerned about the needs of the saints and elders, and God will use the saints and elders to draw the attention of the churches to his needs.

We must avoid all propaganda in connection with the work. With utter honesty of heart we must trust in God and make our requirements known to Him alone. Should the Lord so lead, we may tell to His glory what He has wrought through us. (See Acts 14:27; 15:3-4.) But nothing must be done by way of advertisement, in the hope of receiving material help. This is displeasing to God and hurtful to ourselves. If in any financial matter our faith grows weak, we shall find it fail when difficulties arising in connection with the work put it to the test. Besides, if we know anything of the power of the cross to deal with the self-life, how can we resort to propaganda for our work and so take things out of the hands of God and carry them on by our own efforts?

I know of works which, at their inception, were on a pure faith basis, and the blessing of the Lord rested on them. Soon the workers felt the need of extending the work, and actually extended it beyond their usual income. Consequently, they had to resort to indirect advertisement in order to meet their liabilities. Let us beware of extending the work ourselves, for if the extension is of man, we shall have to use man-made methods to meet the new demands. If God sees the work needs extension, He Himself will extend it, and if He extends it, He will be responsible to meet the increased needs. It is because human methods are employed to extend a work, that human means must be devised to meet its fresh requirements; so advertisement and propaganda are resorted to in order to solve the problem. Circular letters, reports, magazines, deputation-work, special agents, and special business centers have been means much used of Christian workers to increase funds for the work. Men are not willing to let God extend it in His own time, and because they cannot wait patiently for its spontaneous development, but force an artificial growth, they have to resort to natural activity to meet the demands of that growth. They have hastened developments, so they have to devise ways and means of procuring increased supplies. The spontaneous growth of the work of God does not necessitate any activities of human nature, for God meets all demands which He creates.

Advertisement has been developed to a fine art in this age, but if we have to take our cue from businessmen and use up-to-date advertising methods to make our work a success, then let us give up our ministry and change our calling. The wisdom of the world declares that "the end justifies the means," but it is never so in the spiritual realm. Our end must be spiritual, but our means must be spiritual too. The cross is no mere symbol; it is a fact and a principle which must govern all God's work.

We must let the Holy Spirit hinder us where He will, and not seek to urge things forward by touching divine work with human hands. There is no need for us to devise means to draw attention to our work. God in His sovereignty and providence can well bear all responsibility. If He moves men to help us, then all is well, but if we seek to move men ourselves, both we and the work will suffer loss. If we truly believe God we shall leave the matter wholly in His hands.

We are all trusting God for our living, but what need is there to make it known? I feel repelled when I hear God's servants emphasize the fact that they are living by faith. Do we really believe in God's sovereignty and in His providence? If we do, surely we can trust Him to make our needs known to His saints, and so to order things that our needs can be met without our trying to make them known. Even should people conclude from our manner of living that we have a private income, and in consequence withhold their gifts, we do not mind. I would counsel my younger brethren in the ministry not to talk of their personal needs, or of their faith in God, so that they may the better be able to prove Him. The more faith there is, the less talk there will be about it.

## AMONG THE FELLOW WORKERS

In the Old Testament we read that though the Levites stood in the place of God to receive tithes from all His people, they themselves offered tithes to Him. The servant of the Lord should learn to give as well as to receive. We praise God for the generous way the workers in days past have given to their fellow laborers, but we still need to be more thoughtful for the material needs of all our brethren in the work. We must remember the words of Paul: "These hands have ministered to my needs and to those who are with me" (Acts 20:34). We must not merely hope to have sufficient to spend on ourselves and our work, but must look to God to provide us with sufficient to give to others too. If we are only occupied with the thought of our personal needs and the needs of our work, and forget the needs of our fellow workers, the plane of our spiritual life is too low. Like Paul, we must constantly think of those with us, and help to minister to their needs. If anyone among us is only a receiver and not a giver, he is unworthy of Him who sent him and those who labor with him.

The scope of our thinking along the line of material needs should always be on the basis of "my needs and to those who are with me." The money God sends to me is not only for me, but also for those with me. A brother once suggested that God would surely supply the needs of all our fellow workers, so we need not feel too concerned about them, especially as we are not a mission and have no financial obligations towards them. But our brother forgot that we are not only responsible for our own needs and the needs of our work, but in a spiritual way we, like Paul, are responsible also for those with us. Whether we are good fellow workers or not will be evidenced by the measure of our thoughtfulness for our brethren in the work.

Since we are not a mission, and have no man-made organization, no headquarters, no centralization of funds, and consequently no distributing center, how can the needs of all our fellow workers be supplied? This question has been repeatedly put to me by interested brethren. The answer is this: all needs will be met if each one realizes his threefold financial responsibility—first, in regard to his personal family and needs; second, in regard to the needs of his work; and third, in regard to the needs of his fellow laborers. We must not only look to God to supply our own wants and all those related to our work, but we must look to

Him just as definitely to send us extra funds to enable us to have something to send to our associates in the work. Of course we have no official obligation towards them, but we cannot ignore our spiritual responsibility.

The requirements of workers vary, and the requirements of the work vary too, besides which, the power of prayer differs in different individuals, and the measure of faith differs also. It follows therefore that our income will not be the same; but every one of us should definitely exercise faith for the supply of sufficient funds to be able to distribute to the necessities of others. The amounts we receive and give may differ, but the same principle applies to us all. Working on such a basis, no headquarters is necessary; for each of us acts as a sort of headquarters and distributing center. Of course that does not mean we must send an equal share to all who are associated with us; that is a matter of individual guidance. We trust in the sovereignty and providence of God, and we leave it to Him to regulate the passing on of gifts so that none will have a surplus and none be left in want. Should God lead us to send money regularly to any particular worker, it would be well to send it through one brother this time and another next time, so that the giver will receive less attention from the receiver.

The principle of God's government in relation to financial things is "he who gathered much had no excess, and he who gathered little had no lack" (2 Cor. 8:15). Anyone who has gathered much must be willing to have nothing over, for only then can he who has gathered little have no lack.

Some of us have proved in experience that when we bear the burden for those who gather little, God sees to it that we gather much; but if we only think of our own needs, the utmost we can hope for is to gather little and have no lack. It is a privilege to be able to help your brethren in the work, and to be able to give away even the greater proportion of your income. Those who have only learned to take seldom receive; but those who have learned to give are always receiving and have always more to give. The more money you spend on others, the more your income will increase; the more you try to save, the more you will troubled by rust and thieves (Matt. 6:19-20).

We must not confine our giving to those immediately associated with us, but must remember workers in other parts and seek to minister to their needs. We must constantly keep the thought of other workers and their needs before the brethren among whom we labor, and encourage them to help them, never fearing that God will bless other workers more than us. We must leave no room for fear or jealousy. Do we really believe in the sovereignty of God? If so, we shall never fear that anything God has intended for us shall fail to reach us. The needs of Paul and his fellow workers were great, and though he only brought the needs of the saints and the elders before the churches, God looked after his needs and the needs of those with him.

If your work is to be conducted along lines well-pleasing to God, then it is absolutely essential that the sovereignty of God be a working factor in your experience, and no mere theory. When you know His sovereignty, then even if men seem to move around you at random and circumstances appear to whirl at the mercy of chance, you will still be confident in the assurance that God is ordering every detail of your way for His glory and for your good. The needs of others may be known to men, while none may know or even care about your wants, but you will have no anxiety if the sovereignty of God is a reality to you; for then you will see all those haphazard circumstances, and all those indifferent folk, and even the opposing hosts of evil, being silently harnessed to His will; and all those unrelated forces will become related as one to serve His purpose, and to serve the purposes of those whose will is one with His. Yes, "We know that all things work together for good to those who love God, to those who are called according to His purpose" (Rom. 8:28).

So the question is not, Are our needs small or great? or, Are they known or unknown? but simply this, Are we in the will of God? Our faith may be tested, and our patience too, but if we are willing to leave things in God's hands and quietly wait for Him, then we shall not fail to see a careful timing of events and an exquisite dovetailing of circumstances, and emerging from a meaningless maze we shall behold a perfect correspondence between our need and the supply.

## WHY NOT A FAITH MISSION?

Some have asked, "Since you believe all God's servants should trust Him for their daily needs, and since you have quite a company of fellow workers, why do you not become an organized faith mission?"

For two reasons: first, in God's Word all association of workers is on a spiritual basis, not on an official one. As soon as you have an official organization, then you change the spiritual relationship which exists among the fellow workers into an official relationship. Second, dependence upon God alone for the meeting of all material needs does not demand as active a faith on the part of an official organization as it does on the part of individuals who are only related in a spiritual fellowship. It is much easier to trust God as a mission than to trust Him as an individual. In Scripture we see individual faith, but we see no such thing as organization-faith. In an organization there is bound to be some income, and every member is sure to receive a share, whether he exercises faith or not. This opens the way for people to join the mission who have no active faith in God. And in the case of those who have faith when they join, there is the likelihood of personal trust in the Lord gradually growing weak through lack of exercise, since supplies come with a certain measure of regularity whether the individual members of the mission exercise faith or not. It is very easy to lose faith in God and simply trust an organization. Those who know the frailty of the flesh realize how prone we are to depend on anything and anyone but God. It is much easier to put our expectation in remittances from the mission than in ravens from heaven. Beloved, is not this the truth? If I have said anything amiss, may God and men both forgive me.

Because of our proneness to look at the bucket and forget the fountain, God has frequently to change His means of supply to keep our eyes fixed on the source. So the heavens that once sent us welcome showers become as brass, the streams that refreshed us are allowed to dry up, and the ravens that brought our daily food visit us no longer; but then God surprises us by meeting our needs through a poor widow, and so we prove the marvelous resources of God. Organization-faith does not stimulate personal trust in God, and that is what He is out to develop.

I know that in an organized body many difficulties vanish automatically. Humanly speaking, it insures a much greater income, for many of God's children prefer to give to organizations rather than to individuals. Besides, organized work comes much more to the notice of the children of God than unorganized. But questions such as these challenge us continually: Do you really believe in God? Must scriptural principles be sacrificed to convenience? Do you really want God's best with all its accompanying difficulties? We do, and so we have no alternative but to work on the ground of the Body of Christ in spiritual association with all others who stand on that same ground.

But we wish to point out that, though we ourselves are not a mission, we are not opposed to missions. Our testimony is positive, not negative. We believe that in God's Word the different groups of sent-out ones who were associated in the work all stood on the ground of the Body, and that no such group was organized into a mission. Still, if our brethren feel led of God to form such an organization, we have nothing to say against it. We only say, God bless them! For us to form a mission because others of God's children do so would be wrong, since we see no scriptural ground for it, and have no leading of the Spirit in that direction. But whether we work in a fellowship whose relationships are only spiritual, or in an organization whose relationships are official, may God make us absolutely one in this, that we do not seek the increase or extension of the companies in which we work, but make it our one aim to work exclusively for the founding and building up of the local churches.

# CHAPTER 9: THE ORGANIZATION OF LOCAL CHURCHES

Having already observed the difference between the work and the churches, between the apostles and the elders, between the basis of a scriptural church and sects, we can now proceed to see how a local church is organized.

According to the present-day conception, three things are regarded as essential to the existence of a church, apart from the group of Christians who constitute its members. These three are—a "minister," a church building, and "church services." The Christian world would question the existence of a church if even one of these three were lacking.

What would one think these days of a church without a "minister"? Call him pastor or anything else you like, but such a man you certainly must have. As a rule he is specially trained for church work, but he may be either a local man, or a worker transferred from some other place. Whatever his background and qualifications, he gives himself exclusively to the affairs of the church. Thus, those in the churches are divided into two classes—the clergy, who make it their business to attend to spiritual matters, and the laity, who devote themselves to secular things. Then of course there must be church services, for which the minister is responsible, and the most essential of these is the Sunday morning gathering. You may call it a service, or a meeting, or whatever you choose, but such a gathering there must be at least every Sunday, when the church members sit in their pews and listen to the sermon their minister has prepared. And naturally there must be a church building. You may term it a hall, a meeting place, a chapel, or a church; but whatever you care to call it, such a place there must be. Otherwise, how could you ever "go to church" on Sundays? But what is considered essential to a church these days, was considered totally unnecessary in the early days of the Church's history. Let us see what the Word of God has to say on the matter.

# THE "MINISTER," OR WORKER, IN CHURCH GOVERNMENT

"Paul and Timothy, slaves of Christ Jesus, to all the saints in Christ Jesus who are in Philippi, with the overseers and deacons" (Phil. 1:1). In not a single scriptural church do we find any mention of a "minister" controlling its affairs; such a position is always occupied by a group of local elders. And nowhere do we get a clearer or more comprehensive presentation of the personnel of a church than in the verse just quoted from the Philippian letter. The church consists of all the saints, the overseers, and the deacons. The deacons are the men appointed to serve tables (Acts 6:26), that is, those who care exclusively for the business side of things. The overseers are the elders, who take the oversight of all church matters. (Acts 20:17, 28, and Titus 1:5, 7 make this quite clear.) And besides the overseers and the deacons, there are all the saints. These three classes comprise the entire church, and no other class of person can be introduced into any church without making it an unscriptural organization.

Before we go on to consider the elders, let us glance for a moment at the deacons. They do not occupy such an important position as the elders, who rule the church; they are chosen by the church to serve it. They are the executors who carry out the decisions of the Holy Spirit through the elders and the church. Because the deacons have actually more to do with assembly life than with the work, we think it sufficient to just make this brief mention of them.

There are two points in connection with the elders that call for special attention. First, they are chosen from among the common brethren. They are not workers who have a special call from God to devote themselves exclusively to spiritual work. As a rule they have their families, and their business duties, and are just ordinary believers of good reputation. Second, elders are chosen from among the local brethren. They are not transferred from other places, but are set apart just in the place where they live, and they are not called to leave their ordinary occupations, but simply to devote their spare time to the responsibilities of the church. The members of the church are local men, and as elders are chosen from among the ordinary members, it follows that they are also local men (Acts 14:23; Titus 1:5).

And since all scriptural elders are local brothers, if we transfer a man from some other place to control a church, we are departing from scriptural ground. Here again we see the difference between the churches and the work. A brother may be transferred to another place to take care of the work there, but no brother can be sent out of his own locality to bear the burdens of the church in another place. The churches of God are all governed by elders, and elders are all chosen from among the local brethren.

If a group of men are saved in a certain place, and a worker is left in charge of them, then it is inaccurate to refer to that company as a church. If affairs are still in the hands of the worker and have not passed into the hands of the local brothers, then it is still his work; it is not a church. Let us make this distinction clear: the work is always in the hands of the workers, and the church is always in the hands of the local brethren. Whenever a worker is in control of affairs, then it is a question of work, not of a church.

It has been pointed out before that in God's Word there are local elders, but no local apostles. When Paul left Titus in Crete, his object was not that Titus should manage church affairs there, but that he should appoint elders in every place so that they could take charge of affairs. The business of the worker is to found churches and appoint elders, never to take direct responsibility in the churches. If in any place an apostle takes responsibility for the affairs of the local church, he either changes the nature of his office or the nature of the church. No apostle coming from another place is qualified for the office of local elder; the post can only be occupied by local men.

Let us who have been called of God to the work be absolutely clear on this point, that we were never called to settle down as pastors in any place. We may revisit the churches we have founded and help the believers we formerly led to the Lord, but we can never become their "minister" and bear the responsibility of spiritual affairs on their behalf. They must be satisfied with the elders appointed by the apostles and learn to honor and obey them. Obviously it needs more grace on the part of the believers to submit themselves to others of their own number and of their own rank, than to yield to the control of a man who comes from another place and has special qualifications for spiritual work. But God has so ordained it, and we bow to His wisdom.

The relationship between the work and the church is really very simple. A worker preaches the gospel, souls are saved, and after a short lapse of time a few of the comparatively advanced ones are chosen from among them to be responsible for local affairs. Thus a church is established! The apostle then follows the leading of the

Spirit to another place, and history is repeated there. So the spiritual life and activity of the local church develops, because the believers bear their own responsibility; and the work extends steadily because the apostles are free to move from place to place preaching the gospel and founding new churches.

The first question usually asked in connection with a church is, "Who is the minister?" The thought in the questioner's mind is, "Who is the man responsible for ministering and administering spiritual things in this church?" The clerical system of church management is exceedingly popular, but the whole thought is foreign to Scripture, where we find the responsibility of the church committed to elders, not to "ministers" as such. And the elders only take oversight of the church work; they do not perform it on behalf of the brethren. If, in a company of believers, the minister is active and the church members are all passive, then that company is a mission, not a church. In a church all the members are active. The difference between the elders and the other members is that the latter work, while the former both work themselves and also oversee the others as they work. Since the question of elders has been dealt with elsewhere, we shall make no further reference to it here.

## THE MEETING PLACE

Another thing which is considered of vital importance to the existence of a church is a church building. The thought of a church is so frequently associated with a church building, that the building itself is often referred to as "the church." But in God's Word it is the living believers who are called the church, not the bricks and mortar (see Acts 5:11; Matt. 18:17). According to Scripture it is not even necessary for a church to have a place definitely set apart for fellowship. The Jews always had their special meeting places, and wherever they went they made a point of building a synagogue in which to worship God. The first apostles were Jews, and the Jewish tendency to build special places of worship was natural to them. Had Christianity required that places be set apart for the specific purpose of worshipping the Lord, the early apostles, with their Jewish background and natural tendencies, would have been ready enough to build them. The amazing thing is that, not only did they not put up special buildings, but they seem to have ignored the whole subject intentionally. It is Judaism, not Christianity, which teaches that there must be sanctified places for divine worship. The temple of the New Testament is not a material edifice; it consists of living persons, all believers in the Lord. Because the New Testament temple is spiritual, the question of meeting places for believers, or places of worship, is one of minor importance. Let us turn to the New Testament and see how the question of meeting places is dealt with there.

When our Lord was on earth, He met with His disciples at times on the hillside and at times by the sea. He gathered them around Him now in a house, again in a boat, and there were times when He drew apart with them in an upper room. But there was no consecrated place, where He habitually met with His own. At Pentecost the disciples were gathered in an upper room, and after Pentecost they either met all together in the temple or separately in different houses (Acts 2:46), or at times in the portico of Solomon (Acts 5:12). They met for prayer in various homes, Mary's being one of them (Acts 12:12), and we read that on a certain occasion they were assembled in a room on the third floor of a building (Acts 20:8). Judging from these passages, the believers assembled in a great variety of places and had no official meeting place. They simply made use of any building that suited their needs, whether a private home, or just a room in a house, or else a large public building such as the temple, or even a wide space like the portico of Solomon. They had no buildings specially set apart for church use; they had nothing which would correspond to the "church" of today.

"And on the first day of the week, when we gathered together to break bread, Paul conversed with them....And there were a considerable number of lamps in the upper room where we were gathered together. And a certain young man named Eutychus was sitting in the window" (Acts 20:7-9). In

Troas we find the believers meeting in the third story of a building. There is a delightfully unofficial air about this gathering, such a contrast to the present-day conventional services, with the church members all sitting stiffly in their pews. But this Troas meeting was a truly scriptural one. There was no official stamp upon it; it bore the marks of real life, in its perfect naturalness and pure simplicity. It was quite all right for some of the saints to sit on the window-ledge, or for others to sit on the floor, as Mary did of old. In our assemblies we must return to the principle of the upper room. The ground floor is a place for business, a place for men to come and go; but there is more of a home atmosphere about the upper room, and the gatherings of God's children are family affairs. The last supper was in an upper room; so was Pentecost, and so again was the meeting here. God wants the intimacy of the upper room to mark the gatherings of His children, not the stiff formality of an imposing public edifice.

That is why in the Word of God we find His children meeting in the family atmosphere of a private home. We read of the church in the house of Prisca and Aquila (Rom. 16:5; 1 Cor. 16:19), the church in the house of Nymphas (Col. 4:15), and the church in the house of Philemon (Philem. 2). The New Testament mentions at least these three different churches that were in the homes of believers.

How did churches come to be in such homes? If in a certain place there were a few believers, and one of them had a house large enough to accommodate them all, they quite naturally assembled there, and the Christians in that locality were called "the church in the house of So-andso."

Everything must begin at the beginning. When a church is founded, the believers from the very outset must learn to meet by themselves, either in their own homes or in some other building which they are able to secure. Of course, not every church is a church in a house, but a church in a house should be encouraged rather than considered as a drawback. If the number of believers is great and the sphere of the locality wide, they might need to meet, as the saints in Jerusalem did, in different houses (which may mean homes, halls, or any other building) instead of in one house. There was only one church in Jerusalem, but its members assembled in different houses. The principle of houses still applies today. This does not mean that the whole church will always meet separately; in fact, it is important, and of great profit, for all the believers to gather together quite regularly in one place (1 Cor. 14:23). To make such meetings possible, they could either borrow or rent a public place for the occasion, or, if they have sufficient means, they could acquire a hall permanently for the purpose. But the meeting place for the believers could generally be in a private home. If this is not available, and not suitable, of course other buildings could be acquired. But we should try to encourage meetings in the homes of the Christians.

The grand edifices of today, with their lofty spires, speak of the world and the flesh rather than of the Spirit, and in many ways they are not nearly as well suited to the purpose of Christian assembly as the private homes of God's people. In the first place, people feel much freer to speak of spiritual things in the unconventional atmosphere of a home than in a spacious church building where everything is conducted in a formal manner; besides, there is not the same possibility for mutual intercourse there. Somehow, as soon as people enter those special buildings, they involuntarily settle down to passivity, and wait to be preached to. A family atmosphere should pervade all gatherings of the children of God, so that the brothers even feel free to ask questions (1 Cor. 14:35). Everything should be under the control of the Spirit, but there should be the liberty of the Spirit too. Further, if the churches are in the private homes of the brethren, they naturally feel that all the interests of the church are their interests. There is a sense of closeness of relationship between themselves and the church. Many Christians feel that church affairs are something quite beyond them. They have no intimate concern in them, because in the first place they have their "minister" who is specially responsible for all such affairs, and then they have a great church building which seems so remote from their homes, and where matters are conducted so systematically and with such precision that one feels overpowered and bound in spirit.

Still further, the meetings in believers' homes can be a fruitful testimony to the neighbors around, and they provide an opportunity for witness and gospel preaching. Many who are not willing to go to a "church" will be glad to go to a private house. And the influence is most helpful for the families of the Christians. From early days the children will be surrounded by a spiritual atmosphere, and will have constant opportunity to see the reality of eternal things. Again, if meetings are in the homes of the Christians, the Church is saved much material loss. One of the reasons the Christians survived the Roman persecutions during the first three centuries of Church history, was that they had no special buildings for worship, but met in cellars and caves and other inconspicuous places. Such meeting places were not readily discovered by their persecutors; but the large and costly edifices of today would be easily located and destroyed, and the churches would be speedily wiped out. The imposing structures of our modern times convey an impression of the world rather than of the Christ whose name they bear. (The halls and other buildings required for the work are quite another matter; we are speaking here only of the churches.)

So the scriptural method of church organization is simple in the extreme. As soon as there are a few believers in a place, they begin to meet in one of their homes. If numbers increase so that it becomes impracticable to meet in one house, then they can meet in several different houses, but the entire company of believers can meet together once in a while in some public place. A hall for such purposes could either be borrowed, rented, or built, according to the financial condition of the church; but we must remember that the ideal meeting places of the saints are their own private homes.

Meetings connected with the work are arranged along totally different lines, and are entirely under the auspices of the workers. They are on the principle of Paul's own rented house in Rome. As we have seen, when Paul reached Rome a church was already in existence there, and the believers already had their regular gatherings. Paul did not use the meeting place of the church for his work, but rented a separate place, as he stayed for a prolonged period in Rome. In Troas he only stayed for a week, so he did not rent a place there, but simply accepted the hospitality of the church. When he went away, the special meetings he had been conducting there ceased, but the brethren in Troas still continued their own meetings. If a worker intends to remain for a considerable period in any place, then he must obtain a separate center for his work and not make use of the church's meeting place. Frequently such a center will require more extensive accommodation than the meeting place of the church. If the Lord calls some of His servants to maintain a permanent testimony in a given place, then the call for a special building in connection with the work may be much greater than the need of premises is in connection with the church. It is almost essential to have a hall if the work is to be carried on in any place, whereas the homes of the brethren will nearly always meet the needs of the church meetings.

## THE MEETING

Before we consider the question of meeting, let us first say a few words concerning the nature of the Church. Christ is the Head of the Church and "we who are many are one body in Christ, and individually members one of another" (Rom. 12:5). Apart from Christ, the Church has no head; all believers are only members, and they are "members one of another." Mutuality expresses the nature of the Church, for all the relationships among believers are of one member to another, never of a head to the members. All those who compose a church take their place as members of the Body, not one occupying the position of head. The whole life of the church, and all its activities, must be stamped by this characteristic of mutuality.

But the nature of the work is quite different from that of the church. In the work there are active and passive groups. The apostles are active, and those among whom they labor are passive, whereas in the church all are active. In the work, activity is one-sided; in the church it is all-round.

When we recognize the fundamental difference between the nature of the work and the church, then we shall easily understand the scriptural teaching concerning the meetings which we are about to consider. There are two different kinds of meetings in Scripture—the church meeting and the apostolic meeting. If we are to differentiate clearly between the two, we must first understand the different nature of church and work. Once we see that clearly, a glance at the nature of any meeting will make it obvious to what sphere it belongs; but if we fail to realize the distinction, we shall constantly confuse the church with the work. In the early Church there were meetings which were definitely connected with the churches, and others that were just as definitely connected with the work. In the latter only one man spoke, and all the others constituted his audience. One stood before the others, and by his preaching directed the thoughts and hearts of those who sat quietly listening. This type of meeting can be recognized at once as a meeting connected with the apostolic work, because it bears the character of the work, that is, activity on the one side and passivity on the other. There is no stamp of mutuality about it. In the church meetings, "each one has a psalm, has a teaching, has a revelation, has a tongue, has an interpretation" (1 Cor. 14:26). Here it is not a case of one leading and all the others following, but of each one contributing his share of spiritual helpfulness. True, only a few of those present take part, but all may; only a few are actual contributors to the meeting, but all are potential contributors. The Scriptures show these two distinct kinds of meetings—apostolic meetings, which are led by one man, and church meetings, in which all the local brethren are free to take part.

The apostolic meetings may be divided into two classes —for believers and for unbelievers. The meeting which was held immediately after the Church came into existence was an apostolic meeting for unbelievers (Acts 2:14). The gatherings in the portico of Solomon (Acts 3:11) and in the house of Cornelius (Acts 10) were of the same nature, and there are still other records of similar meetings in the book of Acts. They were clearly apostolic meetings, not church meetings, because one man spoke and all the others listened. Paul's preaching at Troas was to the brethren (Acts 20). Whether it was in the church or not, it was still apostolic in nature, for it was one-sided, the apostle alone speaking to the whole assembly, and not the various members taking part for their mutual edification. Paul preached to the brethren at Troas because he was passing through that place, and any apostle passing through a place as he did would be free to respond to an invitation from the brethren to help them spiritually. Then when Paul was in Rome, the believers came to his rented room to hear him witness (Acts 28:23, 30-31). This work again is specifically apostolic in nature, because one man is active, while the others are passive.

The second kind of meeting is mentioned in the first Epistle to the Corinthians:

If therefore the whole church comes together in one place, and all speak in tongues, and some unlearned in tongues or unbelievers enter, will they not say that you are insane?....What then, brothers? Whenever you come together, each one has a psalm, has a teaching, has a revelation, has a tongue, has an interpretation. Let all things be done for building up. If anyone speaks in a tongue, it should be by two, or at the most three, and in turn, and one should interpret; but if there is no interpreter, he should be silent in the church, and speak to himself and to God. And as to prophets, two or three should speak, and the others discern. But if something is revealed to another sitting by, the first should be silent. For you can all prophesy one by one that all may learn and all may be encouraged. And the spirits of prophets are subject to prophets; for God is not a God of confusion but of peace. As in all the churches of the saints (4:23, 26-33).

This is obviously a church meeting, because it is not one man leading while all the others follow, but each gifted one contributing to the meeting as the Spirit directs. In the apostolic meetings there is a definite distinction between the preacher and his audience, but in this kind of meeting any gifted member of the church may be preacher and any may be audience. Nothing is determined by man, and each takes part as the Spirit leads. It is not an "all-man" ministry, but a Holy Spirit ministry. The prophets and teachers minister the Word as the Lord gives it, while others minister to the assembly in other ways. Not all can prophesy and teach, but all can seek to prophesy and teach (v. 1). An opportunity is given to each member of the church to help others, and an opportunity is given to each one to be helped. One brother may speak at one stage of the gathering and another later on; you may be chosen of the Spirit to help the brethren this time, and I next time. Everything in the meeting is governed throughout by the principle of "two or three" (vv. 27, 29). Even the same two or three prophets are not permanently appointed to minister to the meetings, but at each meeting the Spirit chooses any two or three from among all the prophets present. That such assemblies are assemblies of the church is seen at a glance, because the stamp of mutuality is clearly upon all the proceedings.

There is only one verse in the New Testament which speaks of the importance of Christians meeting together; it is Hebrews 10:25: "Not abandoning our own assembling together, as the custom with some is, but exhorting one another; and so much the more as you see the day drawing near." This verse shows that the object of such assembling is to exhort "one another." This is obviously not an apostolic meeting, for it is not a case of one man exhorting the entire assembly, but all the members bearing equal responsibility to exhort one another. A church meeting has the stamp of "one another" upon it.

There are several purposes for which the church meets, as recorded in Scripture. First, for prayer (Acts 2:42; 4:24, 31; 12:5); second, for reading (Col. 4:16; 1 Thes. 5:27; Acts 2:42; 15:21, 30-31); third, for the breaking of bread— which are not meetings presided over by a single individual who bears all responsibility, since reference is made to "the cup of blessing which we bless...the bread which we break" (1 Cor. 10:16-17; Acts 2:42; 20:7); and fourth, for the exercise of spiritual gifts (1 Cor. 14). The last type of meeting is a church meeting, for the phrase "in the church" is used repeatedly in the passage which describes it (vv. 28, 34-35). Of this meeting it is said that all may prophesy. How different from one man preaching and all the others sitting quietly in the pew listening to his sermon! That meeting has no place among the different gatherings of the church, for its nature makes it evident that it is an apostolic meeting, and being an apostolic meeting, it belongs to the sphere of the work, not of the church. Meetings where activity is one-sided do not come within the scope of the church, for they lack the distinctive feature of all church gatherings; and where any attempt is made to fit them into the church program, much trouble is sure to result.

Today, alas! this style of meeting is the chief feature of the churches. No meeting is attended with such regularity as this one. Who is considered a really good Christian? Is it not one who comes to church fifty-two Sunday mornings in the year to hear the minister preach? But this is passivity, and it heralds death. Even he who has attended "church" fifty-two Sundays in the year has not really been once to a church meeting. He has only gone to a meeting in connection with the work. I do not imply that we should never have this kind of meeting, but the point is that such a meeting is part of the work and is not part of the church. If you have a worker in the locality, then you may have this type of meeting, not otherwise. The local church, as a church, has no such meetings. Where they are found in connection with a church, we must discourage them and help believers to see that church meetings are conducted by the church. If apostolic meetings take the place of church meetings, then the church members become passive and indolent, always expecting to be helped, instead of seeking, in dependence upon the Spirit, to be helpful to the other members. It is contrary to the New Testament principles of mutual help and mutual edification. The reason the churches in China are still so weak, after a hundred years of Christian missions, is that God's servants have introduced into the local churches a type of meeting that really belongs to the work, and the church members have naturally concluded that if they attend such services and just passively receive all that is taught them there, they have performed the chief part of their Christian duty. Individual responsibility has been lost sight of, and passivity has hindered the development of spiritual life throughout the churches.

Further, to maintain the Sunday morning preaching, you must have a good preacher. Therefore, a worker is not only needed to manage church affairs, but also to maintain the meetings for spiritual uplift. It is only natural, if a good address is to be delivered every Sunday, that the churches hope for someone who is better qualified to preach than recently converted local brothers. How could they be expected to produce a good sermon once a week? And who could be expected to preach better than a specially called servant of God? So an apostle settles down to pastor the church, and consequently the churches and the work both lose their distinctive features.

The result is serious loss in both directions. On the one hand, the brethren become lazy and selfish because their thought is only centered on themselves and the help they can receive, and on the other hand, unevangelized territories are left without workers because apostles have settled down to be elders. For lack of activity the spiritual growth of the churches is arrested, and for lack of apostles the extension of the work is arrested too.

Since so much havoc has been wrought by introducing a feature of the work into the churches, and thus robbing both of their true nature, we must differentiate clearly between meetings that belong specifically to the work and those that belong specifically to the church. When God blesses our efforts in any place to the salvation of souls, we must see to it that the saved ones understand, from the outset, that the meetings which resulted in their salvation belong to the work and not to the church, and that they are the church and must therefore have their own church meetings. They must meet in their homes or in other places to pray, study the Word, break bread, and exercise their spiritual gifts; and in such meetings their object must be mutual helpfulness and mutual edification. Each individual must bear his share of responsibility and pass on to the others what he himself has received from the Lord. The conduct of the meetings should be the burden of no one individual, but all the members should bear the burden together, and they should seek to help one another depending upon the teaching and leading of the Spirit, and depending upon His empowering too. As soon as believers are saved, they should begin to assemble themselves regularly. Such gatherings of local believers are true church meetings.

Meetings connected with the work are only a temporary institution (unless the object is to maintain a special testimony in a special place). But the assembling of the believers for fellowship and mutual encouragement is something permanent. Even should the believers be very immature, and their meetings seem quite childish, they must learn to content themselves with what help they receive from one another and must not always hope to be able to sit down and listen to a good sermon. They should seek revelation, spiritual gifts, and utterance from God; and if their need casts them upon Him, it will result in the enrichment of the whole church. Meetings of recently saved believers will naturally bear the stamp of immaturity at the beginning, but for the worker to take over the responsibility of such meetings will stunt their growth, not foster it. It is the condition of the church meetings, not of the meetings connected with the work, that indicates the spiritual state of a church in any locality. When an apostle is preaching a grand sermon, and all the believers are nodding assent and adding their frequent and fervent "Amens," how deeply spiritual the congregation seems! But it is when they meet by themselves that their true spiritual state comes to light.

The apostolic meeting is not an intrinsic part of the church life; it is merely a piece of work, and it ceases with the departure of the worker. But the church meetings go on uninterrupted, whether the worker is present or absent. It is because the difference has not been realized between meetings for the church and for the work, that it has ever occurred to the brethren to cease to assemble themselves when the worker goes. One of the fruitful sources of spiritual failure today is that the children of God consider the church to be a part of the work; so when there is a sermon to hear, they constitute a willing audience, but if there is no preacher, the meetings automatically cease, and there is no thought of simply gathering together to help one another.

But how can the local believers be equipped to minister one to the other? In the apostolic days it was taken for granted that the Spirit would come upon all believers as soon as they turned to the Lord, and with the oncoming of the Spirit, spiritual gifts were imparted, through the exercise of which the churches were edified. The usual method which God has ordained for building up the churches is the ordinary church gatherings, not the meetings conducted by the workers. The reason the churches are so weak these days is that workers seek to build them up, through the meetings under their care, instead of leaving it to their own responsibility to edify each other through proper church meetings. Why has it come about that the church meetings of

156

1 Corinthians 14 are no longer a part of church life? Because so many of God's people lack the experience of the Spirit's oncoming, without which a meeting conducted along the lines of 1 Corinthians 14 is a mere empty form. Unless all those we lead to the Lord have a definite experience of the Holy Spirit coming upon them, it will be of little use instructing them how to conduct their church meetings, for such meetings will be powerless and ineffective. If the Holy Spirit is upon the believers, as in the days of the early Church, He will give gifts to men, and such men will be able to strengthen the saints and to build up the Body of Christ. We see from Paul's first Corinthian Epistle that God so equipped believers with spiritual gifts that they were able to carry on the work of building up the churches quite independently of the apostles. (This does not imply that they needed no further apostolic help. They decidedly did.) Alas! that nowadays many of God's people set more store by God's servants than by His Holy Spirit! They are content to be ministered to by the gifts of a worker, instead of seeking for themselves the gifts of the Spirit; so true church meetings have given place to meetings under the auspices of the workers.

In 1 Corinthians 14, where a church meeting is in view, apostles have been left out of account altogether! There is no place for them in the meetings of a local church! When the members of a church assemble and the spiritual gifts are in use, prophecy and other gifts are exercised, but there is no mention of apostles for the simple reason that apostles are appointed no place in the meetings of the local church; they are appointed to the work. When the local church meets, it is the gifts that are brought into use; office has no place here, not even that of an apostle. But this does not preclude a visiting apostle from speaking at all in a church meeting. This is illustrated by the fact that Paul took part in the Troas meeting. But the point to be noted is that Paul was only passing through Troas, so his speaking there was merely a temporary arrangement in order that the local saints might benefit by his spiritual gifts and knowledge of the Lord; it was not a permanent institution.

Apostles, as apostles, represent an office in the work, and not any particular gift; therefore, here they are ignored altogether. Not a mention is made of them in this local church gathering. In the organization of the church they have no place at all, because their ministry, as apostles, was not for the churches but for the work. As we have already observed, apostles had no say in the management of the business affairs of any church; but from the fact that no part is allotted them even in the local gatherings for mutual edification, it is clear that God did not even intend that they should bear the responsibility of the spiritual ministry in the churches. God gave gifts to the local brethren so that they could be prophets, evangelists, shepherds and teachers, and, thus equipped, could carry the burden of spiritual ministry in the locality. Apostles do not bear responsibility either for the spiritual or material side of affairs in any church; the elders are responsible for the local management, and the prophets and other ministers for the local ministry.

Then have apostles nothing to do with the local church? Surely! There is still plenty of scope for them to help the churches, but not in the capacity of apostles. On the business side of things they can help indirectly by giving counsel to the elders, who deal directly with the church affairs; and on the spiritual side in the church meetings they can minister with any spiritual gifts they may possess, such as prophecy or teaching. Their apostolic office is of no account in a church meeting for the exercise of spiritual gifts. As apostles they cannot exercise any apostolic gift, but as brothers they can minister to their fellow believers by the use of any gift with which the Spirit may have endowed them.

Not only apostles, but even elders as such, have no part in the meetings. In this chapter (1 Cor. 14), elders have no place at all. They are not even mentioned. We have already pointed out that elders are for office, not for ministry. They are appointed for church government, and not for ministry. Office is for government, and gifts are for ministry. In the meetings which are for ministry, it is those who have been gifted by God that count, not those who hold office; so in the church meetings it is the prophets, teachers, and evangelists who take the lead, not the elders. They are the gifted ones of the church.[2]

We must differentiate between the work of the elders, and the work of the prophets and teachers. Their work is different, but they are not necessarily different persons. It is quite possible for one person to act in both capacities. The elders are those who hold office in a local church; the prophets and teachers are the gifted ministers in a local church. The elders are for church government at all times; the prophets and teachers are for ministry in church meetings. Whenever there is a church, the Lord not only appoints elders for its government, but also gives gifts to some brothers to constitute them ministers for the meetings. But this does not mean that elders have nothing to do with the meetings. Whenever government in the meetings is necessary, they can exercise authority there. As to ministry, though they cannot minister as elders, yet, if they are also prophets or teachers, they can minister in that capacity. *It is almost imperative that elders be prophets and teachers; otherwise, they cannot rule the church effectively.*

The point to be remembered is that church meetings are the sphere for the ministry of the Word, not the sphere for the exercise of any office. It is for the exercise of gifts unto edification. Since both apostleship and eldership are offices, one in the work and one in the church, so both of the officers, as such, are altogether out of the meetings. But God will be gracious to His church to give it gifts for its upbuilding. The church meetings are the place for the use of these gifts for mutual help.

All meetings on the "round-table" principle are church meetings, and all meetings on the "pulpit-and-pew" principle are meetings belonging to the work. The latter may be of a passing nature, and not necessarily a permanent institution, whereas the former are a regular feature of church life. A round-table enables you to pass something to me and me to pass something to you. It affords opportunity for an expression of mutuality, that essential feature of all relationships in the church. In the local churches we must discourage all meetings on the "pulpit-and-pew" principle, so that, on the one hand, God's workers shall be free to travel far and wide proclaiming the glad tidings to sinners, and, on the other hand, the new converts shall be cast on the Lord for all needed equipment to serve one another. Thus the churches, having to bear their own responsibility, will develop their own spiritual life and gifts through exercise. It is all right to have an apostolic meeting when a worker visits the locality, but when he goes, meetings of the pulpit-type should be discontinued. Prophets, teachers, and evangelists in the local church may also take such meetings from time to time, but they should be regarded as exceptional, for they foster passivity and do not on the whole make for the spiritual development of the churches.

Let us consult the book of Acts in order to see the example God set for His Church in the beginning. "And they continued steadfastly in the teaching and the fellowship of the apostles, in the breaking of bread and the prayers....And day by day, continuing steadfastly with one accord in the temple and breaking bread from house to house, they partook of their food with exultation and simplicity of heart" (Acts 2:42, 46). Such were conditions in the early days of the Church's history. The apostles did not establish a central meeting place for the believers, but these "continued steadfastly in the teaching and fellowship of the apostles, in the breaking of bread and the prayers." They moved from house to house having fellowship one with another.

We can now draw our own conclusions from the three points we have considered. (1) Wherever there is a group of believers in any place, a few of the more mature are chosen from their number to care for the others, after which all local responsibility rests upon them. From the very outset it should be made clear to the new converts that it is by divine appointment that the management of the church is entrusted to local elders and not to any worker from another place.

(2) There is no official meeting place necessary for the church. The members meet in one or more houses, according as their numbers require, and should it be necessary to meet in several houses, it is well for the whole church to congregate from time to time in one place. For such meetings a special place could be obtained either for the occasion, or permanently, according to existing church conditions. (3) The church meetings are not the responsibility of the workers. Local believers should learn to use the spiritual gifts with which God has entrusted them to minister to their fellow believers. The principle on which all church meetings are conducted is that of the "roundtable," not of the "pulpit-and-pew." When any apostle visits a place, he could lead a series of meetings for the local church, but such meetings are exceptional. In the usual church gatherings the brethren should all make their special contributions in the power and under the leading of the Spirit. But to make such meetings of definite value it is essential that the believers receive spiritual gifts, revelation, and utterance; therefore, the workers should make it a matter of real concern that all their converts experience the power of the outpoured Spirit.

If the examples God has shown us in His Word are followed, then no question will ever arise in the churches regarding self-government, selfsupport, and selfpropagation. And the churches in the different localities will consequently be saved much unnecessary expenditure, which will enable them to come freely to the help of the poor believers, as the Corinthians did, or to the help of the workers, as did the Philippians. If the churches follow the lines God Himself has laid down for them, His work will go forward unhindered and His kingdom be extended on earth.

## THE MINISTRY, THE WORK, AND THE CHURCHES

In the earlier chapters of this book we have already seen what the ministry, the work, and the local churches are. In this chapter we have seen the connection between the ministry and the local church, and also the difference between the church and the work. Now we can consider more minutely the relationship between the ministry, the work, and the churches, in order to see clearly how they stand, how they function, what their respective spheres are, and how they are interrelated.

In Acts 13 we saw that God had established one of His churches in a certain locality; then He gave gifts to a few individuals in that church to equip them to minister there as prophets and teachers, so that the church might be built up. These prophets and teachers constituted the ministry in that church. When in life and in gift these ministers had reached a certain stage of spiritual maturity, God sent two of their number to work in other places; and history repeated itself in the churches established by these two apostles.

Do you not see here the relationship between the churches, the ministry, and the work? (1) God establishes a church in a locality. (2) He raises up gifted men in the church for the ministry. (3) He sends some of these specially equipped men out into the work. (4) These men establish churches in different places. (5) God raises up other gifted men among these churches for the ministry of building them up. (6) Some of these in turn are thrust forth to work in other fields. Thus, the work directly produces the churches, and the churches indirectly produce the work. So the churches and the work progress, moving in an ever-recurring cycle—the work always resulting directly in the founding of churches, and the churches always resulting indirectly in further work.

As to the gifted men raised up of God for the ministry, they labor both in the churches and in the work. When they are in their own locality, they seek to edify the church. When they are in other places, they bear the burden of the work. When they are in the local church, they are prophets and teachers. When they are sent to other places, they are apostles. The men are the same, at home or abroad, but their ministries differ according to the sphere of their service. The prophets and teachers (and shepherds and evangelists), whose sphere is local, plus the apostles, whose sphere is extralocal, constitute the ministry. As the former serve the churches, and the latter the work, the ministry is designed of God to meet the spiritual need in both spheres. Here again we see the relationship between the churches, the ministry, and the work. The work is produced by the churches, the churches are founded as a result of the work, and the ministry serves both the churches and the work.

In Ephesians 4 we see that the sphere of the ministry is the Body of Christ, which may be expressed locally as a church, or extra-locally as the work. It is for this reason also that apostles, prophets, evangelists, and teachers are linked together, though actually the sphere of an apostle's work is quite different from that of the other three. But all belong to the one ministry, whose sphere of service is the Body of Christ. These two groups of men are responsible for the work of the ministry, the one being gifted by the Spirit that they may be enabled to serve the local church, the other called from among these gifted ones to serve Him in different places and given an office in addition to their gifts. Those who have been gifted use their gifts to serve the Church by serving the church in their locality. Those who have both gifts and apostolic commission serve the Church by serving the churches in different localities.

God uses these men to impart His grace to the Church. Their various gifts enable them to transmit grace from the Head to the Body. Spiritual ministry is nothing less than ministering Christ to His people. God's thought in giving these men as a gift to His Church was that a Christ, personally known and experienced by them, might through the gifts of the Spirit, be ministered to His people. They were given to the Church "for the perfecting of the saints unto the work of the ministry, unto the building up of the Body of Christ."

Thus, in the ministry we have the prophets and other ministers using their gifts to serve the local church, while the apostles, by their office and gifts, serve all the churches. The ministry of these two groups of men is of great importance, because all the work of God—local and extra-local—is in their hands. That is why God's Word declares that the Church of God is built upon the foundation of the apostles and prophets.

And in the offices instituted by God, we have the elders occupying the chief place in the local church, while apostles hold no office at all there. Apostles, on the other hand, hold the chief office in the work, while the elders have no place there. Apostles rank foremost in the universal Church, and elders rank foremost in the local church. When we see the distinction between the respective offices of apostles and elders, then we shall understand why the two are constantly linked together (Acts 15:2, 4, 6, 2223). Apostles and elders are the highest representative of the Church and the churches. Apostles hold the highest office in the work, but in the local church they—as apostles— hold no office at all; elders, on the other hand, hold the chief office in the local church, but as elders they have no place in the work.

And in the local church, there are two departments of service, one relating to business management, the other to spiritual ministry. Offices are

162

connected with the management of the church and are held by the elders and the deacons. Gifts are connected with the ministry of the church and are exercised by the prophets and teachers (and evangelists). The elders and deacons are responsible for the management of the church, while the prophets and teachers concern themselves chiefly with the meetings of the church. Should the deacons and elders also be prophets and teachers, then they could manage church affairs and at the same time, minister to the church in the meetings. We must differentiate between the elders and the ministers. In everyday life, it is the elders who rule the church, but in the meetings for edification, the ministers are the ones ordained by God to serve the church. It should be repeated that elders, as such, are appointed for church government, and not for meetings to edify the church. In 1 Corinthians 14, where meetings are in view, elders do not come in at all. But elders, in order to be effective, should also have the gift of a prophet, teacher, shepherd, or evangelist. Yet it must be remembered that when they minister in the meetings they do so, not in the capacity of elders, but as prophets, or teachers, or other ministers. It is in the latter capacity that they have part in the ministry. First Timothy 5:17 makes it clear that the usual sphere of their service is to rule, but some of them (not necessarily all) may also teach and minister.

So the ministry, the work, and the churches are quite different in function and sphere, but they are really coordinated and interrelated. Ephesians 4 speaks of the Body of Christ, but no discrimination is made there between the churches, the work, and the ministry. The saints of the churches, the apostles of the work, and the different ministers of the ministry are all considered in the light of, and in relation to, the Body of Christ. Because whether it be the local church, the ministry, or the work, all are in the Church. They are really one; so while it is necessary to distinguish between them in order to understand them better, we cannot really separate them. Those who are in the different spheres of the Church need to see the reality of the Body of Christ and act relatedly as a body. They should not, because of difference of responsibilities, settle themselves into watertight compartments. "The church, which is His Body," includes the churches, the ministry, and the work. The churches are the Body expressed locally, the ministry is the Body in function, and the work is the Body seeking increase. All three are different manifestations of the one Body, so they are all interdependent and interrelated. None can move, or even exist, by itself. In fact, their relationship is so intimate and vital that none can be right itself without being rightly adjusted to the others. The church cannot go on without receiving the help of the ministry and without giving help to the work; the work cannot exist without the sympathy of the ministry and the backing of the church; and the ministry can only function when there is the church and the work.

This is most important. In the previous chapters we have sought to show their respective functions and spheres; now the danger is lest, failing to understand the spiritual nature of the things of God, we should not only try to distinguish between them, but sever them into separate units, thus losing the interrelatedness of the Body. However clear the distinction between them, we must remember that they are all in the Church. Consequently, they must move and act as one, for no matter what their specific functions and spheres, they are all in one Body.

So on the one hand, we differentiate between them in order to understand them, and on the other hand, we bear in mind that they are all related as a body. It is not that a few gifted men, recognizing their own ability, take it upon themselves to minister with the gifts they possess; nor that a few persons, conscious of call, form themselves into a working association; nor is it that a number of like-minded believers unite and call themselves a church. All must be on the ground of the Body. The church is the life of the Body in miniature; the ministry is the functioning of the Body in service; the work is the reaching out of the Body in growth. Neither church, ministry, nor work can exist as a thing by itself. Each has to derive its existence from, find its place in, and work for the good of the Body. All three are from the Body, in the Body, and for the Body. If this principle of relatedness to the Body and interrelatedness among its members is not recognized, there can be no church, no ministry, and no work. The importance of this principle cannot be over-emphasized, for without it everything is man-made, not God-created. The basic principle of the ministry is the Body. The basic principle of the work is the Body. The basic principle of the churches is the Body. The Body is the governing law of the life and work of the children of God today.

# THE NORMAL
# CHRISTIAN LIFE

# WATCHMAN NEE

# FOREWORD

Today society is messy because people's lives are messy. The problems we have as a society arise because we don't know what is normal or correct. We need to ask God again how to order our life. His word can teach us to live an orderly life and in this book Watchaman Nee shows us how through his word we can find order and that order can give us a life in harmony.

This book establishes a biblical foundation that every Christian needs to live.

The Normal Christian Life is a book by Watchman Nee first delivered as a series of addresses to Christian workers who were gathered in Denmark for special meetings in 1938 and 1939. The messages were first published chapter by chapter in the magazine A Witness and A Testimony published by Theodore Austin-Sparks. The first chapter was published in the November–December 1940 issue. This first publication of the book can be viewed in the original magazines on Austin-Sparks.Net. The messages were later compiled into a book by Angus Kinnear in 1957 in Bombay, India.

In The Normal Christian Life, Watchman Nee presents foundational principles for the Christian life and walk drawing primarily from the book of Romans. The book is generally regarded by many as the first introduction of Watchman Nee to the Western world. As of 2009, this book has sold over 1 million copies and is available in many editions and languages.

# CHAPTER 1: THE BLOOD OF CHRIST

What is the normal Christian life? We do well at the outset to ponder this question. The object of these studies is to show that it is something very different from the life of the average Christian. Indeed a consideration of the written Word of God -- of the Sermon on the Mount for example -- should lead us to ask whether such a life has ever in act been lived upon the earth, save only by the Son of God Himself. But in that last saving clause lies immediately the answer to our question.

The Apostle Paul gives us his own definition of the Christian life in Galations 2:20. It is "no longer I, but Christ". Here he is not stating something special or peculiar -- a high level of Christianity. He is, we believe, presenting God's normal for a Christian, which can be summarized in the words: I live no longer, but Christ lives His life in me.

God makes it quite clear in His Word that He has only one answer to every human need -- His Son, Jesus Christ. In all His dealings with us He works by taking us out of the way and substituting Christ in our place. The Son of God died instead of us for our forgiveness: He lives instead of us for our deliverance. So we can speak of two substitutions -- a Substitute on the Cross who secures our forgiveness and a Substitute within who secures our victory. It will help us greatly, and save us from much confusion, if we keep constantly before us this fact, that God will answer all our questions in one way only, namely, by showing us more of His Son.

## OUR DUAL PROBLEM: SINS AND SIN

We shall take now as a starting-point for our study of the normal Christian life that great exposition of it which we find in the first eight chapters of the Epistle to the Romans, and we shall approach our subject from a practical and experimental point of view. It will be helpful first of all to point out a natural division of this section of Romans into two, and to note certain striking differences in the subject-matter of its two parts.    The first eight chapters of Romans form a self-contained unit. The four-and-a-half chapters from 1:1 to 5:11 form the first half of this unit and the three-and-a-half chapters from 5:12 to 8:39 the second half. A careful reading will show us that the subject-matter of the two halves is not the same. For example, in the argument of the first section we find the plural word 'sins' given prominence. In the second section, however, this changed, for while the word 'sins' hardly occurs once, the singular word 'sin' is used again and again and is the subject mainly dealt with. Why is this?

It is because in the first section it is a question of the sins I have committed before God, which are many and can be enumerated, whereas in the second it is a question of sin as a principle working in me. No matter how many sins I commit, it is always the one sin principle that leads to them. I need forgiveness for my sins, but I need also deliverance from the power of sin. The former touches my conscience, the latter my life. I may receive forgiveness for all my sins, but because of my sin I have, even then, no abiding peace of mind.

When God's light first shines into my heart my one cry is for forgiveness, for I realize I have committed sins before Him; but when once I have received forgiveness of sins I make a new discovery, namely, the discovery of sin, and I realize not only that I have committed sins before God but that there is something wrong within. I discover that I have the nature of a sinner. There is an inward inclination to sin, a power within that draws to sin. When that power breaks out I commit sins. I may seek and receive forgiveness, but then I sin once more. So life goes on in a vicious circle of sinning and being forgiven and then sinning again. I appreciate the blessed fact of God's forgiveness, but I want something more than that: I want deliverance. I need forgiveness for what I have done, but I need also deliverance from what I am.

## GOD'S DUAL REMEDY: THE BLOOD AND THE CROSS

Thus in the first eight chapters of Romans two aspects of salvation are presented to us: firstly, the forgiveness of our sins, and secondly, our deliverance from sin. But now, in keeping with this fact, we must notice a further difference.

In the first part of Romans 1 to 8, we twice have reference to the Blood of the Lord Jesus, in chapter 3:25 and in chapter 5:9. In the second, a new idea is introduced in chapter 6:6, where we are said to have been "crucified" with Christ. The argument of the first part gathers round that aspect of the work of the Lord Jesus which is represented by 'the Blood' shed for our justification through "the remission of sins". This terminology is however not carried on into the second section, where the argument centers now in the aspect of His work represented by 'the Cross', that is to say, by our union with Christ in His death, burial and resurrection. This distinction is a valuable one. We shall see that the Blood deals with what we have done, whereas the Cross deals with what we are. The Blood disposes of our sins, while the Cross strikes at the root of our capacity for sin. The latter aspect will be the subject of our consideration in later chapters.

## THE PROBLEM OF OUR SINS

We begin, then, with the precious Blood of the Lord Jesus Christ and its value to us in dealing with our sins and justifying us in the sight of God. This is set forth for us in the following passages: "All have sinned" (Romans 3:23).

> *"God commendeth his own love toward us, in that, while we were yet sinners, Christ died for us. Much more then, being now justified by his blood, shall we be saved from the wrath of God through him" (Romans 5:8,9).*

> *"Being justified freely by his grace through the redemption that is in Christ Jesus: whom God set forth to be a propitiation, through faith, by his blood, to shew his righteousness, because of the passing over of the sins one aforetime, in the forbearance of God; for the shewing, I say, of his righteousness at this present season: that he might himself be just, and the justifier of him that hath faith in Jesus" (Romans 3:24-26).*

We shall have reason at a later stage in our study to look closely at the real nature of the fall and the way of recovery. At this point we will just remind ourselves that when sin came in it found expression in an act of disobedience to God (Romans 5:19). Now we must remember that whenever this occurs the thing that immediately follows is guilt.

Sin enters as disobedience, to create first of all a separation between God and man whereby man is put away from God. God can no longer have fellowship with him, for there is something now which hinders, and it is that which is known throughout Scripture as `sin'. Thus it is first of all God who says, "They are all under sin" (Romans 3:9). Then, secondly, that sin in man, which henceforth constitutes a barrier to his fellowship with God, gives rise in him to a sense of guilt -- of estrangement from God. Here it is man himself who, with the help of his awakened conscience, says, "I have sinned" (Luke 15:18). Nor is this all, for sin also provides Satan with his ground of accusation before God, while our sense of guilt gives him his ground of accusation in our hearts; so that, thirdly, it is `the accuser of the brethren' (Rev. 12:10) who now says, `You have sinned'.

To redeem us, therefore, and to bring us back to the purpose of God, the Lord Jesus had to do something about these three questions of sin and of guilt and of Satan's charge against us. Our sins had first to be dealt with, and this was effected by the precious Blood of Christ. Our guilt has to be dealt with and our guilty conscience set at rest by showing us the value of that Blood. And finally the attack of the enemy has to be met and his accusations answered. In the Scriptures the Blood of Christ is shown to operate effectually in these three ways, Godward, manward and Satanward. There is thus an absolute need for us to appropriate these values of the Blood if we are to go on. This is a first essential. We must have a basic knowledge of the fact of the death of the Lord Jesus as our Substitute upon the Cross, and a clear apprehension of the efficacy of His Blood for our sins, for without this we cannot be said to have started upon our road. Let us look then at these three matters more closely.

## THE BLOOD IS PRIMARILY FOR GOD

The Blood is for atonement and has to do first with our standing before God. We need forgiveness for the sins we have committed, lest we come under judgment; and they are forgiven, not because God overlooks what we have done but because He sees the Blood. The Blood is therefore not primarily for us but for God. If I want to understand the value of the Blood I must accept God's valuation of it, and if I do not know something of the value set upon the Blood by God I shall never know what its value is for me. It is only as the estimate that God puts upon the Blood of Christ is made known to me by His Holy Spirit that I come into the good of it myself and find how precious indeed the Blood is to me. But the first aspect of it is Godward. Throughout the Old and New Testaments the word `blood' is used in connection with the idea of atonement, I think over a hundred times, and throughout it is something for God.

In the Old Testament calendar there is one day that has a great bearing on the matter of our sins and that day is the Day of Atonement. Nothing explains this question of sins so clearly as the description of that day. In Leviticus 16 we find that on the Day of Atonement the blood was taken from the sin offering and brought into the Most Holy Place and there sprinkled before the Lord seven times. We must be very clear about this. On that day the sin offering was offered publicly in the court of the tabernacle. Everything was there in full view and could be seen by all. But the Lord commanded that no man should enter the tabernacle itself except the high priest. It was he alone who took the blood and, going into the Most Holy Place, sprinkled it there to make atonement before the Lord. Why? Because the high priest was a type of the Lord Jesus in His redemptive work (Hebrews 9:12,12), and so, in figure, he was the one who did the work. None but he could even draw near to enter in. Moreover, connected with his going in there was but one act, namely, the presenting of the blood to God as something He had accepted, something in which He could find satisfaction. It was a transaction between the high priest and God in the Sanctuary, away from the eyes of the men who were to benefit by it. The Lord required that.

The Blood is therefore in the first place for Him.

Earlier even than this there is described in Exodus 12:13 the shedding of the blood of the passover lamb in Egypt for Israel's redemption. This is again, I think, one of the best types in the Old Testament of our redemption. The blood was put on the lintel and on the door-posts, whereas the meat, the flesh of the lamb, was eaten inside the house; and God said: "When I see the blood, I will pass over you". Here we have another illustration of the fact that the blood was not meant to be presented to man but to God, for the blood was put on the lintel and on the door-posts, where those feasting inside the house would not see it.

## God Is Satisfied

It is God's holiness, God's righteousness, which demands that a sinless life should be given for man. There is life in the Blood, and that Blood has to be poured out for me, for my sins. God is the One who requires it to be so. God is the One who demands that the Blood be presented, in order to satisfy His own righteousness, and it is He who says: `When I see the blood',

I will pass over you.' The Blood of Christ wholly satisfies God.     Now I desire to say a word at this point to my younger brethren in the Lord, for it is here that we often get into difficulties. As unbelievers we may have been wholly untroubled by our conscience until the Word of God began to arouse us. Our conscience was dead, and those with dead consciences are certainly of no use to God. But later, when we believed, our awakened conscience may have become acutely sensitive, and this can constitute a real problem to us. The sense of sin and guilt can become so great, so terrible, as almost to cripple us by causing us to lose sight of the true effectiveness of the Blood. It seems to us that our sins are so real, and some particular sin may trouble us so many times, that we come to the point where to us our sins loom larger than the Blood of Christ.

Now the whole trouble with us is that we are trying to sense it; we are trying to feel its value and to estimate subjectively what the Blood is for us. We cannot do it; it does not work that way. The Blood is first for God to see. We then have to accept God's valuation of it. In doing so we shall find our valuation. If instead we try to come to a valuation by way of our feelings we get nothing; we remain in darkness. No, it is a matter of faith in God's Word. We have to believe that the Blood is precious to God because He says it is so (1 Peter 1:18,19). If God can accept the Blood as a payment for our sins and as the price of our redemption, then we can rest assured that the debt has been paid. If God is satisfied with the Blood, then the Blood must be acceptable. Our valuation of it is only according to His valuation -- neither more nor less. It cannot, of course, be more, but it must not be less. Let us remember that He is holy and He is righteous, and that a holy and righteous God has the right to say that the Blood is acceptable in His eyes and has fully satisfied Him.

## THE BLOOD AND THE BELIEVER'S ACCESS

The Blood has satisfied God; it must satisfy us also. It has therefore a second value that is manward in the cleansing of our conscience. When we come to the Epistle to the Hebrews we find that the Blood does this. We are to have "hearts sprinkled from an evil conscience" (Hebrews 10:22). This is most important. Look carefully at what it says. The writer does not tell us that the Blood of the Lord Jesus cleanses our hearts, an then stop there in his statement. We are wrong to connect the heart with the Blood in quite that way. It may show a misunderstanding of the sphere in which the Blood operates to pray, 'Lord, cleanse my heart from sin by Thy Blood'. The heart,

172

God says, is "desperately sick" (Jeremiah 17:9), and He must do something more fundamental than cleanse it: He must give us a new one.

We do not wash and iron clothing that we are going to throw away. As we shall shortly see, the `flesh' is too bad to be cleansed; it must be crucified. The work of God within us must be something wholly new. "A new heart also will I give you, and a new spirit will I put within you" (Ezekiel 36:26).

No, I do not find it stated that the Blood cleanses our hearts. Its work is not subjective in that way, but wholly objective, before God. True, the cleansing work of the Blood is seen here in Hebrew 10 to have reference to the heart, but it is in relation to the conscience. "Having our hearts sprinkled from a evil conscience". What then is the meaning of this?    It means that there was something intervening between myself and God, as a result of which I had an evil conscience whenever I sought to approach Him. It was constantly reminding me of the barrier that stood between myself and Him. But now, through the operation of the precious Blood, something new has been effected before God which has removed that barrier, and God has made that fact known to me in His Word. When that has been believed in and accepted, my conscience is at once cleared and my sense of guilt removed, and I have no more an evil conscience toward God.

Every one of us knows what a precious thing it is to have a conscience void of offense in our dealings with God. A heart of faith and a conscience clear of any and every accusation are both equally essential to us, since they are interdependent. As soon as we find our conscience is uneasy our faith leaks away and immediately we find we cannot face God. In order therefore to keep going on with God we must know the up-to-date value of the Blood. God keeps short accounts, and we are made nigh by the Blood every day, every hour and every minute. It never loses its efficacy as our ground of access if we will but lay hold upon it. When we enter the most Holy Place, on what ground dare we enter but by the Blood?

But I want to ask myself, am I really seeking the way into the Presence of God by the Blood or by something else? What do I mean when I say, `by the Blood'? I mean simply that I recognize my sins, that I confess that I have need of cleansing and of atonement, and that I come to God on the basis of the finished work of the Lord Jesus. I approach God through His merit alone, and never on the basis of my attainment; never, for example, on the ground that I have been extra kind or patient today, or that I have done something for the Lord this morning. I have to come by way of the Blood every time. The temptation to so many of us when we try to approach God is to think that because God has been dealing with us -- because He has been taking steps to bring us into something more of Himself and has been teaching us deeper lessons of the Cross -- He has thereby set before us new standards, and that only by attaining to these can we have a clear conscience before Him. No! A clear conscience is never based upon our attainment; it can only be based on the work of the Lord Jesus in the shedding of His Blood.

I may be mistaken, but I feel very strongly that some of us are thinking in terms such as these: `Today I have been a little more careful; today I have been doing a little better; this morning I have been reading the Word of God in a warmer way, so today I can pray better!' Or again, `Today I have had a little difficulty with the family; I began the day feeling very gloomy and moody; I am not feeling too bright now; it seems that there must be something wrong; therefore I cannot approach God.'  What, after all, is your basis of approach to God? Do you come to Him on the uncertain ground of your feeling, the feeling that you may have achieved something for God today? Or is your approach based on something far more secure, namely, the fact that the Blood has been shed, and that God looks on that Blood and is satisfied? Of course, were it conceivably possible for the Blood to suffer any change, the basis of your approach to God might be less trustworthy. But the Blood has never changed and never will. Your approach to God is therefore always in boldness; and that boldness is yours through the Blood and never through your personal attainment. Whatever be your measure of attainment today or yesterday or the day before, as soon as you make a conscious move into the Most Holy Place, immediately you have to take your stand upon the safe and only ground of the shed Blood. Whether you have had a good day or a bad day, whether you have consciously sinned or not, your basis of approach is always the same -- the Blood of Christ. That is the ground upon which you may enter, and there is no other.

As with many other stages of our Christian experience, this matter of access to God has two phases, an initial and a progressive one. The former is presented to us in Ephesians 2 and the latter in Hebrews 10. Initially, our standing with God was secured by the Blood, for we are "made nigh in the blood of Christ" (Eph. 2:13). But thereafter our ground of continual access is still by the Blood, for the apostle exhorts us: "Having therefore...boldness to enter into the holy place by the blood of

Jesus... let us draw near" (Heb. 10:19,22). To begin with I was made nigh by the Blood, and to continue in that new relationship I come through the Blood every time. It is not that I was saved on one basis and that I now maintain my fellowship on another. You say, 'That is very simple; it is the A.B.C. of the Gospel.' Yes, but the trouble with many of us is that we have moved away from the A.B.C. We have thought we had progressed and so could dispense with it, but we can never do so. No, my initial approach to God is by the Blood, and every time I come before Him it is the same. Right to the end it will always and only be on the ground of the Blood.

This does not mean at all that we should live a careless life, for we shall shortly study another aspect of the death of Christ which shows us that anything but that is contemplated. But for the present let us be satisfied with the Blood, that it is there and that it is enough.

We may be weak, but looking at our weakness will never make us strong. No trying to feel bad and doing penance will help us to be even a little holier. There is no help there, so let us be bold in our approach because of the Blood: 'Lord, I do not know fully what the value of the Blood is, but I know that the Blood has satisfied Thee; so the Blood is enough for me, and it is my only plea. I see now that whether I have really progressed, whether I have really attained to something or not, is not the point. Whenever I come before Thee, it is always on the ground of the precious Blood. Then our conscience is really clear before God. No conscience could ever be clear apart from the Blood. It is the Blood that gives us boldness.

> *"No more conscience of sins": these are tremendous words of Hebrews 10:2. We are cleansed from every sin; and we may truly echo the words of Paul: "Blessed is the man to whom the Lord will not reckon sin" (Romans 4:8).*

## OVERCOMING THE ACCUSER

In view of what we have said we can now turn to face the enemy, for there is a further aspect of the Blood which is Satanward. Satan's most strategic activity in this day is as the accuser of the brethren (Rev. 12:10) and it is as this that our Lord confronts him with His special ministry as High Priest "through his own blood" (Hebrews 9:12).    How then does the Blood operate against Satan? It does so by putting God on the side of man against him. The Fall brought something into man which gave Satan a footing within him, with the result that God was compelled to withdraw Himself. Man is now outside the garden -- beyond reach of the glory of God (Romans 3:23) -- because he is inwardly estranged from God. Because of what man has

175

done, there is something in him which, until it is removed, renders God morally unable to defend him. But the Blood removes that barrier and restores man to God and God to man. Man is in favour now, and because God is on his side he can face Satan without fear. You remember that verse in John's first Epistle -- and this is the translation of it I like best: "The blood of Jesus his Son cleanses us from every sin"[1] It is not exactly "all sin" in the general sense, but every sin, every item. What does it mean? Oh, it is a marvelous thing! God is the light, and as we walk in the light with Him everything is exposed and open to that light, so that God can see it all -- and yet the Blood is able to cleanse from every sin. What a cleansing! It is not that I have not a profound knowledge of myself, nor that God has not a perfect knowledge of me. It is not hat I try to hide something nor that God tries to overlook something. No, it is that He is in the light and I too am in the light, and that there the precious Blood cleanses me from every sin. The Blood is enough for that! Some of us, oppressed by our own weakness, may at times have been tempted to think that there are sins which are almost unforgivable. Let us remember the word: "The blood of Jesus Christ his Son cleanses us from every sin." Big sins, small sins, sins which may be very black and sins which appear to be not so black, sins which I think can be forgiven and sins which seem unforgivable, yes, all sins, conscious or unconscious, remembered or forgotten, are included in those words: "every sin". "The blood of Jesus his Son cleanses us from every sin", and it does so because in the first place it satisfies God.

Since God, seeing all our sins in the light, can forgive them on the basis of the Blood, what ground of accusation has Satan? Satan may accuse us before Him, but, "If God is for us, who is against us?" (Romans 8:31). God points him to the Blood of His dear Son. It is the sufficient answer against which Satan has no appeal. "Who shall lay anything to the charge of God's elect? It is God that justifieth; who is he that shall condemn? It is Christ Jesus that died, yea rather, that was raised from the dead, who is at the right hand of God, who also maketh intercession for us" (Romans 8:33,34).    So here again our need is to recognize the absolute sufficiency of the precious Blood. "Christ having come a high priest...through his own blood, entered in once for all into the holy place, having obtained eternal redemption" (Hebrews 9:11,12). He was Redeemer once. He has been High Priest and Advocate for nearly two thousand years. He stands there in the presence of God, and "he is the propitiation for our sins" (1 John 2:1,2). Note the words

---

[1] 1 John 1:7: Marginal reading of New Translation by J.N. Darby.

of Hebrews 9:14: "How much more shall the blood of Christ..." They underline the sufficiency of His ministry. It is enough for God. What then of our attitude to Satan? This is important, for he accuses us not only before God but in our own conscience also. `You have sinned, and you keep on sinning. You are weak, and God can have nothing more to do with you.' This is his argument. And our temptation is to look within and in self-defense to try to find in ourselves, in our feelings or our behavior, some ground for believing that Satan is wrong. Alternatively we are tempted to admit our helplessness and, going to the other extreme, to yield to depression and despair. Thus accusation becomes one of the greatest and most effective of Satan's weapons. He points to our sins and seeks to charge us with them before God, and if we accept his accusations we go down immediately.

Now the reason why we so readily accept his accusations is that we are still hoping to have some righteousness of our own.. The ground of our expectation is wrong. Satan has succeeded in making us look in the wrong direction. Thereby he wins his point, rendering us ineffective. But if we have learned to put no confidence in the flesh, we shall not wonder if we sin, for the very nature of the flesh is to sin. Do you understand what I mean? It is because we have not come to appreciate our true nature and to see how helpless we are that we still have some expectation in ourselves, with the result that, when Satan comes along and accuses us, we go down under it.

God is well able to deal with our sins; but He cannot deal with a man under accusation, because such a man is not trusting in the Blood. The Blood speaks in his favour, but his is listening instead to Satan. Christ is our Advocate but we, the accused, side with the accuser. We have not recognized that we are unworthy of anything but death; that, as we shall shortly see, we are only fit to be crucified anyway. We have not recognized that it is God alone that can answer the accuser, and that in the precious Blood He has already done so.

Our salvation lies in looking away to the Lord Jesus and in seeing that the Blood of the Lamb has met the whole situation created by our sins and has answered it. That is the sure foundation on which we stand. Never should we try to answer Satan with our good conduct but always with the Blood. Yes, we are sinful, but, praise God! the Blood cleanses us from every sin. God looks upon the Blood whereby His Son has met the charge, and Satan has no more ground of attack. Our faith in the precious Blood and our refusal to be moved from that position can alone silence his charges and put him to flight (Romans 8:33,34); and so it will be, right on to the end (Revelation

12:11). Oh, what an emancipation it would be if we saw more of the value of God's eyes of the precious Blood of His dear Son!

# CHAPTER 2: THE CROSS OF CHRIST

We have seen that Romans 1 to 8 falls into two sections, in the first of which we are shown that the Blood deals with what we have done, while in the second we shall see that the Cross[2] deals with what we are. We need the Blood for forgiveness; we need also the Cross for deliverance. We have dealt briefly above with the first of these two and we shall move on now to the second; but before we do so we will look for a moment at a few more features of this passage which serve to emphasize the difference in subject matter and argument between the two halves.

## SOME FURTHER DISTINCTIONS

Two aspects of the resurrection are mentioned in the two sections, in chapters 4 and 6. In Romans 4:25 the resurrection of the Lord Jesus is

---

[2] Note - The author uses 'the Cross' here and throughout these studies in a special sense. Most readers will be familiar with the current use of the expression 'the Cross' to signify, firstly, the entire redemptive work accomplished historically in the death, burial, resurrection and ascension of the Lord Jesus Himself (Phil. 2:8,9), and secondly, in a wider sense, the union of believers with Him therein through grace (Rom. 6:4; Eph. 2:5,6). Clearly in that use of the term the operation of 'the Blood' in relation to forgiveness of sins (as dealt with in Chapter 1 of this book) is, from God's viewpoint, included (with all that follows in these studies) as a part of the work of the Cross. In this and the following chapters, however, the author is compelled, for lack of an alternative term, to use 'the Cross' in a more particular and limited doctrinal sense in order to draw a helpful distinction, namely, that between substitution and identification, as being, from the human angle, two separate aspects of the doctrine of redemption. Thus the name of the whole is of necessity used for one of its parts. The reader should bear this in mind in what follows. -- Ed.

mentioned in relation to our justification: "Jesus our Lord...was delivered up for our trespasses, and was raised for our justification." Here the matter in view is that of our standing before God. But in Romans 6:4 the resurrection is spoken of as imparting to us new life with a view to a holy walk: "That like as Christ was raised from the dead...so we also might walk in newness of life." Here the matter before us is behaviour. Again, peace is spoken of in both sections, in the fifth and eighth chapters. Romans 5 tells of peace with God which is the effect of justification by faith in His Blood: "Being therefore justified by faith, we have peace with God through our Lord Jesus Christ." (5:1mg.) This means that, now that I have forgiveness of sins, God will no longer be a cause of dread and trouble to me. I who was an enemy to God have been "reconciled...through the death of his Son" (5:10). I very soon find, however, that I am going to be a great cause of trouble to myself. There is still unrest within, for within me there is something that draws me to sin. There is peace with God, but there is no peace with myself. There is in fact civil war in my own heart. This condition is well depicted in Romans 7 where the flesh and the spirit are seen to be in deadly conflict within me. But from this the argument leads in chapter 8 to the inward peace of a walk in the Spirit. "The mind of the flesh is death", because it "is enmity against God", "but the mind of the spirit is life and peace" (Romans 8:6,7). Looking further still we find that the first half of the section deals generally speaking with the question of justification (see, for example, Romans 3:24-26; 4:5,25), while the second half has as its main topic the corresponding question of sanctification (see Rom. 6:19,22). When we know the precious truth of justification by faith we still know only half of the story. We still have only solved the problem of our standing before God. As we go on, God has something more to offer us, namely, the solution of the problem of our conduct, and the development of thought in these chapters serves to emphasize this. In each case the second step follows from the first, and if we know only the first then we are still leading a sub-normal Christian life. How then can we live a normal Christian life? How do we enter in? Well, of course, initially we must have forgiveness of sins, we must have justification, we must have peace with God: these are our indispensable foundation. But with that basis truly established through our first act of faith in Christ, it is yet clear from the above that we must move on to something more.

So we see that objectively the Blood deals with our sins. The Lord Jesus has borne them on the Cross for us as our Substitute and has thereby obtained for us forgiveness, justification and reconciliation. But we must now go a step further in the plan of God to understand how He deals with the sin principle in us. The Blood can wash away my sins, but it cannot wash away my 'old man'. It needs the Cross to crucify me. The Blood deals with the sins, but the Cross must deal with the sinner.

You will scarcely find the word 'sinner' in the first four chapters of Romans. This is because there the sinner himself is not mainly in view, but rather the sins he has committed. The word 'sinner' first comes into prominence only in chapter 5, and it is important to notice how the sinner is there introduced. In that chapter a sinner is said to be a sinner because he is born a sinner; not because he has committed sins. The distinction is important. It is true that often when a Gospel worker wants to convince a man in the street that he is a sinner, he will use the favourite verse Romans 3:23, where it says that "all have sinned"; but this use of the verse is not strictly justified by the Scriptures. Those who so use it are in danger or arguing the wrong way round, for the teaching of Romans is not that we are sinners because we commit sins, but that we sin because we are sinners. We are sinners by constitution rather than by action. As Romans 5:19 expresses it: "Through the one man's disobedience the man were made (or 'constituted') sinners".

How were we constituted sinners? By Adam's disobedience. We do not become sinners by what we have done but because of what Adam has done and has become. I speak English, but I am not thereby constituted on Englishman. I am in fact a Chinese. So chapter 3 draws our attention to what we have done -- "all have sinned" -- but it is not because we have done it that we become sinners.

I once asked a class of children. 'Who is a sinner?' and their immediate reply was, 'One who sins'. Yes, one who sins is a sinner, but the fact that he sins is merely the evidence that he is already a sinner; it is not the cause. One who sins is a sinner, but it is equally true that one who does not sin, if he is of Adam's race, is a sinner too, and in need of redemption. Do you follow me? There are bad sinners and there are good sinners, there are moral sinners and there are corrupt sinners, but they are all alike sinners. We sometimes think that if only we had not done certain things all would be well; but the trouble lies far deeper than in what we do: it lies in what we are. A Chinese may be born America and be unable to speak Chinese at all, but he is a Chinese for all that, because he was born a Chinese. It is birth that counts. So I am a sinner not of my behaviour but of my heredity, my parentage. I am not a sinner because I sin, but I sin because I come of the wrong stock. I sin because I am a sinner.    We are apt to think that what we have done is very bad, but that we ourselves are not so bad. God is taking pains to show us that we ourselves are wrong, fundamentally wrong. The root trouble is the sinner; he must be dealt with. Our sins are dealt with by the Blood, but we ourselves are dealt with by the Cross. The Blood procures our pardon for what we have done; the Cross procures our deliverance from what we are.

## MAN'S STATE BY NATURE

We come therefore to Romans 5:12-21. In this great passage, grace is brought into contrast with sin and the obedience of Christ is set against the disobedience of Adam. It is placed at the beginning of the second section of Romans (5:12 to 8:39) with which we shall now be particularly concerned, and its argument leads to a conclusion which lies at the foundation of our further meditations. What is that conclusion? It is found in verse 19 already quoted: "For as through the one man's disobedience the many were made sinners, even so through the obedience of the one shall the many be made righteous." Here the Spirit of God is seeking to show us first what we are, and then how we came to be what we are.

At the beginning of our Christian life we are concerned with our doing, not with our being; we are distressed rather by what we have done than by what we are. We think that if only we could rectify certain things we should be good Christians, and we set out therefore to change our actions. But the result is not what we expected. We discover to our dismay that it is something more than just a case of trouble on the outside -- that there is in fact more serious trouble on the inside. We try to please the Lord, but find something within that does not want to please Him. We try to be humble, but there is something in our very being that refuses to be humble. We try to be loving, but inside we feel most unloving. We smile and try to look very gracious, but inwardly we feel decidedly ungracious. The more we try to rectify matters on the outside the more we realize how deep-seated the trouble is within. Then we come to the Lord and say, `Lord, I see it now!

Not only what I have done is wrong; I am wrong.'

The conclusion of Romans 5:19 is beginning to dawn upon us. We are sinners. We are members of a race of people who are constitutionally other than what God intended them to be. By the Fall a fundamental change took place in the character of Adam whereby he became a sinner, one constitutionally unable to please God; and the family likeness which we all share is no merely superficial one but extends to our inward character also. We have been "constituted sinners". How did this come about? "By the disobedience of one", says Paul. Let me try to illustrate this.

My name is Nee. It is a fairly common Chinese name. How did I come by it? I did not choose it. I did not go through the list of possible Chinese names and select this one. That my name is Nee is in fact not my doing at all, and, moreover, nothing I can do can alter it. I am a Nee because my father was a Nee, and my father was a Nee because my grandfather was a Nee.

If I act like a Nee I am a Nee, and if I act unlike a Nee I am still a Nee. If I become President of the Chinese Republic I am a Nee, or if I become a beggar in the street I am still a Nee. Nothing I do or refrain from doing will make me other than a Nee.

We are sinners not because of ourselves but because of Adam. It is not because I individually have sinned that I am a sinner but because I was in Adam when he sinned. Because by birth I come of Adam, therefore I am a part of him. What is more, I can do nothing to alter this. I cannot by improving my behaviour make myself other than a part of Adam and so a sinner.     In China I was once talking in this strain and remarked, `We have all sinned in Adam'. A man said, `I don't understand', so I sought to explain it in this way. `All Chinese trace their descent from Huang-ti', I said. `Over four thousand years ago he had a war with Si-iu. His enemy was very strong, but nevertheless Huang-ti overcame and slew him. After this Huang-ti founded the Chinese nation. Four thousand years ago therefore our nation was founded by Huang-ti. Now what would have happened if Huang-ti had not killed his enemy, but had been himself killed instead? Where would you be now?' `There would be no me at all', he answered. `Oh, no! Huang-ti can die his death and you can live your life.' `Impossible!' he cried, `If he had died, then I could never have lived, for I have derived my life from him.'

Do you see the oneness of human life? Our life comes from Adam. If your great-grandfather had died at the age of three, where would you be? You would have died in him! Your experience is bound up with his. Now in just the same way the experience of every one of us is bound up with that of Adam. None can say, `I have not been in Eden' for potentially we all were there when Adam yielded to the serpent's words. So we are all involved in Adam's sin, and by being born "in Adam" we receive from him all that he became as a result of his sin -- that is to say, the Adam-nature which is the nature of a sinner. We derive our existence from him, and because his life became a sinful life, a sinful nature, therefore the nature which we derive from him is also sinful. So, as we have said, the trouble is in our heredity, not in our behaviour. Unless we can change our parentage there is no deliverance for us.

But it is in this very direction that we shall find the solution of our problem, for that is exactly how God has dealt with the situation.

## AS IN ADAM SO IN CHRIST

In Romans 5:12 to 21 we are not only told something about Adam; we are told also something about the Lord Jesus. "As through the one man's disobedience the many were made sinners, even so through the obedience of the one shall the many be made righteous." In Adam we receive everything that is of Adam; in Christ we receive everything that is of Christ. The terms `in Adam' and `in Christ' are too little understood by Christians, and, at the risk of repetition, I wish again to emphasize by means of an illustration the hereditary and racial significance of the term `in Christ'. This illustration is to be found in the letter to the Hebrews. Do you remember that in the earlier part of the letter the writer is trying to show that Melchizedek is greater than Levi? You recall that the point to be proved is that the priesthood of Christ is greater than the priesthood of Aaron who was of the tribe of Levi. Now in order to prove that, he has first to prove that the priesthood of Melchizedek is greater than the priesthood of Levi, for the simple reason that the priesthood of Christ is "after the order of Melchizedek" (Heb. 7:14-17), while that of Aaron is, of course, after the order of Levi. If the writer can demonstrate to us that Melchizedek is greater than Levi, then he has made his point. That is the issue, and he proves it in a remarkable way.

He tells us in Hebrews chapter 7 that one day Abraham, returning from the battle of the kings (Genesis 14), offered a tithe of his spoils to Melchizedek and received from him a blessing. Inasmuch as Abraham did so, Levi is therefore of less account than Melchizedek. Why? Because the fact that Abraham offered tithes to Melchizedek. But if that is true, then Jacob also `in Abraham' offered to Melchizedek, which in turn means that Levi `in Abraham' offered to Melchizedek. It is evident that the lesser offers to the greater (Hebrews 7:7). So Levi is less in standing than Melchizedek, and therefore the priesthood of Aaron is inferior to that of the Lord Jesus. Levi at the time of the battle of the kings was not yet even thought of. Yet he was "in the loins of his father" Abraham, and, "so to say, through Abraham", he offered (Hebrews 7:9,10).

Now his is the exact meaning of 'in Christ'. Abraham, as the head of the family of faith, includes the whole family in himself. When he offered to Melchizedek, the whole family offered in him to Melchizedek. They did not offer separately as individuals, but they were in him, and therefore in making his offering he included with himself all his seed.    So we are presented with a new possibility. In Adam all was lost. Through the disobedience of one man we were all constituted sinners. By him sin entered and death through sin, and throughout the race sin has reigned unto death from that day on. But now a ray of light is cast upon the scene. Through the obedience of Another we may be constituted righteous. Where sin abounded grace did much more abound, and as sin reigned unto death, even so may grace reign through righteousness unto eternal life by Jesus Christ our Lord (Romans 5:19-21). Our despair is in Adam; our hope is in Christ.

## THE DIVINE WAY OF DELIVERANCE

God clearly intends that this consideration should lead to our practical deliverance from sin. Paul makes this quite plain when he opens chapter 6 of his letter with the question: "Shall we continue in sin?" His whole being recoils at the very suggestion. "God forbid!", he exclaims. How could a holy God be satisfied to have unholy, sin-fettered children? And so "how shall we any longer live therein?" (Romans 6:1,2). God has surely therefore made adequate provision that we should be set free from sin's dominion.

But here is our problem. We were born sinners; how then can we cut off our sinful heredity? Seeing that we were born in Adam, how can we get out of Adam? Let me say at once, the Blood cannot take us out of Adam. There is only one way. Since we came in by birth we must go out by death. To do away with our sinfulness we must do away with our life. Bondage to sin came by birth; deliverance from sin comes by death -- and it is just this way of escape that God has provided. Death is the secret of emancipation.

"We...died to sin" (Romans 6:2).

But how can we die? Some of us have tried very hard to get rid of this sinful life, but we have found it most tenacious. What is the way out? It is not by trying to kill ourselves, but by recognizing that God has dealt with us in Christ. This is summed up in the apostle's next statement: "All we who were baptized into Christ Jesus were baptized into his death" (Romans 6:3). But if God has dealt with us 'in Christ Jesus' then we have got to be in Him for this to become effective, and that now seems just as big a problem. How are we to 'get into' Christ? Here again God comes to our help. We have in fact no way of getting in, but, what is more important, we need not try to get in, for we are in. What we could not do for ourselves God has done for us. He has put us into Christ. Let me remind you of I Corinthians 1:30. I think that is one of the best verses of the whole New Testament: 'Ye are in Christ'. How? "Of him (that is, 'of God') are ye in Christ." Praise God! it is not left to us either to devise a way of entry or to work it out. We need not plan how to get in. God has planned it; and He has not only planned it but He has also performed it. 'Of him are ye in Christ Jesus'. We are in; therefore we need not try to get in. It is a Divine act, and it is accomplished.

Now if this is true, certain things follow. In the illustration from Hebrews 7 which we considered above we saw that 'in Abraham' all Israel -and therefore Levi who was not yet born -- offered tithes to Melchizedek. They did not offer separately and individually, but they were in Abraham when he offered, and his offering included all his seed. This, then, is a true figure of ourselves as 'in Christ'. When the Lord Jesus was on the Cross all of us died -- not individually, for we had not yet been born -but, being in Him, we died in Him. "One died for all, therefore all died" (2 Cor. 5:14). When He was crucified all of us were crucified.

Many a time when preaching in the villages of China one has to use very simple illustrations for deep Divine truth. I remember once I took up a small book and put a piece of paper into it, and I said to those very simple ones, 'Now look carefully. I take a piece of paper. It has an identity of its own, quite separate from this book. Having no special purpose for it at the moment I put it into the book. Now I do something with the book. I post it to Shanghai. I do not post the paper, but the paper has been put into the book. Then where is the paper? Can the book go to Shanghai and the paper remain here? Can the paper have a separate destiny from the book? No! Where the book goes the paper goes. If I drop the book in the river the paper goes too, and if I quickly take it out again I recover the paper also. Whatever experience the book goes through the paper goes through with it, for it is in the book.'

"Of him are ye in Christ Jesus." The Lord God Himself has put us in Christ, and in His dealing with Christ God has dealt with the whole race. Our destiny is bound up with His. What He has gone through we have gone through, for to be 'in Christ' is to have been identified with Him in both His death and resurrection. He was crucified: then what about us? Must we ask God to crucify us? Never! When Christ was crucified we were crucified; and His crucifixion is past, therefore ours cannot be future. I challenge you to find one text in the New Testament telling us that our crucifixion is in the future. All the references to it are in the Greek aorist, which is the 'once-for-all' tense, the 'eternally past' tense. (See: Romans 6:6; Galations 2:20; 5:24; 6:14). And just as no man could ever commit suicide by crucifixion, for it were a physical impossibility to do so, so also, in spiritual terms, God does not require us to crucify ourselves. We were crucified when He was crucified, for God put us there in Him. That we have died in Christ is not merely a doctrinal position, it is an eternal fact.

## HIS DEATH AND RESURRECTION REPRESENTATIVE AND INCLUSIVE

The Lord Jesus, when He died on the Cross, shed His Blood, thus giving His sinless life to atone for our sin and to satisfy the righteousness and holiness of God. To do so was the prerogative of the Son of God alone. No man could have a share in that. The Scripture has never told us that we shed our blood with Christ. In His atoning work before God He acted alone; no other could have a part. But the Lord did not die only to shed His Blood: He died that we might die. He died as our Representative. In His death He included you and me.

We often use the terms 'substitution' and 'identification' to describe these two aspects of the death of Christ. Now many a time the use of the word 'identification' is good. But identification would suggest that the thing begins from our side: that I try to identify myself with the Lord. I agree that the word is true, but it should be used later on. It is better to begin with the fact that the Lord included me in His death. It is the 'inclusive' death of the Lord which puts me in a position to identify myself, not that I identify myself in order to be included. It is God's inclusion of me in Christ that matters. It is something God has done. For that reason those two New Testament words "in Christ" are always very dear to my heart.

The death of the Lord Jesus is inclusive. The resurrection of the Lord Jesus is alike inclusive. We have looked at the first chapter of I Corinthians to establish the fact that we are "in Christ Jesus". Now we will go to the end of the same letter to see something more of what this means. In I Corinthians

15:45,47 two remarkable names or titles are used of the Lord Jesus. He is spoken of there as "the last Adam" and He is spoken of too as "the second man". Scripture does not refer to Him as the second Adam but as "the last Adam"; nor does it refer to Him as the last Man, but as "the second man". The distinction is to be noted, for it enshrines a truth of great value.

As the last Adam, Christ is the sum total of humanity; as the second Man He is the Head of a new race. So we have here two unions, the one relating to His death and the other to His resurrection. In the first place His union with the race as "the last Adam" began historically at Bethlehem and ended at the cross and the tomb. In it He gathered up into Himself all that was in Adam and took it to judgment and death. In the second place our union with Him as "the second man" begins in resurrection and ends in eternity -- which is to say, it never ends -- for, having in His death done away with the first man in whom God's purpose was frustrated, He rose again as Head of a new race of men, in whom that purpose shall be fully realized.   When therefore the Lord Jesus was crucified on the cross, He was crucified as the last Adam. All that was in the first Adam was gathered up and done away in Him. We were included there. As the last Adam He wiped out the old race; as the second Man He brings in the new race. It is in His resurrection that He stands forth as the second Man, and there too we are included. "For if we have become united with him by the likeness of his death, we shall be also by the likeness of his resurrection" (Romans 6:5). We died in Him as the last Adam; we live in Him as the second Man. The Cross is thus the power of God which translates us from Adam to Christ.

# CHAPTER 3: THE PATH OF PROGRESS: KNOWING

Our old history ends with the Cross; our new history begins with the resurrection. "If any man is in Christ, he is a new creature: the old things are passed away; behold they are become new" (2 Cor 5:17). The Cross terminates the first creation, and out of death there is brought a new creation in Christ, the second Man. If we are 'in Adam' all that is in Adam necessarily devolves upon us; it becomes ours involuntarily, for we have to do nothing to get it. There is no need to make up our minds to lose our temper or to commit some other sin; it comes to us freely and despite ourselves. In a similar way, if we are 'in Christ' all that is in Christ comes to us by free grace, without effort on our part but on the ground of simple faith.

But to say that all we need comes to us in Christ by free grace, though true enough, may seem unpractical. How does it work out in practice? How does it become real in our experience?

As we study chapters 6, 7 and 8 of Romans we shall discover that the conditions of living the normal Christian life are fourfold. They are: (a) Knowing, (b) Reckoning, (c) Presenting ourselves to God, and (d) Walking in the Spirit, and they are set forth in that order. If we would live that life we shall have to take all four of these steps; not one nor two nor three, but all four. As we study each of them we shall trust the Lord by His Holy Spirit to illumine our understanding; and we shall seek His help now to take the first big step forward.

## OUR DEATH WITH CHRIST A HISTORIC FACT

Romans 6:1-11 is the passage before us now. In these verses it is made clear that the death of the Lord Jesus is representative and inclusive. In His death we all died. None of us can progress spiritually without seeing this. Just as we cannot have justification if we have not seen Him bearing our sins

189

on the Cross, so we cannot have sanctification if we have not seen Him bearing us on the Cross. Not only have our sins been laid on Him but we ourselves have been put into Him.

How did you receive forgiveness? You realized that the Lord Jesus died as your Substitute and bore your sins upon Himself, and that His Blood was shed to cleanse away your defilement. When you saw your sins all taken away on the Cross what did you do? Did you say, `Lord Jesus, please come and die for my sins'? No, you did not pray at all; you only thanked the Lord You did not beseech Him to come and die for you, for you realized that He had already done it.

But what is true of your forgiveness is also true of your deliverance. The work is done. There is no need to pray but only to praise. God has put us all in Christ, so that when Christ was crucified we were crucified also. Thus there is no need to pray: `I am a very wicked person; Lord, please crucify me'. That is all wrong. You did not pray about your sins; why pray now about yourself? Your sins were dealt with by His Blood, and you were dealt with by His Cross. It is an accomplished fact. All that is left for you to do is to praise the Lord that when Christ died you died also; you died in Him. Praise Him for it and live in the light of it. "Then believed they his words: they sang his praise" (Psalm 106:12).

Do you believe in the death of Christ? Of course you do. Well, the same Scripture that says He died for us says also that we died with Him. Look at it again: "Christ died for us" (Romans 5:8). That is the first statement, and that is clear enough; but is this any less clear? "Our old man was crucified with him" (Romans 6:6). "We died with Christ" (Romans 6:8). When are we crucified with Him? What is the date of our old man's crucifixion? Is it tomorrow? Yesterday? Today? In order to answer this it may help us if for a moment I turn Paul's statement round and say, `Christ was crucified with (i.e. at the same time as) our old man'. Some of you came here in twos. You traveled to this place together. You might say, My friend came here with me', but you might just as truly say, `I came here with my friend'. Had one of you come three days ago and the other only today you could not possibly say that; but having come together you can make either statement with equal truth, because both are statements of fact. So also in historic fact we can say, reverently but with equal accuracy, `I was crucified when Christ was crucified' or `Christ was crucified when I was crucified', for they are not two historical events, but one. My crucifixion was "with him".[3] Has Christ been crucified? Then can I be otherwise? And if He was crucified nearly two thousand years ago, and I with Him, can my crucifixion be said to take place tomorrow? Can His be past and mine be present or future? Praise the Lord, when He died in my stead, but He bore me with Him to the Cross, so that when He died I died. And if I believe in the death of the Lord Jesus, then I can believe in my own death just as surely as I believe in His.

Why do you believe that the Lord Jesus died? What is your ground for that belief? Is it that you feel He has died? No, you have never felt it. You believe it because the Word of God tells you so. When the Lord was crucified, two thieves were crucified at the same time. You do not doubt that they were crucified with Him, either, because the Scripture says so quite plainly.

You believe in the death of the Lord Jesus and you believe in the death of the thieves with Him. Now what about your own death? Your crucifixion is more intimate than theirs. They were crucified at the same time as the Lord but on different crosses, whereas you were crucified on the self same cross as He, for you were in Him when He died. How can you know? You can know for the one sufficient reason that God has said so. It does not depend on your feelings. If you feel that Christ has died, He has died; and if you do not feel that he died, He has died. If you feel that you have died, you have died; and if you do not feel that you have died, you have nevertheless just as surely died. These are Divine facts. That Christ has died is a fact, that the two thieves have died is a fact, and that you have died is a fact also.

Let me tell you, You have died! You are done with! You are ruled out! The self you loathe is on the Cross in Christ. And "he that is dead is freed from sin" (Romans 6:7, A.V.). This is the Gospel for Christians. Our crucifixion can never be made effective by will or by effort, but only be accepting what the Lord Jesus did on the Cross. Our eyes must be opened to see the finished work of Calvary. Some of you, prior to your salvation, may have tried to save yourselves. You read the Bible, prayed, went to Church, gave alms. Then one day your eyes were opened and you saw that a full salvation had already been provided for you on the Cross. You just accepted that and thanked God, and peace

---

[3] The expression "with him" in Romans 6:6 carries of course a doctrinal as well as historical, or temporal sense. It is only in the historical sense that the statement is reversible. W.N.

and joy flowed into your heart. Now salvation and sanctification are on exactly the same basis. You receive deliverance from sin in the same way as you receive forgiveness of sins.

For God's way of deliverance is altogether different from man's way. Man's way is to try to suppress sin by seeking to overcome it; God's way is to remove the sinner. Many Christians mourn over their weakness, thinking that if only they were stronger all would be well. The idea that, because failure to lead a holy life is due to our impotence, something more is therefore demanded of us, leads naturally to this false conception of the way of deliverance. If we are preoccupied with the power of sin and with our inability to meet it, then we naturally conclude that to gain the victory over sin we must have more power. 'If only I were stronger', we say, 'I could overcome my violent outbursts of temper', and so we plead with the Lord to strengthen us that we may exercise more self-control.    But this is altogether wrong; this is not Christianity. God's means of delivering us from sin is not by making us stronger and stronger, but by making us weaker and weaker. That is surely rather a peculiar way of victory, you say; but it is the Divine way. God sets us free from the dominion of sin, not by strengthening our old man but by crucifying him; not by helping him to do anything but by removing him from the scene of action. For years, maybe, you have tried fruitlessly to exercise control over yourself, and perhaps this is still your experience; but when once you see the truth you will recognize that you are indeed powerless to do anything, but that in setting you aside altogether God has done it all. Such a revelation brings human self-effort to an end.

## THE FIRST STEP: "KNOWING THIS..."

The normal Christian life must begin with a very definite 'knowing', which is not just knowing something about the truth nor understanding some important doctrine. It is not intellectual knowledge at all, but an opening of the eyes of the heart to see what we have in Christ.

How do you know your sins are forgiven? Is it because your pastor told you so? No, you just know it. If I ask you how you know, you simply answer, 'I know it!' Such knowledge comes by Divine revelation. It comes from the Lord Himself. Of course the fact of forgiveness of sins is in the Bible, but for the written Word of God to become a living Word from God to you He had to give you "a spirit of wisdom and revelation in the knowledge of him" (Eph. 1:17). What you needed was to know Christ in that way, and it is always so. So there comes a time, in regard to any new apprehension of Christ, when you know it in your own heart, you `see' it in your spirit. A light has shined into your inner being and you are wholly persuaded of the fact. What is true of the forgiveness of your sins is no less true of your deliverance from sin. When once the light of God dawns upon your heart you see yourself in Christ. It is not now because someone has told you, and not merely because Romans 6 says so. It is something more even than that. You know it because God has revealed it to you by His Spirit. You may not feel it; you may not understand it; but you know it, for you have seen it. Once you have seen yourself in Christ, nothing can shake your assurance of that blessed fact.

If you ask a number of believers who have entered upon the normal Christian life how they came by their experience, some will say in this way and some will say in that. Each stresses his own particular way of entering in and produces Scripture to support his experience; and unhappily many Christians are using their special experiences and their special scriptures to fight other Christians. The fact of the matter is that, while Christians may enter into the deeper life by different ways, we need not regard the experiences or doctrines they stress as mutually exclusive, but rather complementary. One thing is certain, that any true experience of value in the sight of God must have been reached by way of a new discovery of the meaning of the Person and work of the Lord Jesus. That is a crucial test and a safe one.

And here in our passage Paul makes everything depend upon such a discovery. "Knowing this, that our old man was crucified with him, that the body of sin might be done away, that so we should no longer be in bondage to sin" (Romans 6:6).

## DIVINE REVELATION ESSENTIAL TO KNOWLEDGE

So our first step is to seek from God a knowledge that comes by revelation -- a revelation, that is to say, not of ourselves but of the finished work of the Lord Jesus Christ on the Cross. When Hudson Taylor, the founder of the China Inland Mission, entered into the normal Christian life it was thus that he did so. You remember how he tells of his long-standing problem of how to live `in Christ', how to draw the sap out of the Vine into himself. For he knew that he must have the life of Christ flowing out through him and yet felt that he had not got it, and he saw clearly enough that his need was to be found in Christ. 'I knew', he said, writing to his sister from Chinkiang in 1869, 'that if only I could abide in Christ, all would be well, but I could not.'

The more he tried to get in the more he found himself slipping out, so to speak, until one day light dawned, revelation came and he saw. 'Here, I feel, is the secret: not asking how I am to get sap out of the Vine into myself, but remembering that Jesus is the Vine -- the root, stem, branches, twigs, leaves, flowers, fruit, all indeed.' Then, in words of a friend that had helped him:

'I have not got to make myself a branch. The Lord Jesus tells me I am a branch. I am part of Him and I have just to believe it and act upon it. I have seen it long enough in the Bible, but I believe it now as a living reality.'

It was as though something which had indeed been true all the time had now suddenly become true in a new way to him personally, and he writes to his sister again:

'I do not know how far I may be able to make myself intelligible about it, for there is nothing new or strange or wonderful -- and yet, all is new! In a word, "whereas once I was blind, now I see"....I am dead and buried with Christ -- aye, and risen too and ascended....God reckons me so, and tells me to reckon myself so. He knows best....Oh, the joy of seeing this truth – I do pray that the eyes of your understanding may be enlightened, that you may know and enjoy the riches freely given us in Christ.'[4] Oh, it is a great thing to see that we are in Christ! Think of the bewilderment of trying to get into a room in which you already are! Think of the absurdity of asking to be put in! If we recognize the fact that we are in, we make no effort to enter. If we had more revelation we should have fewer prayers and more praises. Much of our praying for ourselves is just because we are blind to what God has done.

I remember one day in Shanghai I was talking with a brother who was very exercised concerning his spiritual state. He said, 'So many are living beautiful, saintly lives. I am ashamed of myself. I call myself a Christian and yet when I compare myself with others I feel I am not one at all. I want to know this crucified life, this resurrection life, but I do not know it and see no way of getting there.' Another brother was with us, and the two of us had been talking for two hours or so, trying to get the man to see that he could

---

[4] The quotations are from Hudson Taylor and the China Inland Mission by Dr. and Mrs. Howard Taylor, Chapter 12, 'The Exchanged Life'. The whole passage should be read. -- Ed.

not have anything apart from Christ, but without success. Said our friend, 'the best thing a man can do is to pray.' 'But if God has already given you everything, what do you need to pray for?' we asked. 'He hasn't', the man replied, 'for I am still losing my temper, still failing constantly; so I must pray more.' 'Well', we said, 'do you get what you pray for?' 'I am sorry to say that I do not get anything', he replied. We tried to point out that, just as he had done nothing for his justification, so he need do nothing for his sanctification.

Just then a third brother, much used of the Lord, came in and joined us. There was a thermos flask on the table, and this brother picked it up and said, 'What is this?' 'A thermos flask.' 'Well, you just imagine for a moment that this thermos flask can pray, and that it starts praying something like this: "Lord, I want very much to be a thermos flask. Wilt Thou make me to be a thermos flask? Lord, give me grace to become a thermos flask. Do please make me one!" What will you say?' 'I do not think even a thermos flask would be so silly,' our friend replied. 'It would be nonsense to pray like that; it is a thermos flask!' Then my brother said, 'You are doing the same thing. God in times past has already included you in Christ. When He died, you died; when He lived, you lived. Now today you cannot say, "I want to die; I want to be crucified; I want to have resurrection life."

The Lord simply looks at you and says, "You are dead! You have new life!" All your praying is just as absurd as that of the thermos flask. You do not need to pray to the Lord for anything; you merely need your eyes opened to see that He has done it all.'

That is the point. We need not work to die, we need not wait to die, we are dead. We only need to recognize what the Lord has already done and to praise Him for it. Light dawned for that man. With tears in his eyes he said, 'Lord, I praise Thee that Thou hast already included me in Christ. All that is His is mine!' Revelation had come and faith had something to lay hold of; and if you could have met that brother later on, what a change you would have found!

## THE CROSS GOES TO THE ROOT OF OUR PROBLEM

Let me remind you again of the fundamental nature of that which the Lord has done on the Cross. I feel I cannot press this point too much for we must see it. Suppose, for the sake of illustration, that the government of your country should wish to deal drastically with the question of strong drink and should decide that the whole country was to go `dry', how could the decision be carried into effect? How could we help? If we were to search every shop and house throughout the land and smash all the bottles of wine or beer or brandy we came across, would that meet the case? Surely not. We might thereby rid the land of every drop of alcoholic liquor it contains, but behind those bottles of strong drink are the factories that produce them, and if we only deal with the bottles and leave the factories untouched, production will still continue and there is no permanent solution of the problem. The drink-producing factories, the breweries and distilleries throughout the land, must be closed down if the drink question is to be permanently settled.

We are the factory; our actions are the products. The Blood of the Lord Jesus dealt with the question of the products, namely, our sins. So the question of what we have done is settled, but would God have stopped there? What about the question of what we are? Our sins were produced by us. They have been dealt with, but how are we going to be dealt with? Do you believe the Lord would cleanse away all our sins and then leave us to get rid of the sin-producing factory? Do you believe He would put away the goods produced but leave us to deal with the source of production?

To ask this question is but to answer it. Of course He has not done half the work and left the other half undone. No, He has done away with the goods and also made a clean sweep of the factory that produces the goods. The finished work of Christ really has gone to the root of our problem and dealt with it. There are no half measures with God. "Knowing this," says Paul, "That our old man was crucified with him, that the body of sin might be done away, that so we should no longer be in bondage to sin" (Rom. 6:6).

"Knowing this"! Yes, but do you know it? "Or are ye ignorant?" (Rom. 6:3).

May the Lord graciously open our eyes.

# CHAPTER 4: THE PATH OF PROGRESS: RECKONING

We now come to a matter on which there has been some confusion of thought among the Lord's children. It concerns what follows this knowledge. Note again first of all the wording of Romans 6:6: "Knowing this, that our old man was crucified with Him". The tense of the verb is most precious for it puts the event right back there in the past. It is final, once-for-all.

The thing has been done and cannot be undone. Our old man has been crucified once and for ever, and he can never be un-crucified. This is what we need to know.

Then, when we know this, what follows? Look again at our passage. The next command is in verse 11: "Even so reckon ye also yourselves to be dead unto sin". This, clearly, is the natural sequel to verse 6. Read them together: 'Knowing that our old man was crucified, ... reckon ye yourselves to be dead'. That is the order. When we know that our old man has been crucified with Christ, then the next step is to reckon it so.

Unfortunately, in presenting the truth of our union with Christ the emphasis has too often been placed upon this second matter of reckoning ourselves to be dead, as though that were the starting point, whereas it should rather be upon knowing ourselves to be dead. God's Word makes it clear that 'knowing' is to precede 'reckoning'. "Knowing this ... reckon." The sequence is most important. Our reckoning must be based on knowledge of divinely revealed fact, for otherwise faith has no foundation on which to rest. When we know, then we reckon spontaneously.

So in teaching this matter we should not over-emphasize reckoning.

People are always trying to reckon without knowing. They have not first had a Spirit-given revelation of the fact; yet they try to reckon and soon they get into all sorts of difficulties. When temptation comes they begin to reckon furiously: 'I am dead; I am dead; I am dead!' but in the very act of reckoning

197

they lose their temper. Then they say, `It doesn't work. Romans 6:11 is no good.' And we have to admit that verse 11 is no good without verse 6. So it comes to this, that unless we know for a fact that we are dead with Christ, the more we reckon the more intense will the struggle become, and the issue will be sure defeat.

For years after my conversion I had been taught to reckon. I reckoned from 1920 until 1927. The more I reckoned that I was dead to sin, the more alive I clearly was. I simply could not believe myself dead and I could not produce the death. Whenever I sought help from others I was told to read Romans 6:11, and the more I read Romans 6:11 and tried to reckon, the further away death was: I could not get at it. I fully appreciated the teaching that I must reckon, but I could not make out why nothing resulted from it. I have to confess that for months I was troubled. I said to the Lord, `If this is not clear, if I cannot be brought to see this which is so very fundamental, I will cease to do anything. I will not preach any more; I will not go out to serve Thee any more; I want first of all to get thoroughly clear here.' For months I was seeking, and at times I fasted, but nothing came through.

I remember one morning -- that morning was a real morning and one I can never forget -- I was upstairs sitting at my desk reading the Word and praying, and I said, `Lord, open my eyes!' And then in a flash I saw it. I saw my oneness with Christ. I saw that I was in Him, and that when He died I died. I saw that the question of my death was a matter of the past and not of the future, and that I was just as truly dead as He was because I was in Him when He died. The whole thing had dawned upon me. I was carried away with such joy at this great discovery that I jumped from my chair and cried, `Praise the Lord, I am dead!' I ran downstairs and met one of the brothers helping in the kitchen and I laid hold of him. `Brother', I said, `do you know that I have died?' I must admit he looked puzzled. `What do you mean?' he said, so I went on: `Do you not know that Christ has died? Do you not know that I died with Him? Do you not know that my death is no less truly a fact than His?' Oh it was so real to me! I longed to go through the streets of Shanghai shouting the news of my discovery. From that day to this I have never for one moment doubted the finality of that word: "I have been crucified with Christ".

I do not mean to say that we need not work that out. Yes, there is an outworking of the death which we are going to see presently, but this, first of all, is the basis of it. I have been crucified: it has been done.     What, then, is the secret of reckoning? To put it in one word, it is revelation. We need revelation from God Himself (Matt. 16:17; Eph. 1:17,18). We need to have our eyes opened to the fact of our union with Christ, and that is something more than knowing it as a doctrine. Such revelation is no vague, indefinite thing. Most of us can remember the day when we saw clearly that Christ died for us, and we ought to be equally clear as to the time when we saw that we died with Christ. It should be nothing hazy, but very definite, for it is with this as basis that we shall go on. It is not that I reckon myself to be dead, and therefore I will be dead. It is that, because I am dead -- because I see now what God has done with me in Christ -therefore I reckon myself to be dead. That is the right kind of reckoning. It is not reckoning toward death but from death.

## THE SECOND STEP: "EVEN SO RECKON..."

What does reckoning mean? `Reckoning' in Greek means doing accounts book-keeping. Accounting is the only thing in the world we human beings can do correctly. An artist paints a landscape. Can he do it with perfect accuracy? Can the historian vouch for the absolute accuracy of any record, or the map-maker for the perfect correctness of any map? They can make, at best, fair approximations. Even in everyday speech, when we try to tell some incident with the best intention to be honest and truthful, we cannot speak with complete accuracy. It is mostly a case of exaggeration or understatement, of one word too much or too little. What then can a man do that is utterly reliable? Arithmetic! There is no scope for error there. One chair plus one chair equals two chairs. That is true in London and it is true in Cape Town. If you travel west to New York or east to Singapore it is still the same. All the world over and for all time, one plus one equals two. One plus one is two in heaven and earth and hell.

Why does God say we are to reckon ourselves dead? Because we are dead. Let us keep to the analogy of accounting. Suppose I have fifteen shillings in my pocket, what do I enter in my account-book? Can I enter fourteen shillings and sixpence or fifteen shillings and sixpence? No, I must enter in my account-book that which is in fact in my pocket. Accounting is the reckoning of facts, not fancies. Even so, it is because I am really dead that God tells me to account it so. God could not ask me to put down in my account-book what was not true. He could not ask me to reckon that I am dead if I am still alive. For such mental gymnastics the word `reckoning' would be inappropriate; we might rather speak of `mis-reckoning'!

Reckoning is not a form of make-believe. It does not mean that, having found that I have only twelve shillings in my pocket, I hope that by entering fifteen shillings incorrectly in my account-book such 'reckoning' will somehow remedy the deficiency. It won't. If I have only twelve shillings, yet try to reckon to myself: 'I have fifteen shillings; I have fifteen shillings; I have fifteen shillings', do you think that the mental effort involved will in any way affect the sum that is in my pocket? Not a bit of it! Reckoning will not make twelve shillings into fifteen shillings, nor will it make what is untrue true. But if, on the other hand, it is a fact that I have fifteen shillings in my pocket, then with great ease and assurance I can enter fifteen shillings in my account-book. God tells us to reckon ourselves dead, not that by the process of reckoning we may become dead, but because we are dead. He never told us to reckon what was not a fact.

Having said, then, that revelation leads spontaneously to reckoning, we must not lose sight of the fact that we are presented with a command: "Reckon ye ...." There is a definite attitude to be taken. God asks us to do the account; to put down 'I have died' and then to abide by it. Why? Because it is a fact. When the Lord Jesus was on the cross, I was there in Him. Therefore I reckon it to be true. I reckon and declare that I have died in Him. Paul said, "Reckon ye also yourselves to be dead unto sin, but alive unto God." How is this possible? "In Christ Jesus." Never forget that it is always and only true in Christ. If you look at yourself you will think death is not there, but it is a question of faith not in yourself but in Him. You look to the Lord, and know what He has done. 'Lord, I believe in Thee. I reckon upon the fact in Thee.' Stand there all the day.

## THE RECKONING OF FAITH

The first four-and-a-half chapters of Romans speak of faith and faith and faith. We are justified by faith in Him (Rom. 3:28; 5:1). Righteousness, the forgiveness of our sins, and peace with God are all ours by faith, and without faith in the finished work of Jesus Christ none can possess them. But in the second section of Romans we do not find the same repeated mention of faith, and it might at first appear that the emphasis is therefore different. It is not really so, however, for where the words 'faith' and 'believe' drop out the work 'reckon' takes their place. Reckoning and faith are here practically the same thing.

What is faith? Faith is my acceptance of God's fact. It always has its foundations in the past. What relates to the future is hope rather than faith, although faith often has its object or goal in the future, as in Hebrews 11. Perhaps for this reason the word chosen here is `reckon'. It is a word that relates only to the past -- to what we look back to as settled, and not forward to as yet to be. This is the kind of faith described in Mark 11:24: "All things whatsoever ye pray and ask for, believe that ye have received them, and ye shall have them." The statement there is that, if you believe that you already have received your requests (that is, of course, in Christ), then `you shall have them'. To believe that you may get something, or that you can get it, or even that you will get it, is not faith in the sense meant here. This is faith -- to believe that you have already got it. Only that which relates to the past is faith in this sense. Those who say `God can' or `God may' or `God must' or `God will' do not necessarily believe at all. Faith always says, `God has done it'.

When, therefore, do I have faith in regard to my crucifixion? Not when I say God can, or will, or must crucify me, but when with joy I say, `Praise God, in Christ I am crucified!'

In Romans 3 we see the Lord Jesus bearing our sins and dying as our Substitute that we might be forgiven. In Romans 6 we see ourselves included in the death whereby He secured our deliverance. When the first fact was revealed to us we believed on Him for our justification. God tells us to reckon upon the second fact for our deliverance. So that, for practical purposes, `reckoning' in the second section of Romans takes the place of `faith' in the first section. The emphasis is not different. The normal Christian life is lived progressively, as it is entered initially, by faith in Divine fact: in Christ and His Cross.

## TEMPTATION AND FAILURE, THE CHALLENGE TO FAITH

For us, then, the two greatest facts in history are these: that all our sins are dealt with by the Blood, and that we ourselves are dealt with by the Cross. But what now of the matter of temptation? What is to be our attitude when, after we have seen and believed these facts, we discover the old desires rising up again? Worse still, what if we fall once more into known sin? What if we lose our temper, or worse? Is the whole position set forth above proved thereby to be false?

Now remember, one of the Devil's main objects is always to make us doubt the Divine facts. (Compare Gen. 3:4) After we have seen, by revelation of the Spirit of God, that we are indeed dead with Christ, and have reckoned it so, he will come and say: 'There is something moving inside. What about it? Can you call this death?' When that happens, what will be our answer? The crucial test is just here. Are you going to believe the tangible facts of the natural realm which are clearly before your eyes, or the intangible facts of the spiritual realm which are neither seen nor scientifically proved?

Now we must be careful. It is important for us to recall again what are facts stated in God' Word for faith to lay hold of and what are not. How does God state that deliverance is effected? Well, in the first place, we are not told that sin as a principle in us is rooted out or removed. To reckon on that will be to miscalculate altogether and find ourselves in the false position of the man we considered earlier, who tried to put down the twelve shillings in his pocket as fifteen shillings in his account-book. No, sin is not eradicated. It is very much there, and, given the opportunity, will overpower us and cause us to commit sins again, whether consciously or unconsciously. That is why we shall always need to know the operation of the precious Blood.

But whereas we know that, in dealing with sins committed, God's method is direct, to blot them out of remembrance by means of the Blood, when we come to the principle of sin and the matter of deliverance from its power, we find instead that God deals with this indirectly. He does not remove the sin but the sinner. Our old man was crucified with Him, and because of this the body, which before had been a vehicle of sin, is unemployed (Romans 6:6).[5] Sin, the old master, is still about, but the slave who served him has been put to death and so is out of reach and his members are unemployed. The gambler's hand is unemployed, the swearer's tongue is unemployed, and these members are now available to be used instead "as instruments of righteousness unto God" (Romans 6:13).

Thus we can say that 'deliverance from sin' is a more scriptural idea than 'victory over sin'. The expressions "freed from sin" and "dead unto sin" in

---

[5] The verb katargeo translated 'destroyed' in Romans 6:6 (A.V.) does not mean 'annihilated', but 'put out of operation', 'made ineffective'. It is from the Creek root argos, 'inactive', 'not working', 'unprofitable', which is the word translated 'idle' in Matthew 20:3,6 of the unemployed laborers in the market place. -- Ed.

Romans 6:7 and 11 imply deliverance from a power that is still very present and very real -- not from something that no longer exists. Sin is still there, but we are knowing deliverance from its power in increasing measure day by day.

This deliverance is so real that John can boldly write: "Whosoever is begotten of God doeth no sin ... he cannot sin" (1 John 3:9), which is, however, a statement that, wrongly understood, may easily mislead us. By it John is not telling us that sin is now no longer in our history and that we shall not again commit sin. He is saying that to sin is not in the nature of that which is born of God. The life of Christ has been planted in us by new birth and its nature is not to commit sin. But there is a great difference between the nature and the history of a thing, and there is a great difference between the nature of the life within us and our history. To illustrate this (though the illustration is an inadequate one) we might say that wood `cannot' sink, for it is not its nature to do so; but of course in history it will do so if a hand hold it under water. The history is a fact, just as sins in our history are historic facts; but the nature is a fact also, and so is the new nature that we have received in Christ. What is `in Christ' cannot sin; what is in Adam can sin and will do so whenever Satan is given a chance to exert his power.

So it is a question of our choice of which facts we will count upon and live by: the tangible facts of daily experience or the mightier fact that we are now `in Christ'. The power of His resurrection is on our side, and the whole might of God is at work in our salvation (Rom. 1:16), but the matter still rests upon our making real in history what is true in Divine fact.     "Now faith is the assurance of things hoped for, the proving of things not seen" (Heb. 11:1), and "the things which are not seen are eternal" (2 Cor. 4:18). I think we all know that Hebrews 11:1 is the only definition of faith in the New Testament, or indeed in the Scriptures. It is important that we should really understand that definition. You are familiar with the common English translation of these words, describing faith as "the substance of things hoped for" (A.V.). However, the word in the Greek has in it the sense of an action and not just of some thing, a `substance', and I confess I have personally spent a number of years trying to find a correct word to translate this. But the New Translation of J.N. Darby is especially good in regard to this word: "Faith is the substantiating of things hoped for". That is much better. It implies the making of them real in experience.     How do we `substantiate' something? We are doing so every day. We cannot live in the world without doing so. Do you know the difference between substance and `substantiating'? A substance is an object, something before me.

'Substantiating' means that I have a certain power or faculty that makes that substance to be real to me. Let us take a simple illustration. By means of our senses we can take things of the world of nature and transfer them into our consciousness so that we can appreciate them. Sight and hearing, for example, are two of my faculties which substantiate to me the world of light and sound. We have colours: red, yellow, green, blue, violet; and these colours are real things. But if I shut my eyes, then to me the colour is no longer real; it is simply nothing -- to me. It is not only that the colour is there, but I have the power to 'substantiate' it. I have the power to make that colour true to me and to give it reality in my consciousness. That is the meaning of 'substantiating'.

If I am blind I cannot distinguish colour, or if I lack the faculty of hearing I cannot enjoy music. Yet music and colour are in fact real things, and their reality is unaffected by whether or not I am able to appreciate them. Now we are considering here the things which, though they are not seen, are eternal and therefore real. Of course we cannot substantiate Divine things with any of our natural senses; but there is one faculty which can substantiate the "things hoped for", the things of Christ, and that is faith. Faith makes the real things to become real in my experience. Faith 'substantiates' to me the things of Christ. Hundreds of thousands of people are reading Romans 6:6: "Our old man was crucified with him". To faith it is true; to doubt, or to mere mental assent apart from spiritual illumination, it is not true.

Let us remember again that we are dealing here not with promises but with facts. The promises of God are revealed to us by His Spirit that we may lay hold of then; but facts are facts and they remain facts whether we believe them or not. If we do not believe the facts of the Cross they still remain as real as ever, but they are valueless to us. It does not need faith to make these things real in themselves, but faith can 'substantiate' them and make them real in our experience.

Whatever contradicts the truth of God's Word we are to regard as the Devil's lie, not because it may not be in itself a very real fact to our senses but because God has stated a greater fact before which the other must eventually yield. I once had an experience which (though not applicable in detail to the present matter) illustrates this principle. Some years ago I was ill. For six nights I had high fever and could find no sleep. Then at length God gave me from the Scripture a personal word of healing, and because of this I expected all symptoms of sickness to vanish at once. Instead of that, not a wink of sleep could I get, and I was not only sleepless but more restless than ever. My temperature rose higher, my pulse beat faster and my head ached more severely than before. The enemy asked, `Where is God's promise? Where is your faith? What about all your prayers?' So I was tempted to thrash the whole matter out in prayer again, but was rebuked, and this Scripture came to mind: "Thy word is truth" (John 17:17). If God' Word is truth, I thought, then what are these symptoms? They must all be lies! So I declared to the enemy, `This sleeplessness is a lie, this headache is a lie, this fever is a lie, this high pulse is a lie. In view of what God has said to me, all these symptoms of sickness are just your lies, and God's Word to me is truth.' In five minutes I was asleep, and I awoke the following morning perfectly well.

Now of course in a particular personal matter such as the above it might be quite possible for me to deceive myself as to what God had said, but of the fact of the Cross there can never be any such question. We must believe God, no matter how convincing Satan's arguments appear. A skillful liar lies not only in word but in gesture and deed; he can as easily pass a bad coin as tell an untruth. The Devil is a skillful liar, and we cannot expect him to stop at words in his lying. He will resort to lying signs and feelings and experiences in his attempts to shake us from our faith in God's Word. Let me make it clear that I do not deny the reality of the `flesh'. Indeed we shall have a good deal more to say about this further on in our study. But I am speaking here of our being moved from a revealed position in Christ. As soon as we have accepted our death with Christ as a fact, Satan will do his best to demonstrate convincingly by the evidence of our day-to-day experience that we are not dead at all but very much alive. So we must choose. Will we believe Satan's lie or God's truth?

Are we going to be governed by appearances or by what God says? I am Mr. Nee. I know that I am Mr. Nee. It is a fact upon which I can confidently count. It is of course possible that I might lose my memory and forget that I am Mr. Nee, or I might dream that I am some other person. But whether I feel like it or not, when I am sleeping I am Mr. Nee and when I am awake I am Mr. Nee; when I remember it I am Mr. Nee and when I forget it I am still Mr. Nee.

Now of course, were I to pretend to be someone else, things would be much more difficult. If I were to try and pose as Miss K. I should have to keep saying to myself all the time, `You are Miss K.; now be sure to remember that you are Miss K.,' and despite much reckoning the likelihood would be that when I was off my guard and someone called, `Mr. Nee!' I should be caught out and should answer to my own name. Fact would triumph over fiction, and all my reckoning would break down at that crucial moment. But I am Mr. Nee and therefore I have no difficulty whatever in reckoning myself to be Mr. Nee. It is a fact which nothing I experience or fail to experience can alter.

So also, whether I feel it or not, I am dead with Christ. How can I be sure? Because Christ has died; and since "one died for all, therefore all died" (2 Cor. 5:14). Whether my experience proves it or seems to disprove it, the fact remains unchanged. While I stand upon that fact Satan cannot prevail against me. Remember that his attack is always upon our assurance. If he can get us to doubt God's Word, then his object is secured and he has us in his power; but if we rest unshaken in the assurance of God's stated fact, assured that He cannot do injustice to His work or His Word, then it does not matter what tactics Satan adopts, we can well afford to laugh at him. If anyone should try to persuade me that I am not Mr. Nee, I could well afford to do the same.

"We walk by faith, not be appearance" (2 Cor. 5:7), mg). You probably know the illustration of Fact, Faith and Experience walking along the top of a wall. Fact walked steadily on, turning neither to right nor left and never looking behind. Faith followed and all went well so long as he kept his eyes focused upon Fact; but as soon as he became concerned about Experience and turned to see how he was getting on, he lost his balance and tumbled off the wall, and poor old Experience fell down after him.

All temptation is primarily to look within; to take our eyes off the Lord and to take account of appearances. Faith is always meeting a mountain, a mountain of evidence that seems to contradict God's Word, a mountain of apparent contradiction in the realm of tangible fact -- of failures in deed, as well as in the realm of feeling and suggestion -- and either faith or the mountain has to go. They cannot both stand. but the trouble is that many a time the mountain stays and faith goes. That must not be. If we resort to our senses to discover the truth, we shall find Satan's lies are often enough true to our experience; but if we refuse to accept as binding anything that contradicts God's Word and maintain an attitude of faith in Him alone, we shall find instead that Satan's lies begin to dissolve and that our experience is coming progressively to tally with that Word.     It is our occupation with Christ that has this result, for it means that He becomes progressively real to us on concrete issues. In a given situation we see Him as real holiness, real resurrection life -- for us. What we see in Him objectively now operates in us subjectively -- but really -- to manifest Him in us in that situation. That is the mark of maturity. That is what Paul means by his words to the Galatians: "I am again in travail until Christ be formed in you" (4:19). Faith is `substantiating' God's facts; and faith is always the `substantiating' of eternal fact -- of something eternally true.

## ABIDING IN HIM

Now although we have already spent long on this matter, there is a further thing that may help to make it clearer to us. the Scriptures declare that we are "dead indeed", but nowhere do they say that we are dead in ourselves. We shall look in vain to find death within; that is just the place where it is not to be found. We are dead not in ourselves but in Christ. We were crucified with Him because we were in Him.     We are familiar with the words of the Lord Jesus, "Abide in me, and I in you" (John 15:4). Let us consider them for a moment. First they remind us once again that we have never to struggle to get into Christ. We are not told to get there, for we are told to stay there where we have been placed. It was God's own act that put us in Christ, and we are to abide in Him. But further, this verse lays down for us a Divine principle, which is that God has done the work in Christ and not in us as individuals. The all-inclusive death and the all-inclusive resurrection of God's Son were accomplished fully and finally apart from us in the first place. It is the history of Christ which is to become the experience apart from Him. The Scriptures tell us that we were crucified "with Him", that we were quickened, raised, and set by God in the heavenlies "in Him", and that we are complete "in Him" (Rom. 6:6; Eph. 2:5,6; Col. 2:10). It is not just something that is still to be effected in us (though it is that, of course).

It is something that has already been effected, in association with Him.

In the Scriptures we find that no Christian experience exists as such. What God has done in His gracious purpose is to include us in Christ. In dealing with Christ God has dealt with the Christian; in dealing with the Head He has dealt with all the members. It is altogether wrong for us to think that we can experience anything of the spiritual life in ourselves merely, and apart from Him. God does not intend that we should acquire something exclusively personal in our experience, and He is not willing to effect anything like that for you and me. All the spiritual experience of the Christian is already true in Christ. It has already been experienced by Christ.

What we call `our' experience is only our entering into His history and His experience.

It would be odd if one branch of a vine tried to bear grapes with a reddish skin, and another branch tried to bear grapes with a green skin, and yet another branch grapes with a very dark purple skin, each branch trying to produce something of its own without reference to the vine. It is impossible, unthinkable. The character of the branches is determined by the vine. Yet certain Christians are seeking experiences as experiences. They think of crucifixion as something, of resurrections as something, of ascension as something, and they never stop to think that the whole is related to a Person. No, only as the Lord opens our eyes to see the Person do we have any true experience. Every true spiritual experience means that we have discovered a certain fact in Christ and have entered into that; anything that is not from Him in this way is an experience that is going to evaporate very soon. `I have discovered that in Christ; then, Praise the Lord, it is mine! I possess it, Lord, because it is in Thee.' Oh it is a great thing to know the facts of Christ as the foundation for our experience.

So God's basic principle in leading us on experimentally is not to give us something. It is not to bring us through something, and as a result to put something into us which we can call `our experience'. It is not that God effects something within us so that we can say, `I died with Christ last March' or `I was raised from the dead on January 1st, 1937,' or even, `Last Wednesday I asked for a definite experience and I have got it'. No, that is not the way. I do not seek experiences in themselves as in this present year of grace. Time must not be allowed to dominate my thinking here. Then, some will say, what about the crises so many of us have passed through? True, some of us have passed through real crises in our lives. For instance George Muller could say, bowing himself down to the ground, `There was a day when George Muller died'. How about that? Well, I am not questioning the reality of the spiritual experiences we go through nor the importance of crises to which God brings us in our walk with Him; indeed, I have already stressed the need for us to be quite as definite ourselves about such crisis in our own lives. But the point is that God does not give individuals individual experiences. All that they have is only an entering into what God has already done. It is the `realizing' in time of eternal things. The history of Christ becomes our experience and our spiritual history; we do not have a separate history from His. The entire work regarding us is not done in us here but in Christ. He does no separate work in individuals apart from what He has done there. Even eternal life is not given to us as individuals: the life is in the Son, and "he that hath the Son hath the life". God has done all in His Son, and He has included us in Him; we are incorporated into Christ.

Now the point of all this is that there is a very real practical value in the stand of faith that says, 'God has put me in Christ, and therefore all that is true of Him is true of me. I will abide in Him.' Satan is always trying to get us out, to keep us out, to convince us that we are out, and by temptations, failures, suffering, trial, to make us feel acutely that we are outside of Christ. Our first thought is that, if we were in Christ, we should not be in this state, and therefore, judging by the feelings we now have, we must be out of Him; and so we begin to pray, 'Lord, put me into Christ'. No! God's injunction is to "abide" in Christ, and that is the way of deliverance. But how is it so? Because it opens the way for God to take a hand in our lives and to work the thing out in us. It makes room for the operation of His superior power -- the power of resurrection (Rom. 6:4,9,10) -- so that the facts of Christ do progressively become the facts of our daily experience, and where before "sin reigned" (Rom. 5:21) we make now the joyful discovery that we are truly "no longer ... in bondage to sin" (Rom. 6:6).

As we stand steadfastly on the ground of what Christ is, we find that all that is true of Him is becoming experimentally true in us. If instead we come onto the ground of what we are in ourselves we will find that all that is true of the old nature remains true of us. If we get there in faith we have everything; if we return back here we find nothing. So often we go to the wrong place to find the death of self. It is in Christ. We have only to look within to find we are very much alive to sin; but when we look over there to the Lord, God sees to it that death works here but that "newness of life" is ours also. We are "alive unto God" (Rom. 6:4,11).

"Abide in me, and I in you." This is a double sentence: a command coupled with a promise. That is to say, there is an objective and a subjective side to God's working, and the subjective side depends upon the objective; the "I in you" is the outcome of our abiding in Him. We need to guard against being over-anxious about the subjective side of things, and so becoming turned in upon ourselves. We need to dwell upon the objective -"abide in me" -- and to let God take care of the subjective. And this He has undertaken to do.

I have illustrated this from the electric light. You are in a room and it is growing dark. You would like to have the light on in order to read. There is a reading-lamp on the table beside you. What do you do? Do you watch it intently to see if the light will come on? Do you take a cloth and polish the bulb? No, you get up and cross over to the other side of the room where the switch is on the wall and you turn the current on. You turn your attention to the source of power and when you have taken the necessary action there the light comes on here.

So in our walk with the Lord our attention must be fixed on Christ. "Abide in me, and I in you" is the Divine order. Faith in the objective facts make those facts true subjectively. As the apostle Paul puts it, "We all ... beholding ... the glory of the Lord, are transformed into the same image" (2 Cor. 3:18 mg.). The same principle holds good in the matter of fruitfulness of life: "He that abideth in me, and I in him, the same beareth much fruit" (John 15:5). We do not try to produce fruit or concentrate upon the fruit produced. Our business is to look away to Him. As we do so He undertakes to fulfill His Word in us.

How do we abide? `Of God are ye in Christ Jesus.' It was the work of God to put you there and He has done it. Now stay there! Do not be moved back onto your own ground. Never look at yourself as though you were not in Christ. Look at Christ and see yourself in Him. Abide in Him. Rest in the fact that God has put you in His Son, and live in the expectation that He will complete His work in you. It is for Him to make good the glorious promise that "sin shall not have dominion over you" (Rom. 6:14).

# CHAPTER 5: THE DIVIDE OF THE CROSS

The kingdom of this world is not this kingdom of God. God had in His heart a world-system - a universe of His creating -- which should be headed up in Christ His Son (col. 1:16,17). But Satan, working through man's flesh, has set up instead a rival system known in Scripture as "this world" -- a system in which we are involved and which he himself dominates. He has in fact become "the prince of this world" (John 12:31).

## TWO CREATIONS

Thus, in Satan's hands, the first creation has become the old creation, and God's primary concern is now no longer with that but with a second and new creation. He is bringing in a new creation, a new kingdom and a new world, and nothing of the old creation, the old kingdom or the old world can be transferred to the new. It is a question now of these two rival realms, and of which realm we belong to.

The apostle Paul, of course, leaves us in no doubt as to which of these two realms is now in fact ours. He tells us that God, in redemption, "delivered us out of the power of darkness, and translated us into the kingdom of the Son of his love" (Col. 1:12,13).

But in order to bring us into His new kingdom, God must do something new in us. He must make of us new creatures. Unless we are created anew we can never fit into the new realm. "That which is born of the flesh is flesh"; and, "flesh and blood cannot inherit the kingdom of God; neither doth corruption inherit incorruption" (John 3:16; 1 Cor. 15:50). However educated, however cultured, however improved it be, flesh is still flesh. Our fitness for the new kingdom is determined by the creation to which we belong. Do we belong to the old creation or the new? Are we born of the flesh or of the Spirit? Our ultimate suitability for the new realm hinges on the question of origin. The question is not `good' or bad?' but `flesh or Spirit?'

211

"That which is born of the flesh is flesh", and it will never be anything else. That which is of the old creation can never pass over into the new.

Once we really understand what God is seeking, namely, something altogether new for Himself, then we shall see clearly that we can never bring any contribution from the old realm into that new thing. God wanted to have us for Himself, but He could not bring us as we were into that which He had purposed; so He first did away with us by the Cross of Christ, and then by resurrection provided a new life for us. "If any man is in Christ, he is a new creature (mg. 'there is a new creation'): the old things are passed away; behold, they are become new" (2 Cor. 5:17). Being now new creatures with a new nature and a new set of faculties, we can enter the new kingdom and the new world.

The Cross was the means God used to bring to an end 'the old things' by setting aside altogether our 'old man', and the resurrection was the means He employed to impart to us all that was necessary for our life in that new world. "We were buried therefore with him through baptism into death: that like as Christ was raised from the dead through the glory of the Father, so we also might walk in newness of life" (Rom. 6:4).

The greatest negative in the universe is the Cross, for with it God wiped out everything that was not of Himself: the greatest positive in the universe is the resurrection, for through it God brought into being all He will have in the new sphere. So the resurrection stands at the threshold of the new creation. It is a blessed thing to see that the Cross ends all that belongs to the first regime, and that the resurrection introduces all that pertains to the second. Everything that had its beginning before resurrection must be wiped out. Resurrection is God's new starting-point.    We have now two worlds before us, the old and the new. In the old, Satan has absolute dominion. You may be a good man in the old creation, but as long as you belong to the old you are under sentence of death, because nothing of the old can go over to the new. The Cross is God's declaration that all is of the old creation must die. Nothing of the first Adam can pass beyond the Cross; it all ends there. The sooner we see that, the better, for it is by the Cross that God has made a way of escape for us from that old creation. God gathered up in the Person of His Son all that was of Adam and crucified Him; so in Him all that was of Adam was done away. Then God made, as it were, a proclamation throughout the universe saying: 'Through the Cross I have set aside all that is not of Me; you who belong to the old creation are all included in that; you too have been crucified with Christ!' None of us can escape that verdict.

This brings us to the subject of baptism. "Are ye ignorant that all we who were baptized into Christ Jesus were baptized into his death? We were buried therefore with him through baptism into death" (Rom. 6:3,4). What is the significance of these words?

Baptism in Scripture is associated with salvation. "He that believeth and is baptized shall be saved" (Mark 16:16). We cannot speak scripturally of 'baptismal regeneration' but we may speak of 'baptismal salvation'. What is salvation? It relates not to our sins nor to the power of sin, but to the cosmos or world-system. We are involved in Satan's world-system. To be saved is to make our exit from his world-system into God's

In the Cross of our Lord Jesus Christ, says Paul, "the world hath been crucified unto me, and I unto the world" (Gal. 6:14). This is the figure developed by Peter when he writes of the eight souls who were "saved through water" (1 Peter 3:20). Entering into the ark, Noah and those with him stepped by faith out of that old corrupt world into a new one. It was not so much that they were personally not drowned, but that they were out of that corrupt system. That is salvation.

Then Peter goes on: "Which also after a true likeness (mg. 'in the antitype') doth now save you, even baptism" (verse 21). In other words, by that aspect of the Cross which is figured in baptism you are delivered from this present evil world, and, by your baptism in water, you confirm this. It is baptism "into his death", ending one creation ; but it is also baptism "into Christ Jesus", having in view a new one (Rom. 6:3). You go down into the water and your world, in figure, goes down with you. you come up in Christ, but your world is drowned.

"Believe on the Lord Jesus, and thou shalt be saved", said Paul at Philippi, and "spake the word of the Lord" to the jailer and his household. And he "was baptized, he and all his, immediately" (Acts 16:31-34). In doing so, he and those with him testified before God, His people and the spiritual powers that they were indeed saved from a world under judgment. As a result, we read, they rejoiced greatly, "having believed in God".

Thus it is clear that baptism is no mere question of a cup of water, nor of a baptistry of water. It is a tremendous thing, relating as it does both to the death and to the resurrection of our Lord; and having in view two worlds. Anyone who has worked in a pagan country knows what tremendous issues are raised by baptism.

## BURIAL MEANS AN END

Peter goes on now to describe baptism in the passage just quoted as "the answer of a good conscience toward God" (1 Peter 3:21 A.V.). Now we cannot answer without being spoken to . If God had said nothing we should have no need to answer. But He has spoken; He has spoken to us by the Cross. By it He has told of His judgment of us, of the world, of the old creation and of the old kingdom. The Cross is not only Christ's personally - - an individual' Cross. It is an all inclusive Cross, a `corporate' Cross, a Cross that includes you and me. God has put us all into His Son, and crucified us in Him. In the last Adam He has wiped out all that was of the first Adam.

Now what is my answer to God's verdict on the old creation? I answer by asking for baptism. Why? In Romans 6:4 Paul explains that baptism means burial: "We were buried therefore with him through baptism". Baptism is of course connected with both death and resurrection, though in itself it is neither death nor resurrection: it is burial. But who qualifies for burial? Only the dead! So if I ask for baptism I proclaim myself dead and fit only for the grave.

Alas, some have been taught to look on burial as a means to death; they try to die by getting themselves buried! Let me say emphatically that, unless our eyes have been opened by God to see that we have died in Christ and been buried with Him, we have no right to be baptized. The reason we step down into the water is that we have recognized that in God's sight we have already died. It is to that that we testify. God's question is clear and simple. `Christ has died, and I have included you there. Now, what are you going to say to that?' What is my answer? `Lord, I believe You have done the crucifying. I say Yes to the death and to the burial to which You have committed me.' He has consigned me to death and the grave; by my request for baptism I give public assent to that fact.

In China a woman lost her husband, but, becoming deranged by her loss, she flatly refused to have him buried. Day after day for a fortnight he lay in the house. `No', she said, `he is not dead; I talk with him every night.' She was unwilling to have him buried because, poor woman, she did not believe him to be dead. When are we willing to bury our dear ones? Only when we are absolutely sure that they have passed away. While there is the tiniest hope that they are alive we will never bury them. So when will I ask for baptism? When I see that God's way is perfect and that I deserved to die, and when I truly believe that God has already crucified me. Once I am fully persuaded that, before God, I am quite dead, then I apply for baptism. I say, `Praise God, I am dead! Lord, You have slain me; now get me buried!'

In China we have two emergency Services, a `Red Cross' and a `Blue Cross' The first deals with those who are wounded in battle but are still alive, to bring them succour and healing; the second deals with those who are already dead in famine, flood or war, to give them burial. God's dealings with us in the Cross of Christ are more drastic than those of the `Red Cross'. He does not set out to patch up the old creation. By Him even the still living are condemned to death and to burial, that they may be raised again to new life. God has done the work of crucifixion so that now we are counted among the dead; but we must accept this and submit to the work of the `Blue Cross', by sealing that death with `burial'.

There is an old world and a new world, and between the two there is a tomb. God has already crucified me, but I must consent to be consigned to the tomb. My baptism confirms God's sentence, passed upon me in the Cross of His Son. It affirms that I am cut off from the old world and belong now to the new. So baptism is no small thing. It means for me a definite conscious break with the old way of life. This is the meaning of Romans 6:2: "We who died to sin, how shall we any longer live therein?" Paul says, in effect, `If you would continue in the old world, why be baptized? You should never have been baptized if you meant to live on in the old realm'. When once we see this, we clear the ground for the new creation by our assent to the burial of the old.

In Romans 6:5, still writing to those who "were baptized" (verse 3), Paul speaks of our being "united with him by the likeness of his death". For by baptism we acknowledge in a future that God has wrought an intimate union between ourselves and Christ in this matter of death and resurrection. One day I was seeking to emphasize this truth to a Christian brother. We happened to be drinking tea together, so I took a lump of sugar and stirred it into my tea. A couple of minutes later I asked, `Can you tell me where the sugar is now, and where the tea?' `No', he said, `you have put them together and the one has become lost in the other; they cannot now be separated.' It was a simple illustration, but it helped him to see the intimacy and the finality of our union with Christ in death. It is God that has put us there, and God's acts cannot be reversed.

What, in fact does this union imply? The real meaning behind baptism is that in the Cross we were `baptized' into the historic death of Christ, so that His death became ours. Our death and His became then so closely identified

215

that it is impossible to divide between them. It is to this historic `baptism' -- this God-wrought union with Him -- that we assent when we go down into the water. Our public testimony in baptism today is our admission that the death of Christ two thousand years ago was a mighty all-inclusive death, mighty enough and all-inclusive enough to carry away in it and bring to an end everything in us that is not of God.

## RESURRECTION UNTO NEWNESS OF LIFE

"If we have become united with him by the likeness of his death, we shall be also be the likeness of his resurrection (Rom. 6:5).

Now with resurrection the figure is different because something new is introduced. I am "baptized into his death", but I do not enter in quite the same way into His resurrection, for, Praise the Lord! His resurrection enters into me, imparting to me a new life. In the death of the Lord the emphasis is solely upon `I in Christ'. With the resurrection, while the same thing is true, there is now a new emphasis upon `Christ in me'. How is it possible for Christ to communicate His resurrection life to me? How do I receive this new life? Paul suggests, I think, a very good illustration with these very same words: "united with him". For the word `united' (A.V. `planted together') may carry in the Greek the sense of `grafted'[6] and it gives us a very beautiful picture of the life of Christ which is imparted to us through resurrection.

In Fukien I once visited a man who owned an orchard of longien[7] trees. He had three or four acres of land and about three hundred fruit trees. I inquired if his trees had been grafted or if they were of the original native

---

[6] Greek sumphtuos `planted or grown along with', `united with'. The word is used in the sense of `grafted' in Classical Greek. in the delightful illustration which follows, the analogy of grafting should perhaps not be pressed too closely, for it is not quite safe to imply, without some qualification, that Christ is grafted into the old stock. But what parable can adequately describe the miracle of the new creation? -- Ed.

[7] long-ien (Euphoria longana) is a tree native to China. Its fruit resembles an apricot in size and has a round central stone, a dry, light brown, papery skin and a delicious white, grape-like pulp. It is eaten either fresh or dried, and is prized by the Chinese both for its flavour and for its food value. -- Ed.

stock. `Do you think', he replied, `that I would waste my land growing ungrafted trees? What value could I ever expect from the old stock?

So I asked him to explain the process of grafting, which he gladly did.

`When a tree has grown to a certain height', he said, `I lop off the top and graft on to it.' Pointing to a special tree he asked, `Do you see that tree? I call it the father tree, because all the grafts for the other trees are taken from that one. If the other trees were just left to follow the course of nature, their fruit would be only about the size of a raspberry, and would consist mainly of thick skin and seeds. This tree, from which the grafts for all the others are taken, bears a luscious fruit the size of a plum, with very thin skin and a tiny seed; and of course all the grafted trees bear fruit like it.' `How does it happen?' I asked. `I simply take a little of the nature of the one tree and transfer it to the other', he explained. `I make a cleavage in the poor tree and insert a slip from the good one. Then I bind it up and leave it to grow.' `But how can it grow?' I asked. `I don't know', he said, `but it does grow.'

Then he showed me a tree bearing miserably poor fruit from the old stock below the graft, and rich juicy fruit from the new stock above the graft. `I have left the old shoots with their useless fruit on them to show the difference', he said. `From it you can understand the value of grafting. You can appreciate, can you not, why I grow only grafted trees?'  How can one tree bear the fruit of another? How can a poor tree bear good fruit? Only by grafting. Only by our implanting into it the life of a good tree. But if a man can graft a branch of one tree into another, cannot God take of the life of His Son and, so to speak, graft it into us?  A Chinese woman burned her arm badly and was taken to hospital. In order to prevent serious contracture due to scarring it was found necessary to graft some new skin over the injured area, but the doctor attempted in vain to graft a piece of the woman's own skin onto the arm. Owing to her age and ill-nourishment the skin graft was too poor and would not `take'. Then a foreign nurse offered a piece of skin and the operation was carried out successfully. The new skin knit with the old, and the woman left the hospital with her arm perfectly healed; but there remained a patch of white foreign skin on her yellow arm to tell the tale of the past. You ask how the skin of another grew on that woman's arm? I do not know how it grew, but I know that it did grow.

If an earthly surgeon can take a piece of skin from one human body and graft it on another,[8] cannot the Divine Surgeon implant the life of His Son into me? I do not know how it is done. "The wind bloweth where it listeth, and thou hearest the voice thereof, but knowest not whence it cometh, and whither it goeth; so is every one that is born of the Spirit" (John 3:8). We cannot tell how God has done His work in us, but it is done. We can do nothing and need do nothing to bring it about, for by the resurrection God has already done it.

God has done everything. There is only one fruitful life in the world and that has been grafted into millions of other lives. We call this the 'new birth'. New birth is the reception of a life which I did not possess before. It is not that my natural life has been changed at all; it is that another life, a life altogether new, altogether Divine, has become my life. God has cut off the old creation by the Cross of His Son in order to bring in a new creation in Christ by resurrection. He has shut the door to that old kingdom of darkness and translated me into the kingdom of His dear Son. My glorying is in the fact that it has been done -- that, through the Cross of our Lord Jesus Christ , that old world has " been crucified unto me, and I unto the world" (Galations 6:14). My baptism is my public testimony to that fact. By it, as by my oral witness, my "confession is made unto salvation" (Romans 10:10).

---

[8] Whatever question medical men may raise as to the account of this unusual incident, the statement which follows is not open to challenge.-- Ed.

# CHAPTER 6: THE PATH OF PROGRESS: PRESENTING OURSELVES TO GOD

Our study has now brought us to the point where we are able to consider the true nature of consecration. We have before us the second half of Romans 6 from verse 12 to the end. In Romans 6:12,13 we read: "Let not sin therefore reign in your mortal body, that ye should obey the lusts thereof: neither present your members unto sin as instruments of unrighteousness; but present yourselves unto God, as alive from the dead, and your members as instruments of righteousness unto God." The operative word here is "present" and this occurs five times, in verses 13, 16 and 19.[9]

Many have taken this word "present" to imply consecration without looking carefully into its content. Of course that is what it does mean, but not in the sense in which we so often understand it. It is not the consecration of our `old man' with his instincts and resources -- our natural wisdom, strength and other gifts -- to the Lord for Him to use.     This will be at once clear from verse 13. Note there the clause "as alive from the dead". Paul says: "Present yourselves unto God, as alive from the dead". This defines for us the point at which consecration begins. For what is here referred to is not the consecration of anything belonging to the old creation, but only of that which has passed through death to resurrection. The `presenting' spoken of

---

[9] Note.--Two Greek verbs paristano and paristemi are translated in these verses by `present' in the R.V. where the A.V. has `yield'. Paristemi occurs frequently with this meaning, e.g. in Rom. 12:1; 2 Cor. 11:2; Col. 1:22,28, and in Luke 2:22 where it is used of the presenting of the infant Jesus to God in the Temple. Both words have an active sense for which the R.V. translation `present' is greatly to be preferred. `Yield' contains a passive idea of `surrender' that has coloured much evangelical thought, but which is not in keeping with the context here in Romans. -- Ed.

is the outcome of my knowing my old man to be crucified. Knowing, reckoning, presenting to God: that is the Divine order.

When I really know I am crucified with Him, then spontaneously I reckon myself dead (verses 6 and 11); and when I know that I am raised with Him from the dead, then likewise I reckon myself "alive unto God in Christ Jesus" (verses 9 and 11), for both the death and the resurrection side of the Cross are to be accepted by faith. When this point is reached, giving myself to Him follows. In resurrection He is the source of my life -- indeed He is my life; so I cannot but present everything to Him, for all is His, not mine. But without passing through death I have nothing to consecrate, nor is there anything God can accept, for He has condemned all that is of the old creation to the Cross. Death has cut off all that cannot be consecrated to Him, and resurrection alone has made consecration possible. Presenting myself to God means that henceforth I consider my whole life as now belonging to the Lord.

## THE THIRD STEP: "PRESENT YOURSELVES ..."

Let us observe that this 'presenting' relates to the members of my body -- that body which, as we say earlier, is now unemployed in respect to sin. "Present yourselves ... and your members", says Paul, and again: "Present your members" (Romans 6:13,19). God requires of me that I now regard all my members, all my faculties, as belonging wholly to Him.

It is a great thing when I discover I am no longer my own but His. If the ten shillings in my pocket belong to me, then I have full authority over them. But if they belong to another who has committed them to me in trust, then I cannot buy what I please with them, and I dare not lose them. Real Christian life begins with knowing this. How many of us know that, because Christ is risen, we are therefore alive "unto God" and not unto ourselves? How many of us dare not use our time or money or talents as we would, because we realize they are the Lord's not ours? How many of us have such a strong sense that we belong to Another that we dare not squander a shilling of our money, or an hour of our time, or any of our mental or physical powers?

On one occasion a Chinese brother was traveling by train and found himself in a carriage together with three non-Christians who wished to play cards in order to while away the time. Lacking a fourth to complete the game, they invited this brother to join them. 'I am sorry to disappoint you', he said, 'but I cannot join your game for I have not brought my hands with me.'

`Whatever do you mean?' they asked in blank astonishment. `This pair of hands does not belong to me', he said, and then there followed the explanation of the transfer of ownership that had taken place in his life. That brother regarded the members of his body as belonging entirely to the Lord. That is true holiness.

Paul says, "Present your members as servants to righteousness unto sanctification (A.V. `holiness')" (Romans 6:19). Make it a definite act. "Present yourselves to God."

## SEPARATED UNTO THE LORD

What is holiness? Many people think we become holy by the eradication of something evil within. No, we become holy by being separated unto God. In Old Testament times, it was when a man was chosen by God to be altogether

His that he was publicly anointed with oil and was then said to be `sanctified'. Thereafter he was regarded as set apart to God. In the same manner even animals or material things -- a lamb, or the gold of the temple -- could be sanctified, not by the eradication of anything evil in them, but by being thus reserved exclusively to the Lord. "Holiness' in the Hebrew sense meant something thus set apart, and all true holiness is holiness "to the Lord" (Exodus 28:36). I give myself over wholly to Christ: that is holiness.

Presenting myself to God implies a recognition that I am altogether His. This giving of myself is a definite thing, just as definite as reckoning. There must be a day in my life when I pass out of my own hands into His, and from that day forward I belong to Him and no longer to myself. That does not mean that I consecrate myself to be a preacher or a missionary. Alas, many people are missionaries not because they have truly consecrated themselves to God but because, in the sense of which we are speaking, they have not consecrated themselves to Him. They have `consecrated' (as they would put it) something altogether different, namely, their own uncrucified natural faculties to the doing of His work; but that is not true consecration. Then to what are we to be consecrated? Not to Christian work, but to the will of God to be and do whatever He wants. David had many mighty men. Some were generals and others were gatekeepers, according as the king assigned them their task. We must be willing to be either generals or gatekeepers, allotted to our parts just as God wills and not as we choose. If you are a Christian, then God has marked out a pathway for you -- a `course' as Paul calls it in 2

Timothy 4:7. Not only Paul's path but the path of every Christian has been clearly marked out by God, and it is of supreme importance that each one should know and walk in the God-appointed course. `Lord, I give myself to Thee with this desire alone, to know and walk in the path Thou hast ordained.' That is true giving. If at the close of a life we can say with Paul: "I have finished my course", then we are blessed indeed. There is nothing more tragic than to come to the end of life and know we have been on the wrong course. We have only one life to live down here and we are free to do as we please with it,

but if we seek our own pleasure our life will never glorify God. A devoted Christian once said in my hearing, `I want nothing for myself; I want everything for God.' Do you want anything apart from God, or does all your desire center in His will? Can you truly say that the will of God is "good and acceptable and perfect" to you? (Romans 12:2)

For it is our wills that are in question here. That strong self-assertive will of mine must go to the Cross, and I must give myself over wholly to the Lord. We cannot expect a tailor to make us a coat if we do not give him any cloth, nor a builder to build us a house if we let him have no building material; and in just the same way we cannot expect the Lord to live out His life in us if we do not give Him our lives in which to live. Without reservations, without controversy, we must give ourselves to Him to do as He pleases with us. "Present yourselves unto God" (Romans 6:13).

## SERVANT OR SLAVE?

If we give ourselves unreservedly to God, many adjustments may have to be made: in family, or business, or church relationships, or in the matter of our personal views. God will not let anything of ourselves remain. His finger will touch, point by point, everything that is not of Him, and He will say: `This must go'. Are you willing? It is foolish to resist God, and always wise to submit to Him. We admit that many of us still have controversies with the Lord. He wants something, while we want something else. Many things we dare not look into, dare not pray about, dare not even think about, lest we lose our peace. We can evade the issue in that way, but to do so will bring us out of the will of God. It is always an easy matter to get out of His will, but it is a blessed thing just to hand ourselves over to Him and let Him have His way with us.

How good it is to have the consciousness that we belong to the Lord and are not our own! There is nothing more precious in the world. It is that which brings the awareness of His continual presence, and the reason is obvious. I must first have the sense of God's possession of me before I can have the sense of His presence with me. When once His ownership is established, then I dare do nothing in my own interests, for I am His exclusive property. "Know ye not, that to whom ye present yourselves as servants unto obedience, his servants ye are whom ye obey?" (Romans 6:16).

The word here rendered 'servant' really signifies a bondservant, a slave. This word is used several times in the second half of Romans 6. What is the difference between a servant and a slave? A servant may serve another, but the ownership does not pass to that other. If he likes his master he can serve him, but if he does not like him he can give in his notice and seek another master. Not so is it with the slave. He is not only the servant of another but he is the possession of another. How did I become the slave of the Lord? On His part He bought me, and on my part I presented myself to Him. By right of redemption I am God's property, but if I would be His slave I must willingly give myself to Him, for He will never compel me to do so. The trouble about many Christians today is that they have an insufficient idea of what God is asking of them. How glibly they say: 'Lord, I am willing for anything.' Do you know that God is asking of you your very life? There are cherished ideals, strong wills, precious relationships, much-loved work, that will have to go; so do not give yourself to God unless you mean it. God will take you seriously, even if you did not mean it seriously.

When the Galilian boy brought his bread to the Lord, what did the Lord do with it? He broke it. God will always break what is offered to Him. He breaks what He takes, but after breaking it He blesses and uses it to meet the needs of others. After you give yourself to the Lord, He begins to break what was offered to Him. Everything seems to go wrong, and you protest and find fault with the ways of God. But to stay there is to be no more than just a broken vessel -- no good for the world because you have gone too far for the world to use you, and no good for God either because you have not gone far enough for Him to use you. You are out of gear with the world, and you have a controversy with God. This is the tragedy of many a Christian.

My giving of myself to the Lord must be an initial fundamental act. Then day by day I must go on giving to Him, not finding fault with His use of me but accepting with praise even what the flesh revolts against. I am the Lord's and now no longer reckon myself to be my own but acknowledge in everything His ownership and authority. That it the attitude God requires, and to maintain it is true consecration. I do not consecrate myself to be a missionary or a preacher; I consecrate myself to God to do His will where I am, be it in school, office or kitchen, counting whatever He ordains for me to be the very best, for nothing but good can come to those who are wholly His.

May we always be possessed by the consciousness that we are not our own.

# CHAPTER 7: THE ETERNAL PURPOSE

We have spoken of the need of revelation, of faith and of consecration, if we are to live the normal Christian life. But unless we see the end God has in view we shall never clearly understand why these steps are necessary to lead us to that end. Before therefore we consider further the question of inward experience, let us first look at the great Divine goal before us. What is God's purpose in creation and what is His purpose in redemption? It may be summed up in two phrases, one from each of our two sections of Romans. It is: "The glory of God" (Romans 3:23), and "The glory of the children of God" (Romans 8:21).

In Romans 3:23 we read: "All have sinned, and fall short of the glory of God". God's purpose for man was glory, but sin thwarted that purpose by causing man to miss God's glory. When we think of sin we instinctively think of the judgment it brings; we invariably associate it with condemnation and hell. Man's thought is always of the punishment that will come to him if he sins, but God's thought is always of the glory man will miss if he sins. The result of sin is that we forfeit God's glory: the result of redemption is that we are qualified again for glory. God's purpose in redemption is glory, glory, glory.

## FIRSTBORN AMONG MANY BRETHREN

This consideration takes us forward into Romans chapter 8 where the topic is developed in verses 16 to 18 and again in verses 29 and 30. Paul says: "We are children of God: and if children, then heirs; heirs of God, and joint-heirs with Christ; if so be that we suffer with him, that we may be also glorified with him. For I reckon that the sufferings of this present time are not worthy to be compared with the glory which shall be revealed to usward" (Romans 8:16-18); and again: "Whom he foreknew, he also foreordained to be conformed to the image of his Son, that he might be the firstborn among many brethren: and whom he foreordained, them he also called: and whom he called, them he also justified: and whom he justified, them he also glorified" (Romans 8:29,30). What was God's objective? It was that His Son Jesus Christ might be the firstborn among many brethren, all of whom should be conformed to His image. How did God realize that objective? "Whom he justified, them he also glorified." God's purpose, then, in creation and redemption was to make Christ the firstborn Son among many glorified sons. That may perhaps at first convey very little to many of us, but let us look into it more carefully.

In John 1:14 we are told that the Lord Jesus was God's only begotten Son: "the Word became flesh, and dwelt among us (and we beheld his glory, glory as of the only begotten from the Father)". That He was God's only begotten Son signifies that God had no other Son but this one. He was with the Father from all eternity. But, we are told, God was not satisfied that Christ should remain the only begotten Son; He wanted also to make Him His first begotten. How could an only begotten Son become a first begotten? The answer is simple: by the Father having more children. If you have but one son then his is the only begotten, but if thereafter you have other children then the only begotten becomes the first begotten.

The Divine purpose in creation and redemption was that God should have many children. He wanted us, and could not be satisfied without us. Some time ago I called to see Mr. George Cutting, the writer of the well-known tract Safety, Certainty and Enjoyment. When I was ushered into the presence of this old saint of ninety-three years, he took my hand in his and in a quiet, deliberate way he said: `Brother, do you know, I cannot do without Him? And do you know, He cannot do without me?' Though I was with him for over an hour, his great age and physical frailty made any sustained conversation impossible. But what remains in my memory of that interview was his frequent repetition of these two questions: `Brother, do you know, I cannot do without Him? And do you know, He cannot do without me?' In reading the story of the prodigal son most people are impressed with all the troubles the prodigal meets; they are occupied in thinking what a bad time he is having. But that is not the point of the parable. "My son ... was lost, and is found" -- there is the heart of the story. It is not a question of what the son suffers but of what the Father loses. He is the sufferer; He is the loser. A sheep is lost: whose is the loss? The shepherd's. A coin is lost: whose is the loss? The woman's. A son is lost: whose is the loss? The Father's. That is the lesson of Luke chapter 15. The Lord Jesus was the only begotten Son, and as the only begotten He had no brothers. But the Father sent the Son in order that the only begotten might also be the first begotten, and the beloved

226

Son have many brethren. There you have the whole story of the Incarnation and the Cross; and there you have at the last the purpose of God fulfilled in His "bringing many sons unto glory" (Heb. 2:10).

In Romans 8:29 we read of "many brethren"; in Hebrews :10 of "many sons". From the point of view of the Lord Jesus it is "brethren"; from the point of view of God the Father it is "sons". Both words in this context convey the idea of maturity. God is seeking full-grown sons; but He does not stop even there. For He does not want His sons to live in a barn or a garage or a field; He wants them in His home; He wants them to share His glory. That is the explanation of Romans 8:30: "Whom he justified, them he also glorified." Sonship -- the full expression of His Son -- is God's goal in the many sons. How could He bring that about? By justifying them and then by glorifying them. In His dealings with them God will never stop short of that goal. He set Himself to have sons, and to have those sons, mature and responsible, with Him in glory. He made provision for the whole of Heaven to be peopled with glorified sons. That was His purpose in redemption.

## THE GRAIN OF WHEAT

But how could God's only begotten Son become His first begotten? The method is explained in John 12:24: "Verily, verily, I say unto you, Except a grain of wheat fall into the earth and die, it abideth by itself alone; but if it die, it beareth much fruit." Who was that grain? It was the Lord Jesus. In the whole universe God had only one `grain of wheat'; He had no second grain. God put His one grain of wheat into the ground and it died, and in resurrection the only begotten grain became the first begotten grain, and from the one grain there have sprung many grains.

In respect of His divinity the Lord Jesus remains uniquely "the only begotten Son of God". Yet there is a sense in which, from the resurrection onward through all eternity, He is also the first begotten, and His life from that time is found in many brethren. For we who are born of the Spirit are made thereby "partakers of the divine nature" (2 Peter 1:4), though not, mark you, as of ourselves but only, as we shall see in a moment, in dependence upon God and by virtue of our being `in Christ'. We have "received the spirit of adoption, whereby we cry, Abba, Father. The Spirit himself beareth witness with our spirit, that we are children of God" (Rom. 8:5,16). It was by way of the Incarnation and the Cross that the Lord Jesus made this possible. Therein was the Father-heart of God satisfied, for in the Son's obedience unto death the Father has secured His many sons. The first and the twentieth chapters of John are in this respect most precious. In the beginning of his Gospel John tells us that Jesus was "the only begotten from the Father". At the end of his Gospel he tells us how, after the Lord Jesus died and rose again, He said to Mary Magdalene, "Go unto my brethren, and say to them, I ascend unto my Father and your Father, and my God and your God" (John 20:17). Hitherto in this Gospel the Lord had spoken often of "the Father" or of "my Father". Now, in resurrection, He add, "... and your Father". It is the eldest Son, the first begotten, speaking. By His death and resurrection many brethren have been brought into God's family, and so, in the same verse He uses this very name for them: "My brethren". "He is not ashamed to call them brethren" (Heb. 2:11).

## THE CHOICE THAT CONFRONTED ADAM

God planted a great number of trees in the garden of Eden, but "in the midst of the garden" -- that is, in a place of special prominence -- He planted two trees, the tree of life and the tree of the knowledge of good and evil. Adam was created innocent; he had no knowledge of good and evil. Think of a grown man, say thirty years old, who has no sense of right or wrong, no power to differentiate between the two! Would you not say such a man was undeveloped? Well, that is exactly what Adam was. And God brings him into the garden and says to him, in effect, 'Now the garden is full of trees, full of fruits, and of the fruit of every tree you may eat freely. But in the very midst of the garden is one tree called "the tree of the knowledge of good and evil"; you must not eat of that, for in the day that you do so you will surely die. But remember, the name of the other tree close by is Life.' What, then, is the meaning of these two trees? Adam was, so to speak, created morally neutral -- neither sinful nor holy, but innocent -- and God put those two trees there so that he might exercise free choice. He could choose the tree of life, or he could choose the tree of the knowledge of good and evil.

Now the knowledge of good and evil, though forbidden to Adam, is not wrong in itself. Without it however Adam is in a sense limited in that he cannot decide for himself on moral issues. Judgment of right and wrong resides not in him but in God, and Adam's only course when faced with any question is to refer it to Jehovah God. Thus you have a life in the garden which is totally dependent on God. These two trees, then, typify two deep principles; they represent two planes of life, the Divine and the human. The "tree of life" is God Himself, for God is life. He is the highest form of life, and He is also the source and goal of life. And the fruit: what is that? It is our Lord Jesus Christ. You cannot eat the tree but you can eat the fruit. No one is able to receive God as God, but we can receive the Lord Jesus. The fruit is the edible part, the receivable part of the tree. So -may I say it reverently? -- the Lord Jesus is really God in a receivable form. God in Christ we can receive.

If Adam should take of the tree of life, he would partake of the life of God and thus become a `son' of God, in the sense of having in him a life that derived from God. There you would have God's life in union with man: a race of men having the life of God in them and living in constant dependence upon God for that life. If on the other hand Adam should turn the other way and take the fruit of the tree of the knowledge of good and evil, then he would develop his own manhood along natural lines apart from God. Reaching a peak of attainment as a self-sufficient being, he would have the power in himself to form independent judgment, but he would have no life from God. So this was the alternative that lay before him. Choosing the way of the Spirit, the way of obedience, he could become a `son' of God, living in dependence upon God for his life; or, taking the natural course, he could put the finishing touch to himself, as it were, by becoming a self-dependent being, judging and acting apart from God. The history of humanity is the outcome of the choice he made.

## ADAM'S CHOICE THE REASON FOR THE CROSS

Adam chose the tree of the knowledge of good and evil and thereby took up independent ground. In doing so he became (as man is now in his own eyes) a `fully developed' man. He could command a knowledge; he could decide for himself; he could go on or stop. From then on he was "wise" (Genesis 3:6). But the consequence for his was death rather than life, because the choice he had made involved complicity with Satan and brought him therefore under the judgment of God. That is why access to the tree of life had thereafter to be forbidden to him.

Two planes of life had been set before Adam: that of Divine life in dependence upon God, and that of human life with its `independent' resources. Adam's choice of the latter was sin, because thereby he allied himself with Satan to thwart the eternal purpose of God. He did so by choosing to develop his manhood -- to become perhaps a very fine man, even by his standards a `perfect' man -- apart from God. But the end was death, because he had not in him the Divine life necessary to realize God's purpose in his being, but had chosen to become instead an `independent' agent of the Enemy. Thus in Adam we all become sinners, equally dominated by Satan, equally subject to the law of sin and death, and equally deserving of the wrath of God.

From this we see the Divine reason for the death and resurrection of the Lord Jesus. We see too the Divine reason for true consecration -- for reckoning ourselves to be dead unto sin but alive unto God in Christ Jesus, and for presenting ourselves unto Him as alive from the dead. We must all go to the Cross, because what is in us by nature is a self-life, subject to the law of sin. Adam chose a self-life rather than a Divine life; so God had to gather up all that was in Adam and do away with it. Our `old man' has been crucified. God has put us all in Christ and crucified Him as the last Adam, and thus all that is of Adam has passed away.

Then Christ arose in new form; with a body still, but `in the Spirit', no longer `in the flesh'. "The last Adam became a life-giving spirit" (1 Cor. 15:45). The Lord Jesus now has a resurrected body, a spiritual body, a glorious body, and since He is no longer in the flesh He can now be received by all. "He that eateth me, he also shall live because of me", said Jesus (John 6:57). The Jews revolted at the thought of eating His flesh and drinking His blood, but of course they could not receive Him then because He was still literally in the flesh. Now that He is in the Spirit every one of us can receive Him, and it is by partaking of His resurrection life that we are constituted children of God. "As many as received him, to them gave he the right to become children of God ... which were born ... of God." (John 1:12,13).

God is not out to reform our life. It is not His thought to bring it to a certain stage of refinement, for it is on a totally wrong plane. On that plane He cannot now bring man to glory. He must have a new man; one born anew, born of God. Regeneration and justification go together.

## HE THAT HATH THE SON HATH THE LIFE

There are various planes of life. Human life lies between the life of the lower animals and the life of God. We cannot bridge the gulf that divides us from the plan above or the plan below, and the distance that separates us from the life of God is vastly greater than that which separates us from the life of the lower animals.

In China one day I called on a Christian leader who was sick in bed, and whom, for the sake of this story, I shall call `Mr. Wong' (though that was not his real name). He was a very learned man, a Doctor of Philosophy, and one esteemed throughout the whole of china for his high moral principles, and he had long been engaged in Christian work. But he did not believe in the need for regeneration; he only proclaimed a social gospel. When I called on Mr. Wong his pet dog was by his bedside, and after speaking with him of the things of God and of the nature of His work in us, I pointed to the dog and inquired his name. He told me he was called Fido. `Is Fido his Christian name or his surname?' I asked (using the common Chinese terms for `personal name' and `family name'). `Oh, that is just his name', he said. `Do you mean that is just his Christian name? Can I call him Fido Wong?' I continued. `Certainly not!' came the emphatic reply. `But he lives in your family', I protested, `Why don't you call him Fido Wong?' Then, indicating his two daughters, I asked `Are your daughters not called Miss Wong?' `Yes!' `Well then, why cannot I call your dog Master Wong?' The Doctor laughed, and I went on: `Do you see what I am getting at? Your daughters were born into your family and they bear your name because you have communicated your life to them. Your dog may be an intelligent dog, a well-behaved dog, and altogether a most remarkable dog; but the question is not, Is he a good or a bad dog? It is merely, Is he a dog? He does not need to be bad to be disqualified from being a member of your family; he only needs to be a dog. The same principle applies to you in your relationship to God. The question is not whether you are a bad man or a good man, more or less, but simply, Are you a man? If your life is on a lower plane than that of God's life, then you cannot belong to the Divine family. Throughout your life your aim in preaching has been to turn bad men into good men; but men as such, whether good or bad, can have no vital relationship with God. Our only hope as men is to receive the Son of God, and when we do so His life in us will constitute us sons of God.' The Doctor saw the truth, and that day he became a member of God's family by receiving the Son of God into his heart.

What we today possess in Christ is more than Adam lost. Adam was only a developed man. He remained on that plane, and never possessed the life of God. But we who receive the Son of God not only receive the forgiveness of sins; we receive also the Divine life which was represented in the garden by the tree of life. By the new birth we receive something Adam never had; we possess what he missed.

## THEY ARE ALL OF ONE

God wants sons who shall be joint-heirs with Christ in glory. That is His goal; but how can He bring that about? Turn now to Hebrews 2:10 and 11: "It became him, for whom are all things, and through whom are all things, in bringing many sons unto glory, to make the author of their salvation perfect through sufferings. For both he that sanctifieth and they that are sanctified are all of one: for which cause he is not ashamed to call them brethren." There are two parties mentioned here, namely, "many sons" and "the author of their salvation", or, in different terms, "he that sanctifieth" and "they that are sanctified". But these two parties are said to be "all of one". The Lord Jesus as Man derived His life from God, and (in another sense, but just as truly) we derive our new life from God. He was "begotten ... of the Holy Ghost" (Matthew 1:20 mg.), and we were "born of .... the spirit", "born ... of God" (John 3:5; 1:13). So, God says, we are all of One. "Of" in the Greek means "out of". The first begotten Son and the many sons are all (though in different senses) "out of" the one Source of life. Do you realize that we have the same life today that God has? The life which He has in Heaven is the life which He has imparted to us here on the earth. That is the precious "gift of God" (Rom. 6:23). It is for that reason that we can live a life of holiness, for it is not our own life that has been changed, but the life of God that has been imparted to us.

Do you notice that, in this consideration of the eternal purpose, the whole question of sin ultimately goes out? It no longer has a place. Sin came in with Adam, and even when it has been dealt with, as it has to be, we are only brought back to the point where Adam was. But in relating us again to the Divine purpose -- in, as it were, restoring to us access to the tree of life -- redemption has given us far more than Adam ever had. It has made us partakers of the very life of God Himself.

# CHAPTER 8: THE HOLY SPIRIT

We have spoken of the eternal purpose of God as the motive and explanation of all His dealings with us. Now, before we return to our study of the phases of Christian experience as set forth in Romans, we must digress yet again in order to consider something which lies at the heart of all our experience as the vitalizing power of effective life and service. I refer to the personal presence and ministry of the Holy Spirit of God.    And here, too, let us take as our starting-point two verses from Romans, one from each of our sections. "The love of God hath been shed abroad in our hearts through the Holy Ghost which was given unto us" (Romans 5:5). "If any man hath not the Spirit of Christ, he is none of us" (Romans 8:9).

God does not give His gifts at random, nor dispense them in any arbitrary fashion. They are given freely to all, but they are given on a definite basis. God has truly "blessed us with every spiritual blessing in the heavenly places in Christ" (Ephesians 1:3), but if those blessings which are ours in Christ are to become ours in experience, we must know on what ground we can appropriate them.

In considering the gift of the Holy Spirit it is helpful to think of this in two aspects, as the Spirit outpoured and the Spirit indwelling, and our purpose now is to understand on what basis this twofold gift of the Holy Spirit becomes ours. I have no doubt that we are right in distinguishing thus between the outward and the inward manifestations of His working, and that as we go on we shall find the distinction helpful. Moreover, when we compare them, we cannot but come to the conclusion that the inward activity of the Holy Spirit is the more precious. But to say this is not for one moment to imply that His outward activity is not also precious, for God only gives good gifts to His children. Unfortunately we are apt to esteem our privileges lightly because of their sheer abundance. The Old Testament saints, who were not as favoured as we are, could appreciate more readily than we do the preciousness of this gift of the outpoured Spirit. In their day it was a gift given only to the select few -- chiefly to priests, judges, kings and prophets

233

-- whereas now it is the portion of every child of God. Think! we who are mere nonentities can have the same Spirit resting upon us as rested upon Moses the friend of God, upon David the beloved king, and upon Elijah the mighty prophet. By receiving the gift of the outpoured Holy Spirit we join the ranks of God's chosen servants of the Old Testament dispensation. Once we see the value of this gift of God, and realize too our deep need of it, we shall immediately ask, How can I receive the Holy Spirit in this way to equip me with spiritual gifts and to empower me for service? Upon what basis has the Spirit been given?

## THE SPIRIT OUTPOURED

Let us turn first to Acts chapter 2 verses 32 to 36:

"(32) This Jesus did God raise up, whereof we all are witnesses. (33) Being therefore by the right hand of God exalted, and having received of the Father the promise of the Holy Ghost, he hath poured forth this, which ye see and hear. (34) For David ascended not into the heavens: but he saith himself, The Lord said unto my Lord, sit thou on my right hand, (35) Till I make thine enemies the footstool of thy feet.(36) Let all the house of Israel therefore know assuredly, that God hath made him both Lord and Christ, this Jesus whom ye crucified."

Let us for the moment set verses 34 and 35 aside and consider verses 33 and 36 together. The former are a quotation from the 110th Psalm and are really a parenthesis, so we shall get the force of Peter's argument better if we ignore them for the time being. In verse 33 Peter states that the Lord Jesus was exalted "at the right hand of God" (mg.). What was the result? He "received of the Father the promise of the Holy Ghost". And what followed? Pentecost! The result of His exaltation was -- "this, which ye see and hear".

What, then, was the basis upon which the Spirit was first given to the Lord Jesus to be poured out upon His people? It was His exaltation to Heaven. This passage makes it absolutely clear that the Holy Spirit was poured out because the Lord Jesus was exalted. The outpouring of the Spirit has no relation to your merits or mine, but only to the merits of the Lord Jesus. The question of what we are does not come into consideration at all here, but only what He is. He is glorified; therefore the Spirit is poured out.

Because the Lord Jesus died on the Cross, I have received forgiveness of sins; because the Lord Jesus rose from the dead, I have received new life;

because the Lord Jesus has been exalted to the right hand of the Father, I have received the outpoured Spirit. All is because of Him; nothing is because of me. Remission of sins is not based on human merit, but on the Lord's crucifixion; regeneration is not based on human merit, but on the Lord's resurrection; and the enduement with the Holy Spirit is not based on human merit, but on the Lord's exaltation. The Holy Spirit has not been poured out on you or me to prove how great we are, but to prove the greatness of the Son of God.

Now look at verse 36. There is a word here which demands our careful attention: the word 'therefore'. How is this word generally used? Not to introduce a statement, but to follow a statement that has already been made. Its use always implies that something has been mentioned before. Now what has preceded this particular 'therefore'? With what is it connected? It cannot reasonably be connected with either verse 34 or verse 35, but it quite obviously relates back to verse 33. Peter has just referred to the outpouring of the Spirit upon the disciples "which ye see and hear", and he says: "Let all the house of Israel therefore know assuredly, that God hath made him both Lord and Christ, this Jesus whom ye crucified". Peter says, in effect, to his audience: 'This outpouring of the Spirit, which you have witnessed with your own eyes and ears, proves that Jesus of Nazareth whom ye crucified is now both Lord and Christ'. The Holy Spirit was poured out on earth to prove what had taken place in Heaven -- the exaltation of Jesus of Nazareth to the right hand of God. The purpose of Pentecost is to prove the Lordship of Jesus Christ.

There was a young man named Joseph, who was dearly loved of his father. One day news reached the father of the death of his son, and for years Jacob lamented Joseph's loss. But Joseph was not in the grave; he was in a place of glory and power. After Jacob had been mourning the death of his son for years, it was suddenly reported to him that Joseph was alive and in a high position in Egypt. At first Jacob could not take it in. It was too good to be true. But ultimately he was persuaded that the story of Joseph's exaltation was really a fact. How did he come to believe in it? He went out, and saw the chariots that Joseph had sent from Egypt.

What do the chariots represent here? They surely typify here the Holy Spirit, sent both to be the evidence that God's Son is in glory and to convey us there. How do we know that Jesus of Nazareth, who was crucified by wicked men nearly two thousand years ago, did not just die a martyr's death but is at the Father's right hand in glory? How can we know for a surety that

He is Lord of lords and King of kings? We can know it beyond dispute because He has poured out His Spirit upon us. Hallelujah! Jesus is Lord!

Jesus is Christ! Jesus of Nazareth is both Lord and Christ!

The exaltation of the Lord Jesus is the basis on which the Spirit has been given. Is it possible then that the Lord has been glorified and you have not received the Spirit? On what basis did you receive forgiveness of sins? Was it because you prayed so earnestly, or because you read your Bible from cover to cover, or because of your regular attendance at Church? Was it because of your merits at all? No! A thousand times, No! On what ground then were your sins forgiven? "Apart from shedding of blood there is no remission" (Hebrews 9:22). The sole ground of forgiveness is the shedding of blood; and since the precious Blood has been shed, your sins have been forgiven.

Now the principle on which we receive the enduement of the Holy Spirit is the very same as that on which we receive forgiveness of sins. The Lord has been crucified, therefore our sins have been forgiven; the Lord has been glorified, therefore the Spirit has been poured out upon us. Is it possible that the Son of God shed His Blood and that your sins, dear child of God, have not been forgiven? Never! Then is it possible that the Son of God has been glorified and you have not received the Spirit? Never!

Some of you may say: I agree with all this, but I have no experience of it. Am I to sit down smugly and say I have everything, when I know perfectly well I have nothing? No, we must never rest content with objective facts alone. We need subjective experience also; but that experience will only come as we rest upon Divine facts. God's facts are the basis of our experience.

Let us go back again to the question of justification. How were you justified? Not by doing anything at all, but by accepting the fact that the Lord had done everything. Enduement with the Holy Spirit becomes yours in exactly the same way as justification, not by your doing anything yourself, but by your putting your faith in what the Lord has already done. If we lack the experience, we must ask God for a revelation of the eternal fact of the baptism of the Holy Spirit as the gift of the exalted Lord to His Church. Once we see that, effort will cease, and prayer will give place to praise. It was a revelation of what the Lord had done for the world that brought to an end our efforts to secure forgiveness of sins, and it is a revelation of what the Lord has done for His Church that will bring to an end our efforts to secure

THE NORMAL CHRISTIAN LIFE

the baptism of the Holy Spirit. We work because we have not seen the work of Christ. But when once we have seen that, faith will spring up in our hearts, and as we believe, experience will follow.

Some time ago a young man, who had only been a Christian for five weeks and who had formerly been violently opposed to the gospel, attended a series of meetings which I was addressing in Shanghai. At the close of one in which I was speaking along the above lines, he went home and began to pray earnestly, 'Lord, I do want the power of the Holy Spirit. Seeing Thou hast now been glorified, wilt Thou not now pour out Thy Spirit upon me?' Then he corrected himself: 'Oh no, Lord, that's all wrong!' and began to pray again: 'Lord Jesus, we are in a life-partnership, Thou and I, and the Father has promised us two things -- glory for Thee, and the Spirit for me. Thou, Lord, hast received the glory; therefore it is unthinkable that I have not received the Spirit. Lord, I praise Thee! Thou hast already received the glory, and I have already received the Spirit.' From that day the power of the Spirit was consciously upon him.

## FAITH IS AGAIN THE KEY

As for forgiveness, so equally for the coming upon us of the Holy Spirit, the whole question is one of faith. As soon as we see the Lord Jesus on the Cross, we know our sins are forgiven; and as soon as we see the Lord Jesus on the Throne, we know the Holy Spirit has been poured out upon us. The basis upon which we receive the enduement of the Holy Spirit is not our praying and fasting and waiting, but the exaltation of Christ. Those who emphasize tarrying and hold 'tarrying meetings' only mislead us, for the gift is not for the 'favoured few' but for all, because it is not given on the ground of what we are at all, but of what Christ is. The Spirit has been poured out to prove His goodness and greatness, not ours. Christ has been crucified, therefore we have been forgiven: Christ has been glorified, therefore we have been endued with power from on high. It is all because of Him.

Suppose an unbeliever expresses the desire to be saved, and you explain to him the way of salvation and pray with him. Suppose then he prays after this fashion: 'Lord Jesus, I believe Thou hast died for me, and that Thou canst blot out all my sins. I truly believe Thou wilt forgive me.' Have you any confidence that that man is saved? When will you rest assured that he has really been born again? Not when he prays: 'Lord, I believe Thou wilt forgive my sins', but when he says: 'Lord, I praise Thee that Thou hast

237

forgiven my sins. Thou hast died for me; therefore my sins are blotted out' You believe a person is saved when prayer turns to praise -- when he ceases to ask the Lord to forgive him, but praises Him that He has already done so because the Blood of the Lamb has already been shed.

In the same way, you can pray and wait for years and never experience the Spirit's power; but when you cease to plead with the Lord to pour out His Spirit upon you, and when instead you trustfully praise Him that the Spirit has been poured out because the Lord Jesus has been glorified, you will find that your problem is solved. Praise God! no single child of His need agonize, nor even wait, for the Spirit to be given. Jesus is not going to be made Lord; He is Lord. Therefore I am not going to receive the Spirit; I have received the Spirit. It is all a question of the faith which comes by revelation. When our eyes are opened to see that the Spirit has already been poured out because Jesus has already been glorified, then prayer turns to praise in our hearts.

All spiritual blessings are given on a definite basis. God's gifts are freely given, but there are conditions which must be fulfilled on our part before the reception of them is possible. There is a passage in God's Word which makes the conditions of the outpoured Spirit perfectly clear: "Repent ye, and be baptized every one of you in the name of Jesus Christ unto the remission of your sins; and ye shall receive the gift of the Holy Ghost. For to you is the promise, and to your children, and to all that are afar off, even as many as the Lord our God shall call unto him" (Acts 2:38,39). Four things are mentioned in this passage: Repentance, Baptism, Forgiveness, and the Holy Spirit. The first two are conditions, the second two are gifts. What are the conditions to be fulfilled if we are to have forgiveness of sins? According to the Word they are two: repentance and baptism.

The first condition is repentance, which means a change of mind. Formerly I thought sin a pleasant thing, but now I have changed my mind about it; formerly I thought the world an attractive place, but now I know better; formerly I regarded it a miserable business to be a Christian, but now I think differently. Once I thought certain things delightful, now I think them vile; once I thought other things utterly worthless, now I think them most precious. That is a change of mind, and that is repentance. No life can be truly changed apart from such a change of mind.

The second condition is baptism. Baptism is an outward expression of an inward faith. When in my heart I truly believe that I have died with Christ, have been buried and have risen with Him, then I ask for baptism. I thereby declare publicly what I believe privately. Baptism is faith in action.    Here

238

then are two divinely appointed conditions of forgiveness -repentance, and faith publicly expressed. Have you repented? Have you testified publicly to your union with your Lord? Then have you received remission of sins and the gift of the Holy Ghost? You say you have only received the first gift, not the second. But, my friend, God offered you two things if you fulfilled two conditions! Why have you only taken one? What are you doing about the second?

Suppose I went into a book-shop, selected a two-volume book, priced at ten shillings, and, having put down a ten-shilling note, walked out of the shop, carelessly leaving one volume on the counter. When I reached home and discovered the oversight, what do you think I should do? I should go straight back to the shop to get the forgotten book, but I should not dream of paying anything for it. I should simply explain to the shopkeeper that both volumes were duly paid for, and ask him if he would therefore kindly let me have the second one; and without any further payment I should march happily out of the shop with my possession under my arm. Would you not do the same under the same circumstances?

But you are under the same circumstances. If you have fulfilled the conditions you are entitled to two gifts, not just one. You have already taken the one; why not just come and take the other now? Say to the Lord, 'Lord, I have complied with the conditions for receiving remission of sins and the gift of the Holy Ghost, but I have foolishly only taken the former. Now I have come back to take the gift of the Holy Ghost, and I praise Thee for it.'

## THE DIVERSITY OF THE EXPERIENCE

But you ask: 'How shall I know that the Holy Spirit is come upon me?' I cannot tell how you will know, but you will know. No description has been given us of the personal sensations and emotions of the disciples at Pentecost. We do not know exactly how they felt, but we do know that their feelings and behaviour were somewhat abnormal, because people seeing them said they were intoxicated. When the Holy Spirit falls upon God's people there will be some things which the world cannot account for. There will be supernatural accompaniments of some kind, though it be no more than an overwhelming sense of the Divine Presence. We cannot and we must not stipulate what particular form such outward expressions will take in any given case, but one thing is sure, that each one upon whom the Spirit of God falls will know it.

When the Holy Spirit came upon the disciples at Pentecost there was something quite extraordinary about their behaviour, and Peter offered an explanation from God's Word to all who witnessed it. This, in substance, is what he said: 'When the Holy Spirit falls upon believers, some will prophesy, some will dream dreams, and others will see visions. This is what God has stated through the prophet Joel.' But did Peter prophesy? Well, hardly in the sense in which Joel meant it. Did the hundred and twenty prophesy or see visions? We are not told that they did. Did they dream dreams? How could they, for were they not all wide awake? Well then, what did Peter mean by using a quotation that seems scarcely to fit the case at all? In the passage quoted (Joel 2:28,29), prophesy, dreams and visions are said to accompany the outpouring of the Spirit, yet these evidences were apparently lacking at Pentecost.

On the other hand, Joel's prophecy said not a word about "a sound as of the rushing of a mighty wind", nor about "tongues parting asunder like as of fire" as accompaniments of the Spirit's outpouring; yet these were manifest in that upper room. And where in Joel do we find mention of speaking in other tongues? And yet the disciples at Pentecost did so.

What did Peter mean? Imagine him quoting God's Word to show that the experience of Pentecost was the outpouring of the Spirit spoken of by Joel, without a single one of the evidences mentioned by Joel being found at Pentecost. What the Book mentioned the disciples lacked, and what the disciples had the Book did not mention! It looks as though Peter's quotation of the Book disproves his point rather than proving it. What is the explanation of this mystery?

Let us recall that Peter was himself speaking under the control of the Holy Spirit. The Book of the Acts was written by the Spirit's inspiration, and not one word was spoken at random. There is no misfit, but a perfect harmony. Note carefully that Peter did not say: 'What you see and hear fulfills what was spoken by the prophet Joel'. What he said was: "This is that which hath been spoken by the prophet Joel" (Acts 2:16). It was not a case of fulfillment, but of an experience of the same order. "This is that" means that 'this which you see and hear is of the same order as that which is foretold'. When it is a case of fulfillment, each experience is reduplicated and prophecy is prophecy, dreams are dreams, and visions are visions; but when Peter says "This is that", it is not a question of the one being a replica of the other, but of the one belonging to the same category as the other. "This" amounts to the same thing as "that"; "this" is the equivalent of "that"; "this is that". What is being emphasized by the Holy Spirit through Peter is the diversity of the experience. The outward evidences may be many and varied, and we have to admit that occasionally they are strange; but the Spirit is one, and He is Lord. (See Corinthians 12:4-6).

What happened to R.A. Torrey when the Holy Spirit came upon him after he had been a minister for years? Let him tell it in his own words: 'I recall the exact spot where I was kneeling in prayer in my study ... It was very quiet moment, one of the most quiet moments I ever knew ... Then God simply said to me, not in any audible voice, but in my heart. "It's yours. Now go and preach." He had already said it to me in His Word in 1 John 5:14,15; but I did not then know my Bible as I know it now, and God had pity on my ignorance and said it directly to my soul... I went and preached, and I have been a new minister from that day to this... Some time after this experience (I do not recall just how long after), while sitting in my room one day ... suddenly ... I found myself shouting (I was not brought up to shout and I am not of a shouting temperament, but I shouted like the loudest shouting Methodist), "Glory to God, glory to God, glory to God", and I could not stop. ... But that was not when I was baptized with the Holy Spirit. I was baptized with the Holy Spirit when I took Him by simple faith in The Word of God."[10]

The outward manifestations in Torrey's case were not the same as those described by Joel or by Peter, but "this is that". It is not a facsimile, yet it is the same thing.

And how did D.L. Moody feel and act when the Spirit came upon him?

'I was crying all the time that God would fill me with His Spirit. Well, one day, in the city of New York -- oh, what a day! -- I cannot describe it, I seldom refer to it; it is almost too sacred an experience to name. Paul had an experience of which he never spoke for fourteen years. I can only say that God revealed Himself to me, and I had such an experience of His love that I had to ask Him to stay His hand. I went preaching again. The sermons were not different; I did not present any new truths; and yet hundreds were converted. I would not now be placed back where I was before that blessed

---

[10] The Holy Spirit, who He is and what He does, by R.A. Torrey, D.D., pp. 198-9.

experience if you should give me all the world - it would be as the small dust of the balance.;[11]

The outward manifestation that accompanied Moody's experience did not tally exactly with Joel's description, or Peter's, or Torrey's, but who could doubt that "this" which Moody experienced was "that" experienced by the disciples at Pentecost? It was not the same in manifestation, but it was the very same in essence.

And what was the experience of the great Charles Finney when the power of the Holy Ghost came upon him?

`I received a mighty baptism of the Holy Ghost without any expectation of it, without ever having the thought in my mind that there was any such thing for me, without any recollection that I had ever heard the thing mentioned by any person in the world, the Holy Spirit descended upon me in a manner that seemed to go through me body and soul. No words can express the wonderful love that was shed abroad in my heart. I wept aloud with joy and love.'[12]

Finney's experience was not a duplicate of Pentecost, nor of Torrey's experience, nor of Moody's; but "this" certainly was "that".

When the Holy Spirit is poured out upon God's people their experiences will differ widely. Some will receive new vision, others will know a new liberty in soul-winning, others will proclaim the Word of God with power, and yet others will be filled with heavenly joy or overflowing praise. "This ... and this ... and this ... is that!" Let us praise the Lord for every new experience that relates to the exaltation of Christ and of which it can truly be said that "this" is an evidence of "that". There is nothing stereotyped about God's dealings with His children. Therefore we must not by our prejudices and preconceptions make a water-tight compartment for the working of His Spirit, either in our own lives or in the lives of others. This applies equally to those who require some particular manifestation (such as `speaking with tongues') as evidence that the spirit has come upon them and to those who deny that any manifestation is given at all. We must leave God free to work as He wills, and to give what evidence He pleases of the work He does. He is Lord, and it is not for us to legislate for Him.    Let us rejoice that Jesus is on the throne, and let us praise Him that, since He has been glorified, the

---

[11] The Life of Dwight L. Moody, by his son, W.R. Moody, p. 149.

[12] Autobiography of Charles E. Finney, chapter 2.

Spirit has been poured out upon us all. As we accept the Divine fact in all the simplicity of faith, we shall know it with such assurance in our own experience that we shall dare to proclaim with confidence -- "This is that!"

## THE SPIRIT INDWELLING

We move on now to the second aspect of the gift of the Holy Spirit, which, as we shall see in our next chapter, is more particularly the subject of Romans 8. It is that which we have spoken of as the Spirit indwelling. "If so be that the Spirit of God dwelleth in you ..." (Romans 8:9). "If the Spirit outpoured, so with the Spirit indwelling, if we are to know in experienced that which is ours in fact, our first need is of Divine revelation. When we see Christ as Lord objectively -- that is, as exalted to the throne in Heaven -- then we shall experience the power of the Spirit upon us. When we see Christ as Lord subjectively -- that is, as effective Ruler within our lives -- then we shall know the power of the Spirit within us.

A revelation of the indwelling Spirit was the remedy Paul offered the Corinthian Christians for their unspirituality. It is important to note that the Christians in Corinth had become preoccupied with the visible signs of the Holy Spirit's outpouring and were making much of `tongues' and miracles, while at the same time their lives were full of contradictions and were a reproach to the Lord's Name. They had quite evidently received the Holy Spirit and yet they remained spiritually immature; and the remedy God offered them for this is the remedy He offers His Church today for the same complaint.

In his letter to them Paul wrote: "Know ye not that ye are a temple of God, and that the Spirit of God dwelleth in you?" (1 Corinthians 3:16). For others he prayed for enlightenment of heart, "...that ye may know" (Ephesians 1:18). A knowledge of Divine facts was the need of the Christians then, and it is no less the need of Christians today. W need the `opening of the eyes of our understanding' that we may know that God Himself through the Holy Spirit has taken up His abode in our hearts. God is present in the person of the Spirit, and Christ is present in the person of the Spirit too. Thus if the Holy Spirit dwells in our hearts we have the Father and the Son dwelling within. That is no mere theory or doctrine, but a blessed reality. We may perhaps have realized that the Spirit is actually within our hearts, but have we realized that He is a Person? Have we understood that to have the Spirit within us it to have the living God within?

To many Christians the Holy Spirit is quite unreal. They regard Him as a mere influence -- and influence for good, no doubt, but just an influence for all that. In their thinking, conscience and the Spirit are more or less identified as some 'thing' within them that brings them to book when they are bad and tries to show them how to be good. The trouble with the Corinthian Christians was not that they lacked the indwelling Spirit but that they lacked the knowledge of His presence. They failed to realize the greatness of the One who had come to make His abode in their hearts; so Paul wrote to them: "Know ye not that ye are a temple of God, and that the Spirit of God dwelleth in you?" Yes, that was the remedy for their unspirituality -- just to know who He really was who dwelt within.

## THE TREASURE IN THE VESSEL

Do you know, my friends, that the Spirit within you is very God? Oh that our eyes were opened to see the greatness of God's gift! Oh that we might realize the vastness of the resources secreted in our own hearts! I could shout with joy as I think, 'The Spirit who dwells within me is no mere influence, but a living Person; He is very God. The infinite God is within my heart!' I am at a loss to convey to you the blessedness of this discovery, that the Holy Spirit dwelling within my heart is a Person. I can only repeat: 'He is a Person!' and repeat it again: 'He is a Person!' and repeat it yet again: 'He is a Person!' Oh, my friends, I would fain repeat it to you a hundred times -- The Spirit of God within me is a Person! I am only an earthen vessel, but in that earthen vessel I carry a treasure of unspeakable worth, even the Lord of glory.

All the worry and fret of God's children would end if their eyes were opened to see the greatness of the treasure hid in their hearts. Do you know, there are resources enough in your own heart to meet the demand of every circumstance in which you will ever find yourself? Do you know there is power enough there to move the city in which you live? Do you know there is power enough to shake the universe? Let me tell you once more -- I say it with the utmost reverence: You who have been born again of the Spirit of God -- you carry God in your heart!

All the flippancy of the children of God would cease too if they realized the greatness of the treasure deposited within them. If you have only ten shillings in your pocket you can march gaily along the street, talking lightly as you go, and swinging your stick in the air. It matters little if you lose your money, for there is not much at stake. But if you carry a thousand pounds in your pocket, the position is vastly different, and your whole demeanour will be different too. There will be great gladness in your heart, but no careless jaunting along the road; and once in a while you will slacken your pace and, slipping your hand into your pocket, you will quietly finger your treasure again, and then with joyful solemnity continue on your way.

In Old Testament times there were hundreds of tents in the camp of Israel, but there was one tent quite different from all the rest. In the common tents you could do just as you pleased -- eat or fast, work or rest, be joyful or sober, noisy or silent. But that other tent was a tent that commanded reverence and awe. You might move in and out of the common tents talking noisily and laughing gaily, but as soon as you neared that special tent you instinctively walked more quietly, and when you stood right before it you bowed your head in solemn silence. No one could touch it with impunity. If man or beast dared to do so, death was the sure penalty. What was so very special about it? It was the temple of the living God. There was little unusual about the tent itself, for it was outwardly of very ordinary material, but the great God had chosen to make it His abode.

Do you realize what happened at your conversion? God came into your heart and made it His temple. In Old Testament days God dwelt in a temple made of stone; today He dwells in a temple composed of living believers. When we really see that God has made our hearts His dwelling place, what a deep reverence will come over our lives! All lightness, all frivolity will end, and all self-pleasing too, when we know that we are the temple of God and that the Spirit of God dwells within us. Has it really come to you that wherever you go you carry with you the Holy Spirit of God? You do not just carry your Bible with you, or even much good teaching about God, but God Himself.

The reason why many Christians do not experience the power of the Spirit, though He actually dwells in their hearts, is that they lack reverence. And they lack reverence because they have not had their eyes opened to the fact of His presence. The fact is there, but they have not seen it. Why is it that some Christians are living victorious lives while others live in a state of constant defeat? The difference is not accounted for by the presence or absence of the Spirit (for He dwells in the heart of every child of God) but by this, that some recognize His indwelling and others do not. True revelation of the fact of the Spirit's indwelling will revolutionize the life of any Christian.

245

"Know ye not that your body is a temple of the Holy Ghost which is in you, which ye have from God? and ye are not your own; for ye were bought with a price: glorify God therefore in your body" (1 Cor. 6:19,20). This verse now takes us a stage further, for, when once we have made the discovery of the fact that we are the dwelling place of God, then a full surrender of ourselves to God must follow. When we see that we are the temple of God we shall immediately recognize that we are not our own. Consecration will follow revelation. The difference between victorious Christians and defeated ones is not that some have the Spirit while others have not, but that some know His indwelling and others do not, and that consequently some recognize the Divine ownership of their lives while others are still their own masters.

Revelation is the first step to holiness, and consecration is the second. A day must come in our lives, as definite as the day of our conversion, when we give up all right to ourselves and submit to the absolute Lordship of Jesus Christ. There may be a practical issue raised by God to test the reality of our consecration, but whether that be so or not, there must be a day when, without reservation, we surrender everything to Him -- ourselves, our families, our possessions, our business and our time. All we are and have becomes His, to be held henceforth entirely at His disposal. >From that day we are no longer our own masters, but only stewards. Not until the Lordship of Jesus Christ is a settled thing in our hearts can the Spirit really operate effectively in us. He cannot direct our lives effectually until all control of them is committed to Him. If we do not give Him absolute authority in our lives, He can be present, but He cannot be powerful. The power of the Spirit is stayed.

Are you living for the Lord or for yourself? Perhaps that is too general a question, so let me be more specific. Is there anything God is asking of you that you are withholding from Him? Is there any point of contention between you and Him? Not till every controversy is settled and the Holy Spirit is given full sway can He reproduce the life of Christ in the heart of any believer.

An American friend, now with the Lord, whose name we will call Paul, cherished the hope from his early youth that one day he would be called `Dr. Paul'. When he was quite a little chap he began to dream of the day when he would enter the university, and he imagined himself first studying for his

M.A. degree and then for his Ph.D. Then at length the glad day would arrive when all would greet him as `Dr. Paul'.

The Lord saved him and called him to preach, and before long he became pastor of a large congregation. By that time he had his degree and was studying for his doctorate, but, despite splendid progress in his studies and a good measure of success as a pastor, he was a very dissatisfied man. He was a Christian, but his life was not Christ-like; he had the Spirit of God within him, but he did not enjoy the Spirit's presence or experience His power. He thought to himself, `I am a preacher of the Gospel and the pastor of a church. I tell my people they should love the Word of God, but I do not really love it myself. I exhort them to pray, but I myself have little inclination to pray. I tell them to live a holy life, but my own life is not holy. I warn them not to love the world, and, though outwardly I shun it, yet in my heart I myself still love it dearly.' In his distress he cried to the Lord to cause him to know the power of the indwelling Spirit, but though he prayed and prayed for months, no answer came. Then he fasted and besought the Lord to show him any hindrance there might be in his life. That answer was not long in coming, and it was this: `I long that you should know the power of My Spirit, but your heart is set on something that I do not wish you to have. You have yielded to me all but one thing, and that one thing you are holding to yourself -- your Ph.D.' Well, to you or me it might be of little consequence whether we were addressed as plain `Mr. Paul' or as `Dr. Paul', but to him it was his very life. He had dreamed of it from childhood and labored for it all through his youth, and now the thing he prized above all was almost within his grasp. In two short months it would be his. So he reasoned with the Lord in this wise: `Is there any harm for me to be a Doctor of Philosophy? Will it not bring much more glory to Thy Name to have a Dr. Paul preaching the Gospel than a plain Mr. Paul?' But God does not change His mind, and all Mr. Paul's sound reasoning did not alter the Lord's word to him. Every time he prayed about the matter he got the same answer. Then, reasoning having failed, he resorted to bargaining with the Lord. He promised to go here or there, to do this or that, if only the Lord would allow him to have his doctor's degree; but still the Lord did not change His mind. And all the while Mr. Paul was becoming more and more hungry to know the fullness of the Spirit. This state of affairs continued to within two days of his final examination.

It was Saturday, and Mr. Paul settled down to prepare his sermon for the following day, but, study as he would, he could get no message. The ambition of a lifetime was just within reach of realization, but God made it clear that he must choose between the power he could sway through a doctor's degree and the power of God's Spirit swaying his life. That evening he yielded. `Lord', he said, `I am willing to be plain Mr. Paul all my days, but I want to know the power of the Holy Ghost in my life.'

He rose from his knees and wrote a letter to his examiners, asking to be excused from the examination on the Monday, and giving his reason. Then he retired, very happy, but not conscious of any unusual experience. Next morning he told his congregation that for the first time in six years he had no sermon to preach, and explained how it came about. The Lord blessed that testimony more abundantly than any of his well-prepared sermons, and from that time God blessed and owned him in an altogether new way. From that day he knew separation from the world, no longer as an outward thing but as a deep inward reality, and in daily experience he knew the blessedness of the Spirit's presence and power.

God is waiting for a settlement of all our controversies with Him. With Mr. Paul it was a question of his doctor's degree, but with us it may be something quite different. Our absolute surrender of ourselves to the Lord generally hinges upon some one particular thing, and God is after that one thing. He must have it, for He must have our all. I was greatly impressed by something a great national leader wrote in his autobiography: `I want nothing for myself; I want everything for my country.' If a man can be willing that his country should have everything and he himself nothing, cannot we say to our God: `Lord, I want nothing for myself; I want all for Thee. I will what Thou willest, and I want to have nothing outside Thy will.' Not until we take the place of a servant can He take His place as Lord. He is not calling us to devote ourselves to His cause: He is asking us to yield ourselves to His will. Are you willing for anything He wills? Another friend of mine, like my friend Mr. Paul, had a controversy with the Lord. before his conversion he fell in love, and as soon as he was saved he sought to win the one he loved to the Lord, but she would have nothing to do with spiritual things. the Lord made it clear to him that his relations with that girl must be broken of, but he was deeply devoted to her, so he evaded the issue and continued to serve the Lord and to win souls for Him. But he became conscious of his need for holiness, and that consciousness marked the beginning of dark days for him. He asked for the Spirit's fullness that he might have power to live a holy life, but the Lord seemed continually to ignore his request.

One morning he had to preach in another city and he spoke from Psalm 73:25: "Whom have I in heaven but thee? And there is none upon earth that

I desire beside thee." On his return home he went to a prayer meeting, and there a sister read out the very same verse from which, unknown to her, he had just preached, and followed it with the question: `Can we truly say: "There is none upon earth that I desire beside thee"?' There was power in that word. It struck right home to his heart and he had to admit to himself that he could not truthfully say that he desired no one in Heaven or earth apart from his Lord. He saw, there and then, that for him everything hinged upon his willingness to give up the girl he loved.

For some it might not have involved much, but for him it was everything. So he began to reason with the Lord: `Lord I will go to Tibet and work for Thee there if I may marry that girl'. But the Lord seemed to care a great deal more about his relationship with that girl than about his going to Tibet, and no amount of reasoning on his part availed to effect any change of emphasis on the part of the Lord. The controversy went on for several months, and when again the young man pleaded for the fullness of the Spirit, the Lord still pointed to the same thing. But that day the Lord triumphed, and that young man looked up to Him and said: `Lord, I can truly say now, "Whom have I in heaven but thee? And there is none upon earth that I desire beside thee".' And that was the beginning of a new life for him.    A forgiven sinner is quite different from an ordinary sinner, and a consecrated Christian is quite different from an ordinary Christian. May the Lord bring us to a definite issue regarding the question of His Lordship. If we do yield wholly to Him and claim the power of the indwelling Spirit, we need wait for no special feelings or supernatural manifestations, but can simply look up and praise Him that something has already happened. We can confidently thank Him that the glory of God has already filled His temple. "Know ye not that ye are the temple of God, and that the Spirit of God dwelleth in you?" "Know ye not that your body is a temple of the Holy Ghost which is in you, which ye have from God?"

# CHAPTER 9: THE MEANING AND VALUE OF ROMANS SEVEN

We must return now to our study of Romans. We broke off at the end of chapter 6 in order to consider two related subjects, namely, God's eternal purpose, which is the motive and goal of our walk with Him, and the Holy Spirit, who supplies the power and resource to bring us to that goal. We come now to Romans 7, a chapter which many have felt to be almost superfluous. Perhaps indeed it would be so if Christians really saw that the old creation has been ruled out by the Cross of Christ, and an entirely new creation brought in by His resurrection. If we have come to the point where we really `know' that, and `reckon' on that, and `present ourselves' on the basis of that, then perhaps we have no need of Romans 7.

Others have felt that the chapter is in the wrong place. They would have put it between the fifth and sixth chapters. After chapter 6 all is so perfect, so straightforward; and then comes breakdown and the cry, "O wretched man that I am!" Could anything be more of an anticlimax? And so some have argued that Paul is speaking here of his unregenerate experience. Well, we must admit that some of what he describes here is not a Christian experience, but none the less many Christians do experience it. What then is the teaching of this chapter?

Romans 6 deals with freedom from sin. Romans 7 deals with freedom from the Law. In chapter 6 Paul has told us how we could be delivered from sin, and we concluded that this was all that was required. Chapter 7 now teaches that deliverance from sin is not enough, but that we also need to know deliverance from the Law. If we are not fully emancipated from the Law we can never know full emancipation from sin. But what is the difference between deliverance from sin and deliverance from the Law? We all see the value of the former, but where is the need for the latter? Well, to appreciate this we must first understand what the Law is and what it does.

## THE FLESH AND MAN'S BREAKDOWN

Romans 7 has a new lesson to teach us. It is found in the discovery that I am "in the flesh" (Rom. 7:5), that "I am carnal" (7:18). This goes beyond the question of sin, for it relates also the matter of pleasing God. We are dealing here not with sin in its forms but with man in his carnal state. The latter includes the former but it takes us a stage further, for it leads to the discovery that in this realm too we are totally impotent, and that "they that are in the flesh cannot please God" (Rom. 8:8). How then is this discovery made? It is made with the help of the Law.

Now let us retrace our steps for a minute and attempt to describe what is probably the experience of many. Many a Christian is truly saved and yet bound by sin. It is not that he is necessarily living under the power of sin all the time, but that there are certain particular sins hampering him continually so that he hears the full Gospel message, that the Lord Jesus not only died to cleanse away our sins, but that when He died He included us sinners in His death; so that not only were our sins dealt with, but we ourselves were dealt with too. The man's eyes are opened and he knows he has been crucified with Christ. Two things follow that revelation. In the first place he reckons that he has died and risen with the Lord, and in the second place, recognizing the Lord's claim upon him, he present himself to God as alive from the dead. He sees that he has no more right over himself. This is the commencement of a beautiful Christian life, full of praise to the Lord. But then he begins to reason as follows: `I have died with Christ and am raised with Him, and I have given myself over to Him for ever; now I must do something for Him, since He has done so much for me. I want to please Him and do His will.' So, after the step of consecration, he seeks to discover the will of God, and sets out to obey Him. Then he makes a strange discovery. He thought he could do the will of God and he thought he loved it, but gradually he finds he does not always like it. At times he even finds a distinct reluctance to do it, and often when he tries to do it he finds he cannot. Then he begins to question his experience. He asks himself: `Did I really know? Yes! Did I really reckon? Yes! Did I really give myself to Him? Yes! Have I taken back my consecration? No! Then whatever is the matter now?' The more this man tries to do the will of God the more he fails. Ultimately he comes to the conclusion that he never really loved God's will at all, so he prays for the desire and the power to do it. He confesses his disobedience and promises never to disobey again. But he has barely got up from his knees before he has fallen once more; before he reaches the point of victory he is conscious of defeat. Then he says to himself: 'Perhaps my last decision was not definite enough. This time I will be absolutely definite.' So he brings all his will-power to bear on the situation, only to find greater defeat than ever awaiting him the next time a choice has to be made. Then at last he echoes the words of Paul: "For I know that in me, that is, in my flesh, dwelleth no good thing: for to will is present with me, but to do that which is good is not. For the good which I would I do not: but the evil which I would not, that I practice" (Rom. 7:18,19).

What The Law Teaches

Many Christians are suddenly launched into the experience of Romans 7 and they do not know why. They fancy Romans 6 is quite enough. Having grasped that, they think there can be no more question of failure, and then to their utmost surprise they suddenly find themselves in Romans 7. What is the explanation?

First let us be quite clear that the death with Christ described in Romans 6 is fully adequate to cover all our need. It is the explanation of that death, with all that follows from it, that is incomplete in chapter 6. We are as yet still in ignorance of the truth set forth in chapter 7. Romans 7 is given to us to explain and make real the statement in Romans 6:14, that: "Sin shall not have dominion over you: for ye are not under law, but under grace." The trouble is that we do not yet know deliverance from law.

What, then, is the meaning of law?

Grace means that God does something for me; law means that I do something for God. God has certain holy and righteous demands which He places upon me: that is law. Now if law means that God requires something of me for their fulfillment, then deliverance from law means that He no longer requires that from me, but Himself provides it. Law implies that God requires me to do something for Him; deliverance from law implies that He exempts me from doing it, and that in grace He does it Himself. I (where 'I' is the 'carnal' man of ch. 7:14) need do nothing for God: that is deliverance from law. The trouble in Romans 7 is that man in the flesh tried to do something for God. As soon as you try to please God in that way, then you place yourself under law, and the experience of Romans 7 begins to be yours.

As we seek to understand this, let it be settled at the outset that the fault does not lie with the Law. Paul says, "the law is holy, and the commandment holy, and righteous, and good" (Rom. 7:12). No, there is nothing wrong with the Law, but there is something decidedly wrong with me. The demands of the Law are righteous, but the person upon whom the demands are made is unrighteous. The trouble is not that the Law's demands are unjust, but that I am unable to meet them. It may be all right for the Government to require payment of 100 shillings but it will be all wrong if I have only ten shillings with which to meet the demand!

I am a man "sold under sin" (Rom. 7:14). Sin has dominion over me. As long as you leave me alone I seem to be rather a fine type of man. It is when you ask me to do something that my sinfulness comes to light. If you have a very clumsy servant and he just sits still and does nothing, then his clumsiness does not appear. If he does nothing all day he will be of little use to you, it is true, but at least he will do no damage that way. But if you say to him: 'Now come along, don't idle away your time; get up and do something', then immediately the trouble begins. He knocks the chair over as he gets up, stumbles over a footstool a few paces further on, then smashes some precious dish as soon as he handles it. If you make no demands upon him his clumsiness is never noticed, but as soon as you ask him to do anything his awkwardness is seen at once. The demands were all right, but the man was all wrong. He was as clumsy a man when he was sitting still as when he was working, but it was your demands that made manifest the clumsiness that was all the time in his make-up, whether he was active or inactive.

We are all sinners by nature. If God asks nothing of us, all seems to go well, but as soon as He demands something of us the occasion is provided for a grand display of our sinfulness. The Law makes our weakness manifest. While you let me sit still I appear to be all right, but when you ask me to do anything I am sure to spoil that thing, and if you trust me with a second thing I will as surely spoil it too. When a holy law is applied to a sinful man, then his sinfulness comes out in full display.

God knows who I am; He knows that from head to foot I am full of sin; He knows that I am weakness incarnate; that I can do nothing. The trouble is that I do not know it. I admit that all men are sinners and that therefore I am a sinner; but I imagine that I am not such a hopeless sinner as some. God must bring us all to the place where we see that we are utterly weak and helpless. While we say so, we do not wholly believe it, and God has to do something to convince us of the fact. Had it not been for the Law we should never have known how weak we are. Paul had reached that point. He makes this clear when he says in Romans 7:7: "I had not known sin, except through the law: for I had not known coveting, except the law had said, Thou shalt not covet". Whatever might be his experience with the rest of the Law, it was the tenth commandment, which literally translated is: "Thou shalt not desire ..." that found him out. There his total failure and incapacity stared him in the face!

The more we try to keep the Law the more our weakness is manifest and the deeper we get into Romans 7, until it is clearly demonstrated to us that we are hopelessly weak. God knew it all along but we did not, and so God had to bring us through painful experiences to a recognition of the fact. We need to have our weakness proved to ourselves beyond dispute. That is why God gave us the Law.

So we can say, reverently, that God never gave us the Law to keep; He gave us the Law to break! He well knew that we could not keep it. We are so bad that He asks no favour and makes no demands. Never has any man succeeded in making himself acceptable to God by means of the Law. Nowhere in the New Testament are men of faith told that they are to keep the Law; but it does say that the Law was given so that there should be transgression. "The law came in ... that the trespass might abound" (Rom. 5:20). The Law was given to make us law-breakers! No doubt I am a sinner in Adam; "Howbeit, I had not know sin, except through the law: ...for apart from the law sin is dead ... but when the commandment came, sin revived, and I died" (Rom. 7:7-9). The Law is that which exposes our true nature. Alas, we are so conceited, and think ourselves so strong, that God has to give us something to test us and prove how weak we are. At last we see it and confess: 'I am a sinner through and through, and I can of myself do nothing whatever to please God.'     No, the Law was not given in the expectation that we would keep it. It was given in the full knowledge that we would break it; and when we have broken it so completely that we are convinced of our utter need, then the Law has served its purpose. It has been our schoolmaster to bring us to

Christ, that He Himself may fulfill it in us (Gal. 3:24).

## CHRIST THE END OF THE LAW

In Romans 6 we saw how God delivered us from sin; in Romans 7 we see how He delivers us from the Law. In chapter 6 we were shown the way of deliverance from sin in the picture of a master and his slave; in chapter 7 we are shown the way of deliverance from the Law in the picture of two husbands and a wife. The relation between sin and the sinner is that of master to slave; the relation between the Law and the sinner is that of husband to wife.

Notice first that in the picture in Romans 7:1-4 by which Paul illustrates our deliverance from the Law there is only one woman, while there are two husbands. The woman is in a very difficult position, for she can only be wife of one of the two, and unfortunately she is married to the less desirable one. Let us make no mistake, the man to whom she is married is a good man; but the trouble lies here, that the husband and wife are totally unsuited to one another. He is a most particular man, accurate to a degree; she on the other hand is decidedly easy-going. With him all is definite and precise; with her all is vague and haphazard. He wants everything just so, while she accepts things as they come. How could there be happiness in such a home?

And then that husband is so exacting! He is always making demands on his wife. And yet one cannot find fault with him, for as a husband he has a right to expect something of her; and besides, all his demands are perfectly legitimate. There is nothing wrong with the man and nothing wrong with his demands; the trouble is that he has the wrong kind of wife to carry them out. The two cannot get on at all; theirs are utterly incompatible natures. Thus the poor woman is in great distress. She is fully aware that she often makes mistakes, but living with such a husband it seems as though everything she says and does is wrong! What hope is there for her? If only she were married to that other Man all would be well. He is no less exacting than her husband, but He also helps much. She would fain marry Him, but her husband is still alive. What can she do? She is "bound by law to the husband" and unless he dies she cannot legitimately marry that other Man. This picture is not drawn by me but by the apostle Paul. The first husband is the Law; the second husband is Christ; and you are the woman. The Law requires much, but offers no help in the carrying out of its requirements. The Lord Jesus requires just as much, yea more (Matt. 5:21-48) but what He requires from us He Himself carries out in us. The Law makes demands and leaves us helpless to fulfill them; Christ makes demands, but He Himself fulfills in us the very demands He makes. Little wonder that the woman desires to be freed from the first husband that she may marry that other Man! But her only hope of release is through the death of her first husband, and he holds on to life most tenaciously. Indeed there is not the least prospect of his passing away. "Till heaven and earth pass away, one jot or one tittle shall in no wise pass away from the law, till all things be accomplished (Matt. 5:18).

The Law is going to continue for all eternity. If the Law will never pass away, then how can I ever be united to Christ? How can I marry a second husband if my first husband simply refuses to die? There is one way out. If he will not die, I can die, and if I die the marriage relationship is dissolved. And that is exactly God's way of deliverance from the Law. The most important point to note in this section of Romans 7 is the transition from verse 3 to verse 4. Verses 1 to 3 show that the husband should die, but in verse 4 we see that in fact it is the woman who dies. The Law does not pass away. God's righteous demands remain for ever, and if I live I must meet those demands; but if I die the Law has lost its claim upon me. It cannot follow me beyond the grave.

Exactly the same principle operates in our deliverance from the Law as in our deliverance from sin. When I have died my old master, Sin, still continues to live, but his power over his slave extends as far as the grave and no further. He could ask me to do a hundred and one things when I was alive, but when I am dead he calls on me in vain. I am for ever freed from his tyranny. So it is with regard to the Law. While the woman lives she is bound to her husband, but with her death the marriage bond is dissolved and she is "discharged from the law of her husband". The Law may still make demands, but for me its power to enforce them is ended.

Now the vital question arises: 'How do I die?' And the preciousness of our Lord's work comes in just here: "Ye also were made dead to the law through the body of Christ" (Rom. 7:4). When Christ died His body was broken, and since God placed me in Him (1 Cor. 1:30), I have been broken too. When He was crucified, I was crucified with Him.

An Old Testament illustration may help to make this clear. It was the veil of testimony that separated the Holy Place from the Most Holy Place, and upon it were embroidered cherubim (Exod. 26:31; 2 Chron. :14) whose faces, by analogy from Ezekiel 1:10 and 10:14, included that of a man as representing the human head of the whole natural creation (Psalm 8:4-8). In Old Testament days God dwelt within the veil and man without. Man could look upon the veil, but not within it. That veil symbolized our Lord's flesh, His body (Heb. 10:20). So in the Gospels men could only look upon the outward form of our Lord; they could not, save by Divine revelation (Matt. 16:16,17), see the God who dwelt within. But when the Lord Jesus died, the veil of the temple was rent from top to bottom (Matt. 27:51) as by the hand of God, so that man could gaze right into the Most Holy Place. Since the death of the Lord Jesus, God is no longer veiled but seeks to reveal Himself (1 Cor. 2:7-10).

But when the veil was rent asunder, what happened to the cherubim? God rent only the veil, it is true, but the cherubim were there in the veil and were one with it, for they were embroidered upon it. It was impossible to rend the veil and preserve them whole. When the veil was rent the cherubim were rent with it. And, in the sight of God, when the Lord Jesus died the whole living creation died too.

"Wherefore, my brethren, ye also were made dead to the law through the body of Christ." That woman's husband may be very well and strong, but if she dies he may make as many demands upon her as he likes; it will not affect her in the slightest. Death has set her free from all her husband's claims. We were in the Lord Jesus when He died, and that inclusive death of His has for ever freed us from the Law. But our Lord did not remain in the grave. On the third day He rose again; and since we are still in Him we are risen too. The body of the Lord Jesus speaks not only of His death but of His resurrection, for His resurrection was a bodily resurrection. Thus "through the body of Christ" we are not only "dead to the law' but alive unto God.

God's purpose in uniting us to Christ was not merely negative; it was gloriously positive -- "that ye should be joined to another" (Rom. 7:4). Death has dissolved the old marriage relationship, so that the woman, driven to despair by the constant demands of her former husband, who never lifted a little finger to help her carry them out, is now set free to marry the other Man, who with every demand He makes becomes in her the power for its fulfillment.

And what is the issue of this new union? "That we might bring forth fruit unto God" (Rom. 7:4). By the body of Christ that foolish, sinful woman has died, but being united to Him in death she is united to Him in resurrection also, and in the power of resurrection life she bring forth fruit unto God. The risen life of the Lord in her empowers her for all the demands God's holiness makes upon her. The Law of God is not annulled; it is perfectly fulfilled, for the risen Lord now lives out His life in her, and His life is always well-pleasing to the Father.

What happens when a woman marries? She no longer bears her own name but that of her husband; and she shares not his name only but his possessions too. "So it is when we are joined to Christ. When we belong to

Him, all that is His becomes ours, and with His infinite resources at our disposal we are well able to meet all His demands.

## OUR END IS GOD'S BEGINNING

Now that we have settled the doctrinal side of the question we must come down to practical issues, staying a little longer with the negative aspect and keeping the positive for our next chapter. What does it mean in everyday life to be delivered from the Law? It means that from henceforth I am going to try to please Him. `What a doctrine!' you exclaim. `What awful heresy! You cannot possibly mean that!'

But remember, if I try to please God `in the flesh', then immediately I place myself under the Law. I broke the Law; the Law pronounced the death sentence; the sentence was executed, and now by death I -- the carnal `I' (Rom. 7:14) -- have been set free from all its claims. There is still a Law of God, and now there is in fact a "new commandment" that is infinitely more exacting than the old, but, Praise God! its demands are being met, for it is Christ who now fulfills them; it is Christ who works in me what is well-pleasing to God. "I came ... to fulfill {the law}" were His words (Matt. 5:17). Thus Paul, from the ground of resurrection, can say: "Work out your own salvation with fear and trembling; for it is God which worketh in you both to will and to work, for his good pleasure" (Phil 2:12,13). It is God that worketh in you. Deliverance from law does not mean that we are free from doing the will of God. It certainly does not mean that we are going to be lawless. Very much the reverse! What it does mean however is that we are free from doing that will as of ourselves. Being fully persuaded that we cannot do it, we cease trying to please God from the ground of the old man. Having at last reached the point of utter despair in ourselves so that we cease even to try, we put our trust in the Lord to manifest His resurrection life in us.

Let me illustrate by what I have seen in my own country. In China some bearers can carry a load of salt weighing 120 kilos, some even 250 kilos. Now along comes a man who can carry only 120 kilos, and here is a load of 250 kilos. He knows perfectly well he cannot carry it, and if he is wise he will say: `I won't touch it!' But the temptation to try is ingrained in human nature, so although he cannot possibly carry it he still tries. As a youngster I used to amuse myself watching ten or twenty of these fellows come along and try, though every one of them knew he could not possibly manage it. In the end he must give up and make way for the man who could. The sooner we too give up trying the better, for I we monopolize the task, then there is no room for the Holy Spirit. But if we say: `I'll not do it; I'll trust Thee to do it for me', then we shall find that a Power stronger than ourselves is carrying us through.

In 1923 I met a famous Canadian evangelist. I had said in an address something along the above lines, and as we walked back to his home afterwards he remarked: `The note of Romans 7 is seldom sounded nowadays; it is good to hear it again. The day I was delivered from the Law was a day of Heaven on earth. After being a Christian for years I was still trying my best to please God, but the more I tried the more I failed. I regarded God as the greatest Demander in the universe, but I found myself impotent to fulfill the least of His demands. Suddenly one day, as I read Romans 7, light dawned and I saw that I had not only been delivered from sin but from the Law as well. In my amazement I jumped up and said: "Lord, are you really making no demands on me? Then I need do nothing more for You!" God's requirements have not altered, but we are not the ones to meet them. Praise God, He is the Lawgiver on the Throne, and He is the Lawkeeper in my heart. He who gave the Law, Himself keeps it. He makes the demands, but He also meets them. My friend could well jump up and shout when he found he had nothing to do, and all who make a like discovery can do the same. As long as we are trying to do anything, He can do nothing. It is because of our trying that we fail and fail and fail. God wants to demonstrate to us that we can do nothing at all, and until that is fully recognized our disappointments and disillusionments will never cease.

A brother who was trying to struggle into victory remarked to me, `I do not know why I am so weak.' `The trouble with you', I said, `is that you are weak enough not to do the will of God, but you are not weak enough to keep out of things altogether. You are still not weak enough. When you are reduced to utter weakness and are persuaded that you can do nothing whatever, then God will do everything.' We all need to come to the point where we say: `Lord, I am unable to do anything for Thee, but I trust Thee to do everything in me.'

I was once staying in a place in China with some twenty other brothers. There was inadequate provision for bathing in the home where we stayed, so we went for a daily plunge in the river. On one occasion a brother had cramp in one leg, and I suddenly saw he was sinking fast, so I motioned to another brother, who was an expert swimmer, to hasten to his rescue. But to my astonishment he made no move. So I grew desperate and called out: 'Don't you see the man is drowning?' and the other brothers, about as agitated as I was, shouted vigorously too. But our good swimmer still did not move. Calm and collected, he remained just where he was, apparently postponing the unwelcome task. Meantime the voice of the poor drowning brother grew fainter and his efforts feebler. In my heart I said: 'I hate that man! Think of his letting a brother drown before his very eyes and not going to the rescue!' But when the man was actually sinking, with a few swift strokes the swimmer was at his side, and both were safely ashore. When I got an opportunity I aired my views. 'I have never seen any Christian who loved his life quite as much as you do', I said. 'Think of the distress you would have saved that brother if you had considered yourself a little less and him a little more.' But the swimmer knew his business better than I did. 'Had I gone earlier', he said, 'he would have clutched me so fast that both of us would have gone under. A drowning man cannot be saved until he is utterly exhausted and ceases to make the slightest effort to save himself.' Do you see it? When we give up the case, then God will take it up. He is waiting until we are at an end of our resources and can do nothing more for ourselves. God has condemned all that is of the old creation and consigned it to the Cross. The flesh profiteth nothing! If we try to do anything in the flesh we are virtually repudiating the Cross of Christ. God has declared us to be fit only for death. When we truly believe that, then we confirm God's verdict by giving up all our fleshly efforts to please Him. Our every effort to do His will is a denial of His declaration in the Cross of our utter worthlessness. Our continued efforts are a misunderstanding on the one hand of God's demands and on the other hand of the source of supply.     We see the Law and we think that we must meet its demands, but we need to remember that, though the Law in itself is all right, it will be all wrong if it is applied to the wrong person. The "wretched man" of Romans 7 tried to meet the demands of God's law himself, and that was the cause of his trouble. The repeated use of the little word 'I' in this chapter gives the clue to the failure. "The good which I would I do not: but the evil which I would not, that I practice" (Rom. 7:19). There was a fundamental misconception in this man's mind. He thought God was asking him to keep the Law, so of course he was trying to keep it. But God was requiring no such thing of him. What was the result? Far from doing what pleased God, he found himself doing what displeased Him. In his very efforts to do the will of God he did exactly the opposite of what he knew to be His will.

I THANK GOD!

Romans 6 deals with "the body of sin", Romans 7 with "the body of this death" (6:6; 7:24). In chapter 6 the whole question before us is sin; in chapter 7 the whole question before us is death. What is the difference between the body of sin and the body of death? In regard to sin (that is, to whatever displeases God) I have a body of sin -- a body, that is to say, which is actively engaged in sin. But in regard to the Law of God (that is, to that which expresses the will of God) I have a body of death. My activity in regard to sin makes my body a body of sin; my failure in regard to all that is wicked, worldly and Satanic I am, in my nature, wholly positive; but in regard to all that pertains to holiness and Heaven and God I am wholly negative.

Have you discovered the truth of that in your life? It is no good merely to discover it in Romans 6 and 7. Have you discovered that you carry the encumbrance of a lifeless body in regard to God's will? You have no difficulty in speaking about wordly matters, but when you try to speak for the Lord you are tongue-tied; when you try to pray you feel sleepy; when you try to do something for the Lord you feel unwell. You can do anything but that which is related to God's will. There is something in this body that does not harmonize with the will of God.

What does death mean? We may illustrate from a well-known verse in the first letter to the Corinthians: "For this cause many among you are weak and sickly, and not a few sleep" (1 Corinthians 11:30). Death is weakness produced to its extremity - weakness, sickness, death. Death means utter weakness; it means you are weak to such a point that you can become no weaker. That I have a body of death in relation to God's will means that I am so weak in regard to serving God, so utterly weak, that I am reduced to a point of dire helplessness. "O wretched man that I am! who shall deliver me out of the body of this death?" cried Paul, and it is good when anyone cries out as he did. There is nothing more musical in the ears of the Lord. This cry is the most spiritual and the most scriptural cry a man can utter. He only utters it when he knows he can do nothing, and gives up making any further resolutions. Up to this point, every time he failed he made a new resolution and doubled and redoubled his will-power. At last he discovers there is no use in his making up his mind any more, and he cries out in desperation: "O wretched man that I am !" Like a man who suddenly awakes to find himself in a burning building, his cry is now for help, for he has come to the point where he despairs of himself.

Have you despaired of yourself, or do you hope that if you read and pray more you will be a better Christian? Bible-reading and prayer are not wrong, and God forbid that we should suggest that they are, but it is wrong to trust even in them for victory. Our help is in Him who is the object of that reading and prayer. Our trust must be in Christ alone. Happily the "wretched man" does not merely deplore his wretchedness; he asks a fine question, namely: "Who shall deliver me?" "Who?" Hitherto he has looked for some thing; now his hope is in a Person. Hitherto he has looked within for a solution to his problem; now he looks beyond himself for a Savior. He no longer puts forth self-effort; all his expectation is now in Another. How did we obtain forgiveness of sins? Was it by reading, praying, almsgiving, and so on? No, we looked to the Cross, believing in what the Lord Jesus had done; and deliverance from sin becomes ours on exactly the same principle, nor is it otherwise with the question of pleasing God. In the matter of forgiveness we look to Him on the Cross; in the matter of deliverance from sin and of doing the will of God we look to Him in our hearts. For the one we depend on what He has done; for the other we depend on what He will do in us; but in regard to both, our dependence is on Him along. He is the One who does it all.

At the time when the Epistle to the Romans was written a murderer was punished in a peculiar and terrible manner. The dead body of the one murdered was tied to the living body of the murderer, head to head, hand to hand, foot to foot, and the living one was bound to the dead one till death. The murderer could go where he pleased, but wherever he went he had to carry the corpse of that murdered man with him. Could punishment be more appalling? Yet this is the illustration Paul now uses. It is as though he were bound to a dead body and unable to get free. Wherever he goes he is hampered by this terrible burden. At last he can bear it no longer and cries: "O wretched man that I am! who shall deliver me ...?" And then, in a flash of illumination, his cry of despair changes to a song of praise. He has found the answer to his question. "I thank God through Jesus Christ our Lord" (Rom. 7:25).

We know that justification is ours through the Lord Jesus and requires no work on our part, but we think sanctification is dependent on our own efforts. We know we can receive forgiveness only by entire reliance on the Lord; yet we believe we can obtain deliverance by doing something ourselves. We fear that if we do nothing, nothing will happen. After salvation the old habit of 'doing' reasserts itself and we begin our old self-efforts again. Then God's word comes afresh to us: "It is finished" (John 19:30). He has done everything on the Cross for our forgiveness and He will do everything in us for our deliverance. In both cases He is the doer. "It is God that worketh in you."

The first words of the delivered man are very precious -- "I thank God". If someone gives you a cup of water you thank the person who gave it, not someone else. Why did Paul say "Thank God"? Because God was the One who did everything. Had it been Paul who did it, he would have said, "Thank Paul". But he saw that Paul was a "wretched man" and that God alone could meet his need; so he said, "Thank God". God wants to do all, for He must have all the glory. If we do some of the work, then we will get some of the glory; but God must have it all Himself, so He does all the work from beginning to end.

What we have said in this chapter might seem negative and unpractical if we were to stop at this point, as though the Christian life were a matter of sitting still and waiting for something to happen. Of course it is very far from being so. All who truly live it know it to be a matter of very positive and active faith in Christ and in an altogether new principle of life -- the law of the Spirit of life. We are now going to look at the effects in us of this new life principle.

# CHAPTER 10: THE PATH OF PROGRESS: WALKING IN THE SPIRIT

Coming now to Romans 8 we may first summarize the argument of our second section of the letter from chapter 5:12 to chapter 8:39 in two phrases, each containing a contrast and each marking an aspect of Christian experience. The are:

Romans 5:12 to 6:23: `In Adam' and `in Christ'.

Romans 7:1 to 8:39: `In the flesh' and `in the Spirit'.

We need to understand the relationship of these four things. The former two are `objective' and set forth our position, firstly as we were by nature and secondly as we now are by faith in the redemptive work of Christ. The latter two are `subjective' and relate to our walk as a matter of practical experience. Scripture makes it clear that the first two give us only a part of the picture and that the second two are required to complete it. We think it enough to be "in Christ", but we learn now that we must also walk "in the Spirit" (Rom. 8:9). The frequent occurrence of "the Spirit" in the early part of Romans 8 serves to emphasize this further important lesson of the Christian life.

The Flesh And The Spirit

The flesh is linked with Adam; the Spirit with Christ. Leaving aside now as settled the question of whether we are in Adam or in Christ, we must ask ourselves: Am I living in the flesh or in the Spirit?

To live in the flesh is to do something `out from'[13] myself as in Adam. It is to derive strength from the old natural source of life that I inherited from him, so that I enjoy in experience all Adam's very complete provision for

---

[13] The author has in mind the Greek preposition ek, the sense of which is not easily conveyed by any single English word. -- Ed.

sinning which all of us have found so effective. Now the same is true of what is in Christ. To enjoy in experience what is true of me as in Him, I must learn what it is to walk in the Spirit. It is a historic fact that in Christ my old man was crucified, and it is a present fact that I am blessed "with every spiritual blessing in the heavenly places in Christ" (Eph. 1:3); but if I do not live in the Spirit, then my life may be quite a contradiction of the fact that I am in Christ, for what is true of me in Him is not expressed in me. I may recognize that I am in Christ, but I may also have to face the fact that my old temper is very much in evidence.      What is the trouble? It is that I am holding the truth merely objectively, whereas what is true objectively must be made true subjectively; and that is brought about as I live in the Spirit.

Not only am I in Christ, but Christ is in me. And just as physically a man cannot live and work in water but only in air, so spiritually Christ dwells and manifests Himself not in `flesh' but in `spirit'. Therefore if I live "after the flesh" I find that what is mine in Christ is, so to say, held in suspense in me. Though in fact I am in Christ, yet if I live in the flesh -- that is, in my own strength and under my own direction -- then in experience I find to my dismay that it is what is in Adam that manifests itself in me. If I would know in experience all that is in Christ, then I must learn to live in the Spirit.

Living in the Spirit means that I trust the Holy Spirit to do in me what I cannot do myself. This life is completely different from the life I would naturally live of myself. Each time I am faced with a new demand from the Lord, I look to Him to do in me what He requires of me. It is not a case of trying but of trusting; not of struggling but of resting in Him. If I have a hasty temper, impure thoughts, a quick tongue or a critical spirit, I shall not set out with a determined effort to change myself, but, reckoning myself dead in Christ to these things, I shall look to the Spirit of God to produce in me the needed purity or humility or meekness. This is what it means to "stand still, and see the salvation of the Lord, which he will work for you" (Exod. 14:13).

Some of you have no doubt had an experience something like the following. You have been asked to go and see a friend, and you knew the friend was not very friendly, but you trusted the Lord to see you through. You told Him before you set out that in yourself you could not but fail, and you asked Him for all that was needed. Then, to your surprise, you did not feel at all irritated, though your friend was far from gracious. On your return you thought over the experience and marveled that you kept so calm, and you wondered if you would be just as calm next time. You were amazed at yourself and sought an explanation. This is the explanation: the Holy Spirit carried you through.

Unfortunately we only have this kind of experience once in while, but it should be a constant experience. When the Holy Spirit takes things in hand there is no need for strain on our part. It is not a case of clenching our teeth and thinking that thus we have controlled ourselves beautifully and have had a glorious victory. No, where there is a real victory there is no fleshly effort. We are gloriously carried through by the Lord. The object of temptation is always to get us to do something. During the first three months of the Japanese war in China we lost a great many tanks and so were unable to deal with the Japanese tanks, until the following scheme was devised. A single shot would be fired at a Japanese tank by one of our snipers in ambush. After a considerable lapse of time the first shot would be followed by a second; then, after a further silence, by another shot; until the tank driver, eager to locate the source of the disturbance, would pop his head out to look around. The next shot, carefully aimed, would put an end to him.

As long as he remained under cover he was perfectly safe. The whole scheme was devised to bring him out into the open. In the same way, Satan's temptations are not primarily to make us do something particularly sinful, but merely to cause us to act in our own energy; and as soon as we step out of our hiding-place to do something on that basis, he has gained the victory over us. If we do not move, if we do not come out of the cover of Christ into the realm of the flesh, then he cannot get us.

The Divine way of victory does not permit of our doing anything at all -- anything, that is to say, outside of Christ. This is because as soon as we move we run into danger, for our natural inclinations take us in the wrong direction. Where, then, are we to look for help? Turn now to Galations 5:17: "The flesh lusteth against the Spirit, and the Spirit against the flesh". In other words, the flesh does not fight against us but against the Holy Spirit, "for these are contrary the one to the other", and it is He, not we, who meets and deals with the flesh. What is the result? "That ye may not do the things that ye would."

I think we have often understood that last clause of this verse in a wrong sense. Let us consider what it means. What 'would we do' naturally? We would move off on some course of action dictated by our own instincts and apart from the will of God. The effect then of our refusal to act out from ourselves is that the Holy Spirit is free to meet and deal with the flesh in us, with the result that we shall not do what we naturally would do; that is, we shall not act according to our natural inclinations; we shall not go off on a course and plan of our own: but shall find instead our satisfaction in His perfect plan. Hence we have the principle: "Walk by the Spirit, and ye shall not fulfill the lust of the flesh" (Gal. 5:16). If we live in the Spirit, if we walk by faith in the risen Christ, we can truly `stand aside' while the Spirit gains new victories over the flesh every day. He has been given to us to take charge of this business. Our victory lies in hiding in Christ, and in counting in simple trust upon His Holy Spirit to overcome in us our fleshly lusts with His own new desires. The Cross has been given to procure salvation for us; the Spirit has been given to produce salvation in us. Christ risen and ascended is the basis of our salvation; Christ in our hearts by the Spirit is its power.

## CHRIST OUR LIFE

"I thank God through Jesus Christ"! That exclamation of Paul's is fundamentally the same as his other words in Galations 2:20 which we have taken as the key to our study: "I live; and yet no longer I, but Christ". We saw how prominent is the word `I' throughout his argument in Romans 7, culminating in the agonized cry: "O wretched man that I am!" Then follows the shout of deliverance: "Thank God ... Jesus Christ"! and it is clear that the discovery Paul has made is this, that the life we live is the life of Christ alone. We think of the Christian life as a `changed life', a `substituted life', and Christ is our Substitute within. "I live; and yet no longer I, but Christ liveth in me." This life is not something which we ourselves have to produce. It is Christ's own life reproduced in us.      How many Christians believe in `reproduction' in this sense, as something more than regeneration? Regeneration means that the life of Christ is planted in us by the Holy Spirit at our new birth. `Reproduction' goes further: it means that new life grows and becomes manifest progressively in us, until the very likeness of Christ begins to be reproduced in our lives. That is what Paul means when he speaks of his travail for the Galations "until Christ be formed in you" (Gal. 4:19).

Let me illustrate with another story. I once arrived in America in the home of a saved couple who requested me to pray for them. I inquired the case of their trouble. `Oh, Mr. Nee, we have been in a bad way lately', they confessed. `We are so easily irritated by the children, and during the past few weeks we have both lost our tempers several times a day. We are really dishonoring the Lord. Will you ask Him to give us patience?' `That is the one thing I cannot do', I said. 'What do you mean?' they asked. 'I mean that one thing is certain', I answered, 'and that is that God is not going to answer your prayer.' At that they said in amazement, 'Do you mean to tell us we have gone so far that God is not willing to hear us when we ask Him to make us patient?' 'No, I do not mean quite that, but I would like to ask you if you have ever prayed in this respect. You have. But did God answer? No! Do you know why? Because you have no need of patience.' Then the eyes of the wife blazed up. She said, 'What do you mean? We do not need patience, and yet we get irritated the whole day long! What do you mean?' 'It is not patience you have need of', I answered, 'it is Christ.'

God will not give me humility or patience or holiness or love as separate gifts of His grace. He is not a retailer dispensing grace to us in doses, measuring out some patience to the impatient, some love to the unloving, some meekness to the proud, in quantities that we take and work on as kind of capital. He has given only one gift to meet all our need -- His Son Christ Jesus, and as I look to Him to live out His life in me, He will be humble and patient and loving and everything else I need -- in my stead. Remember the word in the first Epistle of John: "God gave unto us eternal life, and this life is in his Son. He that hath the Son hath the life; and he that hath not the Son of God hath not the life" (1 John 5:11,12). The life of God is not given us as a separate item; the life of God is given us in the Son. It is "eternal life in Christ Jesus our Lord" (Rom. 6:23). Our relationship to the Son is our relationship to the life.

It is a blessed thing to discover the difference between Christian graces and Christ: to know the difference between meekness and Christ, between patience and Christ, between love and Christ. Remember again what is said in 1 Corinthians 1:30: "Christ Jesus ... was made unto us wisdom from God, and righteousness and sanctification, and redemption." The common conception of sanctification is that every item of the life should be holy; but that is not holiness, it is the fruit of holiness. Holiness is Christ. It is the Lord Jesus being made over to us to be that. So you can put in anything there: love, humility, power, self-control. Today there is a call for patience: He is our patience! Tomorrow the call may be for purity: He is our purity! He is the answer to every need. That is why Paul speaks of "the fruit of the Spirit" as one (Gal. 5:22) and not of 'fruits' as separate items. God has given us His Holy Spirit, and when love is needed the fruit of the Spirit is love; when joy is needed the fruit of the Spirit is joy. It is always true. It does not matter what your personal deficiency, or whether it is a hundred and one different things, God has one sufficient answer -His Son Jesus Christ, and He is the answer to every human need.    How can we know more of Christ in this way? Only by way of an increasing awareness of need. Some are afraid to discover deficiency in themselves and so they never grow. Growth in grace is the only sense in which we can grow, and grace, we have said, is God doing something for us. We all have the same Christ dwelling within, but revelation of some new need will lead us spontaneously to trust Him to live out His life in us in that particular. Greater capacity means greater enjoyment of God's supply. Another letting go, a fresh trusting in Christ, and another stretch of land is conquered. `Christ my life' is the secret of enlargement.

We have spoken of trying and trusting, and the difference between the two. Believe me, it is the difference between Heaven and hell. It is not something just to be talked over as a good thought; it is stark reality. `Lord, I cannot do it, therefore I will no longer try to do it.' This is the point where most of us fail. `Lord, I cannot; therefore I will take my hands off; from now on I trust Thee for that.' I refuse to act; I depend on Him to act and then I enter fully and joyfully into the action He initiates. It is not passivity; it is a most active life, trusting the Lord like that; drawing life from Him, taking Him to be my very life, letting Him out His life in me.

## THE LAW OF THIS SPIRIT OF LIFE

"There is therefore now no condemnation to them that are in Christ Jesus, who walk not after the flesh, but after the Spirit. For the law of the Spirit of life in Christ Jesus hath made free from the law of sin and death" (Rom. 8:1,2, A.V.).

It is in chapter 8 that Paul presents to us in detail the positive side of life in the Spirit. "There is therefore now no condemnation", he begins, and this statement may at first seem out of place here. Surely condemnation was met by the Blood through which we found peace with God and salvation from wrath (Rom. 5:1,9). But there are two kinds of condemnation, namely, that before God and that before myself (just as earlier we saw there are two kinds of peace) and the second may at times seem to use even more awful than the first. When I see that the Blood of Christ has satisfied God, then I know my sins are forgiven, and there is for me no more condemnation before God. Yet I may still be knowing defeat, and the sense of inward condemnation on this account may be very real, as Romans 7 shows. But if I have learned to live by Christ as my life, then I have learned the secret of victory, and, praise God! "there is therefore now no condemnation". "The mind of the spirit is life and peace" (Rom. 8:6), and this becomes my experience as I learn to walk in the Spirit. With peace in my heart I have no time to feel condemned, but only to praise Him who leads me on from victory to victory.    But what lay behind my sense of condemnation? Was it not the experience of defeat and the sense of helplessness to do anything about it? Before I saw that Christ is my life, I labored under a constant sense of handicap; limitation dogged my steps; I felt disabled at every turn. I was always crying out: `I cannot do this! I cannot do that!' Try as I would, I found that I "cannot please God" (Rom. 8:8). But there is no `I cannot' in Christ. Now it is: "I can do all things in him that strenghtheneth me" (Phil. 4:13).

How can Paul be so daring? On what ground does he declare that he is now free from limitation and "can do all things"? Here is his answer: "For the law of the Spirit of life in Christ Jesus made me free from the law of sin and of death" (Rom. 8:2). Why is there no more condemnation? "For ...": there is a reason for it; there is something definite to account for it. The reason is that there is a law called "the law of the Spirit of life" and it has proved stronger than another law called `the law of sin and death". What are these laws? How do they operate? And what is the difference between sin and the law of sin, and between death and the law of death? First let us ask ourselves, What is a law? Well, strictly speaking, a law is a generalization examined until it is proved that there is no exception. We might define it more simply as something which happens over and over again. Each time the thing happens it happens in the same way. We can illustrate this both from statutory and from natural law. For example, in this land, if I drive a car on the right hand side of the road the traffic police will stop me. Why? Because it is against the law of the land. If you do it you will be stopped too. Why? For the same reason that I would be stopped: it is against the law and the law makes no exceptions. It is something which happens repeatedly and unfailingly. Or again, we all know what is meant by gravity. If I drop my handkerchief in London it falls to the ground. That is the effect of gravity. But the same is true if I drop it in New York or Hong Kong. No matter where I let it go, gravity operates, and it always produces the same results. Whenever the same conditions prevail the same effects are seen. There is thus a `law' of gravity.

Now what of the law of sin and death? If someone passes an unkind remark about me, at once something goes wrong inside me. That is not law; that is sin. But it, when different people pass unkind remarks, the same `something' goes wrong inside, then I discern a law within -- a law of sin. Like the law of gravity, it is something constant. It always works the same

270

way. And so too with the law of death. Death, we have said, is weakness produced to its limit. Weakness is 'I cannot'. Now if when I try to please God in this particular matter I find I cannot, and if when I try to please Him in that other thing I again find I cannot, then I discern a law at work. There is not only sin in me but a law of sin; there is not only death in me but a law of death.

Then again, not only is gravity a law in the sense that it is constant, admitting of no exception, but, unlike the rule of the road, it is a 'natural' law and not the subject of discussion and decision but of discovery. The law is there, and the handkerchief 'naturally' drops by itself without any help from me. And the "law" discovered by the man in Romans 7:23 is just like that. It is a law of sin and of death, opposed to that which is good, and crippling the man's will to do good. He 'naturally' sins according to the "law of sin" in his members. He wills to be different, but that law in him is relentless and no human will can resist it. So this brings me to the question, How can I be set free from the law of sin an death? I need deliverance from sin, and still more do I need deliverance from death, but most of all I need deliverance from the law of sin and of death. How can I be delivered from the constant repetition of weakness and failure? In order to answer this question let us follow out our two illustration further.

One of our great burdens in China used to be the likin tax, a law which none could escape, originating in the Ch'in Dynasty and operating right down to our own day. It was an inland tax on the transit of goods, applied throughout the empire and having numerous barriers for collection, and officers enjoying very large powers. The result was that the charge on goods passing through several provinces might become very heavy indeed. But a few years ago a second law came into operation which set aside the likin law. Can you imagine the feelings of relief in those who had suffered under the old law? Now there was no need to think or hope or pray; the new law was already there and had delivered us from the old law. No longer was there need to think beforehand what one would say if one met a likin officer tomorrow!

And as with the law of the land, so it is with natural law. How can the law of gravity be annulled? With regard to my handkerchief that law is at work clearly enough, pulling it down, but I have only to place my hand under the handkerchief and it does not drop. Why? The law is still there. I do not deal with the law of gravity; in fact I cannot deal with the law of gravity. Then why does my handkerchief not fall to the ground? Because there is a power keeping it from doing so. The law is there, but another law superior to it is operation to overcome it, namely the law of life. Gravity can do its utmost but the handkerchief will not drop, because another law is working against the law of gravity to maintain it there. We have all seen the tree which was once a small seed fallen between the slabs of a paving, and which has grown until heavy stone blocks have been lifted by the power of the life within it. That is what we mean by the triumph of one law over another.

In just such a manner God delivers us from one law by introducing another law. The law of sin and death is there all the time, but God has put another law into operation - the law of the Spirit of life in Christ Jesus, and that law is strong enough to deliver us from the law of sin and death. You see, it is a law of life in Christ Jesus -- the resurrection life that in Him has met death in all its forms and triumphed over it (Eph. 1:19,20). The Lord Jesus dwells in our hearts in the person of His Holy Spirit, and if we let Him have a clear way and commit ourselves to Him we shall find that He will keep us from the old law. We shall learn what it is to be kept, not by our own power, but "by the power of God" (1 Peter 1:5).

## THE MANIFESTATION OF THE LAW OF LIFE

Let us seek to make this practical. We touched earlier on the matter of our will in relation to the things of God. Even older Christians do not realize how great a part will-power plays in their lives. That was part of Paul's trouble in Romans 7. His will was good, but all his actions contradicted it, and however much he made up his mind and set himself to please God, it led him only into worse darkness. `I would do good', but "I am carnal, sold under sin". That is the point. Like a car without petrol, that has to be pushed and that stops as soon as it is left alone, many Christians endeavour to drive themselves by will-power, and then think the Christian life a most exhausting and bitter one. Some even force themselves to say `Hallelujah!' because others do it, while admitting there is no meaning in it to them. They force themselves to be what they are not, and it is worse than trying to make water run up-hill. For after all, the very highest point the will can reach is that of willingness (Matt. 26:41). If we have to exert so much effort in our Christian living, it simply says that we are not really like that at all. We don't need to force ourselves to speak our native language. In fact we only have to exert will-power in order to do things we do not do naturally. We may do them for a time, but the law of sin and death wins in the end. We may be able to say: `To will is present with me, and I perform that which is good for

272

two weeks', but eventually we shall have to confess: 'How to perform it I know not'. No, what I already am I do not long to be. If I "would" it is because I am not.

You ask, Why do men use will-power to try to please God? There may be two reasons. They may of course never have experienced the new birth, in which case they have no new life to draw upon; or they may have been born again and the life be there, but they have not learned to trust in that life. It is this lack of understanding that results in habitual failure and sinning, bringing them to the place where they almost cease to believe in the possibility of anything better.

But because we have not believed fully, that does not mean that the feeble life we intermittently experience is all God has given us. Romans 6:23 states that "the free gift of God is eternal life in Christ Jesus our Lord", and now in Romans 8:2 we read that "the law of the Spirit of life in Christ Jesus" has come to our aid. So Romans 8:2 speaks not of a new gift but of the life already referred to in Romans 6:23. In other words, it is a new revelation of what we already have. I feel I cannot emphasize this too much. It is not something fresh from God's hand, but a new unveiling of what He has already given. It is a new discovery of a work already done in Christ, for the words "made me free" are in the past tense. If I really see this and put my faith in Him, there is no absolute necessity for Romans 7 to be repeated in me -- either the experience or the conduct, and certainly not the tremendous display of will-power.

If we will let go our own wills and trust Him, we shall not fall to the ground and break, but we shall fall into a different law, the law of the Spirit of life. For He has given us not only life but a law of life. And just as the law of gravity is a natural law and not the result of human legislation, so the law of life is a 'natural' law, similar in principle to the law that keeps our heart beating or that controls the movement of our eyelids. There is no need for us to think about our eyes, or to decide that we must blink every so often to keep them cleansed; and still less do we bring our will to bear upon our heart. Indeed to do so might rather harm than help it. No, so long as it has life it works spontaneously. Our wills only interfere with the law of life. I discovered that fact once in the following way.

I used to suffer from sleeplessness. Once after several sleepless nights, when I had prayed much about it and exhausted all my resources, I confessed at length to God that the fault must lie with me and asked to be shown where. I said to God: 'I demand an explanation'. He answer was: 'Believe in nature's

273

laws'. Sleep is as much a law as hunger is, and I realized that though I had never thought of worrying whether I would get hungry or not, I had been worrying about sleeping. I had been trying to help nature, and that is the chief trouble with most sufferers from sleeplessness. But now I trusted not only God but God's law of nature, and slept well.

Should we not read the Bible? Of course we should or our spiritual life will suffer. But that should not mean forcing ourselves to read. There is a new law in us which gives us a hunger for it. Then half an hour can be more profitable than five hours of forced reading. And it is the same with giving, with preaching, with testimony. Forced preaching is apt to result in preaching a warm gospel with a cold heart, and we all know what men mean by `cold charity'.

If we will let ourselves live in the new law we shall be less conscious of the old law. It is still there, but it is no longer governing and we are no longer in its grip. That is why the Lord says in Matthew 6: "Behold the birds ... Consider the lilies". If we could ask the birds whether they were not afraid of the law of gravity, how would they reply? They would say: `We never heard the name of Newton. We know nothing about his law. We fly because it is the law of our life to fly.' Not only is there in them a life with the power of flight, but that life has a life has a law which enables these living creatures quite spontaneously and consistently to overcome the law of gravity. Yet gravity remains. If you get up early one morning when the cold is intense and the snow thick on the ground, and there is a dead sparrow in the courtyard, you are reminded at once of the persistence of that law. But while birds live they overcome it, and the life within them is what dominates their consciousness.

God has been truly gracious to us. He has given us this new law of the Spirit, and for us to `fly' is no longer a question of our will but of His life. Have you noticed what a trial it is to make an impatient Christian patient? To require patience of him is enough to make him ill with depression. But God has never told us to force ourselves to be what we are not naturally: to try by taking thought to add to our spiritual stature. Worrying may possibly decrease a man's height, but it certainly never added anything to it. "Be not anxious", are His words. "Consider the lilies, ... they grow." He is directing our attention to the new law of life in us. Oh, for a new appreciation of the life that is ours!

What a precious discovery this is! It can make altogether new men of us, for it operates in the smallest things as well as in the bigger ones. It checks us when, for example, we put out a hand to look at a book in someone else's room, reminding us that we have not asked permission and have no right to do so. We cannot, the Holy Spirit tells us, encroach thus upon the rights of others.

Once I was talking to a Christian friend and he turned to me and said:

'Do you know, I believe that if anyone is willing to live by the law of the Spirit of life, such a man will become truly refined.' 'What do you mean?' I asked. He replied: 'That law has the power to make a man a perfect gentleman. Some scornfully say: "you can't blame those people for the way they act; they are just country folk and have no educational advantages". But the real question is, Have they the life of the Lord within? For I tell you, that life can say to them: "Your voice is too loud", or, "That laughter was not right", or, "Your motive in passing that remark was wrong." In a thousand details the Spirit of life can tell them how to act, so producing in them a true refinement. There is no such inherent power in education.' And yet my friend was himself an educationalist!

But it is true. Take the example of talkativeness. Are you a person of too many words? When you stay with people, do you say to yourself: 'What shall I do? I am a Christian; but if I am to glorify the name of the Lord, I simple must not talk so much. So today let me be extra careful to hold myself in check.'? And for an hour or two you succeed -- until on some pretext you loose control and, before you know where you are, find yourself once again in difficulty with your garrulous tongue. Yes, let us be fully assured that the will is useless here. For me to exhort you to exercise your will in this matter would be but to offer you the vain religion of the world, not the life in Christ Jesus. For consider again: a talkative person remains just that, though he keep silent all day, for there is a 'natural' law of talkativeness governing him (or her!), just as a peach tree is a peach tree whether or not it bears peaches. But as Christians we discover a new law in us, the law of the spirit of life, which transcends all else and which has already delivered us from the 'law' of our talkativeness. If, believing the Lord's Word, we yield ourselves to that new law, it will tell us when we should stop talking -- or not start! -- and it will empower us to do so. On that basis you can go to your friend's house for two or three hours, or stay for two or three days, and experience no difficulty. On your return you will just thank God for His new law of life.

It is this spontaneous life that is the Christian life. It manifests itself in love for the unlovely -- for the brother whom on natural grounds we would not like and certainly could not love. It works on the basis of what the Lord sees of possibility in that brother. `Lord, You see he is lovable and You love him. Love him, now, through me!' And it manifests itself in reality of life -- in a true genuineness of moral character. There is too much hypocrisy in the lives of Christians, too much play-acting. Nothing takes away from the effectiveness of Christian witness as does a pretense of something that is not really there, for the man in the street unfailingly penetrates such a disguise in the end and finds us out for what we are. Yes, pretense gives way to reality when we trust the law of life.

## THE FOURTH STEP: "WALK ... AFTER THE SPIRIT"

"For what the law could not do, in that it was weak through the flesh, God, sending his own Son in the likeness of sinful flesh and as an offering for sin, condemned sin in the flesh: that the ordinance of the law might be fulfilled in us, who walk not after the flesh, but after the Spirit" (Rom. 8:34).

Every careful reader of these two verses will see that there are two things presented here. They are, firstly, what the Lord Jesus has done for us, and secondly, what the Holy Spirit will do in us. "The flesh" is "weak"; consequently the ordinance of the law cannot be fulfilled in us "after the flesh". (Remember, it is again here a question not of salvation but of pleasing God.) Now, because of our inability God took two steps. In the first place, He intervened to deal with the heart of our problem. He sent His Son in the flesh, who died for sin and in doing so "condemned sin in the flesh". That is to say, He took to death representatively all that belonged to the old creation in us, whether we speak of it as `our old man', `the flesh', or the carnal `I'. Thus God struck at the very root of our trouble by removing the fundamental ground of our weakness. This was the first step.

But still "the ordinance of the law" remained to be fulfilled "in us". How could this be done? It required God's further provision of the indwelling Holy Spirit. It is He who is sent to take care of the inward side of this thing, and He is able to do so, we are told, as we "walk ... after the Spirit".

What does it mean to walk after the Spirit? It means two things. Firstly, it is not a work; it is a walk. Praise God, the burdensome and fruitless effort I involved myself in when I sought `in the flesh' to please God gives place to a blessed and restful dependence on "his working, which worketh in me mightily" (Col. 1:29). That is why Paul contrasts the "works" of the flesh with the "fruit" of the Spirit (Gal. 5:19,22).

Then secondly, to "walk after" implies subjection. Walking after the flesh means that I yield to the dictates of the flesh, and the following verses in Romans 8:5-8 make clear where that leads me. It only brings me into conflict with God. To walk after the Spirit is to be subject to the Spirit. There is one thing that the man who walks after the Spirit cannot do, and that is be independent of Him. I must be subject to the Holy Spirit. The initiative of my life must be with Him. Only as I yield myself to obey

Him shall I find the "law of the Spirit of life" in full operation and the "ordinance of the law" (all that I have been trying to do to please God) being fulfilled -- no longer by me but in me. "As many as are led by the Spirit of God, these are sons of God" (Rom. 8:14).

We are all familiar with the words of the benediction in 2 Corinthians 13:14: "The grace of the Lord Jesus Christ, and the love of God, and the communion of the Holy Ghost, be with you all". The love of God is the source of all spiritual blessing; the grace of the Lord Jesus has made it possible for that spiritual wealth to become ours; and the communion of the Holy Ghost is the means whereby it is imparted to us. Love is something hidden in the heart of God; grace is that love expressed and made available in the Son; communion is the importation of that grace by the Spirit. What the Father has devised concerning us the Son has accomplished for us, and now the Holy Spirit communicates it to us. When therefore we discover something fresh that the Lord Jesus has procured for us in His Cross, let us, for its realization, look in the direction that God has indicated, and, by our steadfast attitude of subjection and obedience to the Holy Spirit, keep wide open the way for Him to impart it to us. That is His ministry. He has come for that very purpose -- that He may make real in us all that is ours in Christ.

We have learned in China that, when leading a soul to Christ, we must be very thorough, for there is no certainty when he will again have the help of other Christians. We always seek to make it clear to a new believer that, when he has asked the Lord to forgive his sins and to come into his life, his heart has become the residence of a living Person. The Holy Spirit of God is now within him, to open to him the Scriptures that he may find Christ there, to direct his prayer, to govern his life, and to reproduce in him the character of his Lord.

I went, late one summer, for a prolonged period of rest to a hill-resort where accommodation was difficult to obtain, and while there it was necessary for me to sleep in one house and take my meals in another, the latter being the home of a mechanic and his wife. For the first two weeks of my visit, apart from asking a blessing at each meal, I said nothing to my hosts about the Gospel; and then one day my opportunity came to tell them about the Lord Jesus. They were ready to listen and to come to Him in simple faith for the forgiveness of their sins. They were born again, and a new light and joy came into their lives, for theirs was a real conversion. I took care to make clear to them what had happened, and then, as the weather turned colder, the time came for me to leave them and return to Shanghai. During the cold winter months the man was in the habit of drinking wine with his meals, and he was apt to do so to excess. After my departure, with the return of the cold weather, the wine appeared on the table again, and that day, as he had become accustomed to do, the husband bowed his head to return thanks for the meal -- but no words would come. After one or two vain attempts he turned to his wife. 'What is wrong?' he asked. 'Why cannot we pray today? Fetch the Bible and see what it has to say about wine drinking.' I had left a copy of the Scriptures with them, but though the wife could read she was ignorant of the Word, and she turned the pages in vain seeking for light on the subject. They did not know how to consult God's Book and it was impossible to consult God's messenger, for I was many miles away and it might be months before they could see me. 'Just drink your wine', said his wife. 'We'll refer the matter to brother Nee at the first opportunity.' But still the man found he just could not return thanks to the Lord for that wine. 'Take it away!' he said at length; and when she had done so, together they asked a blessing on their meal.

When eventually the man was able to visit Shanghai he told me the story. Using an expression familiar in Chinese: 'Brother Nee', he said, 'Resident Boss[14] wouldn't let me have that drink!' 'Very good, brother', I said. 'You always listen to Resident Boss!'

Many of us know that Christ is our life. We believe that the Spirit of God is resident in us, but this fact has little effect upon our behaviour. The question is, do we know Him as a living Person, and do we know Him as 'Boss'?

---

[14] 'Resident Boss' -- The author's own rendering of li-mien tang-chia tih. -- Ed.

# CHAPTER 11: ONE BODY IN CHRIST

Before we pass on to our last important subject we will review some of the ground we have covered and summarize the steps taken. We have sought to make things simple, and to explain clearly some of the experiences which Christians commonly pass through. But it is clear that the new discoveries that we make as we walk with the Lord are many, and we must be careful to avoid the temptation to over-simplify the work of God. To do so may lead us into serious confusion.

There are children of God who believe that all our salvation, in which they would include the matter of leading a holy life, lies in an appreciation of the value of the precious Blood. They rightly emphasize the importance of keeping short accounts with God over known specific sins, and the continual efficacy of the Blood to deal with sins committed, but they think of the Blood as doing everything. They believe in a holiness which in fact means only separation of the man from his past; that, through the up-to-date blotting out of what he has done on the ground of the shed Blood, God separates a man out of the world to be His, and that is holiness; and they stop there. Thus they stop short of God's basic demands, and so of the full provision He has made. I think we have by now seen clearly the inadequacy of this.

Then there are those who go further and see that God has included them in the death of His Son on the Cross, in order to deliver them from sin and the Law by dealing with the old man. These are they who really exercise faith in the Lord, for they glory in Christ Jesus and have ceased to put confidence in the flesh (Phil. 3:3). In them God has a clear foundation on which to build. And from this as starting-point, many have gone further still and recognized that consecration (using that word in the right sense) means giving themselves without reserve into His hands and following Him. All these are first steps, and starting from them we have already touched upon other phases of experience set before us by God and enjoyed by many. It is always essential for us to remember that, while each of them is a precious

279

fragment of truth, no single one of them is by itself the whole of truth. All come to us as the fruit of the work of Christ on the Cross, and we cannot afford to ignore any.

## A GATE AND A PATH

Recognizing a number of such phases in the life and experience of a believer, we note now a further fact, namely that, though these phases do not necessarily occur always in a fixed and precise order, they seem to be marked by certain recurring steps or features. What are these steps? First there is revelation. As we have seen, this always precedes faith and experience. Through His Word God opens our eyes to the truth of some fact concerning His Son, and then only, as in Faith we accept that fact for ourselves, does it become actual as experience in our lives. Thus we have:

1. Revelation (Objective).
2. Experience (Subjective).

Then further, we note that such experience usually takes the two-fold form of a crisis leading to a continuous process. It is most helpful to think of this in terms of John Bunyan's 'wicket gate' through which Christian entered upon a 'narrow path'. Our Lord Jesus spoke of such a gate and a path leading unto life (Matt. 7:14), and experience accords with this.

So now we have:
1. Revelation.
2. Experience:

a) A Wicket gate (Crisis)

b) A narrow path (Process)

Now let us take some of the subjects we have been dealing with and see how this helps us to understand them. We will take first our justification and new birth. This begins with a revelation of the Lord Jesus in His atoning work for our sins on the Cross; there follows the crisis of repentance and faith (the wicket gate), whereby we are initially "made nigh" to God (Eph. 2:13); and this leads us into a walk of maintained fellowship with Him (the narrow path), for which the ground of our day-to-day access is still the precious Blood (Heb 10:29,22). When we come to deliverance from sin, we again have three steps: the Holy Spirit's work of revelation, or 'knowing' (Rom. 6:6); the crisis of faith, or 'reckoning' (Rom. 6:11); and the continuing process of consecration, or 'presenting ourselves' to God (Rom. 6:13) on the basis of a walk in newness of life. Consider next the gift of the Holy Spirit. This too begins with a new 'seeing' of the Lord Jesus as exalted to the throne, which issues in the dual experience of the Spirit outpoured and the Spirit in dwelling. Going a stage further, to the matter of pleasing God, we find again the need for spiritual illumination, that we may see the values of the Cross in regard to 'the flesh' -- the entire self-life of man. Our acceptance of this by faith leads at once to a 'wicket gate' experience (Rom. 7:25), in which we initially cease from 'doing' and accept by faith the mighty working of the life of Christ to satisfy God's practical demands in us. This in turn leads us into the 'narrow path' of a walk in obedience to the Spirit (Rom. 8:4).    The picture is not identical in each case, and we must beware of forcing any rigid pattern upon the Holy Spirit's working; but perhaps any new experience will come to us more or less on these lines. There will certainly always be first an opening of our eyes to some new aspect of Christ and His finished work, and then faith will open a gate into a pathway. Remember, too, that our division of Christian experience into various subjects: justification, new birth, the gift of the spirit, deliverance, sanctification, etc., is for our clearer understanding only. It does not mean that these stages must or will always follow one another in a certain prescribed order. In fact, if a full presentation of Christ and His Cross is made to us at the very outset, we may well step into a great deal of experience from the first day of our Christian life, even though the full explanation of much of it may follow later. Would that all Gospel preaching were of such a kind!

One thing is certain, that revelation will always precede faith. When we see something that God has done in Christ our natural response is: 'Thank you, Lord !' and faith follows spontaneously. Revelation is always the work of the Holy Spirit, who is given to come along-side and, by opening the Scriptures to us, to guide us into all the truth (John 16:13). Count upon Him, for He is here for that very thing; and when such difficulties as lack of understanding or lack of faith confront you, address those difficulties directly to the Lord: 'Lord, open my eyes. Lord, make this new thing clear to me. Lord, help Thou my unbelief!' He will not fail you.

## THE FOURFOLD WORK OF CHRIST IN HIS CROSS

We are now in a position to go a step further still and to consider how great a range is compassed by the Cross of the Lord Jesus Christ. In the light of Christian experience and for the purpose of analysis, it may help us if we recognize four aspects of God's redemptive work. But in doing so it is essential to keep in mind that the Cross of Christ is one Divine work -not many. Once in Judaea two thousand years ago the Lord Jesus died and rose again, and He is now "by the right hand of God exalted" (Acts 2:33). The work is finished and need never be repeated, nor can it be added to.    Of the four aspects of the Cross which we shall now mention, we have already dealt with three in some detail. The last will be considered in the two succeeding chapters of our study. They may be briefly summarized as follows:

1.  The Blood of Christ to deal with sins and guilt.
2.  The Cross of Christ to deal with sin, the flesh and the natural man.
3.  The Life of Christ made available to indwell, re-create and empower man.
4.  The Working of Death in the natural man that that indwelling Life may be progressively manifest.

The first two of these aspects are remedial. They relate to the undoing of the work of the Devil and the undoing of the sin of man. The last two are not remedial but positive, and relate more directly to the securing of the purpose of God. The first two are concerned with recovering what Adam lost by the Fall; the last two are concerned with bringing us into, and bringing into us, something that Adam never had. Thus we see that the achievement of the Lord Jesus in His death and resurrection comprises both a work which provided for the redemption of man and a work which made possible the realization of the purpose of God.

We have dealt at some length in earlier chapters with the two aspects of His death represented by the Blood for sins and guilt and the Cross for sin and the flesh. In our discussion of the eternal purpose we have also looked briefly at the third aspect -- that represented by Christ as the grain of wheat -- and in our last chapter, in our consideration of Christ as our life, we have seen something of its practical outworking. Before, however, we pass on to the fourth aspect, which I shall call `bearing the cross', we must say a little more about this third side, namely, the release of the life of Christ in resurrection for man's indwelling and empowering for service.

We have spoken already of the purpose of God in creation and have said that it embraced far more than Adam ever came to enjoy. What was that purpose? God wanted to have a race of men whose members were gifted with a spirit whereby communion would be possible with Himself, who is

Spirit. That race, possessing God's own life, was to co-operate in securing His purposed end by defeating every possible uprising of the enemy and undoing his evil works. That was the great plan. How will it now be effected? The answer is again to be found in the death of the Lord Jesus. It is a mighty death. It is something positive and purposive, going far beyond the recovery of a lost position; for by it, not only are sin and the old man dealt with and their effects annulled, but something more, something infinitely greater is introduced.

## THE LOVE OF CHRIST

Now we must have before us two passages of the Word, one from Genesis 2 and one from Ephesians 5, which are of great importance in this connection. "And the Lord God caused a deep sleep to fall upon the man, and he slept; and he took one of his ribs, which the Lord God had taken from the man, made he a woman, and brought her unto the man. And the man said, This is now bone of my bones, and flesh of my flesh: she shall be called Woman (Heb. ishshah), because she was taken out of Man (Heb. ish)" (Gen. 2:21-23). "Husbands, love your wives, even as Christ also loved the church, and gave himself up for it; that he might sanctify it, having cleansed it by the washing of water with the word, that he might present the church to himself a glorious church, not having spot or wrinkle or any such thing; but that it should be holy and without blemish" (Eph. 5:25-27).

In Ephesians 5 we have the only chapter in the Bible which explains the passage in Genesis 2. What we have presented to us in Ephesians is indeed very remarkable, if we reflect upon it. I refer to what is contained in those words: "Christ ... loved the church". There is something most precious here.

We have been taught to think of ourselves as sinners needing redemption. For generations that has been instilled into us, and we praise the Lord for that as our beginning; but it is not what God has in view as His end. God speaks here rather of "a glorious church, not having spot or wrinkle or any such thing; but .. holy and without blemish". All too often we have thought of the Church as being merely so many 'saved sinners'. It is that; but we have made the terms almost equal to one another, as though it were only that, which is not the case. Saved sinners -- with that thought you have the whole background of sin and the Fall; but in God's sight the Church is a Diving creation in His Son. The one is largely individual, the other corporate. With the one the view is negative, belonging to the past; with the other it is positive, looking forward. The "eternal purpose" is something in the mind of God from eternity concerning His Son, and it has as its objective that the Son should have a Body to express His life. Viewed from that standpoint -- from the standpoint of the heart of God -- the Church is something which is beyond sin and has never been touched by sin. So we have an aspect of the death of the Lord Jesus in Ephesians which we do not have so clearly in other places. In Romans things are viewed from the standpoint of fallen man, and beginning with `Christ died for sinners, enemies, the ungodly' (Rom. 5) we are led progressively to "the love of Christ" (Rom. 8:35). In Ephesians, on the other hand, the standpoint is that of God "before the foundation of the world" (Eph. 1:4), and the heart of the gospel is: "Christ ... loved the church, and gave himself up for it" (Eph. 5:25). Thus, in Romans it is "we sinned", and the message is of God's love for sinners (Rom. 5:8); whereas in Ephesians it is "Christ loved", and the love here is the love of husband for wife. That kind of love has fundamentally nothing to do with sin as such. What is in view in this passage is not atonement for sin but the creation of the Church, for which end it is said that He "gave himself".

There is thus an aspect of the death of the Lord Jesus which is altogether positive and a matter particularly of love to His Church, where the question of sin and sinners does not directly appear. To bring this fact home Paul takes that incident in Genesis 2 as illustration. Now this is one of the marvelous things in the Word, and if our eyes have been opened to see it we will certainly worship.

From Genesis 3 onwards, from the `coats of skins' to Abel's sacrifice, and on from there through the whole Old Testament, there are numerous types which set forth the death of the Lord Jesus as an atonement for sin; yet the apostle does not appeal here to any of those types of His death, but to this one in Genesis 2. Note that; and then recall that it was not until Genesis 3 that sin came in. There is one type of the death of Christ in the Old Testament which has nothing to do with sin, for it is not subsequent to the Fall but prior to it, and that type is here in Genesis 2. Let us look at it for a moment.

Could we say that Adam was put to sleep because Eve had committed a serious sin? Is that what we have here? Certainly not, for Eve was not yet even created. There were as yet no moral issues involved and no problems at all. No, Adam was put to sleep for the express purpose that something might be taken out of him to be made into someone else. His sleep was not for her sin but for her existence. That is what is taught in these verses. This experience of Adam had as its object the creation of Eve, as something determined in the Divine counsels. God wanted an ishshah. He put the man (ish) to sleep, took a rib from his side and made it into ishshah, a woman, and brought her to the man. That is the picture which God is giving us. It foreshadows an aspect of the death of the Lord Jesus that is not primarily for atonement, but answerable to the sleep of Adam in this chapter. God forbid that I should suggest that the Lord Jesus did not die for purposes of atonement. Praise God, He did. We must remember that today we are in fact in Ephesians 5 and not in Genesis 2. Ephesians was written after the Fall, to men who had suffered from its effects, and in it we have not only the purpose in Creation but also the scars of the Fall -- or there would need to be no mention of "spot or wrinkle". Because we are still on the earth and the Fall is a historic fact, 'cleansing' is needed.

But we must always view redemption as an interruption, an 'emergence' measure, made necessary by a catastrophic break in the straight line of the purpose of God. Redemption is big enough, wonderful enough, to occupy a very large place in our vision, but God is saying that we should not make redemption to be everything, as though man were created to be redeemed. The Fall is indeed a tragic dip downwards in that line of purpose, and the atonement a blessed recovery whereby our sins are blotted out and we are restored; but when it is accomplished there yet remains a work to be done to bring us into possession of that which Adam never possessed, and to give God that which His heart desires. For God has never forsaken the purpose which is represented by that straight line. Adam was never in possession of the life of God as presented in the tree of life. But because of the one work of the Lord Jesus in His death and resurrection (and we must emphasize again that it is all one work) His life was released to become ours by faith, and we have received more than Adam ever possessed. The very purpose of God is brought within reach of fulfillment by our receiving Christ as our life. Adam was put to sleep. We remember that it is said of believers that they fall asleep, rather than that they die. Why? Because whenever death is mentioned sin is there in the background. In Genesis 3 sin entered into the world and death through sin, but Adam's sleep preceded that. So the type of the Lord Jesus here is not like other types on the Old Testament. In relation to sin and atonement there is a lamb or a bullock slain; but here Adam was not slain, but only put to sleep to awake again. Thus he prefigures a death that is not on account of sin, but that has in view increase in resurrection. Then too we must note that Eve was not created as a separate entity by a separate creation, parallel to that of Adam. Adam slept, and Eve was created out of Adam. That is God's method with the Church. God's second Man' has awakened from His `sleep' and His Church is created in Him and of Him, to draw her life from Him and to display that resurrection life.     God has a Son who is known to be the only begotten, and God is seeking that the only begotten Son should have brethren. From the position of only begotten He will become the first begotten, and instead of the Son alone God will have many sons. One grain of wheat has died and many grains will spring up. The first grain was once the only grain; now it is changed to be the first grain of many. The Lord Jesus laid down His life, and that life emerged in many lives. These are the Biblical figures we have used hitherto in our study to express this truth. Now, in the figure just considered, the singular takes the place of the plural. The outcome of the Cross is a single person: a Bride for the Son. Christ loved the Church and gave Himself up for it.

## ONE LIVING SACRIFICE

We have said that there is an aspect of the death of Christ presented to us in Ephesians 5 which is to some extent different from that which we have been studying in Romans. Yet in fact this aspect is the very end to which our study of Romans has been moving, and it is into this that the letter is leading us as we shall now see, for redemption leads us back into God's original line of purpose.

In chapter 8 Paul speaks to us of Christ as the firstborn Son among many Spirit-led "sons of God" (Rom. 8:14). "For whom he foreknew, he also foreordained to be conformed to the image of his Son, that he might be the firstborn among many brethren: and whom he foreordained, them he also called: and whom he called, them he also justified: and whom he justified, them he also glorified" (Rom. 8:29,30). Here justification is seen to lead on to glory, a glory that is expressed not in one or more individuals but in a plurality: in many who manifest the image of One. And this object of our redemption is further set forth, as we have seen, in "the love of Christ" for His own, which is the subject of the last verses of the chapter (8:35-39). But what is implicit here in chapter 8 becomes explicit as we move over into chapter 12, the subject of which is the Body of Christ. After the first eight chapters of Romans, which we have been studying, there follows a parenthesis in which God's sovereign dealings with Israel are taken up and dealt with, before the theme of the first chapters is resumed. Thus, for our present purpose, the argument of chapter 12 follows that of chapter 8 and not of chapter 11. We might very simply summarize these chapters thus: Our sins are forgiven (ch. 5), we are dead with Christ (ch. 6), we are by nature utterly helpless (ch. 7), therefore we rely upon the indwelling Spirit (ch. 8). After this, and as a consequence of it: "We ... are one body in Christ" (ch. 12). It is as though this were the logical outcome of all that has gone before, and the thing to which it has all been leading.

Romans 12 and the following chapter contain some very practical instructions for our life and walk. These are introduced with an emphasis once again on consecration. In chapter 6:13 Paul has said: "Present yourselves unto God, as alive from the dead, and your members as instruments of righteousness unto God". But now in chapter 12:1 the emphasis is a little different: "I beseech you therefore, brethren, by the mercies of God, to present your bodies a living sacrifice, holy, acceptable to God, which is your reasonable service". This new appeal for consecration is made to us as "brethren", linking us in thought to the "many brethren" of chapter 8:29. It is a call to us for a united step of faith, the presenting of our bodies as one "living sacrifice" unto God.

This is something that goes beyond the merely individual, for it implies contribution to a whole. The `presenting' is personal but the sacrifice is corporate; it is one sacrifice. Intelligent service to God is one service. We need never feel our contribution is not needed, for if it contributes to the service, God is satisfied. And it is through this kind of service that we prove "what is the good and acceptable and perfect will of God" (ch. 12:2), or, in other words, realize God's eternal purpose in Christ Jesus. So Paul's appeal "to every man that is among you" (12:3) is in the light of this new Divine fact, that "we, who are many, are one body in Christ, and severally members one of another" (12:5), and it is on this basis that the practical instructions follow.

The vessel through which the Lord Jesus can reveal Himself in this generation is not the individual but the Body. "God hath dealt to each man a measure of faith" (12:3), but alone in isolation man can never fulfill God's purpose. It requires a complete Body to attain to the stature of Christ and to display His glory. Oh that we might really see this!

So Romans 12:3-6 draws from the figure of the human body the lesson of our inter-dependence. Individual Christians are not the Body but are members of the Body, and in a human body "all the members have not the same office". The ear must not imagine itself to be an eye. No amount of prayer will give sight to the ear -- but the whole body can see through the eye. So (speaking figuratively) I may have only the gift of hearing, but I can see through others who have the gift of sight; or, perhaps I can walk but cannot work, so I receive help from the hands. An all-too-common attitude to the things of the Lord is that, 'What I know, I know; and what I don't know, I don't know, and can do quite well without.' But in Christ, the things we do not know others do, and we may know them and enter into the enjoyment of them through others.

Let me stress that this is not just a comfortable thought. It is a vital factor in the life of God's people. We cannot get along without one another. That is why fellowship in prayer is so important. Prayer together brings in the help of the Body, as must be clear from Matthew 18:19,20. Trusting the Lord by myself may not be enough. I must trust Him with others. I must learn to pray "Our Father ..." on the basis of oneness with the Body, for without the help of the Body I cannot get through. In the sphere of service this is even more apparent. Alone I cannot serve the Lord effectively, and He will spare no pains to teach me this. He will bring things to an end, allowing doors to close and leaving me ineffectively knocking my head against a blank wall until I realize that I need the help of the Body as well as of the Lord. For the life of Christ is the life of the Body, and His gifts are given to us for work that builds up the Body. The Body is not an illustration but a fact. The Bible does not just say that the Church is like a body, but that it is the Body of Christ. "We, who are many, are one body in Christ, and severally members one of another." All the members together are one Body, for all share His life -- as though He were Himself distributed among His members. I was once with a group of Chinese believers who found it very hard to understand how the Body could be one when they were all separate individual men and women who made it up. One Sunday I was about to break the bread at the Lord's table and I asked them to look very carefully at the loaf before I broke it. Then, after it had been distributed and eaten, I pointed out that though it was inside all of them it was still one loaf -- not many. The loaf was divided, but Christ is not divided even in the sense in which that loaf was. He is still one Spirit in us, and we are all one in Him.

This is the very opposite of man's condition by nature. In Adam I have the life of Adam, but that is essentially individual. There is no union, no fellowship in sin, but only self-interest and distrust of others. As I go on with the Lord I soon discover, not only that the problem of sin and of my natural strength has to be dealt with, but that there is also a further problem created by my 'individual' life, the life that is sufficient in itself and does not recognize its need for and union in the Body. I may have got over the problems of sin and the flesh, and yet still be a confirmed individualist. I want holiness and victory and fruitfulness for myself personally and apart, albeit from the purest motives. but such an attitude ignores the Body, and so cannot provide God with satisfaction. he must deal with me therefore in this matter also, or I shall remain in conflict with His ends. God does not blame me for being an individual, but for my individualism. His greatest problem is not the outward divisions and denominations that divide His Church but our own individualistic hearts.     Yes, the Cross must do its work here, reminding me that in Christ I have died to that old life of independence which I inherited from Adam, and that in resurrection I have become not just an individual believer in Christ but a member of His Body. There is a vast difference between the two. When I see this, I shall at once have done with independence and shall seek fellowship. The life of Christ in me will gravitate to the life of Christ in others. I can no longer take an individual line. Jealousy will go. Competition will go. Private work will go. My interests, my ambitions, my preferences, all will go. It will no longer matter which of us does the work. All that will matter will be that the Body grows.

I said: `When I see this ...' That is the great need: to see the Body of Christ as another great Divine fact; to have it break in upon our spirits by heavenly revelation that "we, who are many, are one body in Christ". Only the Holy Spirit can bring this home to us in all its meaning, but when He does it will revolutionize our life and work.

## MORE THAN CONQUERORS THROUGH HIM

We only see history back to the Fall. God sees it from the beginning. There was something in God's mind before the Fall, and in the ages to come that thing is to be fully realized. God knew all about sin and redemption; yet in His great purpose for the Church set forth in Genesis 2 there is no view of sin. It is as though (to speak in finite terms) He leaps in thought right over the whole story of redemption and sees the Church in future eternity, having a ministry and a (future) history which is altogether apart from sin and wholly of God. It is the Body of Christ in glory, expressing nothing of fallen man but only that which is the image of the glorified Son of man. This is the Church that has satisfied God's heart and has attained dominion.

In Ephesians 5 we stand within the history of redemption, and yet through grace we still have this eternal purpose of God in view as expressed in the statement that He will `present unto himself a glorious Church'. But now we note that the water of life and the cleansing Word are needed to prepare the Church (now marred by the Fall) for presentation to Christ in glory. For now there are defects to be remedied and wounds to be healed. And yet how precious is the promise and how gracious are the words used of her: "not having spot" -- the scars of sin, whose very history is now forgotten; "or wrinkle" -- the marks of age and of time lost, for all is now made up and all is new; and "without blemish" -- so that Satan or demons or men can find no ground for blame in her.

This is where we are now. The age is closing, and Satan's power is greater than ever. Our warfare is with angels and principalities and powers (Rom. 8:38); Eph. 6:12) who are set to withstand and destroy the work of God in us by laying many things to the charge of God's elect. Alone we could never be their match, but what we alone cannot do the Church can. Sin, self-reliance and individualism were Satan's master-strokes at the heart of God's purpose in man, and in the Cross God has undone them. As we put our faith in what He has done -- in "God that justifieth" and in "Christ Jesus that died" (Rom. 8:33,34) -- we present a front against which the very gates of Hades shall not prevail. We, His Church, are "more than conquerors through him that loved us" (Rom. 8:37).

# CHAPTER 12: THE CROSS AND THE SOUL LIFE

God has made full provision for our redemption in the Cross of Christ, but He has not stopped there. In that Cross He has also made secure beyond possibility of failure that eternal plan which Paul speaks of as having been from all the ages "hid in God who created all things". That plan He has now proclaimed "to the intent that now unto the principalities and the powers in the heavenly places might be made known through the church the manifold wisdom of God, according to the eternal purpose which he purposed in Christ Jesus our Lord" (Eph. 3:9-11).

We have said that the work of the Cross has two consequences which bear directly upon the realizing of that purpose in us. On the one hand it has issued in the release of His life that it may find expression in us through the indwelling Spirit. On the other hand it has made possible what we speak of as `bearing the cross'; that is, our co-operation in the daily inworking of His death whereby way is made in us for the manifestation of that new life, through the bringing of the `natural man' progressively into his right place of subjection to the Holy Spirit. Clearly these are the positive and the negative sides of one thing. Equally clearly we are now touching more particularly on the matter of progress in a life lived for God. Hitherto in dealing with the Christian life we have placed our main emphasis upon the crisis by which it is entered. Now our concern is more definitely with the walk of the disciple, having especially in view his training as a servant of God. It is of him that the Lord Jesus said: "Whosoever doth not bear his own cross, and come after me, cannot be my disciple" (Luke 14:27). So we come to a consideration of the natural man and the `bearing of the cross'. To understand this we must, at the risk of being tedious, go back once more to Genesis and consider what it was that God sought to have in man at the beginning and how His purpose was frustrated. In this way we shall be able to grasp the principles by which we can come again to live in line with that purpose.

## THE TRUE NATURE OF THE FALL

If we have even a little revelation of the plan of God we shall always think much of the word `man'. We shall say with the Psalmist, "What is man, that thou art mindful of him?" The Bible makes it clear that what God desires above all things is a man -- a man who will be after His own heart.    So God created a man. In Genesis 2:7 we learn that Adam was created a living soul, with a spirit inside to commune with God and with a body outside to have contact with the material world. (Such New Testament verses as 1 Thessalonians 5:23 and Hebrews 4:12 confirm this threefold character of man's being.) With his spirit Adam was in touch with the spiritual world of God; with his body he was in touch with the physical world of material things. He gathered up these two sides of God's creative act into himself to become a personality, an entity living in the world, moving by itself and having powers of free choice. Viewed thus as a whole, he was found to be a self-conscious and self-expressing being, "a living soul".

We saw earlier that Adam was created perfect -- by which we mean that he was without imperfections because by God -- but that he was not yet perfected. He needed a finishing touch somewhere. God had not yet done all that He intended to do in Adam. There was more in view, but it was as yet in abeyance. God was moving towards the fulfillment of His purpose in creating man, a purpose which went beyond man himself, for it had in view the securing to God of all His rights in the universe through man's instrumental in this? Only by a co-operation that sprang from living union with God. God was seeking to have not merely a race of men of one blood upon the earth, but a race which had, in addition, His life resident within its members. Such a race will eventually compass the downfall of Satan and bring to fulfillment all that God has set His heart upon. It is that that was in view with the creation of man.

Then again, we saw that Adam was created neutral. He had a spirit which enabled him to hold communion with God; but as man he was not yet, so to speak, finally orientated; he had powers of choice and he could, if he liked, turn the opposite way. God's goal in man was `sonship', or, in other words, the expression of His life in human beings. That Divine life was represented in the garden by the tree of life, bearing a fruit that could be accepted, received, taken in. If Adam, created neutral, were voluntarily to turn that way and, choosing dependence upon God, were to receive of the tree of life (representing God's own life), God would then have that life in union with men; He would have realized 'sonship'. But if instead Adam should turn to the tree of the knowledge of good and evil, he would as a result be 'free' to develop himself on his own lines apart from God. Because, however, this latter choice involved complicity with Satan, Adam would thereby put beyond his reach the attaining of his God-appointed goal.

## THE ROOT QUESTION: THE HUMAN SOUL

Now we know the course that Adam chose. Standing between the two trees, he yielded to Satan and took of the fruit of the tree of knowledge. This determined the lines of his development. From then on he could command a knowledge; he 'knew'. But -- and here we come to the point -- the fruit of the tree of knowledge made the first man over-developed in his soul. The emotion was touched, because the fruit was pleasant to the eyes, making him 'desire'; the mind with its reasoning power was developed, for he was 'made wise'; and the will was strengthened, so that in future he could always decide which way he would go. The whole fruit ministered to the expansion and full development of the soul, so that not only was the man a living soul, but from henceforth man will live by the soul. It is not merely that man has a soul, but that from that day on the soul, with its independent powers of free choice, takes the place of the spirit as the animating power of man.

We have to distinguish here between two things, for the difference is most important. God does not mind -- in fact He intends -- that we should have a soul such as He gave to Adam. But what God has set Himself to do is to reverse something. There is something in man today which is not just the fact of having a soul, but which constitutes a living by the soul. It was this that Satan brought about in the Fall. He trapped man into taking a course by which he could develop his soul so as to derive his very life from it.

We must however be careful. To remedy this does not mean that we are going to cross out the soul altogether. You cannot do that. When today the Cross is really working in us, we do not become inert, insensate, characterless. No, we still possess a soul, and whenever we receive something from God the soul will still be used in relation to it, as an instrument, a faculty, in a true subjection to Him. But the point is, Are we keeping within God's appointed limit -- within the bounds set by Him in the

Garden at the beginning -- with regard to the soul, or are we getting outside those bounds?

What God is now doing is the pruning work of the vinedresser. In our souls there is an uncontrolled development, an untimely growth, that has to be checked and dealt with. God must cut that off. So now there are two things before us to which our eyes must be opened. On the one hand God is seeking to bring us to the place where we live by the life of His Son. On the other hand He is doing a direct work in our hearts to undo that other natural resource that is the result of the fruit of knowledge. Every day we are learning these two lessons: a rising up of the life of this One, and a checking and a handing over to death of that other soul-life. These two processes go on all the time, for God is seeking the fully developed life of His Son in us in order to manifest Himself, and to that end He is bringing us back, as to our soul, to Adam's starting-point. So Paul says: "We which live are always delivered unto death for Jesus' sake, that the life also of Jesus may be manifested in our mortal flesh" (2 Cor. 4:11).

What does this mean? It simply means that I will not take any action without relying on God. I will find no sufficiency in myself. I will not take any step just because I have the power to do so. Even though I have that inherited power within me, I will not use it; I will put no reliance in myself. By taking the fruit, Adam became possessed of an inherent power to act, but a power which played right into Satan's hands. You lose that power to act when you come to know the Lord. The Lord cuts it off and you find you can no longer act on your own initiative. You have to live by the life of Another; you have to draw everything from Him.

Oh, friends, I think we all know ourselves in measure, but many a time we do not truly tremble at ourselves. We may, in a manner of courtesy to God, say: `If the Lord does not want it, I cannot do it', but in reality our subconscious thought is that really we can do it quite well ourselves, even if God does not ask us to do it nor empower us for it. Too often we have been caused to act, to think, to decide, to have power, apart from Him. Many of us Christians today are men with over-developed souls. We have grown too big in ourselves. We have become `big-souled'. When we are in that condition, the life of the Son of God in us is confined and almost crowded out of action.

## NATURAL ENERGY IN THE WORK OF GOD

The power, the energy of the soul is present with us all. Those who have been taught by the Lord repudiate that principle as a life principle; they refuse to live by it; they will not let it reign, nor allow it to be the power-spring of the work of God. But those who have not been taught of God rely upon it; they utilize it; they think it is the power.

Let us take first an obvious illustration of this. Far too many of us in the past have reasoned as follows. Here is a delightfully good-natured man, with a clear brain, splendid managing powers and sound judgment. In our hearts we say, `If that man could be a Christian, what an asset he would be to the Church! If only he were the Lord's, what a lot it would mean to His cause!'

But think for a moment. Where did that man's good nature come from? Whence are those splendid managing powers and that good judgment? Not form new birth, for he is not yet born again. We know we have all been born of the flesh; therefore we need a new birth. But the Lord Jesus had something to say about this in John 3:6: "That which is born of the flesh is flesh". Everything which comes not by new birth but my natural birth is flesh and will only bring glory to man, not God. That statement is not very palatable, but it is true.

We have spoken of soul-power or natural energy. What is this natural energy? It is simply what I can do, what I am of myself, what I have inherited of natural gifts and resources. We are none of us without the power of the soul, and our first need is to recognize it for what it is. Take for example the human mind. I may have by nature a keen mind. Before my new birth I had it naturally, as something developed from my natural birth. But the trouble arises here. I become converted, I am born anew, a deep work is effected in my spirit, and essential union with God that has been set up in my spirit, but at the same time I carry over with me something which I derive from my natural birth. Now what am I going to do about it?

The natural tendency is this. Formerly I used to use my mind to pore over history, over business, over chemistry, over questions of the world, or literature, or poetry. I used my keen mind to get the best out of those studies. But now my desire has been changed, so henceforth I employ the same mind in the things of God. I have therefore changed my subject of interest, but I have not changed my method of working. That is the whole point. My interests have been utterly changed (praise God for that!), but now I utilize the same power to study Corinthians and Ephesians that I used before to pursue history and geography. But that power is not of God; and God will not allow that. The trouble with so many of us is that we have changed the channel into which our energies are directed, but we have not changed the source of those energies.

You will find there are many such things which we carry over into the service of God. Consider the matter of eloquence. There are some men who are born orators; they can present a case very convincingly indeed. Then they become converted, and, without asking ourselves where they really stand in relation to spiritual things, we put them on the platform and make preachers of them. We encourage them to use their natural powers for preaching, and again it is a change of subject but the same power. We forget that, in the matter of our resource for handling the things of God, it is a question not of comparative value but of origin -- of where the resource springs from. It is not so much a matter of what we are doing, but of what powers we are employing to do it. We think too little of the source of our energy and too much of the end to which it is directed, forgetting that with God the end never justifies the means.

The following hypothetical case will help us to test the truth of our argument. Mr. A. is a very good speaker: he can talk fluently and most convincingly on any subject, but in practical things he is a very bad manager. Mr. B., on the other hand, is a poor speaker: he cannot express himself clearly but wanders all round his subject, never coming to a point; yet on the other hand he is a splendid manager, most competent in all matters of business. Both these men get converted, and both become earnest Christians. Let us suppose now that I call on them both and ask them to speak at a convention, and that both accept.

Now what will happen? I have asked the self-same thing of both men, but who do you think will pray the harder? Certainly Mr. B. Why? Because he is no speaker. In the matter of eloquence he has no resources of his own to depend upon. He will pray: `Lord, if you do not give me power for this, I cannot do it'. Of course Mr. A. will pray too, but maybe not in the same way as Mr. B. because he has something of natural resource upon which to rely. Now let us suppose that, instead of asking them to speak, I ask them both to take charge of the practical side of affairs at the convention. What will happen? The position will be exactly reversed. Now it will be Mr. A.'s turn to pray hard, for he knows full well that he has no organizing ability. Br. B. of course will pray too, but perhaps without quite the same urgency, for though he knows his need of the Lord he is not nearly so conscious of his need in business matters as is Mr. A.

Do you see the difference between natural and spiritual gifts? Anything we can do without prayer and without an utter dependence upon God must come from that spring of natural life, and is suspect. We must see this clearly. Of course it is not true that those only are suited for a particular work who lack the natural gift for it. The point is that, whether naturally gifted or not, they must know the touch of the Cross in death upon all that is of nature, and their complete dependence upon the God of resurrection. All too readily do we envy our neighbor who has some outstanding natural gift, and fail to realize that our own possession of it, apart from such a working of the Cross, may easily prove a barrier to the very thing that God is seeking to manifest in us.

Shortly after my conversion I went out preaching in the villages. I had had a good education and was well versed in the Scriptures, so I considered myself thoroughly capable of instructing the village folk, among whom were quite a number of illiterate women. But after several visits I discovered that, despite their illiteracy, those women hand an intimate knowledge of the Lord. I knew the Book they haltingly read; they knew the One of whom the Book spoke. I had much in the flesh; they had much in the Spirit. How many Christian teachers today are teaching others as I was then, very largely in the strength of their carnal equipment!

Once I met a young brother -- young, that is to say, in years, but who had learned a good deal of the Lord. The Lord had brought him through much tribulation to gain that knowledge of Himself. As I was talking to him I said, `Brother, what has the Lord really been teaching you these days?' He said, `Only one thing: that I can do nothing apart from him.' `Do you really mean', I said, `that you can do nothing?' `Well, no', he replied. `I can do many things! In fact that has been just my trouble. Oh, you know, I have always been so confident in myself. I know I am well able to do lots of things.' So I asked, `What then do you mean when you say you can do nothing apart from Him?' He answered, `The Lord has shown me that I can do anything, but that He has said, "Apart from me ye can do nothing". So it comes to this, that everything I have done and can do apart from Him is nothing!' We have to come to that valuation. I do not mean to say we cannot do a lot of things, for we can. We can take meetings, and build churches, we can go to the ends of the earth and found missions, and we can seem to bear fruit; but remember that the Lord's word is: "Every plant which my heavenly Father planted not, shall be rooted up" (Matt. 15:13). God is the only legitimate Originator in the universe (Gen. 1:1). Anything that you plan and set on foot has its origin in the flesh, and it will never reach the realm of the Spirit however earnestly you seek God's blessing on it. It may last for years, and then you may think you will adjust here and improve there and maybe bring it on a better plane, but it cannot be done.

Origin determines destination, and what was "of the flesh" originally will never be made spiritual by any amount of 'improvement'. That which is born of the flesh is flesh, and it will never be otherwise. Anything for which we are sufficient in ourselves is 'nothing' in God's estimate, and we have to accept His estimate and write it down as nothing. "The flesh profiteth nothing." It is only what comes from above that will abide. We cannot see this simply by being told it. God must teach us what is meant, by putting His finger on something which He sees and saying: 'This is natural; this has its source in the old creation; this cannot abide.' Until He does so, we may agree in principle but we can never really see it. We may assent to, and even enjoy, the teaching, but we shall never truly loathe ourselves.

But there will come a day when God opens our eyes. Facing a particular issue we shall have to say, as by revelation: 'It is unclean, it is impure; Lord, I see it!' The word 'purity' is a blessed word. I always associate it with the Spirit. Purity means something altogether of the Spirit. Impurity means mixture. When God opens our eyes to see that the natural life is something He can never use in His work, then we find we do not enjoy the doctrine any longer. Rather we loathe ourselves for the impurity that is in us; but when that point is reached, God begins His work of deliverance. We are going on shortly to look at the provision He has made for that deliverance, but we must stay for a little longer with this matter of revelation.

## THE LIGHT OF GOD AND KNOWLEDGE

Of course, if one does not set out to serve the Lord whole-heartedly, one does not feel the necessity for light. It is only when one has been apprehended by God, and seeks to go forward with Him, that one finds how necessary light is. There is a fundamental need of light in order for us to know the mind of God; to know what is of the spirit and what is of the soul; to know what is Divine and what is merely of man; to discern what is truly heavenly and what is only earthly; to understand the difference between things which are spiritual and things which are carnal; to know whether God is really leading us or whether we are walking by our feelings, senses or imaginations. It is when we have reached a position where we would like to follow God fully that we find light to be the most necessary thing in the Christian life.

In my conversations with younger brothers and sisters one question comes up again and again. It is: How can I know that I am walking in the Spirit? How do I distinguish which prompting within me is from the Holy Spirit and which is from myself? It seems that all are alike in this; but some have gone further. They are trying to look within, to differentiate, to discriminate to analyze, and in doing so are bringing themselves into deeper bondage. Now this is a situation which is really dangerous to Christian life, for inward knowledge will never be reached along the barren path of self-analysis.

We are never told in the Word of God to examine our inward condition.[15] That way ends only to uncertainty, vacillation and despair. Of course we have to have self-knowledge. We have to know what is going on within. We do not want to live in a fool's paradise; to have gone altogether wrong and yet not know we have gone wrong; to have a spartan will and yet think we are pursuing the will of God. But such self-knowledge does not come by our turning within; by our analyzing our feelings and motives and everything that is going on inside, and then trying to pronounce whether we are walking in the flesh or in the Spirit.

There are several passages in the Psalms which illumine this subject.

The first is in Psalm 36:9: "In thy light shall we see light". I think that is one of the best verses in the old Testament. There are two lights there. There is "thy light", and then , when we have come into that light, we shall "see light".

---

[15] The two apparent exceptions to this are found in 1 Corinthians 11:28,31 and 2 Corinthians 13:5. But the former passage calls upon us to discern ourselves as to whether we recognize the Lord's body or not, and this is in particular connection with the Lord's table. It is not concerned with self-knowledge as such. The strong command of Paul in the latter passage is to examine ourselves as to whether or not we are "in the faith". It is a question of the existence or otherwise in us of a fundamental faith; of whether, in fact, we are Christians. This is in no way related to our daily walk in the Spirit, or to self-knowledge. -- W.N.

Now those two lights are different. We might say that the first is objective and the second subjective. The first light is the light which belongs to God but is shed upon us; the second is the knowledge imparted by that light. "In thy light shall we see light": we shall know something; we shall be clear about something; we shall see. No turning within, no introspective self-examination will ever bring us to that clear place. No, it is when there is light coming from God that we see.

I think it is so simple. If we want to satisfy ourselves that our face is clean, what do we do? Do we feel it carefully all over with our hands? No, of course not. We find a mirror and we bring it to the light. In that light everything becomes clear. No sight ever came by feeling or analyzing. Sight only comes by the light of God coming in; and when once it has come, there is no loner need to ask if a thing is right or wrong. We know.      You remember again how in Psalm 139:23 the writer says: "Search me, O God, and know my heart". You realize, do you not, what it means to say `Search me'? It certainly does not mean that I search myself. `Search me' means `You search me!' That is the way of illumination. It is for God to come in and search; it is not for me to search. Of course that will never mean that I may go blindly on, careless of my true condition. That is not the point. The point is that however much my self-examination may reveal in me that needs putting right, such searching never really gets below the surface. My true knowledge of self comes not from my searching myself but from God searching me.

But, you ask, what does it mean in practice for us to come into the light? How does it work? How do we see light in His light? Here again the Psalmist comes to our help. "The entrance of Thy words giveth light; it giveth understanding unto the simple" (psalm 119:130 A.V.). In spiritual things we are all `simple'. We are dependent upon God to give us understanding, and especially is this so in the matter of our own true nature. And it is here that the Word of God operates. In the New Testament the passage which states this most clearly is in the Epistle to the Hebrews: "The word of God is living, and active, and sharper than any two-edged sword, and piercing even to the dividing of soul and spirit, of both joints and marrow, and quick to discern the thoughts and intents of the heart. And there is no creature that is not manifest in his sight: but all things are naked and laid open before the eyes of him with whom we have to do" (Heb. 4:12,13). Yes, it is the Word of God, the penetrating Scripture of Truth, that settles our questions. It is that which discerns our motives and defines for us their true source in soul or spirit.

With this I think we can pass on from the doctrinal to the practical side of things. Many of us, I am sure, are living quite honestly before God. We have been making progress, and we do not know of anything much wrong with us. Then one day, as we go on, we meet with a fulfillment of that word: "The entrance of Thy words giveth light". Some servant of God has been used by Him to confront us with His living Word, and that Word has made an entrance into us. Or perhaps we ourselves have been waiting before God and, whether from our memory of Scripture or from the page itself, His Word has come to us in power. Then it is we see something which we have never seen before. We are convicted. We know where we are wrong, and we look up and confess: 'Lord, I see it. There is impurity there. There is mixture. How blind I was! Just fancy that for so many years I have been wrong there and have never known it!' Light comes in and we see light. The light of God brings us to see the light concerning ourselves, and it is an abiding principle that every knowledge of self comes to us in that way.

It may not always be the Scriptures. Some of us have known saints who really knew the Lord, and through praying with them or talking with them, in the light of God radiating from them, we have seen something which we never say before. I have met one such, who is now with the Lord, and I always think of her as a 'lighted' Christian. If I did but walk into her room, I was brought immediately to a sense of God. In those days I was very young and had been converted about two years, and I had lots of plans, lots of beautiful thoughts, lots of schemes for the Lord to sanction, a hundred and lone things which I thought would be marvelous if they were all brought to fruition. With all these things I came to her to try to persuade her; to tell her that this or that was the thing to do.

Before I could open my mouth she would just say a few words in quite an ordinary way. Light dawned! It simply put me to shame. My 'doing' was all so natural, so full of man. Something happened. I was brought to a place where I could say: 'Lord, my mind is set only in creaturely activities, but here is someone who is not out for them at all'. She had but one motive, one desire, and that was for God. Written in the front of her Bible were these words: 'Lord, I want nothing for myself', Yes, she lived for God alone, and where that is the case you will find that such a one is bathed in light, and that that light illuminates others. That is real witness.[16]

Light has one law: it shines wherever it is admitted. That is the only requirement. We may shut it out of ourselves; it fears nothing else. If we throw ourselves open to God, He will reveal. The trouble comes when we have closed areas, locked and barred places in our hearts, where we think with pride that we are right. Our defeat lies then not only in our being wrong but in our not knowing that we are wrong. Wrong may be a question of natural strength; ignorance of it is a question of light. You can see the natural strength in some but they cannot see it themselves. Oh, we need to be sincere and humble, and to open ourselves before God! Those who are open can see. God is light, and we cannot live in His light and be without understanding. Let us say again with the Psalmist: "O send out Thy light and Thy truth: let them lead me" (Psalm 43:3).

We praise God that sin is being brought to the notice of Christians today more than hitherto. In many places the eyes of Christians have been opened to see that victory over sins, as items, is important in Christian life, and in consequence many are walking closer to the Lord in seeking deliverance and victory over them. Praise the Lord for any movement toward Himself, any movement back to real holiness unto God! But that is not enough. There is one thing that must be touched, and that is the very life of the man, not merely his sins. The question of the personality of the man, of his soul-power, is the heart of the matter. To make the question of sins to be everything is still to be on the surface. Holiness, if you only regard sins, is still something on the outside, still superficial. You have not yet got to the root of the evil.

Adam did not let sin into the world by committing murder. That came later. Adam let in sin by choosing to have his soul developed to a place where he cold go on by himself apart from God. When, therefore, God secures a race of men who will be to His glory, and who will be His instrument to accomplish His purpose in the universe, they will be a people whose life - yea, whose very breath -- is dependent upon Him. He will be the "tree of life" to them.

---

[16] This is one of several references by the author to the late Miss Maragaret E. Barber of Pagoda Anchorage, Foochow. See also pp. 95-6, 239, 256-7, 266-7. -- Ed.

What I feel more and more the need of in myself, and what I feel that we all as the Lord's children need to seek from God, is a real revelation of ourselves. I repeat that I do not mean we should be for ever looking in on ourselves and asking: `Now, is this soul or is it spirit?' That will never get us anywhere; it is darkness. No, Scripture shows us how the saints were brought to self-knowledge. It was always by light from God, and that light is God Himself. Isaiah, Ezekiel, Daniel, Peter, Paul, John, all came to a knowledge of themselves because the Lord flashed Himself upon them, and that flash brought revelation and conviction. (Isa. 6:5; Ezek. 1:28; Dan. 10:8; Luke 22:61, 62; Acts 9:3-5; Rev. 1:17).

We can never know the hatefulness of sin and the hatefulness of ourselves unless there is that flash of God upon us. I speak not of a sensation but of an inward revelation of the Lord Himself through His Word.

It does for us what doctrine alone can never do.

Christ is our light. He is the living Word, and when we read the Scriptures that life in Him brings revelation. "The life was the light of men" (John 1:4). Such illumination may not come to us all at once, but gradually; but it will be more and more clear and searching, until we see ourselves in the light of god and all our self-confidence is gone. For light is the purest thing in the world. It cleanses. It sterilizes. It kills what should not be there. In its radiance the `dividing asunder of joints and marrow' becomes to us a fact and no mere teaching. We know fear and trembling as we recognize the corruption of man's nature, the hatefulness of our own selves, and the real threat to the work of God of our unrestrained soul-life and energy. As never before, we wee now how much of us needs God's drastic dealing if He is to use us, and we know that, apart from Him, as servants of God we are finished.

But here the Cross, in its widest meaning, will come to our help again, and we shall seek now to examine an aspect of its work which meets and deals with our problem of the human soul. For only a thorough understanding of the Cross can bring us to that place of dependence which the Lord Jesus Himself voluntarily took when He said: "I can of myself do nothing: as I hear, I judge: and my judgment is righteous; because I seek not mine own will, but the will of him that sent me" (John 5:30).

# CHAPTER 13: THE PATH OF PROGRESS: BEARING THE CROSS

In our previous chapter we have touched several times upon the matter of service for the Lord. As we come now to look at the provision that God has made to meet the problem created by the soul-life of man, it will be helpful if we approach that problem by considering first the principles which govern our work for Him and from which no one who tries to serve Him may deviate. The basis of our salvation, as we well know, is the fact of our Lord's death and resurrection; but the conditions of our service are no less definite. Just as the fact of the death and resurrection of the Lord is the ground of our acceptance with God, so the principle of death and resurrection is the basis of our life and service for Him.

## THE BASIS OF ALL TRUE MINISTRY

No one can be a true servant of God without knowing the principle of death and the principle of resurrection. Even the Lord Jesus Himself served on that basis. You will find in Matthew 3 that, before His public ministry ever began, our Lord was baptized. He was baptized not because He had any sin, or anything which needed cleansing. No, we know the meaning of baptism: it is a figure of death and resurrection. The ministry of the Lord did not begin until He was on that ground. After He had been baptized and had voluntarily taken the ground of death and resurrection, the Holy Spirit came upon Him, and then He ministered.

What does this teach us? Our Lord was a sinless Man. None but He has trodden this earth and known no sin. Yet as Man He had a separate personality from His Father. Now we must tread very carefully when we touch our Lord; but remember His words: "I seek not mine own will, but the will of him that sent me". What does this mean? It certainly does not mean that the Lord had no will of His own. He had a will, as His own words show.

As Son of man He had a will, but He did not do it; He came to do the will of the Father. So this is the point. That thing in Him which is in distinction from the Father is the human soul, which He assumed when He was "found in fashion as a man". Being a perfect Man our Lord had a soul, and of course a body, just as you and I have a soul and a body, and it was possible for Him to act from the soul -- that is, from Himself.

You remember that immediately after the Lord's baptism, and before His public ministry began, Satan came and tempted Him. He tempted Him to satisfy His essential needs by turning stones to bread; to secure immediate respect for His ministry by appearing miraculously in the temple court; to assume without delay the world dominion destined for Him; and you are inclined to wonder why he tempted Him to do such strange things. He might rather, you feel, have tempted Him to sin in a more thoroughgoing way. But he did not; he knew better. He only said: "If thou art the Son of God, command that these stones become bread". What did it mean? The implication was this: `If You are the Son of God You must do something to prove it. Here is a challenge. Some will certainly raise a question as to whether Your claim is real or not. Why do You not settle the matter finally now by coming out and proving it?'

The whole subtle object of Satan was to get the Lord to act for Himself -- that is, from the soul -- and, by the stand He took, the Lord Jesus absolutely repudiated such action. In Adam, man had acted from himself apart from God; that was the whole tragedy of the garden. Now in a similar situation the Son of man takes another ground. Later He defines it as His basic life-principle -- and I like the word in the Greek: "The Son can do nothing out from himself" (John 5:19). That total denial of the soul-life was to govern all His ministry.

So we can safely say that all the work which the Lord Jesus did on earth, prior to His actual death on the cross, was done with the principle of death on the cross, and resurrection as basis, even though as an actual event Calvary still lay in the future. Everything He did was on that ground. But if this is so -- if the Son of man has to go through death and resurrection (in figure and in principle) in order to work, can we do otherwise? Surely no servant of the Lord can serve Him without himself knowing the working of that principle in his life. It is of course out of the question. The Lord made this very clear to His disciples when He left them. He had died and He was risen, and He told them to wait in Jerusalem for the Spirit to come upon them. Now what is this power of the Holy Spirit, this "power from on high" of which He spoke? It is nothing less than the virtue of His death, resurrection and ascension. To use another figure, the Holy Spirit is the Vessel in whom all the values of the death, resurrection and exaltation of the Lord are deposited, that they may be brought to us. He is the one who 'contains' those values and mediates them to men. That is the reason why the Spirit could not be given before the Lord had been glorified. Then only could He rest upon men and women that they might witness; and without the values of the death and resurrection of Christ no such witness is possible.

If we turn to the Old Testament we find the same thing is there. I would refer you to a familiar passage in the seventeenth chapter of Numbers. The matter of Aaron's ministry has been contested. There is a question among the people as to whether Aaron is truly the chosen of God. They have entertained a suspicion, and have said in effect: 'Whether that man is ordained of God or not, we do not know!' and so God sets out to prove who is His servant and who is not. How does He do so? Twelve dead rods are put before the Lord in the sanctuary over against the testimony, and they are there for a night. Then, in the morning, the Lord indicates His chosen minister by the rod which buds, blossoms and bears fruit. We all know the meaning of that. The budding rod speaks of resurrection. It is death and resurrection that marks God-recognized ministry. Without that you have nothing. The budding of Aaron's rod proved him to be on a true basis, and God will only recognize as His ministers those who have come through death to resurrection ground.

We have seen that the death of the Lord works in different ways and has different aspects. We know how His death has worked in regard to the forgiveness of our sins. We all know that our forgiveness is based upon the shed Blood, and that without the shedding of Blood there is no remission. Then we have come further and in Romans 6 have seen how death works to meet the power of sin. We have learned that our old man has been crucified in order that henceforth we should not serve sin, and we have praised the Lord that here too His death has worked for our deliverance. Further on still the question of human self-will arises, and the need for consecration is apparent; and we find death working that way to bring about in us a willingness to let go our own wills and obey the Lord. That indeed constitutes a starting point for our ministry, but still it does not touch the core of the question. There may still be the lack of knowledge of what is meant by the soul.

Then another phase is presented to us in Romans 7 where the question of holiness of life is in view -- a living, personal holiness. There you find a true man of God trying to please God in righteousness, and he comes under the law and the law finds him out. He is trying to please God by using his own carnal power, and the Cross has to bring him to the place where he says, `I cannot do it. I cannot satisfy God with my powers; I can only trust the Holy Spirit to do that in me.' I believe some of us have passed through deep waters to learn this, and to discover the value of the death of the Lord working in this way.

Now mark you, there is still a great difference between "the flesh", as spoken of in Romans 7 in relation to holiness of life, and the working of the natural energies of the soul-life in the service of the Lord. With all the above being known -- and known in experience -- there still remains this one sphere more which the death of the Lord must enter before we are actually of use to Him in service. Even with all these experiences we are still unsafe for Him to use until this further thing is effected in us. How many of God's servants are used by Him, as we say in China, to build twelve feet of wall, only, when they have done so, to undo it all by themselves pulling down fifteen feet! We are used in a sense, but at the same time we destroy our own work, and sometimes that of others also, because of there being somewhere something undealt with by the Cross.

Now we have to see how the Lord has set out to deal with the soul, and then more particularly how this touches the question of our service for Him.

## THE SUBJECTIVE WORKING OF THE CROSS

We must keep before us now four passages from the Gospels They are: Matthew 10:34-39; Mark 8:32-25; Luke 17:32-34; and John 12:24-26. These four passages have something in common. In each you have the Lord Himself speaking to us concerning the soul-activity of man, and in each a different aspect or manifestation of the soul-life is touched upon. In these verses He makes it very plain that the soul of man can be dealt with in one way and in one way only, and that is by our bearing the cross daily and following Him. As we have just seen, the soul-life or natural life that is here in view is something further than what we have in those passages which are concerned with the old man or the flesh. We have sought to make quite clear that, in respect of our old man, God emphasizes the thing He has done once for all in crucifying us with Christ on the Cross. We have seen that three times in the Epistle to the Galations the `crucifying' aspect of the Cross is referred to as a thing accomplished; and in Romans 6:6 we have the clear statement that "our old man was crucified", which, if the tense of the word means anything, we might well paraphrase: `Our old man has been finally and for ever crucified'. It is something done, to be apprehended by Divine revelation and then appropriated by faith.

But there is a further aspect of the Cross, namely that implied in the expression `bearing his cross daily', which is before us now. The Cross has borne me; now I must bear it; and this bearing of the Cross is an inward thing. It is this that we mean when we speak of `the subjective working of the Cross'. Moreover it is a daily process; it is a step by step following after Him. It is this which is now brought before us in relation to the soul, and let us note that the emphasis here is not quite the same as with the old man. We do not have here the `crucifixion' of the soul itself, in the sense that our natural gifts and faculties, our personality and our individuality, are to be put away altogether. Were it so it could hardly be said of us, as it is in Hebrews 10:39, that we are to "have faith unto the saving of the soul". (Compare 1 Peter 1:9; Luke 21:19.) No, we do not lose our souls in this sense, for to do so would be to lose our individual existence completely. The soul is still there with its natural endowments, but the Cross is brought to bear upon it to bring those natural endowments into death -- to put the mark of His death upon them -- and thereafter, as God may please, to give them back to us in resurrection.

It is in this sense that Paul, writing to the Philippians, expresses the desire "that I may know him, and the power of his resurrection, and the fellowship of his sufferings, becoming conformed unto his death" (Phil. 3:10). The mark of death is upon the soul all the time to bring it to the place where it is always subordinate to the Spirit and never independently asserts itself. Only the Cross, working in such a way, could make a man of the calibre of Paul, and with the natural resources hinted at in Philippians 3, so distrust his own natural strength that he could write to the Corinthians: "I determined not to know anything among you, save Jesus Christ, and him crucified. And I was with you in weakness, and in fear, and in much trembling. And my speech and my preaching were not in persuasive words of wisdom, but in demonstration of the Spirit and of power: that your faith should not stand in the wisdom of men, but in the power of God" (1 Cor. 2:2,3).

The soul is the seat of the affections, and what a great part of our decisions and actions is influenced by these! There is nothing deliberately sinful about them, mind you, but it is simply that there is something in us which can go out in natural affection to another person and which as a result can influence wrongly our whole course of action. So in the first of the four passages before us the Lord has to say: "He that loveth father or mother more than me is not worthy of me; and he that loveth son or daughter more than me is not worthy of me. And he that doth not take his cross and follow after me, is not worthy of me" (Matt. 10:37,38). You note that to follow the Lord in the way of the Cross is set before us as His normal, His only way for us. What immediately follows? "He that findeth his soul shall lose it; and he that loseth his soul for my sake shall find it" (Matt. 10:39, mg.).

The secret danger lies in that subtle working of the affections to turn us away from the pathway of God; and the key to the matter is the soul. The Cross has to deal with that. I have to "lose" my soul in the sense in which the Lord meant those words, and which we are seeking here to explain. Some of us know well what it means to lose our soul. We can no longer fulfill its desire; we cannot give in to it; we cannot gratify it: that is the `loss' of the soul. We are going through a painful process to discourage what the soul is asking for. And many a time we have to confess that it is not any definite sin that is keeping us from following the Lord to the end. We are held up because of some secret love somewhere, some perfectly natural affection diverting our course. Yes, affection plays a great part in our lives, and the Cross has to come in there and do its work.

Then we pass to the reference in Mark chapter 8. I think that is a most important passage. Our Lord had just taught His disciples at Caesarea Philippi that He was going to suffer death at the hands of the elders of the Jews, and then Peter, with all his love for his Master, came up and rebuked Him and said to Him: `Lord, do not do it; pity Thyself: this shall never come to Thee!' Out of his love for the Lord he appealed to Him to spare Himself; and the Lord rebuked Peter, as He would rebuke Satan, for caring for the things of men and not the things of God. And then to all present the word was spoken once more: "If any man would come after me, let him deny himself, and take up his cross, and follow me. For whosoever will save his soul shall lose it; and whosoever shall lose his soul for my sake and the gospel's shall save it" (Mark 8:34,35, mg.).

The whole question at issue is again that of the soul, and here it is particularly of the soul's desire for self-preservation. There is that subtle working of the soul which says, `If I could be allowed to live I would do anything, be willing for anything; but I must be kept alive!' There you have the soul almost crying out for help. `Going to the Cross, being crucified -- oh that is really too much! Have mercy on yourself; pity yourself! Do you mean to say you are going against yourself and going with God?' Some of us know well that in order to go on with God we have many a time to go against the voice of the soul- our own or other people's -- and to let the Cross come in to silence that appeal for self-preservation. Am I afraid of the will of God? The dear saint whom I have already mentioned as having had such an influence upon the course of my life, many times asked me the question: `Do you like the will of God?' It is a tremendous question. She did not ask, `Do you do the will of God?' she always asked, `Do you like the will of God?' That question cuts deeper than anything else. I remember once she was having a controversy with the Lord over a certain matter. She knew what the Lord wanted, and in her heart she wanted it too. But is was difficult, and I heard her pray like this: `Lord, I confess I don't like it, but please do not give in to me. Just wait, Lord -- and I will give in to Thee.' She did not want the Lord to yield to her and to reduce His demands upon her. She wanted nothing but to please Him. Many a time we have to come to the place where we are willing to let go things we think to be good and precious -- yes, and even, it may be, the very things of God themselves -- that His will may be done. Peter's concern was for his Lord and was dictated by his natural love for Him. We might feel that Peter had a marvelous love for his Lord, sufficient even for him to dare to rebuke Him. Only a strong love could bring one to attempt that! Yes, but when there is purity of spirit without that mixture of soul, you will not be led into Peter's mistake. You will recognize the will of God and you will find that that is what your heart delights in alone. You will no longer even shed a tear in sympathy with the flesh. Yes, the Cross cuts deeply, and we see here once more how utterly it has to deal with the soul. Once again the Lord Jesus deals with the matter of the soul in Luke chapter 17, and now it is in relation to His return. Speaking of "the day that the Son of man is revealed", He draws a parallel between that day and "the day that Lot went out from Sodom" (verses 29, 30). A little later He speaks of the `rapture' in the twice repeated words: "One shall be taken, and the other shall be left" (verses 34,35). But between His reference to the calling of Lot out of Sodom and this allusion to the rapture, the Lord says these remarkable words: "In that day, he which shall be on the housetop, and his goods in the house, let him not go down to take them away: and let him that is in the field likewise not return back. Remember Lot's wife" (verses 31, 32). Remember Lot's wife! Why? because "whosoever shall seek to gain his soul shall lose it: but whosoever shall lose his soul shall save it alive" (verse 33, mg.).

If I mistake not, this is the one passage in the New Testament that tells of our reaction to the rapture call. We may have thought that when the Son of man comes we shall be taken up automatically, as it were, because of what we read in 1 Corinthians 15:51, 52: "We shall all be changed, in a moment, in the twinkling of an eye, at the last trump ..." Well, however we reconcile the two passages, this one in Luke's Gospel should at least make us pause and reflect; for the emphasis is here very strongly upon one being taken and the other left. It is a matter of our reaction to the call to go, and on the basis of this a most urgent appeal is made to us to be ready (compare Matt. 24:42).

There is surely a reason for this. Clearly that call is not going to produce a miraculous last-minute change in us out of all relation to our previous walk with the Lord. No, in that moment we shall discover our heart's real treasure. If it is the Lord Himself, then there will be no backward look. A backward glance decides everything. It is so easy to become more attached to the gifts of God than to the Giver -- and even, I should add, to the work of God than to God Himself.

Let me illustrate. At the present time [17] I am writing a book. I have finished eight chapters and I have another nine to write, about which I am very seriously exercised before the Lord. But if the call to `come up hither' should come and my reaction were to be `What about my book?' the answer might well be, `All right, stay down and finish it!' That precious thing which we are doing downstairs `in the house' can be enough to pin us down, a peg that holds us to earth.

It is all a question of our living by the soul or by the spirit. Here in this passage in Luke, we have depicted the soul-life in its engagement with the things of the earth -- and mark you, not sinful things either. The Lord only mentioned marrying, planting, eating, selling -- all perfectly legitimate activities with which there is nothing essentially wrong. But it is occupation with them, so that your heart goes out to them, that is enough to pin you down. The way out of that danger is by the losing of the soul. This is beautifully illustrated in the action of Peter when he recognized the risen Lord Jesus by the lake-side. Though with the others he had returned to his former employment, there was now no thought of the ship, nor even of the net full of fishes so miraculously provided. When he heard John's cry of recognition: "it is the Lord", we read that "he cast himself into the sea".

---

[17] 1938. -- Ed.

That is true detachment. The question at issue is always, Where is my heart? The cross has to work in us a true spiritual detachment from anything and anyone outside of the Lord Himself.

But, even here, we are as yet only dealing with the more outward aspects of the soul's activity. The soul giving rein to its affections, the soul asserting itself and trying to manipulate things, the soul becoming preoccupied with things, the soul becoming preoccupied with things on the earth: these are still small things, and do not yet touch the real heart of the matter. There is something which is deeper yet, and which I will try now to explain.

## THE CROSS AND FRUITFULNESS

Let us read again John 12:24,25. "Verily, verily, I say unto you, Except a grain of wheat fall into the earth and die, it abideth by itself alone; but if it die, it beareth much fruit. He that loveth his life (Greek `soul', as in the above passages) loseth it; and he that hateth his life (`soul') in this world shall keep it unto life eternal."

Here we have the inward working of the Cross of which we have been speaking -- the losing of the soul -- linked with and likened to that aspect of the death of the Lord Jesus Himself which we have already seen depicted in the grain of wheat, namely, His death with a view to increase. The end in view is fruitfulness. There is a grain of wheat with life in it, but "it abideth alone". It has the power to impart its life to others; but to do so it must go down into death.

Now we know the way the Lord Jesus took. He passed into death, and, as we saw earlier, His life emerged in many lives. The Son died, and came forth as the first of "many sons". He let go His life that we might receive it. It is in this aspect of His death that we are called to die. It is here that He makes clear the value of conformity to His death, which is that we lose our own natural life, our soul, in order that we may become life-imparters, sharing thereafter with others the new life of God which is in us. This is the secret of ministry, the path of real fruitfulness to God. As Paul says: "We which live are always delivered unto death for Jesus' sake, that the life also of Jesus may be manifested in our mortal flesh. So then death worketh in us, but life in you" (2 Cor. 4:11,12).

We are coming to our point. There is new life in us, if we have received Christ. We all have that precious possession, the treasure in the vessel. Praise the Lord for the reality of His life within us! But why is there so little expression of that life? Why is there an `abiding alone'? Why is it not overflowing and imparting life to others? Why is it scarcely making itself apparent even in our own lives? The reason why there is so little sign of life where life is present is that the soul in us is enveloping and confining that life (as the husk envelopes the grain of wheat) so that it cannot find outlet. We are living in the soul; we are working and serving in our own natural strength; we are not drawing from God. It is the soul that stands in the way of the springing up of life. Lose it; for that way lies fullness.

## A Dark Night -- A Resurrection Morn

So we come back to the almond rod, which was brought into the sanctuary for a night -- a dark night in which there was nothing to be seen -- and then in the morning it budded. There you have set forth the death and resurrection, the life yielded up and the life fained, and there you have the ministry attested. But how does this work out in practice? How do I recognize that God is dealing with me in this way?

First we must be clear about one thing: the soul with its fund of natural energy and resource will continue with us until our death. Till then there will be an unending day-by-day need for the Cross to operate in us, dredging deeply that well-spring of nature. This is the life-long condition of service that is laid down in the words: "Let him deny himself, and take up his cross, and follow me" (Mark 8:34). We never get past that. He who evades it "is not worthy of me" (Matt. 10:38); he "cannot be my disciple" (Luke 14:27). Death and resurrection must remain an abiding principle of our lives for the losing of the soul and the uprising of the Spirit.

Yet here too there may be a crisis that, once reached and passed, can transform our whole life and service for God. It is a wicket gate by which we may enter upon an entirely new pathway. Such a crisis occurred in the life of Jacob at Peniel. It was the `natural man' in Jacob that was seeking to serve God and to attain His end. Jacob knew well that God had said: "The elder shall serve the younger", but he was trying to compass that end through his own ingenuity and resource. God had to cripple that strength of nature in Jacob, and that He did when He touched the sinew of Jacob's thigh. Jacob continued to walk thereafter, but he continued to be lame. He was a different Jacob, as his change of name implies. He had his feet and he could use them, but the strength had been touched, and he limped from an injury from which he would never quite recover.

God must bring us to a point -- I cannot tell you how it will be, but He will do it -- where, through a deep and dark experience, our natural power is touched and fundamentally weakened, so that we no longer dare trust ourselves. He has had to deal with some of us very harshly, and take us through difficult and painful ways, in order to get us there. At length there comes a time when we no longer 'like' to do Christian work -- indeed we almost dread to do things in the Lord's Name. But then at last it is that He can begin to use us.

I can tell you this, that for a year after I was converted I had a lust to preach. It was impossible to stay silent. It was as though there was something moving within me that drove me forward, and I had to keep going. Preaching had become my very life. The Lord may graciously allow you to go on a long while like that -- and not only so but with a fair measure of blessing -- until one day that natural force impelling you is touched, and from then on you no longer do it because you want to do it but because the Lord wants it. Before that experience you preached for the sake of satisfaction you got from serving God in that way; and yet sometimes the Lord could not move you to do one thing that He wanted done. You were living by the natural life, and that life varies a good deal. It is the slave of your temperament. When emotionally you are set on His way you go ahead at full speed, but when your emotions are directed the other way you are reluctant to move at all, even when duty calls. You are not pliable in the Lord's hands. He has therefore to weaken that strength of preference, of like and dislike, in you, until you will do a thing because He wants it and not because you like it. You may enjoy it or you may not, but you will do it just the same. It is not that you can derive a certain satisfaction from preaching or from doing this or that work for God, and therefore you do it. No, you do it now because it is the will of God, and regardless of whether or not it gives you conscious joy. The true joy you know in doing His will lies deeper than your variable emotions.

God is bringing you to the place where He has but to express a wish and you respond instantly. That is the spirit of the Servant (Psalm 40:7,8), but such a spirit does not come naturally to any of us. It comes only when our soul, the seat of our natural energy and will and affections, has known the touch of the Cross. Yet such a servant-spirit is what He seeks and will have in us all. The way to it may be a painful, long-drawn-out process with some of us, or it may be just one stroke; but God has His ways and we must have regard to them.

Every true servant of God must know at some time that disabling from which he can never recover; he can never be quite the same again. There must be that established in you which means that from henceforth you will really fear yourself. You will fear to do anything 'out from' yourself, for, like Jacob, you know what kind of sovereign dealing you will incur if you do it; you know what a bad time you will have in your own heart before the Lord if you move out on the impulse of your soul. You have known something of the chastening hand of a loving God upon you, a God who "dealeth with you as with sons" (Heb. 12:7). The Spirit Himself bears witness in your spirit to that relationship, and to the inheritance and glory that are ours "if so be that we suffer with him" (Rom. 8:16,17); and your response to the 'Father of our spirits' is: "Abba, Father".

But when this is really established in you, you have come to a new place which we speak of as 'resurrection ground'. Death in principle may have had to be wrought out to a crisis in your natural life, but when it has, then you find God releases you into resurrection. You discover that what you have lost is coming back -- though not as before. The principle of life is at work in you now -- something that empowers and strengthens you, something that animates you, giving you life. From henceforth what you have lost will be brought back - but now under discipline, under control. Let me make this quite clear again. If we want to be spiritual people, there is no need for us to amputate our hands or feet; we can still have our body. In the same way we can have our soul, with the full use of its faculties; and yet the soul is not now our life-spring. We are no longer living in it, we are no longer drawing from it and living by it; we use it. When the body becomes our life we live like beasts. When the soul becomes our life we live as rebels and fugitives from God -- gifted, cultured, educated, no doubt, but alienated from the life of God. But when we come to live our life in the Spirit and by the Spirit, though we still use our soul faculties just as we do our physical faculties, they are now the servants of the Spirit; and when we have reached that point God can really use us. But the difficulty with many of us is that dark night. The Lord graciously laid me aside once in my life for a number of months and put me, spiritually, into utter darkness. It was almost as though He had forsaken me -- almost as though nothing was going on and I had really come to the end of everything. And then by degrees He brought things back again. The temptation is always to try to help God by taking things back ourselves;

but remember, there must be a full night in the sanctuary -- a full night in darkness. It cannot be hurried; He knows what He is doing.

We would like to have death and resurrection put together within one hour of each other. We cannot face the thought that God will keep us aside for so long a time; we cannot bear to wait. And I cannot tell you how long He will take, but in principle I think it is quite safe to say this, that there will be a definite period when He will keep you there. It will seem as though nothing is happening; everything you valued is slipping from your grasp. There confronts you a blank wall with no door in it. Seemingly everyone else is being blessed and used, while you yourself have been passed by and are losing out. Lie quiet. All is in darkness, but it is only for a night. It must indeed be a full night, but that is all. Afterwards you will find that everything is given back to you in glorious resurrection; and nothing can measure the difference between what was before and what now is! I was sitting one day at supper with a young brother to whom the Lord had been speaking on this very question of our natural energy. He said to me, `It is a blessed thing when you know the Lord has met you and touched you in that fundamental way, and that disabling touch has been received.' There was a plate of biscuits between us on the table, and I picked one up and broke it in half as though to eat it. Then, fitting the two pieces together again carefully, I said, `It looks all right, but it is never quite the same again, is it? When once your back is broken, you will yield ever after to the slightest touch from God.'

That is it. The Lord knows what He is doing with His own, and He has left no aspect of our need unmet in His Cross, that the glory of the Son may be manifested in the sons. Disciples who have gone this way can, I believe, truly echo the words of the apostle Paul, who could claim to serve God "in my spirit in the gospel of his Son" (Rom. 1:9). They have learned, as he had, the secret of such a ministry: "We ... worship by the Spirit of God, and glory in Christ Jesus, and have no confidence in the flesh" (Phil. 3:3).    Few can have led a more active life than Paul's. To the Romans he puts it on record that he has preached the Gospel from Jerusalem to Illyricum (Rom. 15:19) and that he is ready now to go on to Rome (1:10) and thence, if possible, to Spain (15:24,28). Yet in all this service, embracing as it does the whole Mediterranean world, his heart is set on one object only -- the uplifting of the One who has made it all possible. "I have therefore my glorying in Christ Jesus in things pertaining to God. For I will not dare to speak of any things save those which Christ wrought through me, for the obedience of the Gentiles, by word and deed" (Rom. 15:17,18). That is spiritual service.

May God make each one of us, as truly as he was, "a bondservant of Jesus Christ".

# CHAPTER 14: THE GOAL OF THE GOSPEL

For our final chapter we will take as our starting-point an incident in the Gospels that occurs under the very shadow of the Cross -- an incident that, in its details, is at once historic and prophetic.

"And while he was in Bethany in the house of Simon the leper, as he sat at meat, there came a woman having an alabaster cruse of ointment of spikenard very costly; and she brake the cruse, and poured it over his head ... Jesus said ... Verily I say unto you, Wheresoever the gospel shall be preached throughout the whole world, that also which this woman hath done shall be spoken of for a memorial of her" (Mark 14:3,6,9).

Thus the Lord ordained that the story of Mary anointing Him with that costly ointment should always accompany the story of the Gospel; that what Mary has done should always be coupled with what the Lord has done. That is His own statement. What does He intend that we should understand by it? I think we all know the story of Mary's action well. From the details given in John chapter 12, where the incident follows not long after her brother's restoration to life, we may gather that the family was not a specially wealthy one. The sisters had to work in the house themselves, for we are told that at this feast "Martha also served" (John 12:2 and compare Luke 10:40).[18] No doubt every penny mattered to them. Yet one of those sisters, Mary, having among her treasures an alabaster cruse containing three hundred pence' worth of ointment, expended the whole thing on the Lord. Human reasoning said this was really too much; it was giving the Lord more than His due. That is why Judas took the lead, and the other disciples supported him, in voicing a general complaint that Mary's action was a wasteful one.

---

[18] The author here takes the fairly common view that the "house of Simon the leper" was the home of Mary, Martha and Lazarus, Simon presumably also being a relative of the two sisters. -- Ed.

WASTE

"But there were some that had indignation among themselves, saying, To what purpose hath this waste of the ointment been made? For this ointment might have been sold for above three hundred pence and given to the poor. And they murmured against her" (Mark 14:4,5). These words bring us to what I believe the Lord would have us consider finally together, namely, that which is signified by the little word "waste".

What is waste? Waste means, among other things, giving more than is necessary. If a shilling will do and you give a point, it is a waste. If two ounces will do and you give a kilogram, it is a waste. If three days will suffice to finish a task well enough and you lavish five days or a week on it, it is a waste. Waste means that you give something too much for something too little. If someone is receiving more than he is considered to be worth, then that is waste.

But remember, we are dealing here with something which the Lord said had to go out with the Gospel, wherever that Gospel should be carried. Why? Because He intends that the preaching of the Gospel should issue in something along the very lines of the action of Mary here, namely, that people should come to Him and waste themselves on Him. This is the result that He is seeking.

We must look at this question of wasting on the Lord from two angles: that of Judas (John 12:4-6) and that of the other disciples (Matt. 26:8,9); and for our present purpose we will run together the parallel accounts.    All the twelve thought is a waste. To Judas of course, who had never called Jesus `Lord", everything that was poured out upon Him was waste. Not only was ointment waste; even water would have been waste. Here Judas stands for the world. In the world's estimation the service of the Lord, and our giving ourselves to Him for such service, is sheer waste. He has never been loved, never had a place in the hearts of the world, so any giving to Him is a waste. Many say: `Such -and-such a man could make good in the world if only he were not a Christian!' Because a man has some natural talent or other asset in the world's eyes, they count such people are really too good for the Lord. `What waste of a useful life!' they say.

Let me give a personal instance. In 1929 I returned from Shanghai to my home town of Foochow. One day I was walking along the street with a stick, very weak and in broken health, and I met one of my old college professors. He took me into a teashop where we sat down. He looked at me from head to foot and from foot to head, and then he said: `Now look here; during your college days we thought a good deal of you and we had hopes that you would achieve something great. Do you mean to tell me that this is what you are?' Looking at me with penetrating eyes, he asked that very pointed question. I must confess that, on hearing it, my first desire was to break down and weep. My career, my health, everything had gone, and here was my old professor who taught me law in the school, asking me: `Are you still in this condition, with no success, no progress, nothing to show?'

But the very next moment -- and I have to admit that in all my life it was the first time -- I really knew what it meant to have the "spirit of glory" resting upon me. The thought of being able to pour our my life for my Lord flooded my soul with glory. Nothing short of the Spirit of glory was on me then. I could look up and without a reservation say: `Lord, I praise Thee! This is the best thing possible; it is the right course that I have chosen!' To my professor it seemed a total waste to serve the Lord; but that is what the Gospel is for -- to bring us to a true estimate of His worth. Judas felt it a waste. `We could manage better with the money by using it in some other way. There are plenty of poor people. Why not rather give it for charity, do some social service for their uplift, help the poor in some practical way? Why pour it out at the feet of Jesus?' (See John 12:4-6.) That is always the way the world reasons. `Can you not do something better with yourself than this? It is going a bit too far to give yourself altogether to the Lord!'

But if the Lord is worthy, then how can it be a waste? He is worthy to be so served. He is worthy for me to be His prisoner. He is worthy for me just to live for Him. He is worthy! What the world says about this does not matter. The Lord says: `Do not trouble her'. So let us not be troubled. Men may say what they like, but we can stand on this ground, that the Lord said: `It is a good work. Every true work is not done on the poor; every true work is done to Me'. When once our eyes have been opened to the real worth of our Lord Jesus, nothing is too good for Him.

But I do not want to dwell too much on Judas. Let us go on to see what was the attitude of the other disciples, because their reaction affects us even more than does his. We do not greatly mind what the world is saying; we can stand that, but we do very much mind what other Christians are saying who ought to understand. And yet we find that they said the same thing as Judas; and they not only said it but they were very upset, very indignant about it. "When the disciples saw it, they had indignation, saying, To what purpose is this waste? For this ointment might have been sold for much, and given to the poor" (Matt. 26:8,9).

Of course we know that the attitude of mind is all too common among Christians which says, `Get all you can for as little as possible'. That however is not what is in view here, but something deeper. Let me illustrate. Has someone been telling you that you are wasting your life be sitting still and not doing much? They say, `Here are people who ought to get out into this or that kind of work. They could be used to help this or that group of people. Why are they not more active?' -- and in saying so, their whole idea is use. Everything ought to be used to the full in ways they understand.

There are those who have been very concerned with some dear servants of the Lord on this very ground, that they are apparently not doing enough. They could do so much more, they think, if they could secure an entry somewhere and enjoy a greater acceptance and prominence in certain circles. They could then be used in a far greater way. I have spoken already of a sister whom I knew for a long time and who, I think, is the one by whom I have been helped most. She was used of the Lord in a very real way during those years when I was associated with her, though to some of us at the time this was not so apparent. The one concern in my heart was this: `She is not used!' Constantly I said to myself, `Why does she not get out and take some meetings, go somewhere, do something? It is a waste for her to be living in that small village with nothing happening!' Sometimes, when I went to see her, I almost shouted at her. I said, `No one knows the Lord as you do. You know the Book in a most living way. Do you not see the need around? Why don't you do something? It is a waste of time, a waste of energy, a waste of money, a waste of everything, just sitting here and doing nothing!' But no, brethren, that is not the first thing with the Lord. He wants you and me to be used, certainly. God forbid that I should preach inactivity or seek to justify a complacent attitude to the world's need. As Jesus Himself says here, "the gospel shall be preached throughout the whole world". But the question is one of emphasis. Looking back today, I realize how greatly the Lord was in fact using that dear sister to speak to a number of us who, as young men, were at that time in His training school for this very work of the Gospel. I cannot thank God enough for her.     What, then, is the secret? Clearly it is this, that in approving Mary's action at Bethany, the Lord Jesus was laying down one thing as a basis of all service: that you pour out all you have, your very self, unto Him; and if that should be all He allows you to do, that is enough. It is not first of all a question of whether `the poor' have been helped or not. The first question is: Has the Lord been satisfied?

There is many a meeting we might address, many a convention at which we might minister, many a Gospel campaign in which we might have a share. It is not that we are unable to do it. We could labor and be used to the full; but the Lord is not so concerned about our ceaseless occupation in work for Him. That is not His first object. The service of the Lord is not to be measured by tangible results. No, my friends, the Lord's first concern is with our position at His feet and our anointing of His head. Whatever we have as an 'alabaster box': the most precious thing, the thing dearest in the world to us -- yes, let me say it, the outflow from us of a life that is produced by the very Cross itself -- we give that all up to the Lord. To some, even of those who should understand, it seems a waste; but that is what He seeks above all. Often enough the giving to Him will be in tireless service, but He reserves to Himself the right to suspend the service for a time in order to discover to us whether it is that or Himself that holds us.

## MINISTERING TO HIS PLEASURE

"Wheresoever the gospel shall be preached ... that also which this woman hath done shall be spoken of" (Mark 14:9).

Why did the Lord say this? Because the Gospel is meant to produce this. It is what the Gospel is for. The Gospel is not just to satisfy sinners. Praise the Lord, sinners will be satisfied! but their satisfaction is, we may say, a blessed by-product of the Gospel and not its primary aim. The Gospel is preached in the first place so that the Lord may be satisfied.     I am afraid we lay too much emphasis on the good of sinners and we have not sufficiently appreciated what the Lord has in view as His goal. We have been thinking how the sinner will fare if there is no Gospel, but that is not the main consideration. Yes, Praise God! the sinner has his part. God meets his need and showers him with blessings; but that is not the most important thing. The first thing is this, that everything should be to the satisfaction of the Son of God. It is only when He is satisfied that we shall be satisfied and the sinner will be satisfied. I have never met a soul who has set out to satisfy the Lord and has not been satisfied himself. It is impossible. Our satisfaction comes unfailingly when we satisfy Him first. But we have to remember this, that He will never be satisfied without our 'wasting' ourselves upon Him. Have you ever given too much to the Lord? May I tell you something? One lesson some of us have come to learn is this, that in Divine service the principle of waste is the principle of power. The principle which determines usefulness is the very principle of scattering. Real usefulness in the hand of

God is measured in terms of 'waste'. The more you think you can do, and the more you employ your gifts up to the very limit (and some even go over the limit!) in order to do it, the more you find that you are applying the principle of the world and not of the Lord. God's ways with us are all designed to establish in us this other principle, namely, that our work for Him springs out of our ministering to Him. I do not mean that we are going to do nothing; but the first thing for us must be the Lord Himself, not His work.

But we must come down to very practical issues. You say: 'I have given up a position; I have given up a ministry; I have foregone certain attractive possibilities of a bright future, in order to go on with the Lord in this way. Now I try to serve Him. Sometimes it seems that the Lord hears me, and sometimes He keeps me waiting for a definite answer. Sometimes He uses me, but sometimes it seems that He passes my by. Then, when this is so, I compare myself with that other fellow who is in a certain big system. He too had a bright future, but he has never given it up. He continues on and he serves the Lord. He sees souls saved and the Lord blesses his ministry. He is successful -- I do not mean materially, but spiritually -- and I sometimes think he looks more like a Christian than I do, so happy, so satisfied. After all, what do I get out of this? He has a good time; I have all the bad time. He has never gone this way, and yet he has much that Christians today regard as spiritual prosperity, while I have all sorts of complications coming to me. What is the meaning of it all? Am I wasting my life? Have I really given too much?'

So there is your problem. You feel that were you to follow in that other brother's steps -- were you, shall we say, to consecrate yourself enough for the blessing but not enough for the trouble, enough for the Lord to use you but not enough for Him to shut you up -- all would be perfectly all right. But would it? You know perfectly well that it would not. Takes your eyes off that other man! Look at your Lord, and ask yourself again what it is that He values most highly. The principle of waste is the principle that He would have govern us. 'She is doing this for Me.' Real satisfaction is brought to the heart of the Son of God only when we are really, as people would think, 'wasting' ourselves upon Him. It seems as though we are giving too much and getting nothing -- and that is the secret of pleasing God.

Oh, friends, what are we after? Are we after 'use' as those disciples were? They wanted to make every penny of those three hundred pence go to its full length. The whole question was one of obvious 'usefulness' to God in terms

323

that could be measured and put on record. The Lord waits to hear us say: `Lord, I do not mind about that. If I can only please Thee, it is enough'.

## ANOINTING HIM BEFOREHAND

"Let her alone; why trouble ye her? She hath wrought a good work on me. For ye have the poor always with you, and whensoever ye will ye can do them good: but me ye have not always. She hath done what she could: she hath anointed my body aforehand for the burying" (Mark 14:6-8).

In these verses the Lord Jesus introduces a time-factor with the word `beforehand', and this is something of which we can have a new application today, for it is as important to us now as it was to her then. We all know that in the age to come we shall be called to a greater work -- not to inactivity. "Well done, good and faithful servant: thou hast been faithful over a few things, I will set thee over many things: enter thou into the joy of thy Lord" (Matthew 25:21; and compare Matthew 24:47 and Luke 19:17). Yes, there will be a greater work; for the work of God's house will go on, just as in the story the care of the poor went on. The poor would always be with them, but they could not always have Him. There was something, represented by this pouring out of the ointment, which Mary had to do beforehand or she would have no later opportunity. I believe that in that day we shall all love Him as we have never done now, but yet that it will be most blessed for those who have poured out their all upon the Lord today. When we see Him face to face I trust that we shall all break and pour out everything for Him. But today -- what are we doing today?

Several days after Mary broke the alabaster box and poured the ointment on Jesus' head, there were some women who went early in the morning to anoint the body of the Lord. Did they do it? Did they succeed in their purpose on that first day of the week? No, there was only one soul who succeeded in anointing the Lord, and it was Mary, who anointed Him before hand. The others never did it, for He had risen. Now I suggest that in just such a way the matter of time may be important to us also, and that the whole question for us is : What am I doing to the Lord today?

Have our eyes been opened to see the preciousness of the One whom we are serving? Have we come to see that nothing less than the dearest, the costliest, the most precious, is fit for Him? Have we come to see that working for the poor, working for the benefit of the world, working for the souls of men and for the eternal good of the sinner -- all these so necessary and valuable things -- are right only if they are in their place? In themselves, as things apart, they are as nothing compared with work that is done to the Lord.

The Lord has to open our eyes to His worth. If there is in the world some precious art treasure, and I pay the high price asked for it, be it one thousand, ten thousand, or even a million pounds, dare anyone say it is a waste? The idea of waste only comes into our Christianity when we underestimate the worth of our Lord. The whole question is: How precious is He to us now? If we do not think much of Him, then of course to give Him anything at all, however small, will seem to us a wicked waste. But when He is really precious to our soul, nothing will be too good, nothing too costly for Him; everything we have, our dearest, our most priceless treasure, we shall pour out upon Him, and we shall not count it a shame to have done so. Of Mary the Lord said: "She hath done what she could". What does that mean? It means that she had given up her all. She had kept nothing in reserve for a future day. She had lavished on Him all she had; and yet on the resurrection morning she had no reason to regret her extravagance. And the Lord will not be satisfied with anything less from us than that we too should have done 'what we could'. By this, remember, I do not mean the expenditure of our effort and energy in trying to do something for Him, for that is not the point here. What the Lord Jesus looks for in us is a life laid at His feet -- and that in view of His death and burial and of a future day. His burial was already in view that day in the home in Bethany. Today it is His crowning that is in view -- when He shall be acclaimed in glory as the Anointed One, the Christ of God. Yes, then we shall pour out our all upon Him! But it is a precious thing -- indeed it is a far more precious thing to Him -- that we should anoint Him now, not with any material oil but with something costly, something from our hearts.

That which is merely external and superficial has no place here. It has already been dealt with by the Cross, and we have given our consent to God's judgment upon it and learnt to know in experience its cutting off. What God is demanding of us now is represented by that flask of alabaster: something mined from the depths, something turned and chased and wrought upon, something that, because it is so truly of the Lord, we cherish as Mary cherished that flask -- and we would not, we dare not break it. It comes now from the heart, from the very depth of our being; and we come to the Lord with that, and we break it and pour it out and say: 'Lord, here it is. It is all Yours, because You are worthy!' -- and the Lord has got what He desired. May He receive such an anointing from us today.

FRAGRANCE

"And the house was filled with the odor of the ointment" (John 12:3). By the breaking of that flask and the anointing of the Lord Jesus, the house was pervaded with the sweetest fragrance. Everyone could smell it and none could be unaware of it. What is the significance of this?

Whenever you meet someone who has really suffered -- someone who has gone through experiences with the Lord that have brought limitation, and who, instead of trying to break free in order to be `used', has been willing to be imprisoned by Him and has thus learned to find satisfaction in the Lord and nowhere else -- then immediately you become aware of something. Immediately your spiritual senses detect a sweet savour of Christ. Something has been crushed, something has been broken in that life, and so you smell the odor. The odor that filled the house that day in Bethany still fills the Church today; Mary's fragrance never passes. It needed but one stroke to break the flask for the Lord, but that breaking and the fragrance of that anointing abides.

We are speaking here of what we are; not of what we do or what we preach. Perhaps you may have been asking the Lord for a long time that He will be pleased to use you in such a way as to impart impressions of Himself to others. That prayer is not exactly for the gift of preaching or teaching.

It is rather that you might be able, in your touch with others, to impart God, the presence of God, the sense of God. Dear friends, you cannot produce such impressions of God upon others without the breaking of everything, even your most precious possessions, at the feet of the Lord Jesus.

But if once that point is reached, you may or may not seem to be much used in an outward way, but God will begin to use you to create a hunger in others. People will scent Christ in you. The least saint in the Body will detect that. He will sense that here is one who has gone with the Lord, one who has suffered, one who has not moved freely, independently, but who has known what it is to let go everything to Him. That kind of life creates impressions, and impressions create hunger, and hunger provokes men to go on seeking until they are brought by Divine revelation into fullness of life in Christ.

God does not set us here first of all to preach or to do work for Him. The first thing for which He sets us here is to create in others a hunger for Himself. That is, after all, what prepares the soil for the preaching.    If you set a delicious cake in front of two men who have just had a heavy meal, what will be their reaction? They will talk about it, admire its appearance, discuss the recipe, argue about the cost -- do everything n fact but eat it! But if they are truly hungry it will not be very long before that cake is gone. And so it is with the things of the Spirit. No true work will ever begin in a life without first of all a sense of need being created. But how can this be done? We cannot inject spiritual appetite by force into others; we cannot compel people to be hungry. Hunger has to be created, and it can be created in others only by those who carry with them the impressions of God.

I always like to think of the words of that "great woman" of Shunem. Speaking of the prophet, whom she had observed but whom she did not know well, she said: "Behold now, I perceive that this is an holy man of God, which passeth by us continually" (2 Kings 4:9). It was not what Elisha said or did that conveyed that impression, but what he was. By his merely passing by she could detect something; she could see. What are people sensing about us? We may leave many kinds of impressions: we may leave the impression that we are clever, that we are gifted, that we are this or that or the other. But no: the impression left by Elisha was an impression of God Himself. This matter of our impact upon others turns upon one thing, and that is the working of the Cross in us with regard to the pleasure of the heart of God. It demands that I seek His pleasure, that I seek to satisfy Him only, and that I do not mind how much it costs me to do so. The sister of whom I have spoken came once into a situation that was very difficult for her: I mean, it was costing her everything. I was with her at the time, and together we knelt down and prayed with wet eyes. Looking up she said: Lord, I am willing to break my heart in order that I may satisfy Thy heart!' To talk thus of heart-break might with many of us be merely romantic sentiment, but in the particular situation in which she was, it meant to her just that. There must be something -- a willingness to yield, a breaking and a pouring out of everything to Him -- which gives release to that fragrance of Christ and produces in other lives an awareness of need, drawing them out and on to know the Lord. This is what I feel to be the heart of everything. The Gospel has as its one object the producing in us sinners of a condition that will satisfy the heart of our God. In order that He may have that, we come to Him with all we have, all we are -- yes, even the most cherished things in our spiritual experience -- and we make known to Him: 'Lord, I am willing to let go all of this for You: not just for Your work, not for Your children, not for anything else, but for Yourself!'

Oh, to be wasted! It is a blessed thing to be wasted for the Lord. So many who have been prominent in the Christian world know nothing of this. Many of us have been used to the full -- have been used, I would say, too much -- but we do not know what it means to be wasted on God. We like to be always `on the go': the Lord would sometimes prefer to have us in prison. We think in terms of apostolic journeys: God dares to put his greatest ambassadors in chains.

"But thanks be unto God, which always leadeth us in triumph in Christ, and maketh manifest through us the savour of his knowledge in every place" (2 Cor. 2:14).

"And the house was filled with the odor of the ointment (John 12:3).

The Lord grant us grace that we may learn how to please Him. When, like Paul, we make this our supreme aim (2 Cor. 5:9), the Gospel will have achieved its end.

## ABOUT THE AUTHOR

Watchman Nee is considered one of the most important indigenous church leaders and thinkers in the history of Chinese Christianity. There are few leaders in the history of Chinese Christianity whose influence is as prevalent as Watchman Nee's. (November 4, 1903 – May 30, 1972)

In 1922, he initiated church meetings in Fuzhou that may be considered the beginning of the local churches. During his thirty years of ministry, Nee published many books expounding the Bible. He established churches throughout China and held many conferences to train Bible students and church workers. Following the Communist Revolution, Nee was persecuted and imprisoned for his faith and spent the last twenty years of his life in prison.

# OTHER WATCHMAN NEE BEST SELLERS

https://www.amazon.com/dp/B09KP4PXQM

https://a.co/98A99LI

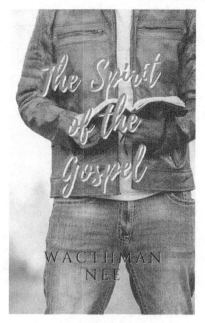

https://a.co/adE7jIC

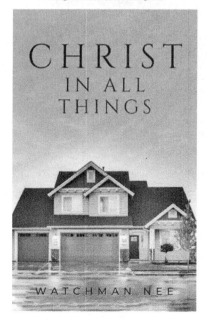

https://a.co/1dXVdrG

https://www.amazon.com/dp/B09RTQ3LLW